VI. THE MOMENT OF TRUTH

Introduction

IN EVERY LIFE—and in the lives of great men especially—there comes a moment when the man stands revealed for what he really is. It may be a great and climactic instant when he encounters a sudden awareness of the whole purpose and direction of his life. It may be a moment of final and irrevocable decision. It may occur at the height of furious action, or it may come at a time of quiet contemplation. But however and whenever it happens, it reveals as nothing else can, the true measure and character of the man.

Turning Point is a collection of these great and moving experiences —these crucial, crystal-clear moments when the turn in the road is reached—and a new path stretches out to the future.

There are hundreds of such stories, some tremendously exciting and vivid, others beautifully told and deeply moving. They are everywhere, some buried in biographies and autobiographies deep in the shelves— and others in more transient media which we only see once and then lose sight of. We have tried to catch a few of these crucial moments, to lift them from the back files and out of the books where they lie hidden. We have edited them only as necessary to hold a feeling of entity, and present them here—the pith, the kernel, the essence of each man.

We have had the whole world to choose from—the people who have made history since history began, to the present day. They are the great and the powerful, the famous and the infamous, the driven and the weary, the mad and the moonstruck—men and women from everywhere and from all time.

> Here is Patrick Henry at his moment of glory crying out for freedom in a land oppressed . . .
>
> Here is Columbus, facing a mutinous crew, but never for an instant doubting his destiny . . .
>
> And Joan of Arc denying her recantation . . .
>
> Here is John Wilkes Booth carrying out the monstrous murder, a crime for which we are all still paying today . . .

Here are the Wright brothers fulfilling man's eternal dream of flight . . .

And Helen Keller, blind, dumb and deaf, "hearing" her first word . . .

They are not all virtuous, these men and women—they are not all famous. Some, like Francisco Pizarro were adventurers and scoundrels of the worst sort—others, like Booth and John Brown were madmen whose only reason for being was the uncontrollable mission that drove them. They are as disparate in background as Andrew Jackson and Lord Cardigan; their interests are as different as those of Babe Ruth were to Beethoven's. What brings them together here is that their stories have been well told—their turning points well lighted.

The divisions we have made are loose ones, and throw together some strange bedfellows: John Brown and Winston Churchill are found together in *The Moment of Triumph*. Yet it is as true that John Brown's victory was culminated by his hanging as that Churchill's was in succeeding to the reins of the British Government.

Here, then, are some fifty men and women at the moment of stress, of revelation, of victory or of adversity—moments which in one way or another light up the inner being of each of them.

THIS IS Philip Dunaway's book. It was his in conception and almost completely his in execution. At the time of his death in September of 1957, Dunaway had collected most of the material for *Turning Point*, the result of fifteen months of searching, reading and editing. I have arranged it and filled in the few gaps he left, always trying to keep the book as he originally planned it. I hope I have succeeded.

GEORGE DE KAY

I. THE MOMENT OF DECISION

Multitudes, multitudes in the valley of decision:

for the day of the Lord is near

in the valley of decision.

JOEL III, 14

ROBERT E. LEE

"Secession is nothing but revolution."

Few men in 1861 had a record of more single-minded dedication to the Union than Robert E. Lee. Yet in February of that year, when he was offered the command of the Union armies, his answer was to resign his commission and retire. It was not a political decision for Lee was not a politically minded man. It had nothing to do with the question of slavery for he had long before freed the slaves he had inherited. Lee's decision was the result of a single loyalty so strong that it transcended all others—his loyalty to his native state of Virginia.

The final effects of Lee's decision can, of course, never be accurately measured. It is sufficient to realize that this man was the greatest military tactician this country ever produced . . . and in the end he fought against the Union he loved. . . .

COLONEL LEE and his guest walked out on the sixty-foot portico of Mrs. Lee's great house on the Virginia hillside to admire the view. Washington seemed quite close today, below them in the pale sunlight of early April. The city's familiar landmarks shone, as if they had been spread there as a view for Arlington:

The half-finished dome of the Capitol wore a crown of scaffolding with a raffish air; the stump of the Washington Monument rose amid acres of stone and rubble; the incomplete Treasury Building was already, they said, quarters for a regiment of cavalry; the fantastic red spires of the Smithsonian Institution bristled from a green plain.

Lee's visitor was Thomas B. Bryan, a friend from Illinois who was soon to join the growing Federal Army. He stood with the colonel beside one of the preposterously large columns copied from an Athenian temple and looked over the lawn where, not so many years before, the aging Lafayette had received his American friends on a farewell tour. Parkland and groves tumbled for half a mile to the Potomac. Water glinted beyond the trees.

The colonel was an arresting figure in plain, neat civilian dress. He was fifty-four years old, but his five feet, eleven inches were held erect. Though he had a deceptively larger look, he weighed not quite 170 pounds. There was a subtle distortion of his physique which escaped all but the sharpest eyes: The upper body was enormous, on a scale to dwarf the narrow hips, slight legs and tiny feet. Chest and shoulders were massive, and his huge head rose from a short, thick neck.

He wore a brush of black mustache, with no beard. There were streaks of gray in his brown hair, but these were scarcely noticeable, despite his protest of thirteen years before, when he had come home from the Mexican War, that his family had stared at the furrows in his face and the white hairs in his head. His complexion was highly colored. There was a quiet animation in his dark brown eyes.

Despite its rather heroic features—a large Roman nose, broad forehead and deep temples—the face was dominated by its expression of calm self-assurance; it was this, perhaps, which had so often inspired confidence in women, children, soldiers, secretaries of war, and the commanding general of the United States Army.

On this spring day only a vague sadness of face gave Lee's visitor a hint of his personal struggle through the weeks when the troubles of the country had been mounting, and the Union seemed to be dissolving.

The colonel gave no impression of wealth or expensive taste, either in his clothing or in the appearance of the manor house. This was accurate enough, for only lately he had so despaired of his low income as to give up the proper landscaping of his wife's home, and was forced to tend only small clearings about the house. It had not been long since he had confessed to his son Custis, "The necessity I daily have for money has, I fear, made me parsimonious."

Lately, too, he had revealed to a cousin a wry feeling of failure in life, of the "small progress I have made on . . . my professional and civil career." Until now, the fact was, his twenty-three years in the army had brought him no higher than the salary of $1,025 a year.

Lee and Bryan were not long on the hillside studying the sights, but there was a brief moment so striking to the visitor that it later seemed prophetic, and he could not forget it. Lee's voice dropped its tone of "almost jovial cheerfulness" to a "deep gravity."

The colonel raised one of his big hands, pointing over the water to the Capitol.

"That beautiful feature of our landscape," he said, "has ceased to charm me as it once did. I fear the mischief that is brewing there."

If there was a proprietary air about his words, it was not strange.

Robert Edward Lee and the city—and the huge house, too—were much of an age. A more imaginative or self-centered man might have been aware of the kinship, whose bonds were much like those of the early history of the country itself. He was the son of Lighthorse Harry Lee, great cavalryman of the Revolution, also Washington's intimate and his funeral orator whose rhetoric seemed likely to endure: "First in war, first in peace . . ."

Robert Lee was born in the mansion Stratford Hall, not far away, in a room where, by family tradition, two signers of the Declaration of Independence had been born before him. His mother was Ann Hill Carter, of the line of old King Carter, one of the wealthiest of Virginia families. His boyhood began with his father's bankruptcy and imprisonment for debt, and had ended with his nursing his invalid mother in her fallen estate at an unpretentious house in Alexandria.

He was an honor cadet at West Point, and had gone to the war with Mexico at the elbow of General Winfield Scott, old Fuss and Feathers, whose admiration for Lee amounted almost to awe. Robert emerged from the Mexican War with a reputation as the army's most talented young officer. He had since filled every choice post to which influence and merit could guide him: He had headed the pet projects of the Engineer Corps in New York harbor, Florida, Baltimore harbor, the Savannah water front, and had battled the Mississippi at St. Louis; he had been West Point's superintendent, had fought Indians on the border; had put down the John Brown raid with the capture of the Kansas fanatic. Until lately, he had been second in command in frontier Texas.

Men even now spoke of Scott's admiration for Lee, quoting the aging warrior: "If war comes, it would be cheap for our country to insure Lee's life for $5,000,000 a year."

Veteran officers remembered the days in Mexico, and some said that Lee's genius for handling troops had enabled Scott to win fame and his war "without coming from his tent."

In the two months since the secession of South Carolina everyone seemed to turn to Lee; everlastingly, they had the same question as to his intentions. It was not surprising to him; this was a matter he had wrestled with long before, without coming to his final painful conclusion.

As long ago as 1856 he had seen the coming storm, and had written:

> Mr. Buchanan, it appears, is to be our next President. I hope he will be able to extinguish fanaticism both North and South, cultivate love for the country and Union, and restore harmony between the different sections.

He had also expressed himself on slavery at about that time:

> There are few, I believe, in this enlightened age, who will not

acknowledge that slavery as an institution is a moral and political evil. . . . I think it a greater evil to the white than to the black race.

He did not, he said, think the Negroes ready for complete freedom:

> The painful discipline they are undergoing is necessary for their further instruction as a race, and I hope will prepare them for better things. . . . Their emancipation will sooner result from the mild and melting influences of Christianity, than from the storms and tempests of controversy.

Not long after he wrote this, Lee had experienced personal distress over slavery; his wife's father, George Washington Parke Custis, died, leaving an involved estate. His will freed his slaves, who were to be given freedom when the estate was settled—within five years at longest. When time dragged on, three of the family Negroes ran away, were captured in Maryland, and sent deeper into Virginia to another plantation.

Several Northern newspapers had excoriated Lee, charging him with guile, and with cruelly whipping his slaves. Old Mr. Custis, one paper said, "had fifteen children by his slave women."

Lee's only recorded reaction was in a letter to his son Custis: "*The N. Y. Tribune* has attacked me for my treatment of your grandfather's slaves, but I shall not reply. He has left me an unpleasant legacy."

In Texas, where Lee was stationed in the winter of 1860, he had clung to hope for the Union. He wrote his family that he would not permit himself to believe that the Union would be wrecked "until all ground for hope is gone." He added a note of hopelessness, however:

> . . . As far as I can judge by the papers, we are between a state of anarchy and civil war. May God avert both of the evils from us!
>
> I fear that mankind for years to come will not be sufficiently Christianized to bear the absence of restraint and force. I see that four states have declared themselves out of the Union; four more will apparently follow. . . . Then, if the border states are brought into the gulf of revolution, one half of the country will be arrayed against the other.
>
> I must try and be patient and await the end, for I can do nothing to hasten or retard it.

Lee was often called upon to declare himself in pre-war Texas, and his statements were unvarying: He stood for the Union, but could not think of making war on Virginia. One officer, R. W. Johnson, who served with Lee on the Indian frontier and was soon to become a Federal general, saw Lee as he was leaving Texas, called to Washington headquarters.

"Colonel, do you intend to go South or remain North?" Johnson asked. "I am very anxious to know just what you propose doing."

Lee replied, "I shall never bear arms against the United States—but it may be necessary for me to carry a musket in defense of my native state, Virginia, in which case I shall try to do my duty."

The Federal commander in Texas, General Twiggs, surrendered his command to state troops, in effect delivering all to the Confederacy. A sharp-eyed woman, Mrs. Caroline Darrow, told Lee the news in San Antonio, and wrote: "His lips trembling and his eyes full of tears, he exclaimed, 'Has it come so soon as this?'" At night, she overheard Lee praying in his hotel room.

Lee did not waver from his course, but he seemed unable to speak or write of it without emotion. In a letter to a son, though it bore the marks of a struggle for calm, he revealed the depths of his feelings. He was by no means one with the Secessionists, but his country was Virginia:

> The South, in my opinion, has been aggrieved by the acts of the North, as you say. I . . . would defend any state if her rights were invaded.
>
> But I can anticipate no greater calamity for the country than a dissolution of the Union. It would be an accumulation of all the evils we complain of, and I am willing to sacrifice everything but honor for its preservation.
>
> I hope . . . that all constitutional means will be exhausted before there is a recourse to force. Secession is nothing but revolution. . . .
>
> It is idle to talk of secession. Anarchy would have been established, and not a government by Washington, Hamilton, Jefferson, Madison and the other patriots of the Revolution. . . . Still, a Union that can only be maintained by swords and bayonets, and in which strife and civil war are to take the place of brotherly love and kindness, has no charm for me.
>
> I shall mourn for my country and for the welfare and progress of mankind. If the Union is to be dissolved and the Government disrupted, I shall return to my native state and share the miseries of my people, and save in defense will draw my sword on none.

And he had come home in that mood, just a few troubled days ago, having declared that he thought the world would have "one soldier less." The days had been full, and the country's tension had mounted rapidly: Twiggs had been dismissed from the army and re-placed, Lincoln had been inaugurated, South Carolina had cut sup-plies from Fort Sumter in Charleston harbor. Near the end of March, Lee had flattering offers: A commission as a full colonel, signed by Lincoln—and a letter from L. P. Walker in Montgomery, Alabama, a lawyer, now styled Secretary of War, Confederate States of America, who offered the rank of brigadier general in the new army, ending rather insistently:

You are requested to signify your acceptance of said appoint-ment, and should you accept you will sign before a magistrate the oath of office herewith and forward the same, with your letter of acceptance to this office.

Many of his brother officers were acting, but Lee could not. For one thing, he was not convinced that Virginia would come to seces-sion; there was wild talk of it everywhere, but he hoped there would be calm heads in Richmond.

Almost his first act, upon returning to Arlington in March, had been to call on General Scott. At the general's office he met an old friend, Lieutenant Colonel Erasmus Keyes, with whom he had served on West Point's Board of Visitors, and who was now secretary to Scott —a post Lee had once been offered. Keyes wrote: "Lee . . . entered my room and inquired if Lieutenant General Scott was disengaged. I stepped quickly forward, seized his hand, greeted him warmly, and said:

" 'Lee, it is reported that you concurred in Twiggs' surrender in Texas; how's that?' "

Lee's manner became one of "great seriousness."

"I am here to pay my respects to General Scott," he said. "Will you be kind enough, Colonel, to show me to his office?"

Lee was alone with the commander for two hours, and when he emerged did not tarry to talk with old army friends.

Keyes thought it a strange interview, for invariably, when Scott had an important talk, he reviewed it in detail for his military secretary. Keyes said:

"On this occasion he told me not a word, and he made no reference to the subject of his conversation with Colonel Lee. His manner that day, when we dined alone, was painfully solemn."

The secretary was positive, however, that Scott had offered to re-sign command of the Federal Army in favor of Lee, and that Lee had declined the offer.

The house to which Lee returned literally shouted of the Union and its great early days. In every room, casually placed, were priceless relics from Mount Vernon: Portraits by famed artists of the young republic, paintings of Martha Washington and Nelly Custis; of Mrs. Lee's ancestor, Colonel Daniel Parke, who had taken Marlborough's victory message from Blenheim to Queen Anne; Washington's camp furniture, china, silver plate, punch bowls, watches—packets of his letters, including one announcing the arrival of the French fleet which had meant independence.

Robert Lee had come here courting, a penniless young aristocrat with an eye for Mary Anne Randolph Custis, one of Virginia's real heiresses, daughter of Washington's adopted son. It was almost thirty years ago; they were grandparents now, and the colonel's "Mim" was an arthritic invalid at fifty-three, looking much older than her years. She was to become the most vehement Confederate in the family, but this spring, in the very week Lincoln went to Washington, she wrote her daughter Mildred:

I pray that the Almighty may listen to the prayers of the faithful in the land and direct their counsels for good and that the designs of ambitious and selfish politicians who would dismember our glorious country may be frustrated, especially that our own State may act right and obtain the mead promised in the Bible to the peace maker.

Mary Lee had been unable to walk normally for years, but she bore her pain with courage, and she often exhibited a strong will. Mary had loved Robert Lee from childhood, apparently, and had overcome her father's objections to marry him. There was every evidence that they were devoted companions throughout marriage. Lee's letters to her during their young married life had not been passionate, but were filled with expressions of affection, both for Mary and their seven children. He once wrote:

You do not know how much I have missed you and the children, my dear Mary. . . . I . . . must again urge you to be very prudent and careful of those dear children. If I could only get a squeeze at that little fellow, turning up his sweet mouth to 'keese baba!'

Then there was a hint of the gentle patriarch:

You must not let him run wild in my absence, and will have to exercise firm authority over all of them. This will not require severity or even strictness, but constant attention and an unwavering course. Mildness and forbearance will strengthen their affection for you, while it will maintain your control over them.

But it was to no avail. The most perceptive of their sons recalled that it was only the father who could command obedience. Yet young Robert never forgot the childhood scenes when Lee tumbled several of his children into bed with him, and made them lie there while he told them stories. He placed his feet in their laps at such times, and literally forced them to tickle his soles as he talked; when they ceased he would nudge them, saying, "No tickling, no story."

Mary had been dowdy and a bit untidy for most of her life, and she was only now beginning to primp and take notice of her appearance. Many years before, writing to prospective guests, Lee had seen fit to warn them that his wife was "somewhat addicted to laziness and forgetfulness" as a housekeeper. Once she had risen from a long illness and, impatient with her snarled hair, had whacked most of it from her head.

But the colonel and "The Mim" were evidently one, and she was soon to organize one of the most faithfully industrious "sewing factories" of the Confederacy in her new home, working for his soldiers at the front.

War closed rapidly upon the Lees of Arlington.

On April twelfth the first shells burst upon Fort Sumter, far away in South Carolina. It was the signal for which the country had waited. The fort surrendered on April fourteenth, and the following day President Lincoln called for 75,000 men to suppress the rebellion which had been thirty years in the brewing. From his Potomac hillside Lee watched. He read *The Alexandria Gazette,* whose longest dispatches were from Richmond, where it was rumored that the convention had closed its doors for secret session. The natural assumption was that secession would follow. Lee learned of the closed meeting on April seventeenth.

On the same day he was called into Washington, by two messages. One was a note from his cousin John Lee, asking him to come tomorrow to meet Francis P. Blair, an old newspaper editor, once chief of *The Congressional Globe,* and a power in the Lincoln administration; Blair was father of the new Postmaster General, Montgomery Blair, who had befriended Lee in St. Louis long before, when he was seeking to tame the flow of the Mississippi.

The other message came from General Scott, a request to report to his office once more.

On the morning of April eighteenth Lee rode down Arlington's hill, across Long Bridge, past squalid cottages on a climbing roadway, along the canal skirting the incomplete monument to Washington, and to the heart of the city. He dismounted at Montgomery Blair's

house at 1651 Pennsylvania Avenue, just opposite the War Department, and went in to meet the elder Blair. They talked alone.

Blair did not mince matters. Lee could have command of the
enormous Federal Army if he wished it. Secretary of War Cameron
had ordered this offer of command through Blair, and there was the
strong impression that the proposal came from Lincoln himself. Lee
dismissed the affair in sparse words:

"After listening to his remarks, I declined to take the offer he made
me, to take command of the army that was to be brought into the
field, stating, as candidly as I could, that though opposed to secession
and deprecating war, I could take no part in an invasion of the Southern states."

Blair did not give up; he pleaded with the colonel for an hour or
more. Blair's son, Montgomery, soon had this tale from the old man,
and wrote his own version of Lee's words:

"Mr. Blair, I look upon secession as anarchy. If I owned four millions of slaves at the South, I would sacrifice them all to the Union;
but how can I draw my sword upon Virginia, my native state?"

Lee also wanted time to talk with his friend General Scott, Blair
remembered.

Lee left Blair and went the short distance to Scott's office, and
looked for the last time at the familiar face with its eyes embedded
in fat. The general lumbered up to meet him, to his height of six
feet six inches.

Scott was the teacher of Lee's youth, and held his respect. Lee told
the general of his refusal of Blair's offer.

"Lee, you have made the greatest mistake of your life," Scott said,
"but I feared it would be so."

Scott's aide, E. D. Townsend, whose desk was in the room with
the general's round table, wrote:

"I quietly arose, keeping my eye on the general, for it seemed probable he might wish to be alone with Lee. He, however, secretly mo-
tioned me to keep my seat."

Townsend recorded the conversation.

"These are times when every officer in the United States should
fully determine what course he will pursue and frankly declare it,"
Scott said. "No one should continue in government employ without
being actively employed."

Lee did not respond.

"Some of the Southern officers are resigning," Scott said, "possibly
with the intention of taking part with their states. They make a fatal
mistake. The contest may be long and severe, but eventually the issue
must be in favor of the Union. . . ."

"I suppose you will go with the rest. If you purpose to resign, it is proper you should do so at once; your present attitude is an equivocal one."

"The property belonging to my children, all they possess, lies in Virginia," Lee said. "They will be ruined, if they do not go with their state. I cannot raise my hand against my children."

Lee left Scott and visited for a time with his older brother, Sidney Smith Lee, a Navy captain, but neither made an immediate decision about leaving the service or enlisting with Virginia.

As Robert left the capital he saw signs of excitement. The Washington papers were screaming the news of Virginia's secession, but it was not yet official.

Lee rode into Alexandria the next day. He saw volunteers at drill on vacant lots, and the more polished Mount Vernon Guards, parading under strange new colors. The rooms of the Young Men's Christian Association were filled with women sewing at uniforms.

Lee saw the dread news in print in *The Alexandria Gazette*: Virginia's secession was approved by the convention; it was true. Within a month the people of the state would vote on the act—they were virtually certain to ratify it. He went into a pharmacy shop to pay a household account, and sighed as he stood at the counter:

"I must say that I am one of those dull creatures that cannot see the good of secession."

The merchant was so struck by these words that he scribbled them on his ledger, adding, "Spoken by Colonel R. E. Lee, when he paid his bill, April 19, 1861."

The colonel went home. After supper, while Mary sat in the well-used old family sitting room, he went upstairs to his own room. She listened as he paced the floor above; she waited through long periods of silence.

At last she heard him drop to his knees for prayer. It was after midnight—long after—when he came down with a letter in his hand.

"Well, Mary," he said, "the question is settled. Here is my resignation and a letter I have written General Scott."

There was a brief note to Secretary of War Cameron, and the longer one to Scott:

                                        Arlington, Va., April 20, 1861
General:
    Since my interview with you on the 18th inst. I have felt that I ought no longer to retain my commission in the Army. I therefore tender my resignation, which I request you will recommend for acceptance. I would have presented it at once, but for the

struggle it has cost me to separate myself from a service to which
I have devoted all the best years of my life and all the ability I
possessed.

During the whole of that time—more than a quarter of a century—I have experienced nothing but kindness from my superiors
and a most cordial friendship from my comrades. To no one,
General, have I been as much indebted as to yourself for uniform kindness and consideration. I shall carry to the grave the
most grateful recollections of your kind consideration, and your
name and fame will always be dear to me.

Save in defence of my native State, I never desire again to draw
my sword.

Be pleased to accept my most earnest wishes for the continu-
ance of your happiness and prosperity, and believe me, most
truly yours,

R. E. Lee

Lee next wrote a letter of explanation to his sister Ann—Mrs. William Louis Marshall, whose husband clung to the Union. He enclosed
a copy of his resignation to Ann, and wrote in part:

Now we are in a state of war which will yield to nothing. The
whole South is in a state of revolution, into which Virginia,
after a long struggle, has been drawn; and, though I recognize
no necessity for this state of things . . . yet in my own person I
had to meet the question whether I should take part against my
native State. . . .

I know you will blame me; but you must think as kindly of me
as you can, and believe that I have endeavored to do what I
thought right. . . .

He also wrote to his brother Smith, explaining that Virginia's secession had forced him to act quickly, and repeating once more the
phrase: "Save in defence of my native State, I have no desire ever
again to draw my sword."

His sons Rooney and Custis were home now, seeking advice from
their father. Both were solemn, and Custis was actually defiant of the
Secessionists; his solution was to fortify Arlington Heights for the
Union, and treat the revolutionists as they deserved.

A woman who rode with Rooney on a train that day remembered
". . . the contrast of his deep depression with the prevalent elation
and jubilancy. He said the people had lost their senses and had no
conception of what a terrible mistake they were making."

A neighbor who talked with one of the Lee daughters described

Arlington on this day, April twentieth: "The house was as if there had been a death in it, for the army was to him home and country."

Nearby Alexandria, like most towns of the South, was seized with joyous delirium.

That day, Mary Lee was able to read lavish praise for her husband in the Alexandria paper, whose editor urged Virginia to call Lee to command, if he should leave the Federal Army:

> There is no man who could command more of the confidence of the people of Virginia . . . and no one under whom the volunteers and militia would more gladly rally. His reputation, his acknowledged ability, his chivalric character, his probity, honor—and, may we add, to his eternal praise—his Christian life and conduct—make his very name 'a tower of strength.' It is a name surrounded by revolutionary and patriotic associations and reminiscences.

Arlington could not know it, but Virginia had been calling for several days. Two messengers had failed to reach the house. And tonight, Saturday, April twentieth, there was a note from Judge John Robertson, who had come up from Richmond. Lee was asked to meet the Judge in Alexandria the next day. Lee replied that he would meet him after church.

He rode into the town with one of his daughters, and after the service at Christ Church, he was approached by three men. They talked for a long time, first isolated in the crowd of churchgoers, and then alone. No one knew the strange men—Judge Robertson was not among them—but the town assumed they were messengers from Richmond. Lee's daughter waited impatiently in a house across the street.

When Lee left the mysterious men, family and neighbors were still in suspense. This was soon to be ended. That night there was another message from Judge Robertson, saying he had been detained in Washington. He asked Lee to accompany him to Richmond the next day.

Lee accepted without hesitation.

On Monday morning, April twenty-second, hangers-on at the Alexandria station watched the colonel, in a high silk hat, climb aboard to ride to Richmond with Judge Robertson. There was little doubt among the townspeople as to his destination.

The cars jerked him down the line of the Orange and Alexandria Railroad across the landscape so soon to be drenched with blood. At the village of Orange he was recognized, and a crowd clamored for him. He went to the rear of the train and bowed.

At Gordonsville, where he changed to the Virginia Central, he was trapped again, and this time was urged to make a speech. E. P. Alexander, later to become one of his generals, remembered its content:

"He responded briefly, advising his hearers not to lounge about stations, but to be putting their affairs in order for a long and bloody war, which was sure to strain all their resources to support it."

The train shuddered and clanked into motion, and fled southward, trailing a pall of woodsmoke. By late afternoon they were in Richmond, and Colonel Lee was installed in the heart of the city's bustle, at the Spotswood Hotel.

Gray Fox: Robert E. Lee and the Civil War, by Burke Davis

CHRISTOPHER COLUMBUS

"It was useless to complain,

since he had come to go to the Indies ..."

The great decision in the life of Christopher Columbus—the decision to sail west to find the Indies—was made when he was a young man sailing in merchant ships in the Mediterranean and along the offshore trade routes of Europe. It was a decision that he held to and which grew as the years went on. Here, launched at last on the journey for which he had spent a lifetime preparing, he finds he must reaffirm his decision once again.

Samuel Eliot Morison's biography of Columbus, from which the following section was taken, won the Pulitzer Prize the year it was published. It remains the finest picture we have of the man and his times.

DURING THE eighth day of October, when "Thanks be to God," says the Admiral, "the air is soft as in April in Seville, and it's a pleasure to be in it, so fragrant it is," the WSW course was maintained. . . . And all night October 9–10 the men could hear flocks of birds flying overhead to the southwestward, and sometimes could see them against the moon. . . .

Notwithstanding this encouraging sign, October 10 was the most critical day of the entire voyage, when the enterprise came nearest to failure through the stubborn conservatism of the men. It is unfair to present the issue between Columbus and his crew as one between a brave man and cowards. Nor was it one between knowledge and ignorance, education and superstition: for if Columbus had had a university education, or listened attentively to the best opinions of his day, he would never have expected Japan to lie 750 leagues west of the Canaries. It was, rather, the inevitable conflict between a man of one great, compelling idea and those who did not share it in anything like the same degree. . . . Their issue with their commander was the eternal one between imagination and doubt, between the spirit that creates and the spirit that denies. . . .

And so, on October 10, when the fleet was steering straight for the Bahamas, and the nearest land was less than 200 miles ahead, all the smoldering discontent of the men flared up into open mutiny. They had done enough and more than enough; the ships should and must turn back. This mutiny, so far as we have any record, was confined to the flagship. . . . What Columbus noted down . . . is short and to the point, and not ungenerous to the men:

"Here the people could stand it no longer, complained of the long voyage; but the Admiral cheered them as best he could, holding out good hope of the advantages they might have; and he added that it was useless to complain, since he had come to go to the Indies, and so had to continue until he found them, with the help of Our Lord." . . .

All day Thursday, October 11, the trade wind still blew a gale, the sea rose higher than at any time on the voyage, and the fleet ran 78 miles between sunrise and sunset, an average speed of 6.7 knots. But signs of land were so many and so frequent that "everyone breathed more freely and grew cheerful." *Niña* picked up a green branch with a little flower that resembled the dog roses on hedges in Castile. *Pinta* gathered quite a collection. . . . These objects . . . served their purpose of stopping complaints, and preparing every man aboard for a speedy end to this first Atlantic crossing.

Sun set under a clear horizon about 5.30, every man in the fleet watching for a silhouette of land against its red disk; but no land was there. All hands were summoned as usual, and after they had said their evening prayers and sung the *Salve Regina* . . . Columbus from the sterncastle made his men a little speech, reminding them of the grace Our Lord has shown them in conducting them so safely and prosperously with fair winds and a clear course . . . ; and he urged the night watch to keep a particularly sharp lookout on the forecastle, reminding them that although he had given orders to do no night sailing after reaching a point 700 leagues from the Canaries, the great desire of all to see land had decided him to carry on that night. Hence all must make amends for this temerity by keeping a particularly good watch, and looking sharp for land, and to him who first sighted it he would then and there give him a silk doublet, in addition to the annuity . . . that the Sovereigns had promised. The gromet then sang his little ditty for changing the watch . . . boatswain Chachu bellowed out the Castilian equivalent to "watch below lay belo-o-w!" and the men took their stations with eyes well peeled. . . .

Anyone who has come onto the land under sail at night from an uncertain position knows how tense the atmosphere aboard ship can be. And this night of October 11–12 was one big with destiny for the human race, the most momentous ever experienced aboard any ship in any sea. Some of the boys doubtless slept, but nobody else. Juan de la Cosa and the Pinzóns are pacing the high poops of their respective vessels, frequently calling down to the men at the tiller a testy order. . . . Lookouts on the forecastles and in the round-tops talking low to each other— Hear anything? Sounds like breakers to me—nothing but the bow wave you fool—I tell you we won't sight land till Saturday, I dreamt it, and my dreams—you and your dreams, here's a hundred maravedis says we raise it by daylight. . . . They tell each other how they would have conducted the fleet—The Old Man never should have set that spritsail, she'll run her bow under—if he'd asked my advice, and I was making my third voyage when he was playing in the streets of Genoa, I'd have told him. . . . Under such circumstances, with everyone's nerves taut as the weather braces, there was almost certain to be a false alarm of land.

An hour before moonrise, at 10 P.M., it came. Columbus, standing on the sterncastle, thought he saw a light, "so uncertain a thing that he did not wish to declare that it was land," but called Pedro Gutiérrez to have a look, and he thought he saw it too. . . . The light, Columbus said, "was like a little wax candle rising and falling," and he saw it only once or twice. . . .

At this juncture one of the seamen . . . thought he saw a light and sang out, "*Lumbre! tierra!*" Pedro de Salcedo, Columbus's page-boy, piped up with "It's already been seen by my master". . . . There is no need to criticize Columbus's seamanship because he sighted an imaginary light, but it is not easy to defend the fact that for this false landfall, which he must have known the next day to have been imaginary, he demanded and obtained the annuity of 10,000 maravedis promised by the Sovereigns to the man who first sighted land. The best we can say in extenuation is to point out that glory rather than greed prompted this act of injustice to a seaman: Columbus could not bear to think that anyone but himself sighted land first. This form of male vanity is by no means absent from the seafaring tribe today.

At 2.00 A.M. October 12 the moon, past full, was . . . just the position to illuminate anything ahead of the ships. . . . On speed the three ships, *Pinta* in the lead, their sails silver in the moonlight. A brave trade wind is blowing and the caravels are rolling, plunging and throwing spray as they cut down the last invisible barrier between the Old World and the New. Only a few moments now, and an era that began in remotest antiquity will end.

Rodrigo de Triana, lookout on *Pinta's* forecastle, sees something like a white sand cliff gleaming in the moonlight on the western horizon, then another, and a dark line of land connecting them. *"Tierra! tierra!"* he shouts, and this time land it is.

Martin Alonso Pinzón, after a quick verification, causes a lombard already loaded and primed to be fired as the agreed signal, and shortens sail in order to wait for the flagship. As soon as *Santa Maria* approached . . . Columbus called out, "Senor Martin Alonso, you have found land!" . . . *Santa Maria, Pinta* and *Niña* jogged off-and-on until daylight. . . .

This first land of the Western Hemisphere . . . sighted by any European since the voyages of the Northmen, was the eastern coast of one of the Bahamas now officially named "San Salvador or Watlings Island." . . .

San Salvador is a coral island about 13 miles long by 6 wide . . . surrounded by dangerous reefs. By daylight Columbus's fleet must have drifted to a point near the Hinchinbrooke Rocks off the southeastern point. Making sail and filling away, they sought an opening through the reef barrier where they might safely anchor and send boats ashore. And the first gap that they could have discovered . . . was on the western shore. . . . Here, rounding a prominent breaking ledge now called Gardiner Reef, the caravels braced their yards sharp and entered a shallow bay. . . . Off a curving beach of gleaming coral sand, they found sheltered anchorage in 5 fathoms of water.

Somewhere on this beach of Long or Fernandez Bay took place the famous Landing of Columbus, often depicted by artists, but never with any respect for the actual topography. Las Casas's abstract of the Journal, and Ferdinand Columbus, who had the Journal before him when he wrote the biography of his father, are the unique sources for this incident. Fitting together the two, we have this description:

"Presently they saw naked people, and the Admiral went ashore in the armed ship's boat with the royal standard displayed. So did the captains of *Pinta* and *Niña* . . . in their boats, with the banners of the Expedition, on which were depicted a green cross with an F on one arm and a Y on the other, and over each his or her crown. And, all having rendered thanks to Our Lord kneeling on the ground, embracing it with tears of joy for the immeasurable mercy of having reached it, the Admiral arose and gave this island the name of *San Salvador*. Thereupon he summoned to him the two captains . . . and all others who came ashore, as witnesses; and in the presence of many natives of that land assembled together, took possession of that island in the name of the Catholic Sovereigns with appropriate words and ceremony. . . . Forthwith the Christians hailed him as Admiral and Viceroy and swore to obey him . . . all begging his pardon for the injuries that through fear and inconstancy they had done him. Many Indians having come together for that ceremony and rejoicing, the Admiral, seeing that they were a gentle and peaceful people and of great simplicity, gave them some little red caps and glass beads which they hung around their necks, and other things of slight worth, which they all valued at the highest price."

Admiral of the Ocean Sea, by Samuel Eliot Morison

HARRY S. TRUMAN

"But the test was now successful."

In April of 1945 Harry S. Truman was called, hastily and under tragic circumstances, to the Presidency of the United States
—and within a few months found himself required to make a decision that must change the course of history. Because of its frightening, unbelievable power the atomic bomb was destined to be not
only the determining factor in all future warfare but also a tremendously important consideration in all fields of world relations even
in peacetime.

The "Manhattan Project" had been under way since 1942, but
such was its secrecy that even the Vice President didn't know of
its existence until he was asked to decide whether—and how—this
deadly force was to be released into the world.

THE HISTORIC message of the first explosion of an atomic bomb was
flashed to me in a message from Secretary of War Stimson on the
morning of July 16. The most secret and the most daring enterprise
of the war had succeeded. We were now in possession of a weapon
that would not only revolutionize war but could alter the course of
history and civilization. This news reached me at Potsdam the day
after I had arrived for the conference of the Big Three.

Preparations were being rushed for the test atomic explosion at
Alamogordo, New Mexico, at the time I had to leave for Europe, and
on the voyage over I had been anxiously awaiting word on the results.
I had been told of many predictions by the scientists, but no one was
certain of the outcome of this full-scale atomic explosion. As I read the
message from Stimson, I realized that the test not only met the most
optimistic expectation of the scientists but that the United States had
in its possession an explosive force of unparalleled power.

Stimson flew to Potsdam the next day to see me and brought with
him the full details of the test. I received him at once and called in
Secretary of State Byrnes, Admiral Leahy, General Marshall, General
Arnold, and Admiral King to join us at my office at the Little White
House. We reviewed our military strategy in the light of this revolu-
tionary development. We were not ready to make use of this weapon

against the Japanese, although we did not know as yet what effect the new weapon might have, physically or psychologically, when used against the enemy. For that reason the military advised that we go ahead with the existing military plans for the invasion of the Japanese home islands.

At Potsdam, as elsewhere, the secret of the atomic bomb was kept closely guarded. We did not extend the very small circle of Americans who knew about it. Churchill naturally knew about the atomic bomb project from its very beginning, because it had involved the pooling of British and American technical skill.

On July 24 I casually mentioned to Stalin that we had a new weapon of unusual destructive force. The Russian Premier showed no special interest. All he said was that he was glad to hear it and hoped we would make "good use of it against the Japanese."

A month before the test explosion of the atomic bomb the service Secretaries and the Joint Chiefs of Staff had laid their detailed plans for the defeat of Japan before me for approval. There had apparently been some differences of opinion as to the best route to be followed, but these had evidently been reconciled, for when General Marshall had presented his plan for a two-phase invasion of Japan, Admiral King and General Arnold had supported the proposal heartily.

The Army plan envisaged an amphibious landing in the fall of 1945 on the island of Kyushu, the southernmost of the Japanese home islands. This would be accomplished by our Sixth Army, under the command of General Walter Krueger. The first landing would then be followed approximately four months later by a second great invasion, which would be carried out by our Eighth and Tenth Armies, followed by the First Army transferred from Europe, all of which would go ashore in the Kanto plains area near Tokyo. In all, it had been estimated that it would require until the late fall of 1946 to bring Japan to her knees.

This was a formidable conception, and all of us realized fully that the fighting would be fierce and the losses heavy. But it was hoped that some of Japan's forces would continue to be preoccupied in China and others would be prevented from reinforcing the home islands if Russia were to enter the war. . . .

General Marshall told me that it might cost half a million American lives to force the enemy's surrender on his home grounds.

But the test was now successful. The entire development of the atomic bomb had been dictated by military considerations. The idea of the atomic bomb had been suggested to President Roosevelt by the famous and brilliant Dr. Albert Einstein, and its development turned out to be a vast undertaking. It was the achievement of the combined efforts of science, industry, labor, and the military, and it had no parallel in history. The men in charge and their staffs worked under extremely high pressure, and the whole enormous task required the services of more than one hundred thousand men and immense quantities of material. It required over two and a half years and necessitated the expenditure of two and a half billions of dollars.

Only a handful of the thousands of men who worked in these plants knew what they were producing. So strict was the secrecy imposed that even some of the highest-ranking officials in Washington had not the slightest idea of what was going on. I did not. Before 1939 it had been generally agreed among scientists that it was theoretically possible to release energy from the atom. In 1940 we had begun to pool with Great Britain all scientific knowledge useful to war, although Britain was at war at that time and we were not. Following this—in 1942— we learned that the Germans were at work on a method to harness atomic energy for use as a weapon of war. This, we understood, was to be added to the V-1 and V-2 rockets with which they hoped to conquer the world. They failed, of course, and for this we can thank Providence. But now a race was on to make the atomic bomb—a race that became "the battle of the laboratories."

It was under the general policy of pooling knowledge between our nation and Great Britain that research on the atomic bomb started in such feverish secrecy. American and British scientists joined in the race against the Germans. We in America had available a great number of distinguished scientists in many related fields of knowledge, and we also had another great advantage. We could provide the tremendous industrial and economic resources required for the project—a vastly expensive project—without injury to our war production program. Furthermore, our plants were far removed from the reach of enemy bombing. Britain, whose scientists had initiated the project and were contributing much of the original atomic data, was constantly exposed to enemy bombing and, when she started the atomic research, also faced the possibility of invasion.

For these reasons Roosevelt and Churchill agreed to pool the research and concentrate all of the work on the development of the project within the United States. Working together with the British, we thus made it possible to achieve a great scientific triumph in the field of atomic energy. Nevertheless, basic and historic as this event was, it had to be considered at the time as relatively incidental to the far-flung war we were fighting in the Pacific at terrible cost in American lives.

We could hope for a miracle, but the daily tragedy of a bitter war crowded in on us. We labored to construct a weapon of such over-powering force that the enemy could be forced to yield swiftly once we could resort to it. This was the primary aim of our secret and vast effort. But we also had to carry out the enormous effort of our basic and traditional military plans.

The task of creating the atomic bomb had been entrusted to a special unit of the Army Corps of Engineers, the so-called Manhattan District, headed by Major General Leslie R. Groves. The primary effort, however, had come from British and American scientists working in laboratories and offices scattered throughout the nation.

Dr. J. Robert Oppenheimer, the distinguished physicist from the University of California, had set up the key establishment in the whole process at Los Alamos, New Mexico. More than any other one man, Oppenheimer is to be credited with the achievement of the completed bomb.

My own knowledge of these developments had come about only after I became President, when Secretary Stimson had given me the full story. He had told me at that time that the project was nearing completion and that a bomb could be expected within another four months. It was at his suggestion, too, that I had then set up a committee of top men and had asked them to study with great care the implications the new weapon might have for us.

Secretary Stimson headed this group as chairman, and the other members were George L. Harrison, president of the New York Life Insurance Company, who was then serving as a special assistant to the Secretary of War; James F. Byrnes, as my personal representative; Ralph A. Bard, Under Secretary of the Navy; Assistant Secretary William L. Clayton for the State Department; and three of our most renowned scientists—Dr. Vannevar Bush, president of the Carnegie Institution of Washington and Director of the Office of Scientific Research and Development; Dr. Karl T. Compton, president of the Massachusetts Institute of Technology and Chief of Field Service in the Office of Scientific Research and Development; and Dr. James B. Conant, president of Harvard University and chairman of the National Defense Research Committee.

This committee was assisted by a group of scientists, of whom those most prominently connected with the development of the atomic bomb were Dr. Oppenheimer, Dr. Arthur H. Compton, Dr. E. O. Lawrence, and the Italian-born Dr. Enrico Fermi. The conclusions reached by these men, both in the advisory committee of scientists and in the larger committee, were brought to me by Secretary Stimson on June 1.

It was their recommendation that the bomb be used against the enemy as soon as it could be done. They recommended further that it should be used without specific warning and against a target that would clearly show its devastating strength. I had realized, of course, that an atomic bomb explosion would inflict damage and casualties beyond imagination. On the other hand, the scientific advisers of the committee reported, "We can propose no technical demonstration likely to bring an end to the war; we see no acceptable alternative to direct military use." It was their conclusion that no technical demonstration they might propose, such as over a deserted island, would be likely to bring the war to an end. It had to be used against an enemy target.

The final decision of where and when to use the atomic bomb was up to me. Let there be no mistake about it. I regarded the bomb as a military weapon and never had any doubt that it should be used. The top military advisers to the President recommended its use, and when I talked to Churchill he unhesitatingly told me that he favored the use of the atomic bomb if it might aid to end the war.

In deciding to use this bomb I wanted to make sure that it would be used as a weapon of war in the manner prescribed by the laws of war. That meant that I wanted it dropped on a military target. I had told Stimson that the bomb should be dropped as nearly as possibly upon a war production center of prime military importance.

Stimson's staff had prepared a list of cities in Japan that might serve as targets. Kyoto, though favored by General Arnold as a center of military activity, was eliminated when Secretary Stimson pointed out that it was a cultural and religious shrine of the Japanese.

Four cities were finally recommended as targets: Hiroshima, Kokura, Niigata, and Nagasaki. They were listed in that order as targets for the first attack. The order of selection was in accordance with the military importance of these cities, but allowance would be given for weather conditions at the time of the bombing. Before the selected targets were approved as proper for military purposes, I personally went over them in detail with Stimson, Marshall, and Arnold, and we discussed the matter of timing and the final choice of the first target.

General Spaatz, who commanded the Strategic Air Forces, which would deliver the bomb on the target, was given some latitude as to when and on which of the four targets the bomb would be dropped. That was necessary because of weather and other operational considerations. In order to get preparations under way, the War Department was given orders to instruct General Spaatz that the first bomb would be dropped as soon after August 3 as weather would permit. The order to General Spaatz read as follows:

24 July 1945

TO: General Carl Spaatz
    Commanding General
    United States Army Strategic Air Forces

1. The 509 Composite Group, 20th Air Force, will deliver its first special bomb as soon as weather will permit visual bombing after about 3 August 1945 on one of the targets: Hiroshima, Kokura, Niigata and Nagasaki. To carry military and civilian scientific personnel from the War Department to observe and record the effects of the explosion of the bomb, additional aircraft will accompany the airplane carrying the bomb. The observing planes will stay several miles distant from the point of impact of the bomb.

2. Additional bombs will be delivered on the above targets as soon as made ready by the project staff. Further instructions will be issued concerning targets other than those listed above.

3. Dissemination of any and all information concerning the use of the weapon against Japan is reserved to the Secretary of War and the President of the United States. No communique on the subject or release of information will be issued by Commanders in the field without specific prior authority. Any news stories will be sent to the War Department for special clearance.

4. The foregoing directive is issued to you by direction and with the approval of the Secretary of War and the Chief of Staff, U.S.A. It is desired that you personally deliver one copy of this directive to General MacArthur and one copy to Admiral Nimitz for their information.

/s/ Thos. T. Handy
General, GSC
Acting Chief of Staff

With this order the wheels were set in motion for the first use of an atomic weapon against a military target. I had made the decision. I also instructed Stimson that the order would stand unless I notified him that the Japanese reply to our ultimatum was acceptable.

A specialized B-29 unit, known as the 509th Composite Group, had been selected for the task, and seven of the modified B-29's, with pilots and crews, were ready and waiting for orders. Meanwhile ships and planes were rushing the materials for the bomb and specialists to assemble them to the Pacific island of Tinian in the Marianas.

On July 28 Radio Tokyo announced that the Japanese government would continue to fight. There was no formal reply to the joint ul-

timatum of the United States, the United Kingdom, and China. There
was no alternative now. The bomb was scheduled to be dropped after
August 3 unless Japan surrendered before that day.

On August 6, the fourth day of the journey home from Potsdam,
came the historic news that shook the world. I was eating lunch with
members of the *Augusta's* crew when Captain Frank Graham, White
House Map Room watch officer, handed me the following message:

TO THE PRESIDENT

FROM THE SECRETARY OF WAR

Big bomb dropped on Hiroshima August 5 at 7:15 P.M. Washington time. First reports indicate complete success which was
even more conspicuous than earlier test.

I was greatly moved. I telephoned Byrnes aboard ship to give him
the news and then said to the group of sailors around me, "This is the
greatest thing in history. It's time for us to get home."

A few minutes later a second message was handed to me. It read
as follows:

Following info regarding Manhattan received. "Hiroshima
bombed visually with only one tenth cover at 052315A. There
was no fighter opposition and no flak. Parsons reports 15 minutes
after drop as follows: 'Results clear cut successful in all respects.
Visible effects greater than in any test. Conditions normal in airplane following delivery.'"

When I had read this I signaled to the crew in the mess hall that I
wished to say something. I then told them of the dropping of a powerful new bomb which used an explosive twenty thousand times as powerful as a ton of TNT. I went to the wardroom, where I told the
officers, who were at lunch, what had happened. I could not keep back
my expectation that the Pacific war might now be brought to a speedy
end.

A few minutes later the ship's radio receivers began to carry news
bulletins from Washington about the atomic bomb, as well as a broadcast of the statement I had authorized just before leaving Germany.
Shortly afterward I called a press conference of the correspondents on
board and told them something of the long program of research and
development that lay behind this successful assault.

My statements on the atomic bomb, which had been released in
Washington by Stimson, read in part as follows:

". . . But the greatest marvel is not the size of the enterprise, its
secrecy, nor its cost, but the achievement of scientific brains in putting
together infinitely complex pieces of knowledge held by many men in
different fields of science into a workable plan. And hardly less marvel-

ous has been the capacity of industry to design, and of labor to operate, the machines and methods to do things never done before, so that the brain child of many minds came forth in physical shape and performed as it was supposed to do. Both science and industry worked under the direction of the United States Army, which achieved a unique success in managing so diverse a problem in the advancement of knowledge in an amazingly short time. It is doubtful if such another combination could be got together in the world. What has been done is the greatest achievement of organized science in history. It was done under high pressure and without failure.

"We are now prepared to obliterate more rapidly and completely every productive enterprise the Japanese have above ground in any city. We shall destroy their docks, their factories, and their communications. Let there be no mistake; we shall completely destroy Japan's power to make war.

"It was to spare the Japanese people from utter destruction that the ultimatum of July 26 was issued at Potsdam. Their leaders promptly rejected that ultimatum. If they do not now accept our terms, they may expect a rain of ruin from the air, the like of which has never been seen on this earth. Behind this air attack will follow sea and land forces in such numbers and power as they have not yet seen and with the fighting skill of which they are already well aware.

". . . The fact that we can release atomic energy ushers in a new era in man's understanding of nature's forces. Atomic energy may in the future supplement the power that now comes from coal, oil, and falling water, but at present it cannot be produced on a basis to compete with them commercially. Before that comes there must be a long period of intensive research.

"It has never been the habit of the scientists of this country or the policy of this Government to withhold from the world scientific knowledge. Normally, therefore, everything about the work with atomic energy would be made public.

"But under present circumstances it is not intended to divulge the technical processes of production or all the military applications, pending further examination of possible methods of protecting us and the rest of the world from the danger of sudden destruction.

"I shall recommend that the Congress of the United States consider promptly the establishment of an appropriate commission to control the production and use of atomic power within the United States.

"I shall give further consideration and make further recommendations to the Congress as to how atomic power can become a powerful and forceful influence towards the maintenance of world peace."

Still no surrender offer came. An order was issued to General Spaatz to continue operations as planned unless otherwise instructed.

Year of Decision, by Harry S. Truman

BENJAMIN FRANKLIN

"... I took upon me to assert my freedom ..."

Even in his own lifetime Benjamin Franklin was revered as a great man and a great American. Statesman, philosopher, inventor, businessman and consummate human being, he was loved and respected not only in his own country but throughout the capitals of Europe. He was the American Renaissance man, and appropriately his beginnings were peculiarly American. Franklin's schooling was limited to two years—but by the time he was 17 he was running a liberal newspaper in Boston. At 26 he had published his first Poor Richard's Almanack, was the public printer for the colony of Pennsylvania and had organized Philadelphia's first volunteer fire department.

The picture of Franklin trudging into Philadelphia carrying the two buns for which he had spent his last shilling has become a symbol of colonial America. Less well known is the story of the journey that took him to that city—told here in his own words.

AT LENGTH, a fresh difference arising between my brother and me, I took upon me to assert my freedom, presuming that he would not venture to produce the new indentures. It was not fair in me to take this advantage, and this I therefore reckon one of the first errata of my life; but the unfairness of it weighed little with me, when under the impressions of resentment for the blows his passion too often urged him to bestow upon me, though he was otherwise not an ill-natured man. Perhaps I was too saucy and provoking.

When he found I would leave him, he took care to prevent my getting employment in any other printing-house of the town, by going round and speaking to every master, who accordingly refused to give me work. I then thought of going to New York, as the nearest place where there was a printer; and I was rather inclined to leave Boston when I reflected that I had already made myself a little obnoxious to the governing party, and from the arbitrary proceedings of the Assembly in my brother's case, it was likely I might, if I stayed, soon bring myself into scrapes; and further, that my indiscreet disputations about religion began to make me pointed at with horror by good people as an infidel or atheist. I determined on the point, but my father now siding with my brother, I was sensible that if I attempted to go openly, means would be used to prevent me. My friend Collins, therefore, undertook to manage a little for me. He agreed with the captain of a New York sloop for my passage under the notion of my being a young acquaintance of his that had got into trouble. So I sold some of my books to raise a little money, was taken on board privately, and as we had a fair wind, in three days I found myself in New York, near three hundred miles from home, a boy of but seventeen, without the least recommendation to, or knowledge of, any person in the place, and with very little money in my pocket.

My inclinations for the sea were by this time worn out, or I might now have gratified them. But, having a trade, and supposing myself a pretty good workman, I offered my service to the printer in the place, old Mr. William Bradford, who had been the first printer in Pennsylvania, but removed from thence upon the quarrel of George Keith. He could give me no employment, having little to do, and help enough already; but says he, "My son at Philadelphia has lately lost his principal hand, Aquila Rose, by death; if you go thither, I believe he may employ you." Philadelphia was a hundred miles further; I set out, however, in a boat for Amboy, leaving my chest and things to follow me round by sea.

In crossing the bay, we met with a squall that tore our rotten sails to pieces, prevented our getting into the Kill, and drove us upon Long Island. In our way, a drunken Dutchman, who was a passenger too, fell overboard; when he was sinking, I reached through the water to his shock pate, and drew him up, so that we got him in again. His ducking sobered him a little, and he went to sleep, taking first out of his pocket a book, which he desired I would dry for him. It proved to be my old favorite author, Bunyan's *Pilgrim's Progress*, in Dutch, finely printed on good paper, with copper cuts, a dress better than I had ever seen it wear in its own language. I have since found that it has been translated into most of the languages of Europe, and suppose it has been more generally read than any other book, except perhaps the Bible. Honest John was the first that I know of who mixed narration and dialogue; a method of writing very engaging to the reader, who in the most interesting parts finds himself, as it were, brought into the company and present at the discourse. De Foe in his *Crusoe*, his *Moll Flanders*, *Religious Courtship*, *Family Instructor*, and other pieces, has imitated it with success, and Richardson has done the same in his *Pamela*, etc.

When we drew near the island, we found it was at a place where there could be no landing, there being a great surf on the stony beach. So we dropped anchor, and swung round towards the shore. Some people came down to the water edge and hallooed to us, as we did to them; but the wind was so high, and the surf so loud, that we could not hear so as to understand each other. There were canoes on the shore, and we made signs, and hallooed that they should fetch us; but they either did not understand us, or thought it impracticable, so they went away, and night coming on, we had no remedy but to wait till the wind should abate; and, in the mean time, the boatman and I concluded to sleep, if we could; and so crowded into the scuttle, with the Dutchman, who was still wet; and the spray beating over the head of our boat, leaked through to us, so that we were soon almost as wet as he. In this manner we lay all night, with very little rest; but the wind abating the next day, we made a shift to reach Amboy before night, having been thirty hours on the water, without victuals, or any drink but a bottle of filthy rum, the water we sailed on being salt.

In the evening I found myself very feverish, and went into bed; but having read somewhere that cold water drank plentifully was good for a fever, I followed the prescription, sweat plentifully most of the night, my fever left me, and in the morning, crossing the ferry, I proceeded on my journey on foot, having fifty miles to Burlington, where I was told I should find boats that would carry me the rest of the way to Philadelphia.

It rained very hard all the day; I was thoroughly soaked, and by noon a good deal tired; so I stopped at a poor inn, where I stayed all night, beginning now to wish that I had never left home. I cut so miserable a figure, too, that I found by the questions asked me, I was suspected to be some runaway servant, and in danger of being taken up on that suspicion. However, I proceeded the next day, and got in the evening to an inn, within eight or ten miles of Burlington, kept by one Dr. Brown. He entered into conversation with me while I took some refreshment, and, finding I had read a little, became very sociable and friendly. Our acquaintance continued as long as he lived. He had been, I imagine, an itinerant doctor, for there was no town in England, or country in Europe, of which he could not give a very particular account. He had some letters, and was ingenious, but much of an unbeliever, and wickedly undertook, some years after, to travesty the Bible in doggerel verse, as Cotton had done Virgil. By this means he set many of the facts in a very ridiculous light, and might have hurt weak minds if his work had been published; but it never was.

At his house I lay that night, and the next morning reached Burlington, but had the mortification to find that the regular boats were gone a little before my coming, and no other expected to go before

Tuesday, this being Saturday; wherefore I returned to an old woman in the town, of whom I had bought gingerbread to eat on the water, and asked her advice. She invited me to lodge at her house till a passage by water should offer; and being tired with my foot traveling, I accepted the invitation. She, understanding I was a printer, would have had me stay at that town and follow my business, being ignorant of the stock necessary to begin with. She was very hospitable, gave me a dinner of ox-cheek with great good-will, accepting only of a pot of ale in return; and I thought myself fixed till Tuesday should come. However, walking in the evening by the side of the river, a boat came by, which I found was going towards Philadelphia, with several people in her. They took me in, and, as there was no wind, we rowed all the way; and about midnight, not having yet seen the city, some of the company were confident we must have passed it, and would row no farther; the others knew not where we were; so we put toward the shore, got into a creek, landed near an old fence, with the rails of which we made a fire, the night being cold, in October, and there we remained till daylight. Then one of the company knew the place to be Cooper's Creek, a little above Philadelphia, which we saw as soon as we got out of the creek, and arrived there about eight or nine o'clock on the Sunday morning, and landed at the Market Street wharf.

I have been the more particular in this description of my journey, and shall be so of my first entry into that city, that you may in your mind compare such unlikely beginnings with the figure I have since made there. I was in my working-dress, my best clothes being to come round by sea. I was dirty from my journey; my pockets were stuffed out with shirts and stockings, and I knew no soul nor where to look for lodging. I was fatigued with traveling, rowing, and want of rest; I was very hungry; and my whole stock of cash consisted of a Dutch dollar, and about a shilling in copper. The latter I gave the people of the boat for my passage, who at first refused it on account of my rowing; but I insisted on their taking it, a man being sometimes more generous when he has but a little money than when he has plenty, perhaps through fear of being thought to have but little.

Then I walked up the street, gazing about till near the market-house I met a boy with bread. I had made many a meal on bread, and inquiring where he got it, I went immediately to the baker's he directed me to, in Second Street, and asked for biscuit, intending such as we had in Boston; but they, it seems, were not made in Philadelphia. Then I asked for a three-penny loaf, and was told they had none such. So not considering or knowing the difference of money, and the greater cheapness nor the names of his bread, I bade him give me three-penny worth of any sort. He gave me, accordingly, three great puffy rolls. I was surprised at the quantity, but took it, and having no room in my pockets, walked off with a roll under each arm, and eating the other. Thus I went up Market Street as far as Fourth Street, passing by the door of Mr. Read, my future wife's father; when she, standing at the door, saw me, and thought I made, as I certainly did, a most awkward, ridiculous appearance. Then I turned and went down Chestnut Street and part of Walnut Street, eating my roll all the way, and coming round, found myself again at Market Street wharf, near the boat I came in, to which I went for a draught of the river water; and being filled with one of my rolls, gave the other two to a woman and her child that came down the river in the boat with us, and were waiting to go farther.

Thus refreshed, I walked again up the street, which by this time had many clean-dressed people in it, who were all walking the same way. I joined them, and thereby was led into the great meeting-house of the Quakers near the market. I sat down among them, and after looking round a while and hearing nothing said, being very drowsy through labor and want of rest the preceding night, I fell fast asleep, and continued so till the meeting broke up, when one was kind enough to rouse me. This was, therefore, the first house I was in or slept in, in Philadelphia. . . .

The Autobiography of Benjamin Franklin

THOMAS MERTON

"It was a moment of crisis ... a moment of searching ... a moment of joy."

As a student Thomas Merton lived a rather aimless life of late parties, long discussions, little constructive work—none of it appearing to lead anywhere. He belonged to that restless generation that grew up in the depression and matured under the lowering shadow of the Second World War. His decision to leave this world for life in a monastery came without apparent warning or conscious planning . . . but when it came it was a final, irrevocable stand.

THE SEPTEMBER days went by, and the first signs of fall were beginning to be seen in the clearing of the bright air. The days of heat were done. It was getting on toward that season of new beginnings, when I would get back to work on my Ph.D., and when I hoped possibly to get some kind of job as an instructor at Columbia, in the College or in Extension.

These were the things I was thinking about when one night Rice and Bob Gerdy and I were in Nick's on Sheridan Square, sitting at the curved bar while the room rocked with jazz. Presently Gibney came in with Peggy Wells, who was one of the girls in that show at the Center Theater, the name of which I have forgotten. We all sat together at a table and talked and drank. It was just like all the other nights we spent in those places. It was more or less uninteresting but we couldn't think of anything else to do and there seemed to be no point in going to bed.

After Rice and Gerdy went home, Gibney and Peggy and I still sat there. Finally it got to be about four o'clock in the morning. Gibney did not want to go out on Long Island, and Peggy lived uptown in the Eighties.

They came to Perry Street, which was just around the corner.

It was nothing unusual for me to sleep on the floor, or in a chair, or on a couch too narrow and too short for comfort—that was the way we lived, and the way thousands of other people like us lived. One stayed up all night, and finally went to sleep wherever there happened to be room for one man to put his tired carcass.

It is a strange thing that we should have thought nothing of it, when if anyone had suggested sleeping on the floor as a penance, for the love of God, we would have felt that he was trying to insult our intelligence and dignity as men! What a barbarous notion! Making yourself uncomfortable as a penance! And yet we somehow seemed to think it quite logical to sleep that way as part of an evening dedicated to pleasure. It shows how far the wisdom of the world will go in contradicting itself. "From him that hath not, it shall be taken away even that which he hath."

I suppose I got some five or six hours of fitful sleep, and at about eleven we were all awake, sitting around dishevelled and half stupefied, talking and smoking and playing records. The thin, ancient, somewhat elegiac cadences of the long dead Beiderbecke sang in the room. From where I sat, on the floor, I could see beyond the roofs to a patch of clear fall sky.

At about one o'clock in the afternoon I went out to get some breakfast, returning with scrambled eggs and toast and coffee in an armful of cardboard containers, different shapes and sizes, and pockets full of new packs of cigarettes. But I did not feel like smoking. We ate and talked, and finally cleared up all the mess and someone had the idea of going for a walk to the Chicken Dock. So we got ready to go.

Somewhere in the midst of all this, an idea had come to me, an idea that was startling enough and momentous enough by itself, but much more astonishing in the context. Perhaps many people will not believe what I am saying.

While we were sitting there on the floor playing records and eating this breakfast the idea came to me: "I am going to be a priest."

I cannot say what caused it: it was not a reaction of especially strong disgust at being so tired and so uninterested in this life I was still leading, in spite of its futility. It was not the music, not the fall air, for this conviction that had suddenly been planted in me full grown was not the sick and haunting sort of a thing that an emotional urge always is. It was not a thing of passion or of fancy. It was a strong and sweet and deep and insistent attraction that suddenly made itself felt, but not as movement of appetite towards any sensible good. It was something in the order of conscience, a new and profound and clear sense that this was what I really ought to do.

How long the idea was in my mind before I mentioned it, I cannot say. But presently I said casually:

"You know, I think I ought to go and enter a monastery and become a priest."

Gibney had heard that before, and thought I was fooling. The statement aroused no argument or comment, and anyway, it was not one to which Gibney was essentially unsympathetic. As far as he was concerned, any life made sense except that of a business man.

As we went out the door of the house I was thinking:

"I am going to be a priest."

When we were on the Chicken Dock, my mind was full of the same idea. Around three or four in the afternoon Gibney left and went home to Port Washington. Peggy and I sat looking at the dirty river for a while longer. Then I walked with her to the subway. In the shadows under the elevated drive over Tenth Avenue I said:

"Peggy, I mean it, I am going to enter a monastery and be a priest."

She didn't know me very well and anyway, she had no special ideas about being a priest. There wasn't much she could say. Anyway, what did I expect her to say?

I was glad, at last, to be alone. On that big wide street that is a continuation of Eighth Avenue, where the trucks run down very fast and loud—I forget its name—there was a little Catholic library and a German bakery where I often ate my meals. Before going to the bakery to get dinner and supper in one, I went to the Catholic library, St. Veronica's. The only book about religious Orders they seemed to have was a little green book about the Jesuits but I took it and read it while I ate in the bakery.

Now that I was alone, the idea assumed a different and more cogent form. Very well: I had accepted the possibility of the priesthood as real and fitting for me. It remained for me to make it, in some sense, more decisive.

What did that mean? What was required? My mind groped for some sort of an answer. What was I supposed to do, here and now?

I must have been a long time over the little book and these thoughts. When I came out into the street again, it was dusk. The side streets, in fact, were already quite dark. I suppose it was around seven o'clock.

Some kind of an instinct prompted me to go to Sixteenth Street, to the Jesuit Church of St. Francis Xavier. I had never been there. I don't know what I was looking for: perhaps I was thinking primarily of talking to some one of the Fathers there—I don't know.

When I got to Sixteenth Street, the whole building seemed dark and empty, and as a matter of fact the doors of the church were locked. Even the street was empty. I was about to go away disappointed, when I noticed a door to some kind of a basement under the church.

Ordinarily I would never have noticed such a door. You went down a couple of steps, and there it was, half hidden under the stairs that led up to the main door of the church. There was no sign that the door was anything but locked and bolted fast.

But something prompted me: "Try that door."

I went down the two steps, put my hand on the heavy iron handle. The door yielded and I found myself in a lower church, and the church was full of lights and people and the Blessed Sacrament was exposed in a monstrance on the altar, and at last I realized what I was supposed to do, and why I had been brought here.

It was some kind of a novena service, maybe a Holy Hour, I don't know: but it was nearly ending. Just as I found a place and fell on my knees, they began singing the *Tantum Ergo.* . . . All these people, workmen, poor women, students, clerks, singing the Latin hymn to the Blessed Sacrament written by St. Thomas Aquinas.

I fixed my eyes on the monstrance, on the white Host.

And then it suddenly became clear to me that my whole life was at a crisis. Far more than I could imagine or understand or conceive was now hanging upon a word—a decision of mine.

I had not shaped my life to this situation: I had not been building up to this. Nothing had been further from my mind. There was, therefore, an added solemnity in the fact that I had been called in here abruptly to answer a question that had been preparing, not in my mind, but in the infinite depths of an eternal Providence.

I did not clearly see it then, but I think now that it might have been something in the nature of a last chance. If I had hesitated or refused at that moment—what would have become of me?

But the way into the new land, the promised land, the land that was not like the Egypt where I persisted in living, was not thrown open again: and I instinctively sensed that it was only for a moment.

It was a moment of crisis, yet of interrogation: a moment of searching, but it was a moment of joy. It took me about a minute to collect my thoughts about the grace that had been suddenly planted in my soul, and to adjust the weak eyes of my spirit to its unaccustomed light, and during that moment my whole life remained suspended on the edge of an abyss: but this time, the abyss was an abyss of love and peace, the abyss was God.

It would be in some sense a blind, irrevocable act to throw myself over. But if I failed to do that . . . I did not even have to turn and look behind me at what I would be leaving. Wasn't I tired enough of all that?

So now the question faced me:

"Do you really want to be a priest? If you do, say so. . . ."

The hymn was ending. The priest collected the ends of the humeral veil over his hands that held the base of the monstrance, and slowly lifted it off the altar, and turned to bless the people.

I looked straight at the Host, and I knew, now, Who it was that I was looking at, and I said:

"Yes, I want to be a priest, with all my heart I want it. If it is Your will, make me a priest—make me a priest."

When I had said them, I realized in some measure what I had done with those last four words, what power I had put into motion on my behalf, and what a union had been sealed between me and that power by my decision.

The Seven Storey Mountain, by Thomas Merton

A. J. CRONIN

"... from that uncertain moment, the flood tide of success."

The chances of any great success for young A. J. Cronin were slight, if you judged only by outward appearances. It was only determination and will power that had taken him through medical school to a poor position as company doctor in a Welsh mining town. It would seem that here in Tregeny he had found his place in life. But in truth it was only the beginning, a first step that was to take him eventually to London and a successful Harley Street practice—and then, almost miraculously, to an entirely new career as a novelist.

Cronin tells his own story in the same engaging style that is responsible for the popularity that has sold millions of copies of his books. It is a story of drive—and a story of brilliance—the story of a man who dared to decide.

TIME WAS fleeting—days, weeks, and months—and I was getting nowhere. In the first flush of my enthusiasm I had promised my darling wife—although now I did not use this term of endearment when her efforts at Welsh cooking made me dose myself with bicarbonate of soda and groan that she was slowly poisoning me—I had promised her, I repeated, riches, position, a house in Harley Street, and, if I recollect correctly, a villa on the Mediterranean. And here we still were, plodding along, trying to save a little money—a depressing state of affairs under any circumstances—never "getting out of the bit," as the Scots say, still buried alive in these wretched mountains. I chafed, used many strong words, and applied for many situations, all without avail. Then, one memorable day, I burst in with a letter.

"We're leaving. At the end of the month."

My partner in distress gazed back at me, wide-eyed.

"Leaving! But I'm just getting to like it here."

Was there ever so perverse a woman, trying to convince me that she had nobly settled down? I restrained myself.

"You'll like it better where we're going. It's a much finer job."

I handed her the letter. It was from the secretary of the Medical Aid Society in a neighbouring valley of Tredegar, offering me a post as doctor to the society. The salary was only slightly more than I was now being paid, but what caught the eye and made the pulse bound was the fact that a house—a real house—was included in the terms of the appointment. Her nobility melted before such a temptation: she could scarcely bear to wait.

We remained long enough to enable the company to secure another doctor . . . then, packing our few belongings into a borrowed truck, we . . . set out over the high ridges for our new home.

Tredegar was a colliery town, too, but it was trim and clean and set on the verge of still unspoiled hill country. There were several decent stores, a public library, and—one could scarcely believe it—a town hall where moving pictures were shown twice a week.

The little house to which my wife had looked forward was stoutly built of red brick, with a gabled roof. Standing in a wild patch of garden beside a clear mountain stream spanned by a wooden bridge, it was appropriately named "The Glen." It seemed almost a mansion after the two rooms we had previously occupied, and although her brief but close association with me no longer permitted her to claim to be a saintly character, she thanked Heaven sincerely for the blessing of at last having a place of her own. To such an end the labour of moving in was as nothing—she greatly enjoyed getting things into shape. . . .

We had come in the month of October, and winter was soon upon us. Then, indeed, the going became fairly rough. Our finances were still so straitened that a car was out of the question, and I would tramp miles through the snow in leggings and oilskins, carrying my heavy black bag. It was a relief when, for fifty pounds, I was able to purchase a secondhand motorcycle. . . .

This was a time of great happiness. Our simple furnishings came from the local store, our rugs were certainly not from Persia, nor were our pictures from the best galleries, yet we had both pride and comfort in our small domain. On the cold nights we sat before our blazing fire—coal was plentiful and free—reading, talking, arguing. We had tremendous arguments. Unbelievably, my wife's cooking improved. She even revealed herself as a skilful gardener, raising tulips and noble hyacinths in the tiny glassed-in porch of the house.

Many sunny days came that winter, and when we were free to explore it we found a wild beauty on the high, bare heath which stretched far and away above "The Glen." A breeze always blew there, intoxicating as wine, which made me misquote Walt Whitman:

"There's a wind on the heath; when I feel it on my cheek I want to live forever." For miles under the racing clouds one would be lost in the exhilarating vastness of this primitive moorland, cut only by a few sheep tracks—then suddenly, breasting a crest, we would see the little town with the colliery headstocks far beneath, and would sit down to rest and to pick out, with pride, the toylike house which was our home.

Much of our outdoor leisure was spent up there. We took prodigious walks, gathered "whinberries" for deep-dish pie in the summer and in the fall, borrowing the colliery undermanager's gun, I went out after the snipe which wheeled and darted and always seemed to elude me.

In my medical knowledge I was progressing steadily, making friends among my patients and, at the cost of a few humiliations, learning that I did not quite know everything. The chief doctor of the district, Dr. Davies, was not only a highly skilled physician, with several exclusive London diplomas, but a brilliantly successful surgeon as well. When he consulted with me over a difficult or serious case, rolling up in his large spotless chauffeur-driven limousine while his younger colleague arrived on foot or on that execrable mud-spattered machine, often he differed, in the kindest manner, yet with authority, with my diagnosis.

After such interviews I would sit all evening, grinding my teeth, muttering invectives against my worthy superior. Then suddenly I would jump up. "Damn it all, he's right and I'm wrong. It *was* t.b. meningitis, and I should have spotted it days ago. I know nothing, absolutely nothing, but I will—I tell you I will!"

To my audience of one, knitting sedately on the other side of the fireplace, this might well have seemed a natural pique, soon to be passed over and forgotten. But no, I was in dead earnest. Davies had shown me my limitations; I knew I should never progress until I had overcome them.

I could sense my spouse wondering how this quest of knowledge would reveal itself. And soon she knew, for presently there began to arrive at "The Glen" a succession of large crates which at first sight looked as though they might contain interesting articles like new sheets or table linen or a set of dinner china (which she badly needed), but which, under my vigorous assaults with the hammer, revealed nothing more exciting than dozens of large, thick, and horribly abstruse-looking medical textbooks. Not having enough spare cash to purchase the books, I had joined the library of the Royal Society in London—in fact, it looked as though the entire library now were here, and it was only the beginning. . . .

After several months it became necessary for me to put in some practical work in biochemistry. The nearest laboratory was in the Health Department of Cardiff, more than fifty miles away. But this did not deter me. I applied to the secretary of the Medical Aid Society for four hours off duty on Thursday afternoons, and when this request was granted I departed every week on my motorcycle for the distant city. By making the journey at breakneck speed, I could secure two full hours in the laboratory before returning to my evening surgery. . . .

Of course, neither of us realised in the slightest the craziness of my project, which was to take no less than three major postgraduate degrees to supplement my M.B., Ch.B.: the M.D., the M.R.C.P., and the D.P.H. of London. For a practitioner commanding the expert teaching and highly technical resources of the great hospitals and universities, this constitutes a formidable enterprise, in which the average failures are more than 75 per cent. For an overworked colliery assistant, equipped only with borrowed books, prepared by no more than a few hasty dashes to a provincial laboratory, the thing was surely an impossibility.

I shall never forget the wet and windy day on which I departed for London to sit the examinations, nor the pessimistic bulletins, each gloomier than its predecessor, which I felt obliged to send home during the ensuing week. It is a strange contradiction in my character that, despite the confidence which sustains me during months of effort, the actual test of that effort finds me dispirited and hopeless. All my striving, my frenzied efforts, my almost hysterical outbursts seemed far away and done with. My brain was inactive, almost dull. I felt that I knew nothing. Indeed, when I began the written part of the examination, which was held at the College of Physicians, in Trafalgar Square, I found myself answering the papers with a blind automatism. I wrote and wrote, never looking at the clock, filling sheet after sheet, until my head reeled. . . .

After the written papers the practical and viva-voce part of the examination began, and I was more afraid of these than anything which had gone before. There were perhaps thirty other candidates, all of them men older than myself, and all with an unmistakable air of assurance and position. The candidate placed next to me, for instance, a man named Harold Beaumont whom I had once or twice spoken to, had an Oxford B.Ch., an out-patient appointment at St. Bartholomew's, and a consulting room in ultrafashionable Brook Street. When I compared Beaumont's charming manners, immaculate professional attire, and obvious standing with my own provincial awkwardness I felt my chances of favourably impressing the examiners to be small indeed.

My practical, at the South London Hospital, went, I thought, well enough. My case was one of bronchiectasis in a young boy of fourteen, which, since I had met this condition in my practice, was a piece of good fortune. I felt I had written a sound report. But when it came to the viva-voce my luck seemed to change completely. The "viva" procedure at the College of Physicians had its peculiarities. On two successive days each candidate was questioned, in turn, by two separate examiners. If at the end of the first session the candidate was found inadequate, he was handed a polite note telling him he need not return on the following day. Faced with the imminence of this fatal missive, I found to my horror that I had drawn as my first examiner a man I had heard Beaumont speak of with apprehension, Dr. Maurice Gadsby.

Gadsby was a spare undersized man with a pigeon chest, a tremendous "ha-ha" manner, and a beribboned monocle in his small, severe eye. Recently elected to his Fellowship, he had none of the tolerance of the older examiners, but seemed to set out deliberately to confuse and confound the candidates who came before him. Somewhat to my surprise, he greeted me, repeated my name several times, then demanded:

"Are you Richard's younger brother? Dick was at Cambridge with me, you know."

When I confessed, reluctantly, that I had no brother, he was plainly disappointed—indeed, almost aggrieved. He inspected me through the monocle.

"Were you at Cambridge?"

"No, sir."

"The other shop?"

"What shop, sir?"

"Oxford, of course."

"No, sir."

"Then what university?"

"Glasgow."

A hollow, devastating silence. He did not deign to comment but, with a supercilious lift to his brows, placed before me six slides. Five of these slides I named correctly, but the sixth I could not name. It was on this slide that Gadsby concentrated with all the contempt of one to whom the mere mention of a Scots university was almost obscene. For five minutes he harassed me on this section—which, it appeared, was the ovum of an obscure West African parasite—then languidly, without interest, he passed me on to the next examiner, who was none other than Lord Dawson of Penn, Physician to the King.

I rose and crossed the room with a pale face and a heavily beating heart. All the lassitude, the inertia I had experienced at the beginning of the week was gone now. I had an almost desperate desire to succeed. But I was convinced that Gadsby would fail me. I raised my eyes to find Lord Dawson contemplating me with a friendly, half-humorous smile.

"What's the matter?" he asked, unexpectedly.

"Nothing, sir," I stammered. "I think I've done rather badly with Dr. Gadsby—that's all."

"Never mind about that. Have a look at these specimens. Then just say anything about them that comes into your head."

Dawson smiled encouragingly. He was a handsome, fair-complexioned man of about sixty with a high forehead and a long, humorous upper lip masked by a cropped moustache. Though now perhaps the second most distinguished physician in Europe, he had known difficulties and sharp struggles in his earlier days when, coming from his native Yarrow, he had encountered prejudice and opposition in London. As he gazed at me, without seeming to do so, he could not but observe my ill-cut suit, the soft collar and shirt, the cheap, ill-knotted tie, above all, the look of strained intensity upon my serious face, and it may have been that memories of his own youth came back to him, instinctively enlisting his sympathy on my behalf. He nodded encouragingly as, with my eyes fixed upon the glass jars before me, I stumbled unhappily through a commentary upon the specimens.

"Good," he said as I concluded. He took up another specimen—it was an aneurism of the ascending aorta—and began in a companionable manner to interrogate me. His questions, from being simple, gradually became wider and more searching in their scope, until finally they came to bear upon a recent specific treatment by the induction of malaria. But, opening out under his sympathetic manner, I answered well.

Finally, as he put down the glass jar, Dawson remarked:

"Can you tell me anything of the history of aneurysm?"

"Ambroise Paré," I answered, and my examiner had already begun his approving nod, "is presumed to have first discovered the condition."

Lord Dawson's face showed surprise.

"Why 'presumed'? Paré did discover aneurysm."

I reddened, then turned pale as I plunged on:

"Well, sir, that's what the textbooks say. You'll find it in every book

—I myself took the trouble to verify that it was in six." A quick breath. "But I happened to be reading Celsus, brushing up my Latin —which needed brushing up, sir—when I definitely came across the word *aneurismus*. Celsus knew aneurysm. He described it in full. And that was a matter of thirteen centuries before Paré!"

There was a silence. I raised my eyes, prepared for kindly satire from His Majesty's physician. Decidedly he was looking at me with a queer expression, and for a long time he was silent.

"Doctor," he exclaimed at last, "you are the first candidate in this examination hall who has ever told me something original, something true, and something which I did not know. I congratulate you."

I turned scarlet again.

"Just tell me one thing more—as a matter of personal curiosity," he concluded. "What do you regard as the main principle—the, shall I say, the basic idea which you keep before you when you are exercising the practice of your profession?"

There was a pause while I reflected desperately. At length, feeling I was spoiling all the good effect I had created, I blurted out:

"I suppose—I suppose I keep telling myself never to take anything for granted."

"Thank you, Doctor. . . . Thank you very much."

A few minutes later I went downstairs with the other candidates. At the foot of the stairs beside his leather-hooded cave a liveried porter stood with a little pile of envelopes before him. As the candidates went past he handed an envelope to each of them. Beaumont, walking out next to me, tore his open quickly. His expression altered; he said quietly, with impeccable good form:

"It would appear I'm not wanted tomorrow." Then, forcing a smile, "How about you?"

My fingers were shaking. I could barely read. Dazedly I heard Beaumont congratulate me. My chances were still alive. I walked down to the A.B.C. and treated myself to a double malted milk. I thought tensely, "If I don't get through now, after all this, I'll—I'll walk in front of a bus. . . ."

At last it was over. At four o'clock in the afternoon I came out of the cloakroom, spent and melancholy, pulling on my coat. Then I became aware of Dawson of Penn standing before the big open fire in the hall. I made to pass. But Dawson, for some reason, was holding out his hand, smiling, speaking to me, telling me—telling me that I was now a Member of the Royal College of Physicians.

Dear God, I had done it! I had *done* it! I was alive again, gloriously alive, my headache gone, all my weariness forgotten. As I dashed down to the nearest post office my heart sang wildly, madly. I was through, I had done it, not from the West End of London, but from an outlandish mining town. My whole being was a surging exultation. It hadn't been for nothing after all: those long nights, those mad dashes down to Cardiff, those racking hours of study. On I sped, bumping and cannoning through the crowds, missing the wheels of taxis and omnibuses, my eyes shining, racing, racing to telephone news of the miracle back home. But no, some latent dramatic instinct made me hold things a little longer in suspense. Instead of the full, effusive message I had planned, I sent simply a brief wire asking my wife to come at once to London . . . no more than that curt command. She obeyed, fearing the worst, expecting to find me sick in hospital, perhaps on the verge of suicide. I met her at Victoria Station, tense and pale, with a dreadful glitter in my eye. Then I smiled and hugged her. Gave her thus, holding her tight, the incredible news, blatantly assured her that we were already on the way to Harley Street.

How good life seemed at that moment! How wonderful to share this joy with one so deeply loved! At first neither of us could speak; then we both started to talk at once. I crowded her into a taxi, whirled off to the Savoy. We celebrated recklessly, my dyspepsia forgotten, on a seven-course spread; went on to a George Edwards musical comedy; then to a champagne supper at the Café Royal, from which we emerged in a state of such sublime elation that the very pavements danced and swayed beneath our feet. We were both exhausted when, late the next evening, we reached the clear cold air of our mountain village and once again saw, under the high vault of heaven, the calm and reassuring stars.

*   *   *

It is a cliché to say that time flies when one is fully occupied, yet clichés have a way of being true. We had now been five years in Bayswater, our two boys were attending kindergarten, our lives moved so regularly and smoothly that my dear wife had the delusion we were permanently settled, that nothing would now arise to ruffle the even course of her life.

Only an inverted modesty, the worst kind of affectation, could make me pretend that we had not succeeded, amazingly, in our assault upon London, which had once intimidated us and seemed so difficult to conquer. The nucleus which I had taken over from Dr. Tanner had grown tenfold, and the practice now extended in scope and character far beyond its original limits. I had come to know many of the leading physicians and surgeons of the day, and called in consultation men like Lord Horder, Sir Arbuthnot Lane, and Sir Morley Fletcher.

Recently I had been appointed medical officer to that great department store, Whitely's Limited.

Yet I was not satisfied: for some time past I had been specializing more and more in eye work, attending several ophthalmic clinics and hospitals. Already I had begun to establish myself in that field, and it was my intention to move, presently, to Harley Street.

One morning, however, my ambition was shaken by an unusually severe attack of indigestion, a condition which I had endured periodically since my student days and which, since doctors are constitutionally indifferent to their own complaints, I had merely staved off with increasing doses of bicarbonate of soda. On this occasion, however, I felt that I might profitably seek a more suitable prescription, and that afternoon, as I was passing his consulting room in Wimpole Street, I stopped in to see my good friend, Dr. Izod Bennett, a physician whose knowledge of the maladies of the human organs of digestion had made him nationally famous.

I expected a bottle of bismuth and an invitation to play golf. Instead I received the shock of my life. He did not treat my symptoms lightly, and after several tests, X-ray examinations, and a barium meal, Bennett told me, seriously, that I had a chronic duodenal ulcer, which would certainly perforate if I did not take myself in hand. With feeble jocularity I protested that it was a breach of medical etiquette to endow a fellow doctor with so unpleasant a complaint, but he was not amused and his sentence, in the traditional manner, was immutable —low diet and, without question, as soon as I could arrange it, six months' complete rest in the country. Shaken, I rose from the couch in his consulting room. . . . How could I possibly leave a practice so completely individual as mine for such a period? With my impatient temperament I had never been able to endure an assistant. A locum tenens—how well I knew the breed—would ruin my years of careful work within six weeks. Then, as I began to put on my shirt, a strange, irrational thought—call it madness, if you wish—suddenly transfixed me. I stood for a moment, with distant eyes and, doubtless, a foolish expression upon my face, looking back toward the longings of my youth. Then, like a Chinese mandarin, I nodded, slowly and solemnly, to myself. It was the most important gesture of my life.

For two weeks I said nothing of my interview with Bennett; then, one spring afternoon, I came in, sat down, gazed at the ceiling, and out of the blue, in that dreamy voice which betokens my most irrational decisions, remarked:

"It's high time we cleared out of here."

My wife stared at me.

"What on earth do you mean?"

"Precisely what I say, my dear."

A strained pause. The sun was streaming into our dining room, pleasantly touching the mauve hyacinths she had planted and the new curtains she had hung only the week before. Outside, the air was warm, the pavements dry, the familiar street filled with agreeable bustle. Bayswater and our home had never looked more attractive. The blood rushed to her head.

"You don't know when you're well off. We're happy here, absolutely settled, with the children and everything. You've always had that bee in your bonnet, never content, wanting to dash off at a minute's notice. You've dragged me around so much since we got married you ought to have bought me a caravan. But I've had enough of it. I won't stand any more." She had to pause for breath. "In any case, you're much too young to think of Harley Street."

"I'm not thinking of Harley Street."

"Then what in heaven's name are you thinking of?"

"Selling the practice."

"You never could sell the practice here." She brought out the argument triumphantly. "It's much too large and personal."

"My dear . . . , please don't get mad. . . . I'm afraid I have sold it."

She turned white. She couldn't believe it. Then she saw that it was true. She was beyond words. She had been reading fairy stories to the children the night before, and now, ridiculously, she thought of Aladdin's wonderful lamp, which had brought its possessor everything he wanted, and which, unappreciated, had been so foolishly, so stupidly flung away.

She whispered palely:

"What are you going to do?"

I was silent with, for once, a shamefaced air.

"As a matter of fact . . . , I'm going . . . to try to write."

"Oh God," she gasped, bursting into tears. "You *have* gone crazy."

At this point I felt I had better establish my sanity. I explained, trying not to alarm her, what Izod Bennett had told me. Then I went on, in a low voice, apologetic yet firm:

"I've always had this queer urge to be a writer . . . ever since I was a youngster. But naturally if I'd told them that back home in Scotland, they'd have thought I was wrong in the head. I had to do something sensible, instead. That's why I went in for medicine. It was safe and practical. Oh, I admit I liked it all right. I like it quite well now, I might even go so far as to say that I'm good at it. But all the time I've felt this other thing at the back of my mind. When I've been attending my patients, seeing people as they really are—yes, even as far back as the Rhondda days, when we came up against life in the raw—I kept thinking what stories I could make out of them. I wanted to describe the characters I was meeting, get something down on paper. Of course, I hadn't the time; you need quiet and detachment for that sort of thing, and we were always tearing so hard to get on. Well, now we have got on. I can take six months, even a year, to give myself a chance to write. At least I'll get the bug out of my system. It's a million to one I'm no good. And if I'm not, I can always come back to the treadmill."

There was a long silence. She could not deny that, through the years, she had suspected in me this desire for self-expression. But she had never taken it seriously. When, after dinner and a hard day's work, I had vaguely mentioned my longing to do a book, she smiled at me kindly over her knitting and led me on to talk about my golf handicap. But this was different. This wild project, this disruption, once again, of our pleasant domesticity, seemed to her sheer lunacy.

And it was all fixed, settled, and arranged. What a man! Had he no thought of the children or of his wife? She boiled with anger and dismay.

"Remember that chap Gaugin," I reminded her diffidently. "The Paris stockbroker who, without warning, suddenly threw up his humdrum life and walked off without warning to paint pictures—and good ones—in Tahiti."

"Tahiti," she moaned, "and after that I suppose it will be Timbuktu. For heaven's sake, be sensible. What did Dr. Bennett say was wrong with you?"

"Oh, just a gastric condition. But I must have a rest."

"Yes . . . , yes . . . ," she murmured unsteadily. "You haven't really been well lately. . . ."

Torn by conflicting emotions, she gazed at me glassily, smiled wanly, then—as upon a previous historic occasion—resolved the crisis by laying her head upon my shoulder and again dissolving into tears.

The place selected for our preposterous adventure was Dalchenna farm, a small steading situated on Loch Fyne, a few miles from Inveraray, in the western Highlands of Scotland. And three weeks later, when all the details of the transfer of the practice had been settled and Dr. Green, the new incumbent, was satisfactorily installed, we set out for this remote spot, the car jammed with our belongings, our two boys wild with excitement.

I will acknowledge that, with suitcases falling on my head at every curve, my mood was scarcely a confident one. Yet as we sped along, that fine June day, my heart lifted—after all, we had not had a real holiday in years. And when at last, after a twelve hours' run,

we reached the moors and mountains of our native countryside, I
stopped the car and turned to my wife. Her glance was as tender as
my own, and suddenly, forgivingly, she threw her arms around my
neck. Lambs were frisking in the meadow, a stream, fretted by the
sunshine, rippled by the roadside, our children, released from the back
seat, were gathering wild daffodils.

"It's wonderful to be back again," she whispered in my ear. "You'll
get well here, dear . . . , well and strong. We'll have a lovely time.
. . . And we'll forget all about that stupid old book."

*   *   *

The Highland clachan of Inveraray, little more than a cluster of
whitewashed cottages huddled about the castle of the Duke of Argyll,
lies among a wild grandeur of mountains at the head of the lovely
inlet of the sea which was once the haunt of that delectable fish, the
Loch Fyne herring. But the herring, for no known reason other than
that it is unpredictable in its habits, had some years before abandoned
these waters, extinguishing a profitable industry, sending the trawler
fleet to Lossiemouth and Frazerburgh, leaving the village in all its
native solitude. Dalchenna farm, which I had rented, was some two
miles down the lonely loch shore, and despite the remoteness of the
scene, we fell in love with it at first sight. The farmhouse was a snug
building, with nasturtiums and scarlet fuchsias climbing its grey stone
walls; on all sides green meadows surrounded us; beyond were woods
of alder carpeted with bluebells and mitred bracken into which, as we
approached, a roe deer bounded; while above towered the heather-
clad hills, source of a stream, filled with trout, that tumbled down in
golden spate toward the loch.

For the two boys, aged four and seven, who really had no recollection of anything but city life, the place was truly a wonderland. Bare-
legged and in kilts, they roamed the woods in company with my wife,
climbed the hills, bathed, boated on the loch, fished in the stream,
chased the rabbits, gathered shells and starfishes on the shore, helped
Will, the herdsman, to milk the cows, and Annie, the dairymaid, to
churn the butter. For the mother and her sons, the day was one long,
perpetual delight—they grew brown as berries, ate like hawks, and
slept like hunters. But for me, alas—for the poor parent who was the
instigator of the scheme—the picture was somewhat different.

Having emphatically declared before my entire household that I
would write a novel—tacitly implying, of course, that it was the fault
of every other member of the household that I had not written twenty
novels—I found myself faced with the unpleasant necessity of justify-
ing my rash remarks. All I could do was to retire, with a show of

courage and deep purpose, to the attic of the house which had been at once selected as "the room for Daddy to write in." Here I was confronted by a square deal table, by a pile of twopenny exercise books, a dictionary, and a thesaurus. Nor must I forget the pablum prescribed by Dr. Bennett and treasured in some suitable domestic background, for I am proud of that bland stimulus. Too often in the bad old days brandy has been the chief inspiration of novelists.

It was the morning following our arrival. Amazingly, for that latitude, the sun shone. Our little dinghy danced entrancingly at anchor on the loch, waiting to be rowed. My car stood in the garage, waiting to be driven. The trout in the river lay head to tail, waiting to be caught. The hills stood fresh and green, waiting to be climbed. And I—I stood at the window of the little upstairs room. Wincingly, I looked at the sun, the loch, the boat, the car, the river, and the mountains; then sadly turned and sat down before my deal table, my exercise books, and my dictionary. "What a fool you are," I said to myself gloomily, and I used an adjective to magnify my imbecility. How often during the next three months was I to repeat that assertion—each time with stronger adjectives.

But in the meantime I was going to begin. Firmly I opened the first exercise book, firmly I jogged my fountain pen out of its habitual inertia. Firmly I poised that pen and lifted my head for inspiration.

It was a pleasant view through that narrow window: a long green field ran down to a bay of the loch. There was movement. Six cows, couched in the shadow of a hawthorn hedge, ruminated with steady rhythm; an old goat with an arresting beard tinkled his bell in search, I thought, of dandelions; a yellow butterfly hovered indecisively above a scarlet spurt of fuchsias; some white hens pottered about, liable to sudden excitements and pursuits.

It had all a seductive, dreamlike interest. I thought I might contemplate the scene for a minute or two before settling down to work. I contemplated. Then somebody knocked at the door and said, "Lunchtime." I started, and searched hopefully for my glorious beginning, only to find that the exercise book still retained its blank virginity.

I rose and went downstairs, and as I descended those white-scrubbed wooden steps I asked myself angrily if I were not a humbug. Was I like the wretched poet d'Argenton in Daudet's *Jack*, with his "Parva domus, magna quies" and his *Daughter of Faust*, which, as the days slipped on, never progressed beyond that stillborn opening sentence: "In a remote valley of the Pyrenees . . . teeming with legends." Was I like that? I carved the mutton glumly. My two young sons, removed by their nurse to a remote distance in order that they might on no account disturb the novelist, had returned in high spirits. The younger, aged four, now lisped breezily:

"Finished your book yet, Daddy?"

The elder, always of a corrective tendency, affirmed with the superior wisdom of his two additional years:

"Don't be silly. Daddy's only half finished."

Whereupon their mother smiled upon them reprovingly:

"No, dears, Daddy can only have written a chapter or two."

I felt not like a humbug, but a criminal. Determinedly I called to mind the aphorism of an old schoolmaster of mine. "Get it down," he used to declare. "If it stays in your head it'll never be anything. Get it down." So after lunch I went straight upstairs and began to get my ideas down.

I could fill a volume with the emotional experiences of those next three months. Although the theme of the novel I wished to write was already outlined in my mind—the tragic record of a man's egotism and bitter pride—I was, beyond these naïve fundamentals, lamentably unprepared. Most novelists who suddenly blaze into print in their thirties have practised their vice secretly for years. But I, until this moment, had written nothing but prescriptions and scientific papers. It took great determination to drive me through my inhibitions, like a circus rider through a paper hoop.

I had no pretensions to technique, no knowledge of style or form. The difficulty of simple statement staggered me. I spent hours looking for an adjective. I corrected and recorrected until the page looked like a spider's web; then I tore it up and started all over again.

Yet once I had begun, the thing haunted me. My characters took shape, spoke to me, excited me. When an idea struck me in the middle of the night I would get up, light a candle—we had, of course, no electricity in this remote spot—and sprawl on the floor until I had translated it to paper. I was possessed by the very novelty of what I did. At first my rate of progress was some eight hundred laboured words a day. By the end of the second month I was readily accomplishing two thousand.

For the next three months, through all that lovely summer, while the others enjoyed themselves, I remained chained to my desk. Despite their pleadings that I should take a day off, I kept myself on the rack relentlessly, all day and part of the night, coming down late for my peptonised meals, answering the children absently, seemingly anxious only to get back to my private treadmill.

Although at the time I maintained a stoic, a sphinxlike silence, I will now confess to the miseries I went through. There were redeeming moments when, carried away by what I had written, living with my characters in the drama they were enacting, I dared to hope that I was doing something fine; but for the most part I felt that all my drudgery was quite useless, that I was wasting my time in sheer futility.

The worst moment came when I was halfway through the book, and the typescript of the first chapters arrived from a secretarial bureau in London. As I read the opening pages, a wave of horror swept over me. I thought, Have I written this awful stuff? No one will ever read it. No one will ever publish it. I simply can't go on!

I had the impulse there and then to throw up the whole project, destroy everything I had written. It was irresistible. I got up with a set face, took the manuscript to the back door, and flung it in the ash heap.

When the news was known, a dire silence fell upon the house. At lunch, the very children were silent. I remember so well—it started to rain, a dank Scots afternoon, and, scared by my scowl, my wife and the two boys left me without a word.

Drawing a sullen satisfaction from my surrender, or, as I preferred to phrase it, my return to sanity, I went for a walk in the drizzling rain. Halfway down the loch shore I came upon old Angus, the farmer, patiently and laboriously ditching a patch of the bogged and peaty heath which made up the bulk of his hard-won little croft. As I drew near, he gazed up at me in some surprise; he knew of my intention and, with that inborn Scottish reverence for "letters," had tacitly approved it. When I told him what I had just done, and why, his weathered face slowly changed, his keen blue eyes, beneath misted sandy brows, scanned me with disappointment and a queer contempt. He was a silent man, and it was long before he spoke. Even then his words were cryptic.

"No doubt you're the one that's right, Doctor, and I'm the one that's wrong. . . ." He seemed to look right through me. "My father ditched this bog all his days and never made a pasture. I've dug it all *my* days and I've never made a pasture. But, pasture or no pasture"—he placed his foot on the spade—"I cannot help but dig. For my father knew and I know that if you only dig enough, a pasture can be made here."

I understood. I watched his dogged figure, working away, determined to see the job through at all costs. In silence I tramped back to the house, drenched, shamed, furious, and picked the soggy bundle from the ash heap. I dried it in the kitchen oven. Then I flung it on the table and set to work again with a kind of frantic desperation. I would not be beaten, I would not give in. Night after night, keeping myself awake by sheer will power, I wrote harder than ever. At last, toward the end of September, I wrote *"Finis."* The relief was unbelievable. I had kept my word. I had created a book. Whether it was good, bad, or indifferent I did not know.

With a sigh of incredible relief, I packed the manuscript in an old cardboard box, tied it with farmyard twine. Then, having found a publisher's address in a two-year-old almanac, I dispatched the untidy parcel and promptly forgot about it. Like a man who has lost a heavy burden, I began to bathe and fish and row with the boys, to roam the hills and the moors with them, to behave once again like a normal human being.

The days succeeded one another, and nothing happened. That nondescript package might well have disappeared forever into the void. By stern parental edict the subject was taboo in the family, and when the younger son inadvertently made innocent reference to "Daddy's book," he received the blackest of looks.

In point of fact, I had no illusions—I was fully aware that aspiring authors acquire rejection slips more readily than cheques, and that first manuscripts usually come back a score of times before being accepted —if indeed they are ever accepted at all. My surprise and delight may therefore be imagined when, one morning in October, I received a wire from the head of the publishing firm which I had selected, informing me that the novel had been accepted for publication, offering an advance of fifty pounds, and asking me to come to London immediately.

As we read the telegram, a stunned awe fell upon the farm living room. Fifty pounds, cash down, seemed a lot of money, and perhaps later there might even be a little more, on account of royalties. Pale and rather shaky, I muttered:

"Maybe, with luck and economy, I can make a living as a writer. Get the timetable and find out when the next train leaves for London."

Looking back upon the events which followed, it seems incredible, even now, how swiftly, how amazingly, from that uncertain moment, the flood tide of success was loosed. This first novel, *Hatter's Castle*, written despairingly on twopenny exercise books, thrown out and rescued from the rubbish heap at the eleventh hour, was published in the spring of 1930. It was acclaimed by critics, chosen by the Book Society, translated into twenty-one languages, serialised, dramatised and filmed. It went into endless editions, has sold, to date, approximately three million copies, and goes on selling still. It launched me upon a literary career with such an impetus that, once and for all, I hung up my stethoscope and put away that little black bag—my medical days were over.

Adventures in Two Worlds, by A. J. Cronin

FLORENCE NIGHTINGALE

"The strongest will be wanted at the wash-tub."

The kind of determination it takes to innovate—and to innovate against barriers set up by generations of tradition—is in itself a kind of genius. Florence Nightingale was the product of conservative, tradition-bound, upper-middle class English society. For a young lady of quality to earn her own living was in itself unthinkable at that time; that she should choose to do so in hospital work was unbelievable. But Florence Nightingale was possessed with a drive that would not be contained in the social channels open to a lady of her upbringing. And as a result of this drive, nursing was changed from a refuge for the incompetent and diseased to the respected profession it is today.

Lytton Strachey drew truthful but not always flattering pictures of the people he chose to write about. Here, then, is Florence Nightingale, not as "The Lady with the Lamp"—the highly romantic "girl crusader" so often pictured in teen-age biographies—but as the driven, efficient and fearless person that she was.

. . . A RESTLESSNESS began to grow upon her. She was unhappy, and at last she knew it. Mrs. Nightingale, too, began to notice that there was something wrong. It was very odd; what could be the matter with dear Flo? Mr. Nightingale suggested that a husband might be advisable; but the curious thing was that she seemed to take no interest in husbands. And with her attractions, and her accomplishments, too! There was nothing in the world to prevent her making a really brilliant match. But no! She would think of nothing but how to satisfy that singular craving of hers to be *doing* something. As if there was not plenty to do in any case, in the ordinary way, at home. There was the china to look after, and there was her father to be read to after dinner. Mrs. Nightingale could not understand it; and then one day her perplexity was changed to consternation and alarm. Florence announced an extreme desire to go to Salisbury Hospital for several months as a nurse. . . . The whole scheme was summarily brushed aside as preposterous; and Mrs. Nightingale, after the first shock of terror, was able to settle down again more or less comfortably to her embroidery. But Florence, who was now twenty-five and felt that the dream of her life had been shattered, came near to desperation.

And, indeed, the difficulties in her path were great. For not only was it an almost unimaginable thing in those days for a woman of means to make her own way in the world and to live in independence, but the particular profession for which Florence was clearly marked out both by her instincts and her capacities was at that time a peculiarly disreputable one. A "nurse" meant then a coarse old woman, always ignorant, usually dirty, often brutal, a Mrs. Gamp, in bunched-up sordid garments, tippling at the brandy-bottle or indulging in worse irregularities. The nurses in the hospitals were especially notorious for immoral conduct; sobriety almost unknown among them; and they could hardly be trusted to carry out the simplest medical duties. Certainly, things have changed since those days; and that they *have* changed is due, far more than to any other human being, to Miss Nightingale herself. . . .

At last the pressure of time told; her family seemed to realise that she was old enough and strong enough to have her way; and she became the superintendent of a charitable nursing home in Harley Street. She had gained her independence, though it was in a meagre sphere enough; and her mother was still not quite resigned: surely Florence might at least spend the summer in the country. At times, indeed, among her intimates, Mrs. Nightingale almost wept. "We are ducks," she said with tears in her eyes, "who have hatched a wild swan." But the poor lady was wrong; it was not a swan that they had hatched; it was an eagle.

Miss Nightingale had been a year in her nursing home in Harley Street, when Fate knocked at the door. The Crimean War broke out; the battle of the Alma was fought; and the terrible condition of our military hospitals at Scutari began to be known in England. It sometimes happens that the plans of Providence are a little difficult to follow, but on this occasion all was plain; there was a perfect coordination of events. For years Miss Nightingale had been getting ready; at last she was prepared—experienced, free, mature, yet still young—she was thirty-four—desirous to serve, accustomed to command: at that precise moment the desperate need of a great nation came, and she was there to satisfy it. If the war had fallen a few years earlier, she would have lacked the knowledge, perhaps even the power, for such a work; a few years later and she would, no doubt, have been fixed in the routine of some absorbing task, and moreover, she would have been growing old. Nor was it only the coincidence of Time that was remarkable. It so fell out that Sidney Herbert was at the War Office and in the Cabinet; and Sidney Herbert was an intimate friend of Miss Nightingale's, convinced, from personal experience in charitable work, of her supreme capacity. After such premises, it hardly seems more than a matter of course that her letter, in which she offered her services for the East, and Sidney Herbert's letter, in which he asked for them, should actually have crossed in the post. Thus it all happened, without a hitch. The appointment was made, and even Mrs. Nightingale, overawed by the magnitude of the venture, could only approve. A pair of faithful friends offered themselves as personal attendants; thirty-eight nurses were collected; and within a week of the crossing of the letters Miss Nightingale, amid a great burst of popular enthusiasm, left for Constantinople. . . .

Dark as had been the picture of the state of affairs at Scutari, revealed to the English public in the despatches of the *Times* correspondent and in a multitude of private letters, yet the reality turned out to be darker still. What had occurred was, in brief, the complete breakdown of our medical arrangements at the seat of war. The origins of this awful failure were complex and manifold; they stretched back through long years of peace and carelessness in England; they could be traced through endless ramifications of administrative incapacity —from the inherent faults of confused systems to the petty bunglings of minor officials, from the inevitable ignorance of Cabinet Ministers to the fatal exactitudes of narrow routine. In the inquiries which followed it was clearly shown that the evil was in reality that worst of all evils—one which has been caused by nothing in particular and for which no one in particular was to blame. The whole organisation of the war machine was incompetent and out of date. The old Duke had sat for a generation at the Horse Guards repressing innovations with an iron hand. There was an extraordinary overlapping of authorities, an almost incredible shifting of responsibilities to and fro. As for such a notion as the creation and the maintenance of a really adequate medical service for the army—in that atmosphere of aged chaos, how could it have entered anybody's head? Before the war, the easygoing officials at Westminster were naturally persuaded that all was well—or at least as well as could be expected; when someone, for instance, actually had the temerity to suggest the formation of a corps of army nurses, he was at once laughed out of court. When the war had begun, the gallant British officers in control of affairs had other things to think about than the petty details of medical organisation. Who had bothered with such trifles in the Peninsula? And surely, on that occasion we had done pretty well. Thus the most obvious precautions were neglected, the most necessary preparations put off from

day to day. The principal medical officer of the army, Dr. Hall, was
summoned from India at a moment's notice, and was unable to visit
England before taking up his duties at the front. And it was not until
after the battle of the Alma, when we had been at war for many
months, that we acquired hospital accommodation at Scutari for more
than a thousand men. Errors, follies, and vices on the part of individuals there doubtless were; but, in the general reckoning, they were of
small account—insignificant symptoms of the deep disease of the body
politic—the enormous calamity of administrative collapse.

Miss Nightingale arrived at Scutari—a suburb of Constantinople, on
the Asiatic side of the Bosphorus—on November 4th, 1854; it was ten
days after the battle of Balaclava, and the day before the battle of
Inkerman. The organisation of the hospitals, which had already given
way under the stress of the battle of the Alma, was now to be subjected to the further pressure which these two desperate and bloody
engagements implied. Great detachments of wounded were already
beginning to pour in. The men, after receiving such summary treatment as could be given them at the smaller hospitals in the Crimea
itself, were forthwith shipped in batches of two hundred across the
Black Sea to Scutari. This voyage was in normal times one of four
days and a half; but the times were no longer normal, and now the
transit often lasted for a fortnight or three weeks. It received, not
without reason, the name of "middle passage." Between, and sometimes on the decks, the wounded, the sick and the dying were
crowded—men who had just undergone the amputation of limbs, men
in the clutches of fever or of frostbite, men in the last stages of dysentery and cholera—without beds, sometimes without blankets, often
hardly clothed. The one or two surgeons on board did what they
could; but medical stores were lacking, and the only form of nursing
available was that provided by a handful of invalid soldiers, who were
usually themselves prostrate by the end of the voyage. There was no
other food beside the ordinary salt rations of ship diet; and even
the water was sometimes so stored that it was out of reach of the weak.
For many months, the average of deaths during these voyages was
seventy-four in the thousand; the corpses were shot out into the waters; and who shall say that they were the most unfortunate? At
Scutari, the landing-stage, constructed with all the perverseness of
Oriental ingenuity, could only be approached with great difficulty,
and, in rough weather, not at all. When it was reached, what remained
of the men in the ships had first to be disembarked, and then conveyed up a steep slope of a quarter of a mile to the nearest of the
hospitals. The most serious cases might be put upon stretchers—for
there were far too few for all; the rest were carried or dragged up the

hill by such convalescent soldiers as could be got together, who were not too obviously infirm for the work. At last the journey was accomplished; slowly, one by one, living or dying, the wounded were carried up into the hospital. And in the hospital what did they find?

Lasciate ogni speranza, voi ch'entrate: the delusive words want, neglect, confusion, misery—in every shape and in every degree of intensity—filled the endless corridors and the vast departments of the gigantic barrack-house, which, without forethought or preparation, had been hurriedly set aside as the chief shelter for the victims of the war. The very building itself was radically defective. Huge sewers underlay it, and cesspools loaded with filth wafted their poison into the upper rooms. The floors were in so rotten a condition that many of them could not be scrubbed; the walls were thick with dirt; incredible multitudes of vermin swarmed everywhere. And, enormous as the building was, it was yet too small. It contained four miles of beds, crushed together so close that there was but just room to pass between them. Under such conditions, the most elaborate system of ventilation might well have been at fault; but here there was no ventilation. The stench was indescribable. "I have been well acquainted," said Miss Nightingale, "with the dwellings of the worst parts of most of the great cities of Europe, but have never been in any atmosphere which I could compare with that of Barrack Hospital at night." The structural defects were equalled by the deficiencies in the commonest objects of hospital use. There were not enough bedsteads; the sheets were of canvas, and so coarse that the wounded men recoiled from them, begging to be left in their blankets; there was no bedroom furniture of any kind, and empty beer-bottles were used for candlesticks. There were no basins, no towels, no soap, no brooms, no mops, no trays, no plates; there were neither slippers nor scissors, neither shoe-brushes nor blacking; there were no knives or forks or spoons. The supply of fuel was constantly deficient. The cooking arrangements were preposterously inadequate, and the laundry was a farce. As for purely medical materials, the tale was no better. Stretchers, splints, bandages—all were lacking; and so were the ordinary drugs.

To replace such wants, to struggle against such difficulties, there was a handful of men overburdened by the strain of ceaseless work, bound down by the traditions of official routine, and enfeebled either by old age or inexperience or sheer incompetence. They had proved utterly unequal to their task. The principal doctor was lost in the imbecilities of a senile optimism. The wretched official whose business it was to provide for the wants of the hospital was tied fast hand and foot by red tape. A few of the younger doctors struggled valiantly, but what could they do? Unprepared, disorganised, with such help only as they could find among the miserable band of convalescent soldiers drafted off to tend their sick comrades, they were faced with disease, mutilation, and death in all their most appalling forms, crowded multitudinously about them in an ever increasing mass. They were like men in a shipwreck, fighting, not for safety, but for the next moment's bare existence—to gain, by yet another frenzied effort, some brief respite from the waters of destruction.

In these surroundings, those who had been long inured to scenes of human suffering—surgeons with a world-wide knowledge of agonies, soldiers familiar with fields of carnage, missionaries with remembrances of famine and plague—yet found a depth of horror which they had never known before. There were moments, there were places, in the Barrack Hospital at Scutari, where the strongest hand was struck with trembling, and the boldest eye would turn away its gaze.

Miss Nightingale came, and she, at any rate, in that Inferno, did not abandon hope. For one thing, she brought material succor. Before she left London she had consulted Dr. Andrew Smith, the head of the Army Medical Board, as to whether it would be useful to take out stores of any kind to Scutari; and Dr. Andrew Smith had told her that "nothing was needed." Even Sidney Herbert had given her similar assurances; possibly, owing to an oversight, there might have been some delay in the delivery of medical stores, which he said had been sent out from England "in profusion," but "four days would have remedied this." She preferred to trust her own instincts, and at Marseilles purchased a large quantity of miscellaneous provisions, which were of the utmost use at Scutari. She came, too, amply provided with money—in all, during her stay in the East, about £7000 reached her from private sources; and in addition, she was able to avail herself of another valuable means of help. At the same time as herself, Mr. McDonald of the *Times*, had arrived in Scutari, charged with the duty of administering the large sums of money collected through the agency of that newspaper in aid of the sick and wounded; and Mr. McDonald had the sense to see that the best use he could make of the *Times* Fund was to put it at the disposal of Miss Nightingale.

> I cannot conceive (wrote an eye witness), as I now calmly look back on the first three weeks after the arrival of the wounded from Inkerman, how it could have been possible to have avoided a state of things too disastrous to contemplate, had not Miss Nightingale been there, with the means placed at her disposal by Mr. McDonald.

But the official view was different. What! Was the public service to admit, by accepting outside charity, that it was unable to discharge its own duties without the assistance of private and irregular benevolence? Never! And accordingly when Lord Stratford de Redcliffe, our Ambassador at Constantinople, was asked by Mr. McDonald to indicate how the *Times* Fund could best be employed, he answered that there was indeed one object to which it might very well be devoted—the building of an English Protestant Church at Pera.

Mr. McDonald did not waste further time with Lord Stratford, and immediately joined forces with Miss Nightingale. But, with such a frame of mind in the highest quarters, it is easy to imagine the kind of disgust and alarm with which the sudden intrusion of a band of amateurs and females must have filled the minds of the ordinary officer and the ordinary military surgeon. They could not understand it; what had women to do with war? Honest Colonels relieved their spleen by the cracking of heavy jokes about "the Bird"; while poor Dr. Hall, a rough terrier of a man, who had worried his way to the top of his profession, was struck speechless with astonishment and at last observed that Miss Nightingale's appointment was extremely droll.

Her position was, indeed, an official one, but it was hardly the easier for that. In the hospitals it was her duty to provide the services of herself and her nurses when they were asked for by the doctors, and not until then. At first some of the surgeons would have nothing to say to her, and, though she was welcomed by others, the majority were hostile and suspicious. But gradually she gained ground. Her good will could not be denied, and her capacity could not be disregarded. With consummate tact, with all the gentleness of supreme strength, she managed at last to impose her personality upon the susceptible, overwrought, discouraged, and helpless group of men in authority who surrounded her. She stood firm, she was a rock in the angry ocean; with her alone was safety, comfort, life. And so it was that hope dawned at Scutari. The reign of chaos and old night began to dwindle; order came upon the scene, and common sense, and forethought, and decision, radiating out from the little room off the great gallery in the Barrack Hospital where day and night the Lady Superintendent was at her task. Progress might be slow, but it was sure. The first sign of a great change came with the appearance of some of those necessary objects with which the hospital had been unprovided for months. The sick men began to enjoy the use of towels and soap, knives and forks, combs and tooth-brushes. Dr. Hall might snort when he heard of it, asking, with a growl, what a soldier wanted with a tooth-brush; but the good work went on. Eventually the whole business of purveying to the hospitals was, in effect, carried out by Miss Nightingale. She alone, it seemed, whatever the contingency, knew where to lay her hands on what was wanted; she alone could dispense her stores with readiness; above all she alone possessed the art of circumventing the pernicious influences of official etiquette. This was her greatest enemy, and sometimes even she was baffled by it. On one occasion 27,000 shirts sent out at her instance by the Home Government arrived, were landed, and were only waiting to be unpacked. But the official "Purveyor" intervened; "he could not unpack them," he said, "without a Board." Miss Nightingale pleaded in vain; the sick and wounded lay half-naked shivering for want of clothing; and three weeks elapsed before the Board released the shirts. A little later, however, on a similar occasion, Miss Nightingale felt that she could assert her authority. She ordered a Government consignment to be forcibly opened, while the miserable "Purveyor" stood by, wringing his hands in departmental agony.

Vast quantities of valuable stores sent from England lay, she found, engulfed in the bottomless abyss of the Turkish Customs House. Other ship-loads, buried beneath munitions of war destined for Bala-clava, passed Scutari without a sign, and thus hospital materials were sometimes carried to and fro three times over the Black Sea, before they reached their destination. The whole system was clearly at fault, and Miss Nightingale suggested to the home authorities that a Government Store House should be instituted at Scutari for the reception and distribution of the consignments. Six months after her arrival this was done.

In the meantime she had reorganized the kitchens and the laundries in the hospitals. The ill-cooked hunks of meat, vilely served at irregular intervals, which had hitherto been the only diet for the sick men were replaced by punctual meals, well prepared and appetising, while strengthening extra foods—soups and wines, and jellies ("preposterous luxuries," snarled Dr. Hall)—were distributed to those who needed them. One thing, however, she could not effect. The separation of the bones from the meat was no part of official cookery; the rule was that the food must be divided into equal portions, and if some of the portions were all bone—well, every man must take his chance. The rule, perhaps, was not a very good one; but there it was. "It would require a new Regulation of the Service," she was told, "to bone the meat." As for the washing arrangements, they were revolutionised. Up to the time of Miss Nightingale's arrival the number of shirts which the authorities had succeeded in washing was seven. The hospital bedding, she found, was "washed" in cold water. She took a Turkish house, had boilers installed, and employed soldiers' wives to do the laundry work. The expenses were defrayed from her own funds and that of the *Times*; and henceforward the sick and wounded had the comfort of clean linen.

Then she turned her attention to their clothing. Owing to military exigencies the greater number of the men had abandoned their kit; their knapsacks were lost forever; they possessed nothing but what was on their persons, and that was usually only fit for speedy destruction. The "Purveyor" of course, pointed out that, according to the regulations, all soldiers should bring with them into hospital an adequate supply of clothing, and he declared that it was no business of his to make good their deficiencies. Apparently, it was the business of Miss Nightingale. She procured socks, boots, and shirts in enormous quantities; she had trousers made, she rigged up dressing gowns. "The fact is," she told Sidney Herbert, "I am now clothing the British Army."

All at once, word came from the Crimea that a great new contingent of sick and wounded might shortly be expected. Where were they to go? Every available inch in the wards was occupied; the affair was serious and pressing, and the authorities stood aghast. There were some dilapidated rooms in the Barrack Hospital, unfit for human habitation, but Miss Nightingale believed they might be made capable of accommodating several hundred beds. One of the doctors agreed with her; the rest of the officials were irresolute; it would be a very expensive job, they said; it would involve building; and who would take the responsibility? The proper course was that a representation should be made to the Director-General of the Army Medical Department in London; then the Director-General would apply to the Horse Guards, the Horse Guards would move the Ordnance, the Ordnance would lay the matter before the Treasury, and, if the Treasury gave its consent, the work might be correctly carried through, several months after the necessity for it had disappeared. Miss Nightingale, however, had made up her mind, and she persuaded Lord Stratford—or thought she had persuaded him—to give his sanction to the required expenditure. A hundred and twenty-five workmen were immediately engaged, and the work was begun. The workmen struck; whereupon Lord Stratford washed his hands of the whole business. Miss Nightingale engaged two hundred other men on her own authority, and paid the bill out of her own resources. The wards were ready by the required date; five hundred sick men were received in them; and all the utensils, including knives, forks, spoons, cans and towels, were supplied by Miss Nightingale.

This remarkable woman was in truth performing the function of an administrative chief. How had this come about? Was she not in reality merely a nurse? Was it not her duty simply to tend to the sick? And indeed, was it not as a ministering angel, a gentle "lady with a lamp" that she actually impressed the minds of her contemporaries? No doubt that was so; and yet it is no less certain that, as she herself said, the specific business of nursing was "the least important of the functions into which she had been forced." It was clear that in the state of disorganisation into which the hospitals at Scutari had fallen the most pressing, the really vital, need was for something more than nursing; it was for the necessary elements of civilised life—the commonest material objects, the most ordinary cleanliness, the rudimentary habits of order and authority. "Oh, dear Miss Nightingale," said one of her party as they were approaching Constantinople, "when we land, let there be no delays, let us get straight to nursing the poor fellows!" "The strongest will be wanted at the wash-tub," was Miss Nightingale's answer. And it was upon the wash-tub and all that the wash-tub stood for, that she expended her greatest energies. Yet to say that is perhaps to say too much. For to those who watched her at work among the sick, moving day and night from bed to bed, with that unflinching courage, with that indefatigable vigilance, it seemed as if the concentrated force of an undivided and unparalleled devotion could hardly suffice for that portion of her task alone. Wherever, in those vast wards, suffering was at its worst and the need for help was greatest, there, as if by magic, was Miss Nightingale. Her superhuman equanimity would, at the moment of some ghastly operation, nerve the victim to endure and almost to hope. Her sympathy would assuage the pangs of dying and bring back to those still living something of the forgotten charm of life. Over and over again her untiring efforts rescued those whom the surgeons had abandoned as beyond the possibility of cure. Her mere presence brought with it a strange influence. A passionate idolatry spread among the men: they kissed her shadow as it passed. They did more. "Before she came," said a soldier, "there was cussin' and swearin', but after that it was as 'oly as a church." The most cherished privilege of the fighting man was abandoned for the sake of Miss Nightingale. In those "lowest sinks of human misery," as she herself put it, she never heard the use of one expression "which could distress a gentlewoman."

She was heroic; and these were the humble tributes paid by those of grosser mould to that high quality. Certainly, she was heroic. Yet her heroism was not of that simple sort so dear to the readers of novels and the compilers of hagiologies—the romantic sentimental heroism with which mankind loves to invest its chosen darlings: it was made of sterner stuff. To the wounded soldier on his couch of agony she might well appear in the guise of a gracious angel of mercy; but the military surgeons, and the orderlies, and her own nurses, and the "Purveyor," and Dr. Hall, and even Lord Stratford himself could tell a different story. It was not by gentle sweetness and womanly self-abnegation that she had brought order out of chaos in the Scutari hospitals, that, from her own resources, she had clothed the British Army, that she had spread her dominion over the serried and reluctant powers of the official world; it was by strict method, by stern discipline, by rigid attention to detail, by ceaseless labour, by the fixed determination of an indomitable will. Beneath her cool and calm demeanour lurked fierce and passionate fires. As she passed through the wards in her plain dress, so quiet, so unassuming, she struck the casual observer simply as the pattern of a perfect lady; but the keener eye perceived something more than that—the serenity of high deliberation in the scope of the capacious brow, the sign of power in the dominating curve of the thin nose, and the traces of a harsh and dangerous temper—something peevish, something mocking, and yet something precise—in the small delicate mouth. There was humour in the face; but the curious watcher might wonder whether it was humour of a very pleasant kind; might ask himself, even as he heard the laughter and marked the jokes with which she cheered the spirits of her patients, what sort of sardonic merriment this same lady might not give vent to, in the privacy of her chamber. As for her voice, it was true of it, even more than of her countenance, that it "had that in it one must fain call master." Those clear tones were in no need of emphasis: "I never heard her raise her voice," said one of her companions. Only, when she had spoken, it seemed that nothing could follow but obedience. Once when she had given some direction, a doctor ventured to remark that the thing could not be done. "But it must be done," said Miss Nightingale. A chance bystander, who heard the words, never forgot through all his life the irresistible authority of them. And they were spoken quietly—very quietly indeed.

Late at night, when the long miles of beds lay wrapped in darkness, Miss Nightingale would sit at work in her little room, over her correspondence. It was one of the most formidable of all her duties. There were hundreds of letters to be written to the friends and relations of soldiers; there was the enormous mass of official documents to be dealt with; there were her own private letters to be answered; and, most important of all, there was the composition of her long and confidential reports to Sidney Herbert. These were by no means official communications. Her soul, pent up all day in the restraint and reserve of a vast responsibility, now at last poured itself out in these letters with all its natural vehemence, like a swollen torrent through an open sluice. Here she painted in her darkest colours the hideous scenes which surrounded her; here she tore away remorselessly the last veils still shrouding the abominable truth. Then she would fill pages with recommendations and suggestions, with criticisms of the minutest details of organisation, with elaborate calculations of contingencies, with exhaustive analyses and statistical statements piled up in breathless eagerness one on the top of the other. And then her pen, in the virulence of its volubility, would rush on to the discussion of individuals, to the denunciation of an incompetent surgeon or the ridicule of a self-sufficient nurse. Her sarcasm searched the ranks of the officials with the deadly and unsparing precision of a machine-gun. . . . "I do well to be angry," was the burden of her cry. How many just men were there at Scutari? How many who cared at all for the sick, or had done anything for their relief? Were there ten? Were there five? Was there even one? She could not be sure. . . .

The fact that during the whole of her stay at Scutari she had the Home Government at her back was her trump card in her dealings with the hospital authorities. Nor was it only the Government that was behind her; public opinion in England early recognised the high importance of her mission, and its enthusiastic appreciation of her work soon reached an extraordinary height. The Queen herself was deeply moved. She made repeated inquiries as to the welfare of Miss Nightingale; she asked to see her accounts of the wounded, and made her the intermediary between the throne and the troops.

Let Mrs. Herbert know (she wrote to the War Minister) that I wish Miss Nightingale and the ladies would tell these poor noble, wounded, and sick men that *no one* takes a warmer interest or feels *more* for their sufferings or admires their courage and heroism *more* than their Queen. Day and night she thinks of her beloved troops. So does the Prince. Beg Mrs. Herbert to communicate these my words to those ladies, as I know that *our* sympathy is much valued by these noble fellows.

The letter was read aloud in the wards by the Chaplain. "It is a very feeling letter," said the men.

And so the months passed, and that fell winter which had begun with Inkerman and had dragged itself out through the long agony of the investment of Sebastopol, at last was over. In May, 1855, after six months of labour, Miss Nightingale could look with something like satisfaction at the condition of the Scutari hospitals. Had they done nothing more than survive the terrible strain which had been put upon them, it would have been a matter for congratulation; but they had done much more than that; they had marvellously improved. The confusion and the pressure in the wards had come to an end; order reigned in them, and cleanliness; the supplies were bountiful and prompt; important sanitary works had been carried out. One simple comparison of figures was enough to reveal the extraordinary change: the rate of mortality among the cases treated had fallen from

42 per cent to 22 per thousand. But still the indefatigable lady was not satisfied. The main problem had been solved—the physical needs of the men had been provided for; their mental and spiritual needs remained. She set up and furnished reading-rooms and recreation-rooms. She started classes and lectures. Officers were amazed to see her treating their men as if they were human beings, and assured her that she would only end by "spoiling the brutes." But that was not Miss Nightingale's opinion, and she was justified. The private soldier began to drink less, and even—though that seemed impossible—to save his pay. Miss Nightingale became a banker for the army, receiving and sending home large sums of money every month. At last, reluctantly, the Government followed suit, and established machinery of its own for the remission of money. Lord Panmure, however, remained sceptical; "it will do no good," he pronounced; "the British soldier is not a remitting animal." But, in fact, during the next six months, £71,000 was sent home.

Amid all these activities, Miss Nightingale took up the further task of inspecting the hospitals in the Crimea itself. The labour was extreme, and the conditions of life were almost intolerable. She spent whole days in the saddle, or was driven over those bleak and rocky heights in a baggage cart. Sometimes she stood for hours in the heavily falling snow, and would only reach her hut at dead of night after walking for miles through perilous ravines. Her powers of resistance seemed incredible, but at last they were exhausted. She was attacked by fever, and for a moment came very near to death. Yet she worked on; if she could not move, she could at least write; and write she did until her mind had left her; and after it had left her, in what seemed the delirious trance of death itself, she still wrote. When, after many weeks, she was strong enough to travel, she was to return to England, but she utterly refused. She would not go back, she said, before the last of the soldiers left Scutari. . . .

It was not until July, 1856—four months after the Declaration of Peace—that Miss Nightingale left Scutari for England. Her reputation was now enormous, and the enthusiasm of the public was unbounded. The Royal approbation was expressed by the gift of a brooch, accompanied by a private letter.

You are, I know, well aware (wrote Her Majesty) of the high sense I entertain of the Christian devotion which you have displayed during this great and bloody war, and I hardly need to repeat to you how warm my admiration is for your services, which are fully equal to those of my dear and brave soldiers, whose sufferings you have had the *privilege* of alleviating in so merciful a manner. I am, however, anxious of marking my feelings in a manner which I trust will be agreeable to you, and therefore send you with this letter a brooch, the form and emblems of which commemorate your great and blessed work, and which I hope you will wear as a mark of the high approbation of your Sovereign!

"It will be a very great satisfaction to me," Her Majesty added, "to make the acquaintance of one who has set so bright an example to our sex."

The brooch, which was designed by the Prince Consort, bore a St. George's cross in red enamel, and the Royal cypher surmounted by diamonds. The whole was encircled by the inscription, "Blessed are the Merciful." . . .

Eminent Victorians, by Lytton Strachey

R.M.S. TITANIC

"The band still plays—but not ragtime: Nearer My God to Thee."

The true test of a man—the test that reveals him as brave or cowardly, weak or strong, selfish or open-hearted—the final test is the
one that comes when he faces death. The Titanic was the unsinkable
ship—the most modern, the most luxurious, the fastest. She was the
pride of the British merchant fleet and her maiden voyage fully
booked months before she was ready to sail. When she sank after
striking an iceberg, 1517 of the 2214 people aboard went down with
her. Here is the story of those final hours—and of the heroes and the
cowards that they made.

THE WHITE STAR liner *Titanic*, largest ship the world had ever known,
sailed from Southampton on her maiden voyage to New York on
April 10, 1912. The paint on her strakes was fair and bright; she was
fresh from Harland and Wolff's Belfast yards, strong in the strength
of her forty-six thousand tons of steel, bent, hammered, shaped, and
riveted through the three years of her slow birth.

There was little fuss and fanfare at her sailing; her sister ship, the
Olympic—slightly smaller than the *Titanic*—had been in service for
some months and to her had gone the thunder of the cheers.

But the *Titanic* needed no whistling steamers or shouting crowds
to call attention to her superlative qualities. Her bulk dwarfed the
ships near her as longshoremen singled up her mooring lines and cast
off the turns of heavy rope from the dock bollards. She was not only
the largest ship afloat, but was believed to be the safest. Carlisle, her
builder, had given her double bottoms and had divided her hull into
sixteen watertight compartments, which made her, men thought, unsinkable. She had been built to be and had been described as a gigantic lifeboat. Her designers' dreams of a triple-screw giant, a luxurious,
floating hotel, which could speed to New York at twenty-three knots,
had been carefully translated from blueprints and mold-loft lines at
the Belfast yards into a living reality.

The *Titanic's* sailing from Southampton, though quiet, was not wholly uneventful. As the liner moved slowly toward the end of her dock that April day, the surge of her passing sucked away from the quay the steamer *New York*, moored just to seaward of the *Titanic's* berth. There were sharp cracks as the manila mooring lines of the *New York* parted under the strain. The frayed ropes writhed and whistled through the air and snapped down among the waving crowd on the pier; the *New York* swung toward the *Titanic's* bow, was checked and dragged back to the dock barely in time to avert a collision. Seamen muttered, thought it an ominous start.

Past Spithead and the Isle of Wight the *Titanic* steamed. She called at Cherbourg at dusk and then laid her course for Queenstown. At 1:30 P.M. on Thursday, April 11, she stood out of Queenstown harbor, screaming gulls soaring in her wake, with 2,214 persons—men, women, and children—aboard.

Occupying the Empire bedrooms and Georgian suites of the first-class accommodations were many well-known men and women— Colonel John Jacob Astor and his young bride; Major Archibald Butt, military aide to President Taft, and his friend, Frank D. Millet, the painter; John B. Thayer, vice-president of the Pennsylvania Railroad, and Charles M. Hays, president of the Grand Trunk Railway of Canada; W. T. Stead, the English journalist; Jacques Futrelle, French novelist; H. B. Harris, theatrical manager, and Mrs. Harris; Mr. and Mrs. Isidor Straus; and J. Bruce Ismay, chairman and managing director of the White Star line.

Down in the plain wooden cabins of the steerage class were 706 immigrants to the land of promise, and trimly stowed in the great holds was a cargo valued at $420,000: oak beams, sponges, wine, calabashes, and an odd miscellany of the common and the rare.

The *Titanic* took her departure on Fastnet Light and, heading into the night, laid her course for New York. She was due at Quarantine the following Wednesday morning.

Sunday dawned fair and clear. The *Titanic* steamed smoothly toward the west, faint streamers of brownish smoke trailing from her funnels. The purser held services in the salon in the morning; on the steerage deck aft the immigrants were playing games and a Scotsman was puffing "The Campbells Are Coming" on his bagpipes in the midst of the uproar.

At 9:00 A.M. a message from the steamer *Caronia* sputtered into the wireless shack:

Captain, *Titanic*—Westbound steamers report bergs growlers

and field ice in 42 degrees N. from 49 degrees to 51 degrees W.
12th April.

Compliments—

Barr.

It was cold in the afternoon; the sun was brilliant, but the *Titanic*,
her screws turning over at seventy-five revolutions per minute, was
approaching the Banks.

In the Marconi cabin Second Operator Harold Bride, earphones
clamped on his head, was figuring accounts; he did not stop to answer when he heard *MWL*, Continental Morse for the near-by Ley-
land liner, *Californian*, calling the *Titanic*. The *Californian* had some
message about three icebergs; he didn't bother then to take it down.
About 1:42 P.M. the rasping spark of those days spoke again across the
water. It was the *Baltic*, calling the *Titanic*, warning her of ice on
the steamer track. Bride took the message down and sent it up to the
bridge. The officer of the deck glanced at it, sent it to the bearded master of the *Titanic*, Captain E. C. Smith, a veteran of the White Star
service. It was lunchtime then; the captain, walking along the promenade deck, saw Mr. Ismay, stopped, and handed him the message without comment. Ismay read it, stuffed it in his pocket, told two ladies
about the icebergs, and resumed his walk. Later, about 7:15 P.M., the
captain requested the return of the message in order to post it in the
chartroom for the information of officers.

Dinner that night in the Jacobean dining room was gay. It was bitter
on deck, but the night was calm and fine; the sky was moonless but
studded with stars twinkling coldly in the clear air.

After dinner some of the second-class passengers gathered in the
salon, where the Reverend Mr. Carter conducted a "hymn sing-
song." It was almost ten o'clock and the stewards were waiting with
biscuits and coffee as the group sang:

"O, hear us when we cry to Thee
For those in peril on the sea."

On the bridge Second Officer Lightoller—short, stocky, efficient—
was relieved at ten o'clock by First Officer Murdoch. Lightoller had
talked with other officers about the proximity of ice; at least five wireless ice warnings had reached the ship; lookouts had been cautioned
to be alert; captain and officers expected to reach the field at any
time after 9:30 P.M. At twenty-two knots, its speed unslackened, the
Titanic plowed on through the night.

Lightoller left the darkened bridge to his relief and turned in. Captain Smith went to his cabin. The steerage was long since quiet; in

the first and second cabins lights were going out; voices were growing still; people were asleep. Murdoch paced back and forth on the bridge, peering out over the dark water, glancing now and then at the compass in front of Quartermaster Hichens at the wheel.

In the crow's-nest Lookout Frederick Fleet and his partner, Leigh, gazed down at the water, still and unruffled in the dim, starlit darkness. Behind and below them the ship, a white shadow with here and there a last winking light; ahead of them a dark and silent and cold ocean.

There was a sudden clang. "Dong-dong. Dong-dong. Dong-dong. Dong!" The metal clapper of the great ship's bell struck out 11:30. Mindful of the warnings, Fleet strained his eyes, searching the darkness for the dreaded ice. But there were only the stars and the sea.

In the wireless room, where Phillips, first operator, had relieved Bride, the buzz of the *Californian's* set again crackled into the earphones:

Californian: "Say, old man, we are stuck here, surrounded by ice."

Titanic: "Shut up, shut up; keep out. I am talking to Cape Race; you are jamming my signals."

Then, a few minutes later—about 11:40 . . .

Out of the dark she came, a vast, dim, white, monstrous shape, directly in the *Titanic's* path. For a moment Fleet doubted his eyes. But she was a deadly reality, this ghastly *thing*. Frantically Fleet struck three bells—*something dead ahead*. He snatched the telephone and called the bridge:

"Iceberg! Right ahead!"

The first officer heard but did not stop to acknowledge the message. "Hard-a-starboard!"

Hichens strained at the wheel; the bow swung slowly to port. The monster was almost upon them now.

Murdoch leaped to the engine-room telegraph. Bells clanged. Far below in the engine room those bells struck the first warning. Danger! The indicators on the dial faces swung round to "Stop!" Then "Full speed astern!" Frantically the engineers turned great valve wheels; answered the bridge bells. . . .

There was a slight shock, a brief scraping, a small list to port. Shell ice—slabs and chunks of it—fell on the foredeck. Slowly the *Titanic* stopped.

Captain Smith hurried out of his cabin.

"What has the ship struck?"

Murdoch answered, "An iceberg, sir. I hard-a-starboarded and re-versed the engines, and I was going to hard-a-port around it; but she was too close. I could not do any more. I have closed the watertight doors."

Fourth Officer Boxhall, other officers, the carpenter, came to the bridge. The captain sent Boxhall and the carpenter below to ascertain the damage.

A few lights switched on in the first and second cabins; sleepy pas-sengers peered through porthole glass; some casually asked the stewards:

"Why have we stopped?"

"I don't know, sir, but I don't suppose it is anything much."

In the smoking room a quorum of gamblers and their prey were still sitting round a poker table; the usual crowd of kibitzers looked on. They had felt the slight jar of the collision and had seen an eighty-foot ice mountain glide by the smoking-room windows; but the night was calm and clear, the *Titanic* was "unsinkable." They hadn't bothered to go on deck.

But far below, in the warren of passages on the starboard side for-ward, in the forward holds and boiler rooms, men could see that the *Titanic's* hurt was mortal. In No. 6 boiler room, where the red glow from the furnaces lighted up the naked, sweaty chests of coal-black-ened firemen, water was pouring through a great gash about two feet above the floor plates. This was no slow leak; the ship was open to the sea; in ten minutes there were eight feet of water in No. 6. Long before then the stokers had raked the flaming fires out of the furnaces and had scrambled through the watertight doors in No. 5 or had climbed up the long steel ladders to safety. When Boxhall looked at the mailroom in No. 3 hold, twenty-four feet above the keel, the mail-bags were already floating about in the slushing water. In No. 5 boiler room a stream of water spurted into an empty bunker. All six compart-ments forward of No. 4 were open to the sea; in ten seconds the ice-berg's jagged claw had ripped a three-hundred-foot slash in the bottom of the great *Titanic*.

Reports came to the bridge; Ismay in dressing gown ran out on deck in the cold, still, starlit night, climbed up the bridge ladder.

"What has happened?"

Captain Smith: "We have struck ice."

"Do you think she is seriously damaged?"

Captain Smith: "I'm afraid she is."

Ismay went below and passed Chief Engineer William Bell fresh from an inspection of the damaged compartments. Bell corroborated the captain's statement, hurried back down the glistening steel ladders to his duty. Man after man followed him—Thomas Andrews, one of the ship's designers, Archie Frost, the builder's chief engineer, and his twenty assistants—men who had no posts of duty in the engine room but whose traditions called them there.

On deck, in corridor and stateroom, life flowed again. Men, women, and children awoke and questioned; orders were given to uncover the lifeboats; water rose into the firemen's quarters; half-dressed stokers streamed up on deck. But the passengers—most of them—did not know that the *Titanic* was sinking. The shock of the collision had been so slight that some were not awakened by it; the *Titanic* was so huge that she must be unsinkable; the night was too calm, too beautiful, to think of death at sea.

Captain Smith half ran to the door of the radio shack. Bride, partly dressed, eyes dulled with sleep, was standing behind Phillips, waiting.

"Send the call for assistance."

The blue spark danced: "CQD—CQD—CQD—CQ—" Miles away Marconi men heard. Cape Race heard it, and the steamships *La Provence* and *Mt. Temple*.

The sea was surging into the *Titanic's* hold. At 12:20 the water burst into the seamen's quarters through a collapsed fore and aft wooden bulkhead. Pumps strained in the engine rooms—men and machinery making a futile fight against the sea. Steadily the water rose.

The boats were swung out—slowly; for the deck hands were late in reaching their stations, there had been no boat drill, and many of the crew did not know to what boats they were assigned. Orders were shouted; the safety valves had lifted, and steam was blowing off in a great rushing roar. In the charthouse Fourth Officer Boxhall bent above a chart, working rapidly with pencil and dividers.

12:25 A.M. Boxhall's position is sent out to a fleet of vessels: "Come at once; we have struck a berg."

To the Cunarder *Carpathia* (Arthur Henry Rostron, Master, New York to Liverpool, fifty-eight miles away): "It's a CQD, old man. Position 41–46 N.; 50–14 W."

The blue spark dancing: "Sinking; cannot hear for noise of steam."

12:30 A.M. The word is passed: "Women and children in the boats." Stewards finish waking their passengers below; life preservers are tied on; some men smile at the precaution. "The *Titanic* is unsinkable." The *Mt. Temple* starts for the *Titanic*; the *Carpathia*, with a double watch in her stokeholds, radios: "Coming hard." The CQD changes the course of many ships—but not of one; the operator of the *Californian*, near by, has just put down his earphones and turned in.

The CQD flashes over land and sea from Cape Race to New York; newspaper city rooms leap to life and presses whir.

On the *Titanic* water creeps over the bulkhead between Nos. 5 and 6 firerooms. She is going down by the head; the engineers—fighting a losing battle—are forced back foot by foot by the rising water. Down the promenade deck Happy Jock Hume, the bandsman, runs with his instrument.

12:45 A.M. Murdoch, in charge on the starboard side, eyes tragic but calm and cool, orders boat No. 7 lowered. The women hang back: they want no boat ride on an ice-strewn sea. "The *Titanic* is unsinkable." The men encourage them, explain that this is just a precautionary measure. "We'll see you again at breakfast." There is little confusion; passengers stream slowly to the boat deck. In the steerage the immigrants chatter excitedly.

A sudden sharp hiss—a streaked flare against the night; Boxhall sends a rocket toward the sky. It explodes, and a parachute of white stars lights up the icy sea. "Rockets!" The band plays ragtime.

No. 8 is lowered, and No. 5. Ismay, still in dressing gown, calls for women and children, handles lines, stumbles in the way of an officer, is told to "get the hell out of here." Third Officer Pitman takes charge of No. 5; as he swings into the boat, Murdoch grasps his hand. "Good-by and good luck, old man."

No. 6 goes over the side. There are only twenty-eight people in a lifeboat with a capacity of sixty-five.

A light stabs from the bridge; Boxhall is calling in Morse flashes, again and again, to a strange ship stopped in the ice jam five to ten miles away. Another rocket drops its shower of sparks above the ice-strewn sea and the dying ship.

1:00 A.M. Slowly the water creeps higher; the foreports of the *Titanic* are dipping into the sea. Rope squeaks through blocks; lifeboats drop jerkily seaward. Through the shouting on the decks comes the sound of the band playing ragtime.

The "Millionaires' Special" leaves the ship—boat No. 1, with a capacity of forty people, carries only Sir Cosmo and Lady Duff Gordon and ten others. Aft, the frightened immigrants mill and jostle and rush for a boat. An officer's fist flies out; three shots are fired in the air, and the panic is quelled. . . . Four Chinese sneak unseen into a boat and hide in its bottom.

1:20 A.M. Water is coming into No. 4 boiler room. Stokers slice and shovel as water laps about their ankles—steam for the dynamos; steam for the dancing spark! As the water rises, great ash hoes rake the flaming coals from the furnaces. Safety valves pop; the stokers retreat aft, and the watertight doors clang shut behind them.

The rockets fling their splendor toward the stars. The boats are more heavily loaded now, for the passengers know the *Titanic* is sinking. Women cling and sob. The great screws aft are rising clear of the sea. Half-filled boats are ordered to come alongside the cargo ports and take on more passengers, but the ports are never opened—and the boats are never filled. Others pull for the steamer's light miles away but never reach it: the lights disappear; the unknown ship steams off.

The water rises and the band plays ragtime.

1:30 A.M. Lightoller is getting the port boats off; Murdoch, the starboard. As one boat is lowered into the sea, a boat officer fires his gun along the ship's side to stop a rush from the lower decks. A woman tries to take her Great Dane into a boat with her; she is refused and steps out of the boat to die with her dog. Millet's "little smile which played on his lips all through the voyage" plays no more; his lips are grim, but he waves good-by and brings wraps for the women.

Benjamin Guggenheim, in evening clothes, smiles and says, "We've dressed up in our best and are prepared to go down like gentlemen."

1:40 A.M. Boat 14 is clear, and then 13, 16, 15, and C. The lights still shine, but the *Baltic* hears the blue spark say, "Engine room getting flooded."

The *Olympic* signals: "Am lighting up all possible boilers as fast as can."

Major Butt helps women into the last boats and waves good-by to them. Mrs. Straus puts her foot on the gunwale of a lifeboat, then she draws back and goes to her husband. "We have been together many years; where you go I will go." Colonel John Jacob Astor puts his young wife in a lifeboat, steps back, taps cigarette on fingernail. "Good-by, dearie; I'll join you later."

1:45 A.M. The foredeck is under water, the fo'c'sle head almost awash; the great stern is lifted high toward the bright stars; and still the band plays. Mr. and Mrs. Harris approach a lifeboat arm in arm.

Officer: "Ladies first, please."

Harris bows, smiles, steps back. "Of course, certainly; ladies first."

Boxhall fires the last rocket, then leaves in charge of boat No. 2.

2:00 A.M. She is dying now; her bow goes deeper, her stern higher. But there must be steam. Below in the stokeholds the sweaty firemen keep steam up for the flaring lights and the dancing spark. The glowing coals slide and tumble over the slanted grate bars; the sea pounds behind that yielding bulkhead. But the spark dances on.

The *Asian* hears Phillips try the new signal—SOS.

Boat No. 4 has left now; boat D leaves ten minutes later. Jacques Futrelle clasps his wife. "For God's sake, go! It's your last chance; go!" Madame Futrelle is half forced into the boat. It clears the side.

There are about 660 people in the boats, and 1,500 still on the sinking *Titanic*.

On top of the officers' quarters men work frantically to get the two collapsibles stowed there over the side. Water is over the forward part of A deck now; it surges up the companionways toward the boat deck. In the radio shack Bride has slipped a coat and life jacket about Phillips as the first operator sits hunched over his key, sending—still sending—"41–46 N.; 50–14 W. CQD—CQD—SOS—SOS—"

The captain's tired white face appears at the radio-room door. "Men, you have done your full duty. You can do no more. Now, it's every man for himself." The captain disappears—back to his sinking bridge, where Painter, his personal steward, stands quietly waiting for orders. The spark dances on. Bride turns his back and goes into the inner cabin. As he does so, a stoker, grimed with coal, mad with fear, steals into the shack and reaches for the life jacket on Phillips's back. Bride wheels about and brains him with a wrench.

2:10 A.M. Below decks the steam is still holding, though the pressure is falling—rapidly. In the gymnasium on the boat deck the athletic instructor watches quietly as two gentlemen ride the bicycles and another swings casually at the punching bag. Mail clerks stagger up the boat-deck stairways, dragging soaked mail sacks. The spark still dances. The band still plays—but not ragtime:

> "Nearer my God to Thee,
> Nearer to Thee . . ."

A few men take up the refrain; others kneel on the slanting decks to pray. Many run and scramble aft, where hundreds are clinging above the silent screws on the great uptilted stern. The spark still dances and the lights still flare; the engineers are on the job. The hymn comes to its close. Bandmaster Hartley, Yorkshireman violinist, taps his bow against a bulkhead, calls for "Autumn" as the water curls about his feet, and the eight musicians brace themselves against the ship's slant. People are leaping from the decks into the near-by water—the icy water. A woman cries, "Oh, save me, save me!" A man answers, "Good lady, save yourself. Only God can save you now." The band plays "Autumn":

> "God of Mercy and Compassion!
> Look with pity on my pain . . ."

The water creeps over the bridge where the *Titanic's* master stands; heavily he steps out to meet it.

2:17 A.M. "CQ—" The *Virginian* hears a ragged, blurred CQ, then an abrupt stop. The blue spark dances no more. The lights flicker out; the engineers have lost their battle.

2:18 A.M. Men run about blackened decks, leap into the night, are swept into the sea by the curling wave which licks up the *Titanic's* length. Lightoller does not leave the ship; the ship leaves him; there are hundreds like him, but only a few who live to tell of it. The funnels still swim above the water, but the ship is climbing to the perpendicular; the bridge is under and most of the foremast; the great stern rises like a squat leviathan. Men swim away from the sinking ship; others drop from the stern.

The band plays in the darkness, the water lapping upwards:

> "Hold me up in mighty waters,
> Keep my eyes on things above,
> Righteousness, divine atonement,
> Peace and everlas . . ."

The forward funnel snaps and crashes into the sea: its steel tons hammer out of existence swimmers struggling in the freezing water. Streams of sparks, of smoke and steam, burst from the after funnels. The ship upends to 50 . . . to 60 degrees.

Down in the black abyss of the stokeholds, of the engine rooms, where the dynamos have whirred at long last to a stop, the stokers and the engineers are reeling against hot metal, the rising water clutching at their knees. The boilers, the engine cylinders, rip from their bedplates; crash through bulkheads; rumble—steel against steel.

The *Titanic* stands on end, poised briefly for the plunge. Slowly she slides to her grave—slowly at first, and then more quickly . . . quickly . . . quickly.

2:20 A.M. The greatest ship in the world has sunk. From the calm, dark waters, where the floating lifeboats move, there goes up, in the white wake of her passing, "one continuous moan."

The boats that the *Titanic* had launched pulled safely away from the slight suction of the sinking ship, pulled away from the screams that came from the lips of the freezing men and women in the water. The boats were poorly manned and badly equipped, and they had been unevenly loaded. Some carried so few seamen that women bent to the oars. Mrs. Astor tugged at an oar handle; the Countess of Rothes took a tiller. Shivering stokers in sweaty, coal-blackened singlets and light trousers steered in some boats; stewards in white coats rowed in others. Ismay was in the last boat that left the ship from the starboard side; with Mr. Carter of Philadelphia and two seamen he tugged at the oars. In one of the lifeboats an Italian with a broken wrist—disguised in a woman's shawl and hat—huddled on the floor boards, ashamed now that fear had left him. In another rode the only baggage saved from the *Titanic*—the carryall of Samuel L. Goldenberg, one of the rescued passengers.

There were only a few boats that were heavily loaded; most of those that were half empty made but perfunctory efforts to pick up the moaning swimmers, their officers and crew fearing they would endanger the living if they pulled back into the midst of the dying. Some boats beat off the freezing victims; fear-crazed men and women struck with oars at the heads of swimmers. One woman drove her fist into the face of a half-dead man as he tried feebly to climb over the gunwale. Two other women helped him in and stanched the flow of blood from the ring cuts on his face.

One of the collapsible boats, which had floated off the top of the officers' quarters when the *Titanic* sank, was an icy haven for thirty or forty men. The boat had capsized as the ship sank; men swam to it, clung to it, climbed upon its slippery bottom, stood knee-deep in water in the freezing air. Chunks of ice swirled about their legs; their soaked clothing clutched their bodies in icy folds. Colonel Archibald Gracie was cast up there. Gracie, who had leaped from the stern as the *Titanic* sank; young Thayer, who had seen his father die; Lightoller, who had twice been sucked down with the ship and twice blown to the surface by a belch of air; Bride, the second operator, and Phillips, the first. There were many stokers, half-naked; it was a shivering company. They stood there in the icy sea, under the far stars, and sang and prayed—the Lord's Prayer. After a while a lifeboat came and picked them off, but Phillips was dead then or died soon afterward in the boat.

Only a few of the boats had lights; only one—No. 2—had a light that was of any use to the *Carpathia*, twisting through the ice field to the rescue. Other ships were "coming hard" too; one, the *Californian*, was still dead to opportunity.

The blue sparks still danced, but not the *Titanic's*. *La Provence* to *Celtic*: "Nobody has heard the *Titanic* for about two hours."

It was 2:40 when the *Carpathia* first sighted the green light from No. 2 boat; it was 4:10 when she picked up the first boat and learned that the *Titanic* had foundered. The last of the moaning cries had just died away then.

Captain Rostron took the survivors aboard, boatload by boatload. He was ready for them, but only a small minority of them required much medical attention. Bride's feet were twisted and frozen; others were suffering from exposure; one died, and seven were dead when taken from the boats, and were buried at sea.

It was then that the fleet of racing ships learned they were too late; the *Parisian* heard the weak signals of *MPA*, the *Carpathia*, report the death of the *Titanic*. It was then—or soon afterward, when her radio operator put on his earphones—that the *Californian*, the ship that had been within sight as the *Titanic* was sinking, first learned of the disaster.

And it was then, in all its white-green majesty, that the *Titanic's* survivors saw the iceberg, tinted with the sunrise, floating idly, pack ice jammed about its base, other bergs heaving slowly near by on the blue breast of the sea.

But it was not until later that the world knew; for wireless then was not what wireless is today, and garbled messages had nourished a hope that all of the *Titanic's* company were safe. Not until Monday evening, when P. A. S. Franklin, vice-president of the International Mercantile Marine Company, received relayed messages in New York that left little hope, did the full extent of the disaster begin to be known. Partial and garbled lists of the survivors; rumors of heroism and cowardice; stories spun out of newspaper imagination, based on a few bare facts and many false reports, misled the world, terrified and frightened it. It was not until Thursday night, when the *Carpathia* steamed into the North River, that the full truth was pieced together.

Flashlights flared on the black river when the *Carpathia* stood up to her dock. Tugs nosed about her, shunted her toward Pier 54. Thirty thousand people jammed the streets; ambulances and stretchers stood on the pier; coroners and physicians waited.

In midstream the Cunarder dropped over the *Titanic's* lifeboats; then she headed toward the dock. Beneath the customs letters on the pier stood relatives of the 711 survivors, relatives of the missing— hoping against hope. The *Carpathia* cast her lines ashore; stevedores looped them over bollards. The dense throngs stood quiet as the first survivors stepped down the gangway. The woman half staggered— led by customs guards—beneath her letter. A "low wailing" moan came from the crowd, fell, grew in volume, and dropped again.

Thus ended the maiden voyage of the *Titanic*. The lifeboats brought to New York by the *Carpathia*, a few deck chairs and gratings awash in the ice field off the Grand Banks eight hundred miles from shore, were all that was left of the world's greatest ship.

R. M. S. *Titanic*, by Hanson Baldwin

HENRY DAVID THOREAU

"It was like travelling into a far country ..."

Henry David Thoreau was a comparatively unknown person in his own lifetime. Most of the works by which we know him were published after his death. A member of the transcendentalist movement who made his self-limited livelihood as a handyman, his life was quiet, almost tranquil. Yet history remembers Thoreau as a great man on two scores—as a naturalist whose journals are of unsurpassed beauty, and as the author of an essay, Resistance to Civil Government, from which this excerpt was taken. Here is a quiet decision—one utterly in keeping with the character of the man— yet it may have profoundly altered the history of the world. For it was this brief essay that crystallized the political philosophy of Mahatma Gandhi and through him set a continent in motion.

I HAVE PAID no poll tax for six years. I was put into a jail once on this account, for one night; and as I stood considering the walls of solid stone, two or three feet thick, the door of wood and iron, a foot thick, and the iron grating which strained the light, I could not help being struck with the foolishness of that institution which treated me as if I were mere flesh and blood and bones, to be locked up. I wondered that it should have concluded at length that this was the best use it could put me to, and had never thought to avail itself of my services in some way. I saw that, if there was a wall of stone between me and my townsmen, there was a still more difficult one to climb or break through, before they could get to be as free as I was. I did not for a moment feel confined, and the walls seemed a great waste of stone and mortar. I felt as if I alone of all my townsmen had paid my tax. They plainly did not know how to treat me, but behaved like persons who are underbred. In every threat and in every compliment there was a blunder; for they thought that my chief desire was to stand on the other side of that stone wall. I could not but smile to see how industriously they locked the door on my meditations, which followed them out again without let or hindrance, and *they* were really all that was dangerous. As they could not reach me, they had resolved to punish my body; just as boys, if they cannot come at some person against whom they have a spite, will abuse his dog. I saw that the State was half-witted, that it was timid as a lone woman with her silver spoons, and that it did not know its friends from its foes, and I lost all my remaining respect for it, and pitied it. . . .

The night in prison was novel and interesting enough. The prisoners in their shirt-sleeves were enjoying a chat and the evening air in the door-way, when I entered. But the jailer said, "Come, boys, it is time to lock up"; and so they dispersed, and I heard the sound of their steps returning into the hollow apartments. My roommate was introduced to me by the jailer as a "first-rate fellow and a clever man." When the door was locked, he showed me where to hang my hat, and how he managed matters there. The rooms were white-washed once a month; and this one, at least, was the whitest, most simply furnished, and probably the neatest apartment in town. He naturally wanted to know where I came from, and what brought me there; and, when I had told him, I asked him in turn how he came there, presuming him to be an honest man, of course; and as the world goes I believe he was. "Why," said he, "they accuse me of burning a barn; but I never did it." As near as I could discover, he had probably gone to bed in a barn when drunk, and smoked his pipe there; and so a barn was burnt. He had the reputation of being a clever man, had been there some three months waiting for his trial to come on, and would have to wait as much longer; but he was quite domesticated and contented, since he got his board for nothing, and thought he was well treated.

He occupied one window, and I the other; and I saw that, if one stayed there long, his principal business would be to look out the window. I had soon read all the tracts that were left there, and examined where former prisoners had broken out, and where a grate had been sawed off, and heard the history of the various occupants of that room; for I found that even here there was a history and a gossip which never circulated beyond the walls of the jail. Probably this is the only house in the town where verses are composed, which are afterward printed in circular form, but not published. I was shown quite a long list of verses which were composed by some young men who had been detected in an attempt to escape, who avenged themselves by singing them.

I pumped my fellow-prisoner as dry as I could, for fear I should never see him again; but at length he showed me which was my bed, and left me to blow out the lamp.

It was like travelling into a far country, such as I had never expected to behold, to lie there for one night. It seemed to me that I never had

heard the town-clock strike before, nor the evening sounds of the village; for we slept with the windows open, which were inside the
grating. It was to see my native village in the light of the middle ages,
and our Concord was turned into a Rhine stream, and visions of
knights and castles passed before me. They were the voices of old
burghers that I heard in the streets. I was an involuntary spectator
and auditor of whatever was done and said in the kitchen of the adjacent village-inn—a wholly new and rare experience to me. It was
a closer view of my native town. I was fairly inside of it. I never had
seen its institutions before. This is one of its peculiar institutions; for
it is a shire town. I began to comprehend what its inhabitants were
about.

In the morning our breakfasts were put through the hole in the
door, in small oblong-square tin pans, made to fit, and holding a pint
of chocolate, with brown bread, and an iron spoon. When they called
for the vessels again, I was green enough to return what bread I had
left; but my comrade seized it and said that I should lay that up for
lunch or dinner. Soon after, he was let out to work at haying in a
neighboring field, whither he went every day, and would not be back
until noon; so he bade me good-day, saying that he doubted if he
should see me again.

When I came out of prison—for some one interfered, and paid the
tax—I did not perceive that great changes had taken place on the common, such as he observed who went in as a youth, and emerged a tot-
tering and gray-headed man; and yet a change had to my eyes come
over the scene—the town, and State and country—greater than any
that mere time could effect. I saw to what extent the people among
whom I lived could be trusted as good neighbors and friends; that
their friendship was for summer weather only; that they did not
greatly purpose to do right; that they were a distinct race from me
by their prejudices and superstitions, as the Chinamen and Malays
are; that, in their sacrifices to humanity, they ran no risks, not even to
their property; that, after all, they were not so noble but they treated
the thief as he had treated them, and hoped, by a certain outward
observance and a few prayers, and by walking in a particular straight
though useless path from time to time, to save their souls. This may
be to judge my neighbors harshly; for I believe that most of them
are not aware that they have such an institution as the jail in their
village.

It was formerly the custom in our village, when a poor debtor came
out of jail, for his acquaintances to salute him, looking through their
fingers, which were crossed to represent the grating of a jail window,
"How do ye do?" My neighbors did not thus salute me, but first looked

at me, and then at one another, as if I had returned from a long journey. I was put into jail as I was going to the shoemaker's to get a
shoe which was mended. When I was let out the next morning, I proceeded to finish my errand, and having put on my mended shoe,
joined a huckleberry party, who were impatient to put themselves under my conduct; and in half an hour—for the horse was soon tackled—
was in the midst of a huckleberry field, on one of our highest hills,
two miles off; and then the State was nowhere to be seen. . . .

Resistance to Civil Government, by Henry David Thoreau

J. W. N. SULLIVAN

"... Life has its dramatic moments."

I*t would have been possible," Sullivan says, "for Mozart to have been brought up in the London of those days [c 1900] without ever discovering he cared for music." The possibility that fate and circumstance play such a large part in all our lives is forever intriguing. In looking at his own life, J. W. N. Sullivan, who in his maturity wrote the definitive work on the life and music of Beethoven, and became one of the most prominent musicologists of his day, points out the moment of turning in his own life. It was "perhaps . . . the cardinal experience of my life"—the day when he is first introduced to great music. Here is Sullivan's turning point . . . more dramatic, perhaps, than most, but surely an experience, remembered or not, that is common to us all.*

IT IS SURELY somewhat odd that I had reached the age of seventeen, three years of which had been spent in the greatest capital of the world, without hearing any good music whatever. The extraordinary scarcity of good music, in London, is incredible. Things may be better now, but at the time I am speaking of, good music could not be heard in London without being deliberately hunted for. And paid for. The piano-playing daughter of the poorer classes, who could often be overheard in the district in which I lived, invariably played rubbish. All the music played, outside "classical concerts," all music-hall songs and restaurant bands, all music sung and whistled in the streets was completely inane. The gulf between great music and the music popular with the English masses seems to me almost greater than the gulf between great literature and the ordinary commercial novel. It would have been possible, I believe, for Mozart to have been brought up in the London of those days without ever discovering that he cared for music. For it must be remembered that the difference between good music and bad music is absolute. The difference is as marked as the difference between the odour of a rose and the stench of a sewer. Music can express our highest aspirations with such closeness and subtlety that it seems to be the very voice of the spirit, and it can express dreadful vulgarity and inanity with the same unequalled power. Sheer vulgarity can hardly be expressed by any other art. For vulgarity without virility, without humour, without any redeeming characteristic, we have to go to music. One never realizes the vulgarity of human beings so acutely as when listening to the mindless bawling of popular songs.

I confess that popular music, what I heard of it, did not distress me in those days. I accepted it, I suppose, as a normal accompaniment of existence as one accepted London fogs, flayed carcasses in butchers' shops, and horse-filth in the streets. This habit of indifference only slowly weakened. It is only of late years that a whiff from the public-house automatic piano, or the raucous singing of hooligans homeward bound, has been actively distressing. But music of this kind can perhaps be explained as due to mere imbecility. The latest type of popular music, jazz music, affects me as deliberately evil. It does not seem to me vulgar by inadvertence; it is propaganda for vulgarity. Its popularity testifies to a widespread *nostalgie de la boue*. If our sociologists were also musicians they would find considerable social significance in the popularity of jazz.

My introduction to music occurred to me on the first occasion that [my employer] Mr. Pyatt invited me to dinner. That occasion is memorable for more than one reason. It was my first introduction not only to music, but to surroundings of culture and comfort. The house was smaller than I had expected, but it had an unmistakable air of unobtrusive wealth. In the hall, against the walls, were shields, daggers, elephants' tusks, and the jaw-bones, complete with teeth, of a shark. These things seemed to confirm the fact, which I knew already, that Mr. Pyatt had travelled extensively. The dining room seemed to me amazingly neat and polished, like something set out in the window of a high-class furniture shop. The dinner, at which Mr. Pyatt and myself were alone, except for the waiting-maid, was unexpectedly easy, although I realised that a fair degree of alertness was essential. For the first time in my life I tasted wine; I also had a liqueur and a cigar. I found the whole experience extremely pleasant, for I liked Mr. Pyatt, I enjoyed the dinner, and I was inwardly very pleased by my own behaviour. In those days I was shy without being humble, and it seemed to me that my behaviour, in these unprecedented surroundings, had just the right air of polite but unenthusiastic acceptance. My conversation was perhaps a little distant and formal, for I knew that I should make a mess of things if I became "natural" for a moment, but it was, I felt, sensible, alert, and far from commonplace. I felt that I had passed a rather searching examination successfully at all points. It did not occur to me, of course, to give Mr. Pyatt any of the credit for this. At the coffee stage we moved into another room, filled with very easy chairs and sofas, and containing a piano-player, a rather novel instrument at that time. Mr. Pyatt suggested trying a few rolls. . . .

Well, life has its dramatic moments. Perhaps any one of Mr. Pyatt's rolls would have produced a great effect on me, but it so happened that the first one he put on was one of the mightiest and most immediately arresting of all compositions, Bach's great organ Toccata and Fugue in D minor. Even as arranged for the piano and played by a mechanical player it is, as I can testify, completely overwhelming. My first hearing of it was a cardinal experience in my life; perhaps, when all is summed up, it will prove to be *the* cardinal experience of my life. For it was my first glimpse of those activities of the human spirit which are, I am convinced, the justification of life, and in which the meaning of life is to be found. Nothing that I had hitherto experienced belonged to that region. I experienced, quite literally, a revelation. All great art, I believe, is the record of a spiritual achievement, of a synthesis of experience, of a degree of understanding, that cannot be communicated in other terms. But, for myself, it is only in certain great music that the revelation is complete and unambiguous. Such music is my substitute for the mystic vision. It is, perhaps, an experience that can never be satisfactorily rationalised, nor ever communicated to others. It is also an experience that can never be denied. No account of life that denies its supreme importance can be even remotely true. In this position, however much it may seem to conflict with my liking for clear reasoning based on verifiable premises, I am quite unshakable. I have heard, and I know.

I passed the rest of the evening in a sort of bewildered happiness. Several more rolls were played—too many for my untrained attention. I cannot remember what they were. After that first shock I listened but vaguely. But it was not until very late that I suddenly became conscious of fatigue and rose to go. Mr. Pyatt shook hands with a pleased smile, obviously finding his experiment completely successful, but, with a tact that could not be missed, he refrained from questioning me about my sensations. The bus ride home was through a transfigured London. How I loved it all—the bright lights, the traffic, the dark trees of the park, the great, impressive buildings! I was in a dreamy ecstasy at the wonder of life, at its range and complexity, its infinite possibilities. Life! The scale of it! The diversity of it! The greatness of this adventure to which the spirit of man is committed! What undreamed of possibilities lie before him, what new ways of thinking, what new knowledge, what new heights of experience! And there, it seemed to me, amongst the farthest reaches of the spirit, lonely and prophetic, was music such as I had heard that night, music informed with the new understanding, the new degree of realisation, that has been achieved by the pioneers of our race. Such thoughts are hardly thoughts, I know. But the experience they try to translate is all-important to those who possess it. Even science itself was, to me, transfigured by that experience. It no longer seemed to me an isolated adventure, an unaccountable predilection on the part of a few unusual individuals. It was merely one of the modes of growth of the human consciousness, one of the roads that leads towards the wider knowledge, the greater state of being, that man is on the way to achieve. Both in their motives and in the end they finally serve, the scientific man and the artist are brothers.

And so began for me an altogether richer and wider life. . . . I soon found that the great nights, to me, were the Friday nights—the Beethoven nights. For years I never missed one. But I did more than listen to music. I made it my business to master musical notation and, although I never learned to play an instrument, I trained myself to read music from a score. In this I was greatly helped by my acquaintance with a Mr. Woods, a young man employed in a music shop in New Oxford Street. This acquaintance, also, I owe to Mr. Pyatt, who took me there on one occasion when he wanted to buy some new piano-rolls. A mutual attraction immediately sprang up between Woods and myself, and by the end of the purchase, which took over an hour, we were on almost friendly terms. Piano-rolls were tried in the basement, a large place almost impassable from the number of second-hand pianos it contained, and Woods had the habit, he informed me, of spending an hour or two there every evening after the shop was shut, playing through various rolls for his own amusement. Like myself, he could not play an instrument, and again like myself, he could not afford a mechanical player. Realising that I was a fellow-enthusiast, he invited me to share these nightly orgies. This invitation I gladly accepted, and in the course of a few weeks I must have heard every good composition that had been arranged, up to that time, for the mechanical player. . . .

Amongst the most vivid of my recollections are the evenings we would spend together, consuming sandwiches and lager beer, in the basement room of the Monico Café, after a Beethoven night at the Promenade Concerts. In those days lager beer was served in "steins," and cost only fivepence! Often, reckless with excitement, we would each drink two in an evening. I cannot say of how many confused aspirations and romantic fancies those noble mugs of lager beer were symbolical. We were students, we were enfranchised, we were familiar with great music and great thoughts. We heard scraps of German all around us, a very stimulating thing in itself. Fellow-countrymen of Beethoven! And I remember that a completely unreal Heidelberg was, in some inexplicable manner, associated with it all. (Years later, when a scientific friend of mine wrote to me saying what he really thought of Heidelberg and Heidelberg students, I remember I was profoundly shocked—and curiously hurt.) On these occasions our conversation dealt very little with our own ambitions. Rather would we work ourselves up into a common ecstasy over the great men of the past. The incredible, the ungraspable imagination and force of Beethoven! The immense masterliness of Bach! The superhuman perfection of Mozart! . . .

There are people, I know, who think that the "great man" is a sort of myth. They will admit a quantitative difference, as it were, between men, but not a qualitative difference. The great man is merely a larger edition of the small man. I think this is true of some men we would have to call great, but I do not think it is generally true. There are artists who express for us what we already know; there are other artists who present to us our familiar world in an entirely new light, and who even reveal to us an entirely new world. The sensibilities of such artists may be essentially familiar to our own, but the synthesis of their experience they have effected is something radically new. The work of such men is, it seems to me, prophetic of the future development of the human consciousness. Personally, I find, as I have said before, the clearest examples of art of this magnitude in music, and particularly in the music of Beethoven's last quartets. I do not, therefore, smile at my youthful hero-worship. I do not dismiss those feelings as belonging to the generous illusions of youth. On the contrary, I find that while they were insufficiently discriminating they were also insufficiently profound. The great men of my youth were truly great men, and greater than I knew.

But for the Grace of God, by J. W. N. Sullivan

EDWARD VIII

"I will not enter now into my private feelings ..."

The abdication of David Windsor, Edward VIII of England, is a classic tragedy brought up to date. As Prince of Wales, Windsor had been a dashing and romantic figure. He had fought in the First World War, forcing his way into action over the protests of the royal family and the parliament. He spent the years between the war and his father's death travelling throughout the world, making friends for England in the Empire and the Commonwealth. Yet despite his position—despite his ability to make people like him—he was a lonely and insecure man. He stammered when he spoke in public and it was evident that he felt inadequate to the job ahead. Further, David Windsor, handsome, athletic, charming, had never married. He was to be a bachelor king.

The story of the new king's love affair with Mrs. Simpson, the twice-married commoner, was the most publicized romance of the century. It precipitated a smouldering political crisis, and the world waited for the outcome with excitement and trepidation. Then Edward made his famous abdication radio address. And it seemed to many who heard him throughout the world that, for the first time, his stammer had disappeared.

KING EDWARD announced his decision to abdicate on Thursday, December 10. The preceding Tuesday and Wednesday gave no fresh themes to the drama. There had been faint hope when Mrs. Simpson's statement was published—that she "wished to avoid any action or proposal which would hurt or damage His Majesty or the throne." She said that she was willing, "if such action would solve the problem," to withdraw from the situation. But nothing would shake the strength of King Edward's purpose, and the world waited, excited and anxious, to know the outcome of the hurried meetings between members of the Royal Family, the meetings of Dominion Ministers and the continued interviews between Mr. Baldwin and the King. The signs were increasingly grave, and renewed gloom settled upon financiers and members of the Stock Exchange. . . .

On Wednesday night King Edward answered Mr. Baldwin. The end had come and his pledges of twenty years died upon the wind. The King wrote, "His Majesty has given the matter his further consideration, but regrets that he is unable to alter his decision."

This was the news with which the Prime Minister faced the House of Commons on Thursday afternoon. The hushed, strained morning ended. Thousands of people stood outside the Houses of Parliament, but they made little sound. The day was cold and it added to the gloom, the sense of anxious meditation which spread over the capital. London seemed to be stunned into silence, knowing that hope was passed. When it was almost four o'clock, Mr. Baldwin rose from his seat and walked to the Bar of the House, carrying three sheets of typescript which bore the royal coat of arms in red. He turned quickly and bowed to the Chair, and then, in a clear, unhesitating voice, he said, "A message from His Majesty the King, sir, signed by His Majesty's own hand."

He handed the three sheets of paper to the Speaker and then walked back to his seat. There was one break in the strained silence as the Speaker began—there was a movement in one of the galleries. The word *Order* was cried and then, with the return of silence, the speaker read the King's message.

"After long and anxious consideration I have determined to renounce the throne to which I succeeded on the death of my father, and I am communicating this, my final and irrevocable decision. Realising as I do the gravity of this step, I can only hope that I shall have the understanding of my peoples in the decision I have taken and the reasons which have led me to take it. I will not enter now into my private feelings, but I would beg that it should be remembered that the burden which constantly rests upon the shoulders of a sovereign is so heavy that it can only be borne in circumstances different from those in which I now find myself." . . .

At ten o'clock a voice announced, over the air, "This is Windsor Castle. His Royal Highness Prince Edward."

Then came another voice, thick and tired, and one was aware of the Prince's will summoning its strength, trying . . . to explain his intimate tragedy to the world. . . .

KING EDWARD VIII'S LAST SPEECH

At long last I am able to say a few words of my own. I have never wanted to withhold anything, but until now it has not been constitutionally possible for me to speak.

A few hours ago I discharged my last duty as King and Emperor, and now that I have been succeeded by my brother, the Duke of York, my first words must be to declare my allegiance to him.

This I do with all my heart.

You all know the reasons which have impelled me to renounce the throne, but I want you to understand that in making up my mind I did not forget the country or the Empire, which as Prince of Wales and lately as King I have for twenty-five years tried to serve.

But you must believe me when I tell you that I have found it impossible to carry the heavy burden of responsibility and discharge my duties as King as I would wish to do without the help and support of the woman I love.

And I want you to know that the decision I have made has been mine and mine alone. This was a thing I had to judge entirely for myself. The other person most nearly concerned has tried up to the last to persuade me to take a different course.

I have made this, the most serious decision of my life, only upon a single thought—of what would in the end be best for all.

This decision has been made less difficult to me by the sheer knowledge that my brother, with his long training in the public affairs of this country and with his fine qualities, will be able to take my place forthwith without interruption or injury to the life and progress of the Empire.

And he has one matchless blessing, enjoyed by so many of you, and not bestowed on me, a happy home with his wife and children.

During these hard days I have been comforted by Her Majesty, my mother, and by my family. The Ministers of the Crown, and in particular Mr. Baldwin, the Prime Minister, have always treated me with full consideration. There has never been any constitutional difference between me and them, and between me and Parliament.

Bred in the constitutional traditions by my father, I should never have allowed any such issue to arise. Ever since I was Prince of Wales, and later on when I occupied the throne, I have been treated with the greatest kindness by all classes of people, wherever I have lived or journeyed throughout the Empire. For that I am very grateful.

I now quit altogether public affairs, and lay down my burden. It may be some time before I return to my native land, but I shall always follow the fortunes of the British race and Empire with profound interest, and if at any time in the future I can be found of service to His Majesty in a private station I shall not fail.

And now we all have a new King. I wish him and you, his people, happiness and prosperity with all my heart. God bless you all. GOD SAVE THE KING!

King Edward VIII, by Hector Bolitho

II. THE POWER OF FAITH

If ye have faith as a grain of mustard seed,

ye shall say unto this mountain,

Remove hence to yonder place;

and it shall remove;

and nothing shall be impossible unto you.

MATTHEW XVII, 20

FREDERICK DOUGLASS

"This day, this spot, this one bright morning was important."

When Frederick Douglass died in 1895 there lay behind him a distinguished career as orator, teacher and diplomat. Yet Douglass had begun life as a slave. The courage and the faith that enabled him to escape his bonds and speak for his people was not his own. It was given to him by a primitive, unlettered man—but a man who knew the power of faith—and what it could accomplish.

THE LONG day was ending. Now that the sun had dropped behind scrawny pine trees, little eddies of dust stirred along the road. A bit of air from the bay lifted the flaccid leaves and lightly rustled the dry twigs. A heap of rags and matted hair that had seemed part of the swampy underbrush stirred. A dark head lifted cautiously. It was bruised and cut, and the deep eyes were wide with terror. For a moment the figure was motionless—ears strained, aching muscles drawn together, ready to dive deeper into the scrub. Then the evening breeze touched the bloated face, tongue licked out over cracked, parched lips. As the head sagged forward, a single drop of blood fell heavily upon the dry pine needles.

Water! The wide nostrils distended gratefully, tasting the moisture in the air—cool like the damp bricks of the well. Cracked fingers twitched as if they wrapped themselves around a rusty cup—the rough red cup with its brimming goodness of cool water. It had stood right at the side of his grandmother's hut—the old well had—its skyward-pointing beam so aptly placed between the limbs of what had once been a tree, so nicely balanced that even a small boy could move it up and down with one hand and get a drink without calling for help. The bundle of rags in the bushes shivered violently. Benumbed limbs were coming alive. He must be quiet, lie still a little longer, breathe slowly.

But the stupor that had locked his senses during the heat of the August day was lifting. Pain which could not be borne made him writhe. He gritted his teeth. His head seemed to float somewhere in space, swelling and swelling. He pressed against the ground, crushing the pine needles against his lips. Faces and voices were blurred in his memory. Sun, hot sun on the road—bare feet stirring the dust. The road winding up the hill—dust in the road. He had watched his grandmother disappear in the dust of the road. His mother had gone too, waving goodbye. The road had swallowed them up. The shadows of the trees were blotting out the road. There were only trees here. He lay still.

Darkness falls swiftly in the pine woods. He raised himself once more and looked about. A squirrel scurried for cover. Then everything was still—no harsh voices, no curses, no baying of hounds. That meant they were not looking for him. With the dogs it would have been easy enough. Covey had not bothered to take time out from work. Covey knew he could not get away.

Masters who sent their slaves to this narrow neck of stubborn land between the bay and the river knew their property was safe. Edward Covey enjoyed the reputation of being a first-rate hand at breaking n.....s. Slaveholders in the vicinity called him in when they had trouble. Since Covey was a poor man his occupation was of immense advantage to him. It enabled him to get his farm worked with very little expense. Like some horsebreakers noted for their skill, who rode the best horses in the country without expense, Covey could have under him the most fiery bloods of the neighborhood. He guaranteed to return any slave to his master well broken.

Captain Auld had turned over to Covey this impudent young buck who had been sent down to the Eastern Shore from Baltimore. Among the items of his wife's property, Captain Auld had found this slave listed as "Frederick."

"Sly and dangerous!" The Captain's voice was hard. "Got to be broken now while he's young."

"Frederick!" Covey had mouthed the syllables distastefully, his small green eyes traveling over the stocky well-formed limbs, broad shoulders and long brown arms. "Too much name—too much head!" The comment was a sort of low growl. But his tones were servile as he addressed the master.

"Know his kind well. Just leave him to me. I'll take it out of him."

"Watch yourself! Don't be bringing him back to me crippled. He'll fetch a fair price in a couple of years. Comes of good stock."

Thomas Auld (why "Captain" no one knew) had not been born a slaveholder. Slaves had come to him through marriage. The stench of the whole thing sickened him, but he despised himself for his weakness. He dreaded his wife's scorn. She had grown up on the Lloyd plantation where there were more slaves than anybody could count and there was always plenty of everything. Colonel Lloyd never had trouble with his slaves, she taunted her husband. Auld would tighten his colorless thin lips. God knows he tried hard enough—starved himself to feed a parcel of no-good, lazy blacks. He thoroughly hated them all. This one now—this sleek young buck—he'd been ruined in the city by Hugh Auld. By his own brother and that milk-faced wife of his. Teaching him to read! Ruining a good, strong field hand! Well, he'd try Covey. See what he could do.

"Take him along!"

That had been shortly after "the Christmas." It was now hot summer. For Frederick a long, long time had passed. He was indeed "broken."

A shuddering groan escaped the boy. Part of Covey's irritation could be understood. He *had* been clumsy and slow about the fields and barn. But he dared not ask questions, and since nobody took the trouble to tell him anything his furrows were shallow and crooked.

He failed at running the treadmill. He had never even seen horned cattle before. So it was not surprising that his worst experiences had been with them. The strong, vicious beasts dragged him about at will, and day after day Covey flogged him for allowing the oxen to get away. Flogging was Covey's one method of instruction.

At first Frederick tortured himself with questions. They knew he'd never learned field work. "Old Marse" had sent him to Baltimore when he was just a pickaninny to look after the favorite grandchild, rosy-cheeked Tommy. He remembered that exciting trip to Baltimore and the moment when Mrs. Auld had taken his hand, and, leading him to her little son, had said, "Look, Tommy, here's your Freddy."

The little slave had shyly regarded his equally small master. The white child had smiled, and instantly two small boys became fast friends. Fred had gone everywhere with Tommy. No watchdog was ever more devoted.

"Freddy's with Tommy," the mother would say with assurance.

It was perfectly natural that when Tommy began to read he eagerly shared the new and fascinating game with his companion. The mother was amused at how quickly the black child caught on. She encouraged both children because she considered the exchange good for Tommy. . . .

The seed was planted. Now he wanted to know, and he developed a cunning far beyond his years. It was not too difficult to salvage school books as they were thrown away. He invented "games" for Tommy and his friends—games which involved reading and spelling. The white boys slipped chalk from their schoolrooms and drew letters and words on sidewalks and fences. By the time Tommy was twelve years old, Freddy could read anything that came his way. . . . Then suddenly Tommy was growing up. It was decided to send him away to school. And so, after seven years, his dark caretaker, no longer a small, wide-eyed pickaninny, was sent back to the Eastern Shore plantation. . . . Fred, arriving at the plantation, had been quiet and obedient. Captain Auld appraised this piece of his wife's inheritance with satisfaction. The boy appeared to be strong and bright—a real value. But before he had a chance to show what he could do, "the Christmas" was upon them and all regular work on the plantation was suspended.

Throughout the South it was customary for everybody to knock off from work in the period between Christmas Day and New Year's. On the big plantations there were boxing, wrestling, foot-racing, a lot of dancing and drinking of whiskey. Masters considered it a good thing for the slaves to "let go" this one time of the year—an exhausting "safety valve." All kinds of wild carousing were condoned. Liquor was brought in by the barrel and freely distributed. Not to be drunk during the Christmas was disgraceful and was regarded by the masters with something like suspicion.

Captain Auld's place was too poor for much feasting; but complete license was given, and into half-starved bodies were poured jugs of rum and corn whiskey. Men and women careened around and sang hoarsely, couples rolled in the ditch, while the overseers shouted with laughter. Everybody had a "good time."

All this was new to the boy, Frederick. He had never witnessed such loose depravity. He was a stranger. Eagerly he inquired for those he had known as a child. No one could tell him anything. "Old Marse's" slaves had been divided, exchanged, sold; and a slave leaves no forwarding address. The youth had no feeling of kinship with the plantation folks. He missed Tommy and wondered how he was getting along without him. On the other hand, the field workers and oyster shuckers looked upon the newcomer as a "house n....r."

For a while he watched the dancing and "jubilee beating," tasted the burning liquid and then, as the afternoon wore on, slipped away. The day was balmy, with no suggestion of winter as known in the north. Frederick had not expected this leisure. He had kept his book hidden, knowing such things were forbidden. Now, tucking it inside his shirt, he walked out across the freshly plowed fields.

So it happened that Captain Auld came upon him stretched out under a tree, his eyes fastened on the book which lay before him on the ground, his lips moving. The boy was so absorbed that he did not hear his name called. Only when the Captain's riding whip came down on his shoulders did he jump up. It was too late then.

And so they had called in Covey, the slave-breaker. All that was seven months ago.

The moon over Chesapeake can be very lovely. This night it was full, and the pine trees pointing to a cloudless sky were bathed in silver. Far out on the water a boat moved with languid grace, her sails almost limp, sending a shimmering ripple to the sandy shore.

The dark form painfully crawling between the trees paused at the edge of the cove. The wide beach out there under the bright moonlight was fully exposed. Should he risk it?

"Water." It was a moan. Then he lifted his eyes and saw the ship sailing away on the water. A *free ship going out to sea. Oh Jesus!* He had heard no sound of footsteps, not the slightest breaking of a twig, but a low voice close beside him said,

"Rest easy, you! I get water."

The boy shrank back, staring. A thick tree trunk close by split in two, and a very black man bent over him.

"I Sandy," the deep voice went on. "Lay down now."

The chilled blood in Frederick's broken body began to race. Once more he lost consciousness. This time he did not fight against it. A friend was standing by.

The black man moved swiftly. Kneeling beside the still figure he slipped his hand inside the rags. His face, inscrutable polished ebony, did not change; but far down inside his eyes a dull light glowed as he tore away the filthy cloth, sticky and stiff with drying blood. Was he too late? Satisfied, he eased the twisted limbs on the pine needles and then hurried down to the river's edge where he filled the tin can that hung from a cord over his shoulders.

Frederick opened his eyes when the water touched his lips. He sighed when Sandy gently wiped the clotted blood from his face and touched the gaping wound in the thick, matted hair. His voice sounded strange to his own ears when he asked, "How come you know?"

"This day I work close by Mr. Kemp. Car'line come. Tell me."

At the name Frederick's bones seemed to melt and flow in tears. Something which neither curses, nor kicks, nor blows had touched gave way. Caroline, Covey's own slave woman, who bore upon her body the marks of his sadistic pleasure, who seldom raised her eyes and always spoke in whispers—Caroline had gone for help.

Sandy did nothing to stay the paroxysm of weeping. He knew it was good, that healing would come sooner. Sandy was very wise. Up and down the Eastern Shore it was whispered that Sandy was "voo-doo," that he was versed in black magic. Sandy was a full-blooded African. He remembered coming across the "great waters." He remembered the darkness, the moans and the awful smells. But he had been fortunate. The chain which fastened his small ankle to the hold of the ship also held his giant mother, and she had talked to him. All through the darkness she had talked to him. The straight, long-limbed woman of the Wambugwe had been a prize catch. The Bantus of eastern Africa were hard to capture. They brought the highest prices in the markets. Sandy remembered the rage of the dealer when his mother was found dead. She had never set foot on this new land, but all during the long journey she had talked—and Sandy had not forgotten. He had not forgotten one word.

This mother's son now sat quietly by on his haunches, waiting. Long ago he had learned patience. The waters of great rivers move slowly, almost imperceptibly; big trees of the forest stand still, yet each year grow; seasons come in due time; nothing stays the same. Sandy knew.

After a long shuddering sigh Frederick lay silent. Then Sandy sprang up.

"We go by my woman's house. Come," he said.

Frederick made an effort to rise. Sandy lifted the boy in his strong arms and stood him on his feet. For a moment he leaned heavily; then, with Sandy supporting him, he was conscious of being half dragged through the thicket. His body was empty of pain, of thought, of emotion. . . .

The woman, Noma, sat in the opening of her hut gazing at the fire. It was burning low. . . . The fire was almost out when she heard him coming through the brush. This was so unusual that she started up in alarm. She did not cry out when he appeared, supporting a bruised and battered form. She acted instantly to get this helpless being out of sight. They carried the boy inside the hut and gently deposited him on the soft pile of reeds in the corner. No time was lost with questions.

Quickly she brought warm water and stripped off the filthy rags. She bathed his wounds and wrapped a smooth green leaf about his head. She poured oil on the back, which all along its smooth flatness lay open and raw, an oozing mass. A rib in his side seemed to be broken. They bound his middle with strips she tore from her skirts.

Then she brought a steaming bowl. Frederick had had nothing to eat all day. For the past six months his food had been "stock" and nothing more. Now he was certain that never had he tasted anything so good as this succulent mixture. Into the pot the woman had dropped bits of pork, crabs and oysters, a handful of crisp seaweed, and from her garden, okra and green peppers and soft, ripe tomatoes. In the hot ashes she had baked corn pone. Frederick ate greedily, smacking his lips. Sandy squatted beside him with his own bowl. A burning pine cone lighted them while they ate, and Sandy smiled at the woman.

But hardly had he finished his bowl when sleep weighted Frederick down. The soothing oil, the sense of security and now this good hot food were too much for him. He fell asleep with the half-eaten pone in his hand.

Then the other two went outside. The woman poked the fire, adding a few sticks. Sandy lay down beside it. He told his wife how that afternoon he had spied Caroline hiding in the bushes near where he worked. She acted like a terrified animal, he explained, so he had gone to her. Bit by bit she told him how Covey had beaten Captain Auld's boy, striking his head and kicking him in the side, and left him in the yard. She had seen the boy crawl away into the woods. Surely this time he would die.

"I do not think he die now. Man die hard." Sandy thought a moment. "I help him."

"How?" Noma's question took in the encircling woods, the bay. How could this boy escape? Sandy shook his head.

"He no go now. This one time, he go back."

The woman waited.

"I hear 'bout this boy—how he read and write. He smart with white man's learning."

"Ah!" said the woman, beginning to understand.

"Tonight I give him the knowing of black men. I call out the strength in his bones—the bones his mother made for him."

Sandy lay silent looking up through the tall trees at the stars. He spoke softly.

"I see in him great strength. Now he must know—and each day he will add to it. When time right—he go. That time he not go alone."

And the woman nodded her head.

It was not the dawn flooding the bay with splendor which woke Frederick, though the sun did come up like a golden ball and the waters turned to iridescent glory. Nor was it the crying of crows high up in the pine trees, nor even the barking of a dog somewhere down on the beach. Rather it was a gradual awareness of flaming words . . . all around him—living things that carried him down wide rivers and over mountains and across spreading plains. Then it was people who were with him—black men, very tall and big and strong. They turned up rich earth as black as their broad backs; they hunted in forests; some of them were in cities, whole cities of black folks. For they were free; they went wherever they wished; they worked as they planned. They even flew like birds, high in the sky. He was up there with them, looking down on the earth which seemed so small. He stretched his wings. He was strong. He could fly. He could fly in a flock of people. . . .

Frederick opened his eyes. The dream persisted—a shaft of brightness surrounding a strange crouching figure swaying there beside him, the flowing sound of words. The light hurt his eyes, but now Frederick realized it was Sandy. He was sitting cross-legged on the floor, head erect, eyes two glowing balls of fire, making low musical sounds. If they were words, they conveyed no meaning to Frederick. Bright sunshine poured through an opening in the cabin where a door hung back. Outside a rooster crowed, and memory jerked Frederick to full consciousness. He raised his hand to his eyes. The flow of sound ceased abruptly, and while the boy stared a mask seemed to fall over the man's shining face, snuffing out the glow and setting the features in stone. For a moment the figure was rigid. Then Sandy was on his feet. He spoke tersely.

"Good. You wake. Time you go."

The words were hard and compelling, and Frederick sat up. His body felt light. His sense of well-being was very real, as real as the smell of pine which seemed to exude from every board of the bare cabin. He looked around. The woman was nowhere in sight, but his eyes fell on a pail of water near by; and then Sandy was back with food. The bowl was warm in his hands, and Sandy stood silent waiting for him to eat. Frederick drew a long breath.

He was remembering: black men, men like Sandy, going places! He must find out—he looked up at Sandy. . . .

"Body sleep, the hurt body. It sleep and heal. But you," Sandy leaned over and with his long finger touched Frederick lightly on the chest, "you not sleep."

"But I— How could I—?" Before the steady gaze of those calm eyes Frederick's protest died. He did not understand, but he was remembering. After a moment he asked simply, "Where am I going?"

This was what it meant. Sandy had a plan for him to run away. Well, he would try it. He was not afraid. Freedom sang in his blood. And so Sandy's reply caught him like a blow.

"Back. Back to Covey's."

"No! No!"

All the horror of the past six months was in his cry.

"Covey will kill me—beat me to death." There was no terror in his voice now, merely an explanation. Sandy shook his head. . . . And his heart was satisfied. *This boy will do,* he thought. *He has patience— patience and endurance. Strength will come. . . .*

Then Sandy reached inside the coarse shirt he was wearing and drew out a small pouch—something tied up in an old piece of cloth.

"Now, hear me well."

Frederick set the bowl down.

"No way you can go now. Wise man face what he must. Big tree bend in strong wind and not break. This time no good. Later day you go. You go far."

Frederick bowed his head. He believed Sandy's words, but at the thought of Covey's lash his flesh quivered in spite of the bright promise. Sandy extended the little bag.

"Covey beat you no more. Wear this close to the body—all the time. No man ever beat you."

Frederick's heart sank. He made no move to take the bag. His voice faltered.

"But—but Sandy, that's voodoo. I don't believe in charms. I'm—I'm a Christian."

Sandy was very still. He gazed hard into the boy's gaunt face below the bloodstained bandage wrapped about his head; he saw the shadow in the wide clear eyes; he thought of the lacerated back and broken rib, and his eyes grew very warm. He spoke softly.

"You be very young."

He untied the bag and carefully shook out its contents into the palm of his hand—dust, fine as powder, a bit of shriveled herb and several smooth, round pebbles. Then he held out the upturned hand to Frederick.

"Look now!" he said. "Soil of Africa—come across the sea close by my mother's breast."

Holding his breath Frederick bent his head. It was as if a great hand lay upon his heart.

"And here"—Sandy's long fingers touched the withered fragment—"seaweed, flowered on great waters, waters of far-off lands, waters of many lands."

Holding Frederick's wrist, Sandy carefully emptied the bits upon the boy's palm, then gently closed his fingers.

"A thousand years of dust in one hand! Dust of men long gone, men who lived so you live. Your dust."

He handed Frederick the little bag. And Frederick took it reverently. With the utmost care, lest one grain of dust be lost, he emptied his palm into it. Then, drawing the cord tight, he placed the pouch inside his rags, fastening the cord securely. He stood up, and his head was clear. Again the black man thought, *He'll do!*

The boy stood speechless. There were things he wanted to say, things he wanted to promise. This day, this spot, this one bright morning was important. This man had saved his life, and suddenly he knew that his life was important. He laid his hand on the black man's arm.

"I won't be forgettin'," he said.

They walked together out into the morning and stood a moment on the knoll, looking down at the bay. Then Frederick turned his back and walked toward the trees. At the edge of the wood he stopped and waved his hand, then disappeared in the hidden lane.

There Was Once a Slave, by Shirley Graham

HELEN KELLER

"That living word awakened my soul, gave it light, hope, joy, set it free!"

Helen Keller was seven years old. She was blind and deaf, and unable to speak. Yet the faith and courage and hard work of her teacher Annie Sullivan and of Helen herself worked the miracle that allowed her to grow up a part of the world. Since her graduation cum laude from Radcliffe College, her writing, teaching and inspiration have helped hundreds of handicapped children to hope. Here are two accounts of the day when the miracle began to happen—Miss Keller's in her autobiography and in a letter from Miss Sullivan.

THE MOST important day I remember in all my life is the one on which my teacher, Anne Mansfield Sullivan, came to me. I am filled with wonder when I consider the immeasurable contrasts between the two lives which it connects. It was the third of March, 1887, three months before I was seven years old.

On the afternoon of that eventful day, I stood on the porch, dumb, expectant. I guessed vaguely from my mother's signs and from the hurrying to and fro in the house that something unusual was about to happen, so I went to the door and waited on the steps. The afternoon sun penetrated the mass of honeysuckle that covered the porch, and fell on my upturned face. My fingers lingered almost unconsciously on the familiar leaves and blossoms which had just come forth to greet the sweet southern spring. I did not know what the future held of marvel or surprise for me. Anger and bitterness had preyed upon me continually for weeks and a deep languor had succeeded this passionate struggle.

Have you ever been at sea in a dense fog, when it seemed as if a tangible white darkness shut you in, and the great ship, tense and anxious, groped her way toward the shore with plummet and sounding-line, and you waited with beating heart for something to happen? I was like that ship before my education began, only I was without compass or sounding-line, and had no way of knowing how near the harbour was. "Light! give me light!" was the wordless cry of my soul, and the light of love shone on me in that very hour.

I felt approaching footsteps. I stretched out my hand as I supposed to my mother. Some one took it, and I was caught up and held close in the arms of her who had come to reveal all things to me, and, more than all things else, to love me.

The morning after my teacher came she led me into her room and gave me a doll. The little blind children at the Perkins Institution had sent it and Laura Bridgman had dressed it; but I did not know this until afterward. When I had played with it a little while, Miss Sullivan slowly spelled into my hand the word "d-o-l-l." I was at once interested in this finger play and tried to imitate it. When I finally succeeded in making the letters correctly I was flushed with childish pleasure and pride. Running downstairs to my mother I held up my hand and made the letters for doll. I did not know that I was spelling a word or even that words existed; I was simply making my fingers go in monkey-like imitation. In the days that followed I learned to spell in this uncomprehending way a great many words, among them *pin, hat, cup* and a few verbs like *sit, stand* and *walk*. But my teacher had been with me several weeks before I understood that everything has a name.

One day, while I was playing with my new doll, Miss Sullivan put my big rag doll into my lap also, spelled "d-o-l-l" and tried to make me understand that "d-o-l-l" applied to both. Earlier in the day we had had a tussle over the words "m-u-g" and "w-a-t-e-r." Miss Sullivan had tried to impress it upon me that "m-u-g" is *mug* and that "w-a-t-e-r" is *water*, but I persisted in confounding the two. In despair she had dropped the subject for the time, only to renew it at the first opportunity. I became impatient at her repeated attempts and, seizing the new doll, I dashed it upon the floor. I was keenly delighted when I felt the fragments of the broken doll at my feet. Neither sorrow nor regret followed my passionate outburst. I had not loved the doll. In the still, dark world in which I lived there was no strong sentiment or tenderness. I felt my teacher sweep the fragments to one side of the hearth, and I had a sense of satisfaction that the cause of my discomfort was removed. She brought me my hat, and I knew I was going out into the warm sunshine. This thought, if a wordless sensation may be called a thought, made me hop and skip with pleasure.

We walked down the path to the well-house, attracted by the fragrance of the honeysuckle with which it was covered. Some one was drawing water and my teacher placed my hand under the spout. As the cool stream gushed over one hand she spelled into the other the word *water*, first slowly, then rapidly. I stood still, my whole attention fixed upon the motions of her fingers. Suddenly I felt a misty consciousness as of something forgotten—a thrill of returning thought; and somehow the mystery of language was revealed to me. I knew then that "w-a-t-e-r" meant the wonderful cool something that was flowing over my hand. That living word awakened my soul, gave it light, hope, joy, set it free! There were barriers still, it is true, but barriers that could in time be swept away.

I left the well-house eager to learn. Everything had a name, and each name gave birth to a new thought. As we returned to the house every object which I touched seemed to quiver with life. That was because I saw everything with the strange, new sight that had come to me. On entering the door I remembered the doll I had broken. I felt my way to the hearth and picked up the pieces. I tried vainly to put them together. Then my eyes filled with tears; for I realized what I had done, and for the first time I felt repentance and sorrow.

I learned a great many new words that day. I do not remember what they all were; but I do know that *mother, father, sister, teacher* were among them—words that were to make the world blossom for me, "like Aaron's rod, with flowers." It would have been difficult to find a happier child than I was as I lay in my crib at the close of that eventful day and lived over the joys it had brought me, and for the first time longed for a new day to come.

*   *   *

The following is from Miss Sullivan's letter to a friend.

April 5, 1887.

I must write you a line this morning because something very important has happened. Helen has taken the second great step in her education. She has learned that *everything has a name, and that the manual alphabet is the key to everything she wants to know.*

In a previous letter I think I wrote you that "mug" and "milk" had given Helen more trouble than all the rest. She confused the nouns with the verb "drink." She didn't know the word for "drink," but went through the pantomime of drinking whenever she spelled "mug" or "milk." This morning, while she was washing, she wanted to know the name for "water." When she wants to know the name of anything, she points to it and pats my hand. I spelled "w-a-t-e-r" and thought no more about it until after breakfast. Then it occurred to me that with the help of this new word I might succeed in straightening out the "mug-milk" difficulty. We went out to the pump-house, and I made Helen hold her mug under the spout while I pumped. As the cold water gushed forth, filling the mug, I spelled "w-a-t-e-r" in Helen's free hand. The word coming so close upon the sensation of cold water rushing over her hand seemed to startle her. She dropped the mug and stood as one transfixed. A new light came into her face. She spelled "water" several times. Then she dropped on the ground and asked for its name and pointed to the pump and the trellis, and suddenly turning round she asked for my name. I spelled "Teacher." Just then the nurse brought Helen's little sister into the pump-house, and Helen spelled "baby" and pointed to the nurse. All the way back to the house she was highly excited, and learned the name of every object she touched, so that in a few hours she had added thirty new words to her vocabulary. Here are some of them: *Door, open, shut, give, go, come,* and a great many more.

P.S.—I didn't finish my letter in time to get it posted last night; so I shall add a line. Helen got up this morning like a radiant fairy. She has flitted from object to object, asking the name of everything and kissing me for very gladness. Last night when I got in bed, she stole into my arms of her own accord and kissed me for the first time, and I thought my heart would burst, so full was it of joy.

The Story of My Life, by Helen Keller

A BRITISH AIRMAN

"No one calling himself a man could do less."

Because we dread the final parting—the final turning point—death is an event for which few people are ever prepared. Even those condemned by tribunal or disease who can foresee the moment with a dreadful certainty will often act as though the future would last forever. . . . The condemned man seldom eats a hearty meal.

Yet there are exceptions. There are those whose faith in God, in themselves, in their times, allow them to prepare for the eventuality of death, just as they had planned for the eventualities of life. The excerpt that follows, and the one after that, are examples of how two men faced the end that they knew was inevitable. They lived nearly three hundred and fifty years apart, these men, and their lives were as different as the disparities of their centuries and their ages could make them. Each of these précis was written in the form of a letter, one to a mother, the other to a wife. They are different in every way except one. Through both of them runs a strong current of faith and calmness—not the calmness of resignation, but the calmness of sure knowledge.

THOUGH I FEEL no premonition at all [mother], events are moving rapidly, and I have instructed that this letter be forwarded to you should I fail to return from one of the raids which we shall shortly be called upon to undertake. You must hope on for a month, but at the end of that time you must accept the fact that I have handed my task over to the extremely capable hands of my comrades of the Royal Air Force, as so many splendid fellows have already done.

First, it will comfort you to know that my role in this war has been of the greatest importance. Our patrols far out over the North Sea have helped to keep the trade routes clear for our convoys and supply ships, and on one occasion our information was instrumental in saving the lives of the men in a crippled lighthouse relief ship. Though it will be difficult for you, you will disappoint me if you do not at least try to accept the facts dispassionately, for I shall have done my duty to the utmost of my ability. No man can do more, and no one calling himself a man could do less.

I have always admired your amazing courage in the face of continual setbacks; in the way you have given me as good an education and background as anyone in the country; and always kept up appearances without ever losing faith in the future. My death would not mean that your struggle has been in vain. Far from it. It means that your sacrifice is as great as mine. Those who serve England must expect nothing from her; we debase ourselves if we regard our country as merely a place in which to eat and sleep.

History resounds with illustrious names, who have given all, yet their sacrifice has resulted in the British Empire, where there is a measure of peace, justice, and freedom for all, and where a higher standard of civilization has evolved, and is still evolving, than anywhere else. But this is not only concerning our own land. To-day we are faced with the greatest organized challenge to Christianity and civilization that the world has seen, and I count myself lucky and honoured to be the right age and fully trained to throw my full weight into the scale. For this I have to thank you. Yet there is more work for you to do. The home front will still have to stand united for years after the war is won. For all that can be said against it, I still maintain that this war is a very good thing; every individual is having the chance to give and dare all for his principle like the martyrs of old. However long time may be, one thing can never be altered—I shall have lived and died an Englishman. Nothing else matters one jot nor can anything ever change it.

You must not grieve for me, for if you really believe in religion and all that it entails that would be hypocrisy. I have no fear of death; only a queer elation. . . . I would have it no other way. The universe is so vast and so ageless that the life of one man can only be justified by the measure of his sacrifice. We are sent to this world to acquire a personality and a character to take with us that can never be taken from us. Those who just eat and sleep, prosper and procreate, are no better than animals if all their lives they are at peace.

I firmly and absolutely believe that evil things are sent into the world to try us; they are sent deliberately by our Creator to test our mettle because He knows what is good for us. The Bible is full of cases where the easy way out has been discarded for moral principles.

I count myself fortunate in that I have seen the whole country and known men of every calling. But with the final test of war I consider my character fully developed. Thus at my early age my earthly mission is already fulfilled and I am prepared to die with just one regret, and one only—that I could not devote myself to making your declining years more happy by being with you; but you will live in peace and freedom and I shall have directly contributed to that, so here again my life will not have been in vain.

An Airman's Letter to His Mother, Anonymous

"Baylie oweth me 200£ and Adrian Gilbert 600£."

A master adventurer in an era of soldiers of fortune, Sir Walter Raleigh used his wit and charm to garner position and honor for himself. A court favorite of Elizabeth I, a lady who could be as open-handed with her friends as she was unrelenting toward her enemies, Raleigh was rewarded out of all proportion to his piratical service against the Spaniards. But in 1603, on the death of Elizabeth and the ascension of James I, he was stripped of his offices and estates and sent to the tower. Expecting death from a court before which he had been falsely accused of plotting against the new king, Raleigh wrote his wife:

YOU SHALL now receive (my dear wife) my last words, in these my last lines. My Love I send you, that you may keep it, when I am dead, and my Counsel that you remember it, when I am no more; I would not by my will present you with Sorrows (Dear Bess). Let them go into the grave with me; and be buried in the dust; and seeing it is not the will of God, that I shall see you any more in this life, bear it patiently, and with an heart like thyself.

First I send you all my thanks, which my heart can conceive, or my words can express for your many travails and Care taken for me, which though they have not taken effect, as you wished, yet my debt to you, is not the less, but pay it I never shall, in this world.

Secondly, I beseech you, for the love you bare me living, do not hide yourself many days, after my death, but by your Travails seek to help your miserable fortunes, and the right of your poor Child. Thy mournings cannot avail me, I am but dust.

Thirdly you shall understand, that my Land was conveyed bona fide to my Child, the writings were drawn at Midsummer twelve months; my honest Cousin Brett can testify so much, and Dalberrie too, can remember somewhat therein. And I trust my blood will quench their

Malice, that have thus cruelly murdered me, and that they will not also seek to kill thee and thine with extreme poverty.

To what friend to direct thee, I know not, for all mine have left me, in the true time of trial; and I plainly perceive, that my death was determined from the first day.

Most sorry I am (God knows) that being thus surprised with death, I can leave you in no better state. God is my witness, I meant you all my office of wines, or all that I could have purchased by selling it, half my stuff, and all my Jewels. But some on't for the Boy, but God hath prevented all my Resolutions, and even that Great God that ruleth all in all; but if you can live free from want, care for no more; the rest is but vanity.

Love God, and begin betimes, to repose your self on him, and therein shall you find true and lasting Riches, and endless Comfort. For the rest when you have travailed and wearied all your thoughts, over all sorts of worldly Cogitations, you shall sit down by sorrow in the end.

Teach your son also to love and fear God whilst he is yet young, that the fear of God may grow up with him; and the same God be a husband to you, and a Father to him; a husband and a Father, which cannot be taken from you.

Baylie oweth me 200£, and Adrian Gilbert 600£. In Jersey, I have also much money owing me. Besides the Arrearages of the Wines will pay my debts. And howsoever you do, for my soul's sake, pay all poor men.

When I am gone, no doubt you shall be sought by many; for the world thinks, that I was very rich. But take heed of the pretences of men, and their affections; for they last not but in honest and worthy Men; and no greater misery can befall you in this life, then to become a prey, and afterwards to be despised; I speak not this (God knows) to dissuade you from marriage, for it will be best for you, both in respect of the world and of God.

As for me, I am no more yours, nor you mine. Death hath cut us asunder and God hath divided me from the World, and you from me.

Remember your poor Child, for his Father's sake, who chose you, and loved you, in his happiest times.

Get those Letters (if it be possible) which I writ to the Lords, wherein I sued for my life. God is my witness, it was for you and yours I desired life. But it is true that I disdain myself for begging it, for know it (dear wife) that your son, is the son of a true man, and one, who in his own respect, despiseth Death, and all his misshapen and ugly shapes.

I cannot write much; God he knows, how hardly, I steal this time, while others sleep; and it is also high time, that I should separate my thoughts from the world.

Beg my dead body, which living was denied thee; and either lay it at Sherbourne (if the Land continue) or in Excester Church by my Father and Mother.

I can say no more, time and death call me away.

The everlasting, powerful, infinite and omnipotent God, that Almighty God, who is goodness itself, the true life, and true light, keep thee and thine; have mercy on me, and teach me to forgive my persecutors and Accusers, and send us to meet in his glorious kingdom.

My dear wife farewell, Bless my poor Boy, Pray for me, and let my Good God hold you both in his arms.

Written with the dying hand of sometimes thy Husband, but now (alas) overthrown

Wa: Raleigh

yours that was, But now not my own.

W: R:

As it happened, Raleigh was never sentenced by the court and lived in the tower with his wife and son until 1616, when he was released (conditionally) to head an expedition that was to seek gold at the mouth of the Orinoco. But Raleigh was over 60 and his luck had left him. The voyage, which had been farfetched from the beginning, turned out to be a disaster. He was thwarted by mutiny, storms and sickness; his son was killed, and when the old adventurer returned empty-handed, he was accused of violating his parole by attacking Spanish possessions in the New World. Under an old sentence, which had been withheld for more than fifteen years, he was beheaded at Whitehall on October 29, 1618.

Letter to His Wife, by Sir Walter Raleigh

LOUIS PASTEUR

"... a hunger for discovery."

The advances in medicine during the nineteenth century were, like the progress made in so many other fields in those years of scientific awakening, phenomenal. Lister, Ehrlich, Semmelweiss, Jenner, Koch, were names that meant new discoveries, new techniques, new approaches that were to save millions of lives and prolong the life span of millions more.

Perhaps the best-known name of this group is that of Louis Pasteur. The story of the French chemist's first successful experiments with inoculation—and of the evolution of the process that bears his name—is a classic today. Pasteur in many ways stands as a symbol of the awakening of medical science, for he was a man typical of the breed that brought science from the middle ages to modern times in a single century. Earnest, hard-working, driven by the belief that God had put him and his fellow scientists on earth to save lives, he had the faith—and the energy—to persevere.

"MAD DOG! Mad dog!" That cry in any country, in any street, is terrifying even today; but how much worse was the cry "Mad wolf!" seventy years ago through the nestling towns of the Jura Mountains! To anxious fathers and mothers looking into the faces of their little children, it brought agonizing pictures: the wildest of creatures abroad in the hills, with glittering eyes and foaming mouth, tearing on and on, and about to descend on their little ones playing in the sun. Very gravely Monsieur and Madame Pasteur cautioned small Louis and his two sisters to stay in the tannery yard close to the house. With big eyes full of reflected fear, the children listened and promised to obey. Their training in truth made them keep the promise. The fears were not groundless. Instead of the poor old wolf wearing himself out in the forest on trees and roots, he came flying through the village; eight people in the neighborhood were bitten; and for a long time every one in the country round was in terror of that mad wolf.

Louis Pasteur had been a Christmas present to his father and mother and four-year-old sister, for he was born in 1822, only two days after Christmas, in the little village of Dôle. I suppose no other present was half so welcome.

Though his parents had little to give him but their love, the child soon found his own playthings. We can imagine him cramming frail bluebells into his grimy little hands for his mother and finding a world of delight in the bits of bark lying round the tannery yard. Before long he began to feel proud of the good leather which his father made, and we can imagine him standing silently by while the ox or goat skins were unloaded from big carts, or the oak bark was being ground for tanning. With a child's wonder he must have followed the long process, from the scraping off of the hairy coats through the many soakings in the big pits, till, drained, dried, and oiled, there was a fine load of leather for the shoemaker. All this takes work and patience. It is sometimes a whole year before an ox skin is ready to be made into a boot. In following this process, Louis's mind grew used to watching and waiting. The lessons of the tannery yard were the beginnings of his training in science. They taught him to look for developments.

Besides this, he had regular lessons in the little school near by. Not till he went to boarding school, however, do we follow his education with any vivid interest.

There was storm in the sky and gloom in his heart the day he left home for the big city school. Under the flood of rain the horses pawed restlessly. They found it cold standing still so long while bags and trunks were hoisted to the top of the coach, and while Louis and his friend, Jules Vercel, said a hundred good-bys to the same dear people. They were still shouting "Au revoir!" and waving their hands buoyantly from under the tarpaulin, as the wheels splashed away down the road. Buoyant they seemed, but their hearts were already swelling with homesickness. Through the mist, they said a silent farewell to the gray tower of Arbois church. Then the hills dipped down and carried them rattling onward, bound for Paris.

But this homesickness was only a taste of the homesickness to come. Jules did not suffer so much as the younger boy, who, poor fellow, though he was fifteen, lay awake night after night in the faraway city saying to himself: "How endless unto watchful anguish night doth seem." The green trees of the tannery yard were far dearer to him than the glitter of Paris. We can well imagine that as the clocks chimed the hour he wondered if they were all asleep at home, and if they dreamed that he was sleeping too. I suppose the moon and stars told him that they were shining down on *them*.

"If I could only get a whiff of the tannery yard," he confided to Jules, "I feel I should be cured."

At last the head master, Monsieur Barbet, after trying everything else, wrote a few plain facts to Louis's father.

And so, one November day, Louis Pasteur was sent for. "They are waiting for you," said a messenger, pointing to a little café on the corner. The much-puzzled boy went over to the café. There at the table, with his head in his hands, sat some one dearly familiar—his father.

"I have come to fetch you." There was no rebuke in the tanner's simple greeting. The love-longing had overwhelmed the knowledge-longing in his son's heart—that was all. The father needed no explanations.

Nevertheless, Louis's knowledge-longing was very strong, and he had no idea of giving up study. At Besançon, forty kilometers (less than twenty-five miles) from Arbois, was a college where there was plenty to learn and where he could be prepared for the École Normale (Normal School). Several times a year his father would go to Besançon to sell his leather. That the father would combine with this business a visit to his son, Louis knew well.

At school, the boy was so careful that people thought him slow. He slighted nothing. Absolute sureness, alone, could satisfy him. "Dear sisters," he would write home, "work hard, love each other. When one is accustomed to work, it is impossible to do without it; besides, everything in this world depends on that." In one of his letters he spoke of studying mathematics till he got a "pretty bad headache." "But those headaches never last long," he quickly added, not willing to worry any one.

At nineteen he reëntered the Barbet boarding school in Paris. No longer a homesick boy, he had grown tall and self-reliant, and he soon proved himself so capable that he was asked to help with the teaching. By this means, his schooling cost him only one-third of the usual price. Outside of study or teaching hours, he and his great friend Chappuis had some good times. But Louis was always in danger of overworking. "You know how we worry about your health; you do work so immoderately," wrote his anxious father. "Are you not injuring your eyesight by so much nightwork?" Then that troubled father would appeal to Chappuis as a kind of caretaker: "Do tell Louis not to work so much; it is not good to strain one's brain," adding with much affection: "Remain two good friends."

Among the young people of today it is the fashion to laugh at the fellow who studies hard. "Resistance to knowledge," as Professor Phelps puts it, is a fad. "Grind" is a term of contempt. The average boy quails before it. But the fellow who delights in study never grinds. A few, like Pasteur, have a real hunger for discovery. Pasteur carried that hunger with him when he entered the École Normale. Here, to save time, his chemistry class did not experiment to get phosphorus;

they were merely told how to get it; and many were satisfied to go no farther. Pasteur, however, worked it out for himself; he bought bones, burnt them to ashes, and then "treated the ashes with sulphuric acid." We can imagine with what pride he wrote the label on his little bottle of homemade phosphorus. "This was his first scientific joy."

By a love for work that was almost a passion, Pasteur, so often called in the scorn of jealous rivals a "mere chemist," went on and on, from questioning lifeless, soulless crystals to waging war for man. His was a long line of interests, and they seem scattered and unrelated. That is because whenever he found a need he tried to meet that need with help. Crystals, acids, the ferments of milk and alcohol, the best way to preserve wine and beer, the diseases of silkworms, hens, goats, pigs, and sheep—cholera, fevers, and hydrophobia. All these seized his eager attention. Scientific zeal, patriotism, and love for service goaded him on to further discoveries. He will be lastingly remembered as the Conqueror of Disease.

The tanner's son, in the hidden village of Arbois—the boy who had been called slow, who had left the Paris school because he was homesick, and had entered the École Normale a little old for his class— through working and waiting had grown very great, great enough to be known by the common people. The vinedressers, who tended their grapes on the sunny hills of France, they knew his name. Because Pasteur had found a way to keep their wines from becoming sour, they could sell their produce and bring home the shining coins to buy blue ribbons for Annette and stout shoes for Pierre. Pasteur had kept their hearts glad and their homes comfortable, and had saved one of the great industries of France.

By and by the shepherds, the goatherds, and the swineherds, even the poultry men, heard his name. "Perhaps," one would say, "he would know what has got into our sheep." Twenty had died out of a hundred, beginning to droop only a few hours beforehand.

"It may be Pasteur could cure my hens," a second would suggest, as he leaned over the poor staggering creatures that seemed to have fallen asleep while they were trying to walk.

How much the tanner's son could do who had begun life by "curing" leather! France was his own land, and the French his own people. In the sight of his eager patriotism, service done for the French was like service done for a big family. We hope that sometimes in the midst of his intensely practical discoveries he rejoiced that hundreds were happier because he had lived and because he had taught them how to get the best results from honest labor.

Of his many works there will be space, in this short sketch, to emphasize only two: his conquest of the silkworm disease, by which he saved one of the great industries of France; and his conquest of hydrophobia, by which he saved human life.

Pasteur had never seen a silkworm when, urged by the French government, he attacked the epidemic that had raged among the silkworms for fifteen years. But the boy Pasteur had known how much depended on the making of leather, and it was easy for the man Pasteur, as he journeyed into southern France, to see that the hopes of hundreds of families depended on successful silkworm culture. What other use had those groves of mulberry trees? With no silk to spin, what would become of the millworkers? Strange as it may sound, Pasteur was in a land where worms seemed more important than people. Three-year-old children understood that, whatever else happened, the fires that warmed the worms must not go out; and since those worms are the *dainty* members of the family, everything that touched them must be perfectly clean. Silkworms will not stay on dirty mulberry leaves. Pasteur, beginning with the tiny eggs, or "seeds" as they are called, used this sure method of protection: The moth, which dies anyway soon after her eggs are laid, was "crushed in a mortar and mixed with a little water; the mixture was examined with the microscope—and, if a germ of the disease was found, the eggs, between 300 and 700 from each moth, were immediately destroyed with everything belonging to them." It was the old law of the survival of the fittest.

Only the eggs from healthy moths are used for hatching, for, as has been said, "from healthy moths healthy eggs were sure to spring; from healthy eggs, healthy worms; from healthy worms, fine cocoons," and of course from the finest cocoons, the best silk. Eggs are said to be *pasteurized* when they are the eggs of a perfectly healthy moth. The word *pasteurize* has worked into our dictionaries from Pasteur's famous name, and by it is meant that anything—milk, for instance—is pure, free from living germs, health-giving. It is something for a man's name to stand in the dictionary, to the end of time, for *health*.

In Pasteur's five years' work to save the silkworms, he had the satisfaction of seeing a disease conquered. He wanted no higher pay. Creeping from millions of seeds came millions of worms, so tiny that the mulberry-leaf food had at first to be shredded. Soon, however, they were feeding away with a whispering noise, as if they were starved. Before long, from a moving mass of life, the separate worms showed themselves—great, grayish, velvety things as big as your little finger, fatter and fatter every day, and ravenously hungry.

By and by they tried to stand on their tails in the feeding racks, and reared and stretched their necks as if asking to climb. Then it was time for little Gustave to bring great bundles of brier brush—the silkworms' ladders. And, at last, clinging to tiny branches, there

> set to work millions of spinning worms
> That in their green shops weave the smooth-haired silk.

The "reels" spun by one worm are anywhere from a thousand feet to more than two miles long. In the light of Pasteur's cure, it is no wonder that, after years of failure, the silkworm husking was a jubilee. The cocoons, "heaped in round flat baskets, ready for market, were glorified, seemingly, into heaps of golden and silvern eggs by the afternoon sun." It was a time for feasting on delicious "homemade cheese, home-grown almonds and olives, and good homemade bread." We can easily imagine that during the laughter-filled feast, Marie dreamed of a fine new jacket and Babette of a knot of bright ribbon, a lace fichu, and a bouquet of artificial flowers.

As for Pasteur, the restorer of all these smiles, it was enough to have brought such joy to unnumbered homes. To him, home had always been sacred. Some one once said: "If you want a definition of happiness, visit the Huxley family." The same thing might have been said of the Pasteurs. Louis had known nothing but love in his father's low-roofed tannery; and he knew nothing but love in the other home which he and his wife had begun, in May, 1849. Sorrows came. They came thick and fast. Though he lost three children, a son and a daughter were left. Meanwhile he fathered many children not his own. Returned to his work of healing, as he entered the zoölogical garden of the Institute, the children would run to him, throw their arms around him, and bless him with their perfect trust. And somehow the silver coins slipped very naturally out of his pockets into theirs.

"Pasteur is a man who would find advantage from living in a glass house," said Mr. G. M. Crawford. It is beautiful to have such a thing true. And if Pasteur had been in a glass house, through its transparent walls we might have seen that he not only tucked shining presents into the children's pockets but patted their heads, clasped their hands, and kissed their tear-stained faces, though the tears were never there for long.

"My child, it is all over!" he would exclaim soothingly—"*Mon enfant! Mon enfant!*" It was hard for him to see even slight suffering, particularly in animals or children—he who had never had the "courage to kill a bird in hunting."

As his step was heard in the hospital, a halting step because he had had a paralytic stroke, the heads on the pillows turned toward him and the faces lighted with smiles of gratitude. It was worth the long hours spent in searching, the slow tests, the patient waiting; it was worth more than medals or degrees, this great love of thankful hearts.

Pasteur had plenty of honors; but he counted them as words and ribbons. He was too great to think himself great. The world was the world, full of struggle and need and woe, and the most he could do in his full life was still very little.

Like Agassiz, he had a passion for scientific study and a great gift for teaching. His pupils came away filled with his love of truth, his unwillingness to state a fact unless proved and proved again. His teaching seemed like inspiration, and utterly tireless. It had been so patiently planned beforehand that all the patient preparation was concealed. It was like poured sunlight. Nevertheless, he would never rob a student of the joy of discovery. As a lad it had meant much to him to make his own phosphorus. "Where will you find a young man," he would ask, "whose curiosity and interest will not immediately be awakened when you put into his hands a potato, when from that potato he may produce sugar, from that sugar he may produce alcohol, from that alcohol ether and vinegar? Where is he who will not be happy to tell his family in the evening that he has just been working out an electric telegraph? Such studies are seldom, if ever, forgotten."

At the root of all his teaching lay the principle of *usefulness*. It was repeated again to hundreds. "One man's life is useless if it is not useful to others." As he grew older and realized too fully that the years would not grant him time to solve all of his problems, he looked to his pupils to carry on his work. In praise of their faithful persistence he would say: "I pointed the way; but I had only conceived hopes, and you bring in solid realities." He craved honors for them far more than for himself. But to his list of saved lives we must add part of the credit of the lives saved by the pupils he had trained.

Let us see him, at last, however, not as a teacher but as a healer. To cure hydrophobia, before he could experiment on man, he had to experiment on animals. Let those who condemn it ask and answer the question: Is it better that a guinea pig should suffer a little or that my only child should die? Pasteur never experimented without using chloroform, and, tenderhearted man that he was, he took the greatest care to save any animal from unnecessary suffering. Never had he shot any animal of any kind for sport. But when human life was at stake "vivisection was a dreadful necessity." Even when he had multiplied his experiments, he said, half fearfully: "I think my hand will tremble when I go on to mankind."

In Pasteur's life the years 1885 and 1886 were marked by wonderful strides toward the conquest of hydrophobia. The terrible memory of the mad wolf of his childhood had never worn away. It came back to him in manhood with fresh horror when, one July morning, an Alsatian mother, poorly dressed and leading a nine-year-old boy by

the hand, entered his laboratory. Little Joseph Meister could hardly
walk, and his small hands were fearfully bitten. In a voice full of restrained suffering and with beseeching eyes, Frau Meister begged
Pasteur to save her child. "He was so small!" she sobbed. "When the
dog flew at him, he knew no more than to stand still and cover his face
with his hands. A man, passing, beat off the beast with an iron bar.
But there was my Joseph!—Oh, the dreadful blood!"

"I am no doctor," answered the scientist humbly. "I am only trying
to discover cures; but I shall do my best for little Joseph." As he spoke,
he gently laid his hand on the child's fair head.

When Joseph found that the treatment was no more than a pinprick, his dreary blue eyes began to shine again; he no longer dreaded
the master's touch. Out in the sunny garden, among the rabbits,
chickens, and guinea pigs, he was very happy, and he generally slept
more peacefully than the scientist, who tossed back and forth in terrible fear that the child would die.

But little Meister got well. And, furthermore, in his long stay at
the laboratory he grew to be such a friend of "Dear Monsieur Pasteur"
that he would run in from the garden, climb into his lap, and beg,
with all kinds of childish pleadings, that some specially playful guinea
pig or pink-nosed rabbit might not be used for experiment. And little
Meister had his way, like many other children who loved Pasteur as
a father.

One beautiful day in the next October, six little shepherd boys had
led their flocks to a green meadow glistening in the sunlight of the
Jura Mountains. Here the juicy grass drew its richness from underground streams, and here the boys found flowery places to stretch out
under the blue sky-roof and talk together in their soft French voices.
From time to time they would move on to keep near their straying
sheep, while bees hummed their way into the flowers' hearts and
turned the bright cups upside down with the weight of their velvet
bodies. The children's shepherd life was full of restful friendliness.
Suddenly one of the boys, pointing to the road, shouted "Chien enragé! Chien enragé!" ("Mad dog! Mad dog!"). Fear raised his voice
to a shriek. As the children scrambled to their feet, they saw a great
creature turn and tear toward them. Though they ran as fast as soft
ground, wooden shoes, and fright would let them, that was not very
fast. The dog came panting on. Then the oldest, a fourteen-year-old
boy named Jupille, turned, to save the rest, and faced their maddened
enemy, alone. With glazed eyes, and slimy turned-back lips, the dog
was close upon him. Leaping into the air, he caught the boy's left
hand between his gleaming teeth. Jupille's mountain training came
in play. The hills had taught him strength and swiftness. In his brave

tussle, he managed to throw the dog to the ground, kneel on his back, and with his right hand force the jaws apart to set his left hand free. Of course his right hand was terribly bitten too; but, at last, he got a grip on the animal's neck, and, calling to his little brother to bring him the whip, dropped in the fight, he fastened the dog's jaws tight with the lash. Then he worked with his wooden sabot till the heaving creature was so nearly dead that he could drag him to the brook and end his life.

White-faced, round-eyed, and trembling, the little huddle of shepherd boys trooped back to the village, all of them sure that Jupille would die, and all but Jupille feeling like murderers. His life was the price of theirs. But the mayor, who had heard of Pasteur, sent the great scientist swift word.

Poor Pasteur! As yet this experimenting was too new; he was not ready to risk men. Little Joseph Meister, whom he had saved, had reached him only two days and a half after the attack. Jupille's wounds would be six days old. However, Jupille would have almost no pain (only a pinprick a day) and it might mean life. The boy was sent for; and not only, by patient watching, was he saved, but through the recommendation of the fatherly Pasteur he received a prize for bravery.

Some of the great scientist's experiments were not successful. He had had a chance to treat Meister and Jupille within a week of the day they were bitten. Long-postponed treatment was not so sure.

The next November, a little girl of ten, Louise Pelletier, was brought to him over a month after the mad dog's attack! Pasteur did all he could; but it was useless.

"I did so wish I could have saved your little one!" he said to the father and mother. Then, as he shut the door on their sorrow, the great man himself burst into tears. He had not explained his bitter disappointment in failure, or his own affection for Louise, nor had he told them that their little girl was just the age of Jeanne—the first child given him and the first child taken away.

Although Pasteur had this sad failure, before long his fame was world-wide. By means of a public subscription, started by the *New York Herald*, four little Americans—children of poor laborers—were sent across the ocean to the wonderful healer. The mother of the youngest went with them. When her little boy, who was only five, felt the simple needle prick he asked wonderingly, "Is this all we have come such a long journey for?" When, healthy and smiling, the four children came back to America, in answer to hundreds of questions about the great man they had no wonderful story. The treatment had been so easy!

But Pasteur had a story. On March 1, 1885, his doubts smothered by success, he could tell France that out of three hundred and fifty patients, only one had died—Louise Pelletier. The victory was wonderful, even taking into consideration that some of the dogs, reported as mad, may not have been so, and that some of the people, who were *not* treated by him, died, not of hydrophobia, but of fear. There were men in his time who tried to lessen his glory by these two arguments; but there were others who, during his lifetime, and since then, have called him, for the lives he saved, the "Greatest Man of the Nineteenth Century." Napoleon, with all his military genius, was not so great, because his business was to destroy life; Pasteur's was to save it. A certain map of the world is dotted all over with Pasteur Institutes for the cure of hydrophobia. And there is at least one man who would call the nineteenth century "The Age of Pasteur."

If ever any one was stimulated by obstacles it was Pasteur; but he removed obstacles for others. He made all healing free. No one was ever turned away. French, Belgians, Spanish, Portuguese, Russians, they came to him in daily crowds. Some came, as people will, just out of curiosity—just to see Pasteur—the stout little man with the short beard and black velvet smoking cap and the great name. He was always hard at work. Till within a few months of the very end, his energy went hand in hand with self-forgetfulness. Breakdowns threatened him constantly; but the *saving of life*—left sometimes to the power of man—was too close to the *giving of life*—in the power of God—for him to let one great chance slip. Even at the last, he kept his youthful *enthusiasm*—that pet word of his, meaning "an inward God." There are few things more divine than lives devoted to the hopes of others, whether they waver over silkworms, or sick sheep, or whether they hang on the life of a little child.

Vallery-Radot, in his beautiful story of Pasteur, gives a peaceful picture of the lifesaver's last days. Though he could hardly walk or speak, his eyes were still bright, and, as he sat out of doors, "his grandchildren around him suggested young rose trees climbing around the trunk of a dying oak." On September 28, 1895, he gave up his long battle. There was a great national funeral: a military band, "infantry, marines, cavalry, artillery, and municipal guards . . . red-robed judges and members of university faculties in orange, red, and crimson robes." It was all more showy than the tanner's son would have asked. His simple gravestone better commemorates his simple start in life. Though his name will always mean intense energetic action, that plain stone speaks of well-earned rest:

Ici repose Pasteur.

More Than Conquerors, by Ariadne Gilbert

ALEXIS C. CARREL

"Her eyes, so dim before, were now wide with ecstasy ..."

That science and faith can live together can seldom have been proven more concretely than in the case of Alexis Carrel, surgeon, scientist and Christian. Carrel was 30 years old and three years out of medical school in 1903 when he visited Lourdes. What he saw there convinced him that there is more to healing than a physician's stethoscope or a surgeon's scalpel can provide. And though he believed in the miracles of science, he also believed in God's miracles.

In 1912, Carrel was awarded a Nobel Prize in physiology and medicine. For more than forty years he continued his research in the baffling problems of living matter. But perhaps nothing in his distinguished career so profoundly affected the lives of so many people as the moving story of the miracle he saw at Lourdes. The young doctor Lerrac is, of course, Carrel.

LERRAC LEANED over the bed and studied Marie Ferrand. She was lying on her back, inert. Her head, with its white, emaciated face, was flung back on the pillow. Her wasted arms lay flat at her sides. Her breathing was rapid and shallow.

"How are you feeling?" Lerrac asked her, gently.

She turned her dim, dark-circled eyes toward him and her gray lips moved in an inaudible reply.

Taking her hand, Lerrac put his fingertips on her wrist. Her pulse was excessively rapid, a hundred and fifty beats a minute, and irregular. Her heart was giving out. . . .

Pulling back the covers, the nurse removed the cradle that held up the bedclothes and the rubber ice bag which hung over the patient's abdomen.

Marie Ferrand's emaciated body lay exposed again. The abdomen was distended, as before. The swelling was almost uniform, but somewhat more pronounced on the left side. Gently he let his hands slide over the smooth surface of the belly, lightly palpating it. The solid

masses were still there; at the center, under the umbilicus, he could
still feel the fluid.

Again Lerrac thought to himself that a small, two-inch incision below the umbilicus would have been more useful than sending her to
Lourdes. . . .

He turned to A.B., who was standing a little way off, visibly moved
by the sight of this sickness and suffering.

"It's just what I told you," said Lerrac, "advanced tubercular peritonitis. The fluid is almost all gone. You can feel the solid masses at
the sides. I told you that both her parents died of tuberculosis. At
seventeen, she was already spitting blood. At eighteen, she had a tubercular pleurisy; more than half a gallon of fluid was drawn from the
left lung. Then she had pulmonary lesions. And now, for the last eight
months, she has had this unmistakable tubercular peritonitis. She is
almost completely wasted away. Her heart is racing madly. Look how
thin she is. Look at the color of her face and hands. She may last a
few days more, but she is doomed. Death is very near."

(*Later at the baths*) A group of pilgrims appeared. A.B., with another volunteer, was carrying a stretcher. On it lay Marie Ferrand.

She lay on her back, all shrunken beneath the dark brown blanket
which made a mound over her distended abdomen. Her breath came
quick and short. . . . The sight of such misery, commonplace in any
hospital, made a shocking impression outdoors where each detail was
so clearly etched.

For a moment, before going to the pool, they lowered the stretcher
to the ground. The sick girl was apparently unconscious. Lerrac put
his hand on her wrist. Her pulse was more rapid than ever. Her face
was ashen. . . .

How utterly impossible it was, he thought, to prophesy the exact
moment when life ends! It was obvious that this young girl was about
to die. But he could not say whether her death would come in an
hour or in three or four days. He wondered how it would affect the
pilgrims if she died in the pool. What would they think of miracles,
then?

The church clock struck two. Groups of little carts drawn by
the stretcher-bearers were approaching, followed by more and more
pilgrims. . . .

Lerrac saw Marie Ferrand carried past. He hurried over to her. Her
condition was unchanged; there was still the same ghastly pallor, the
shrunken form under the blanket still had the same distended abdomen, but apparently no more pronounced. . . .

Lerrac turned back to the enclosure. The priest was kneeling down,
facing the line of patients and the crowds beyond. He lifted his arms

and held them out like a cross. He was young; his fleshy white face, dripping with sweat, was covered with red blotches. Only the childlike expression in his eyes and the evident intensity of his faith saved him from absurdity. His voice was so raucous, sincere, and impassioned that it seemed as if the Virgin could not fail to hear him.

"Holy Virgin, heal our sick," he cried out, his child's mouth twisted with emotion.

"Holy Virgin, heal our sick," the crowd responded with a cry like the rolling of waves.

"Holy Virgin," intoned the priest, "hear our prayers!"

"Jesus, we love Thee!"

"Jesus, we love Thee!"

The voice of the crowd thundered on. Here and there, people held out their arms. The sick half-raised themselves on their stretchers. The atmosphere was tense with expectancy.

Then the priest stood up.

"My brothers, let us lift our arms in prayer!" he called.

A forest of arms was raised. A wind seemed to blow through the crowd; intangible, silent, powerful, irresistible, it swept over the people, lashing them, like a mountain storm. Lerrac felt its impact. It was impossible to describe, but it caught at his throat and sent a tremor along his spine. Suddenly, he wanted to cry.

If a strong, healthy man could be carried away, what must be the effect on sick and suffering people in all their weakness? Anxiously, Lerrac studied the faces of the patients, especially the faces of the neurasthenics. He expected to see these nervous cases rise from their stretchers and joyously announce their recovery. But no one stirred.

He walked past the lines of little carts and through the crowd toward the Grotto. Pausing for a moment at the edge of the stream, he observed the crowd. A young intern from Bordeaux, Mr. M., whom Lerrac had met the day before, greeted him.

"Have you had any cures?" Lerrac asked him.

"No," replied M. "A few of the hysteria cases have recovered, but there has been nothing unexpected, nothing that one can't see any day in a hospital."

"Come and look at my patient," said Lerrac. "Her case is not unusual, but I think she is dying. She is at the Grotto."

"I saw her a few minutes ago," said M. "What a pity they let her come to Lourdes. She should have been operated. Bringing her to the Grotto does not seem to have helped her."

It was now about half-past two. Beneath the rock of Massabielle, the Grotto glittered in the light of its thousand candles. The entrance and the walls were hung with rosaries and crutches. Beyond the high iron grille was a statue of the Virgin, standing in the hollowed rock where Bernadette once saw the glowing vision of the lady in white, the Immaculate Conception.

Before the statue of the Virgin, a large square space was fenced off; it was reserved as the place of honor for the sick. Volunteers of Our Lady of Salvation were on duty to prevent crowding and confusion among the little carts and stretchers.

In front of the iron grille and almost touching it, a stretcher was already lying. . . . He and M. made their way toward the Grotto where they could have a close view of the sick and the pilgrims. They stopped near Marie Ferrand's stretcher and leaned against the low wall. She was motionless, her breathing still rapid and shallow; she seemed to be at the point of death. More pilgrims were approaching the Grotto. . . .

Volunteers and stretcher-bearers came crowding in. The little carts were being wheeled from the pools to the Grotto. . . .

Lerrac glanced again at Marie Ferrand. Suddenly he stared. It seemed to him that there had been a change, that the harsh shadows on her face had disappeared, that her skin was somehow less ashen.

Surely, he thought, this was a hallucination. But the hallucination itself was interesting psychologically, and might be worth recording. Hastily he jotted down the time in his notebook. It was twenty minutes before three o'clock.

But if the change in Marie Ferrand was a hallucination, it was the first one Lerrac had ever had. He turned to M.

"Look at our patient again," he said. "Does it seem to you that she has rallied a little?"

"She looks much the same to me," answered M. "All I can see is that she is no worse."

Leaning over the stretcher, Lerrac took her pulse again and listened to her breathing.

"The respiration is less rapid," he told M., after a moment.

"That may mean that she is about to die," said M.

A non-believer, the young intern could see nothing miraculous in this change.

Lerrac made no reply. To him it was obvious that there was a sudden improvement of her general condition. Something was taking place. . . . A priest was preaching to the assembled throngs of pilgrims and patients; hymns and prayers burst out sporadically; and in this atmosphere of fervor, under Lerrac's cool, objective gaze, the face of Marie Ferrand slowly continued to change. Her eyes, so dim before, were now wide with ecstasy as she turned them toward the Grotto. The change was undeniable. . . .

Suddenly, Lerrac felt himself turning pale. The blanket which covered Marie Ferrand's distended abdomen was gradually flattening out.

"Look at her abdomen!" he exclaimed to M.

M. looked.

"Why yes," he said, "it seems to have gone down. It's probably the folds in the blanket that give that impression."

The bell of the basilica had just struck three. A few minutes later, there was no longer any sign of distension in Marie Ferrand's abdomen.

Lerrac felt as though he were going mad.

Standing beside Marie Ferrand, he watched the intake of her breath and the pulsing at her throat with fascination. The heartbeat, though still very rapid, had become regular.

This time, for sure, something was taking place.

"How do you feel?" he asked her.

"I feel very well," she answered in a low voice. "I am still weak, but I feel I am cured."

There was no longer any doubt: Marie Ferrand's condition was improving so much that she was scarcely recognizable. . . .

Lerrac stood there in silence, his mind a blank. This event, exactly the opposite of what he had expected, must surely be nothing but a dream. . . .

Abruptly, Lerrac moved off. Making his way through the crowd of pilgrims whose loud prayers he hardly heard, he left the Grotto. It was now about four o'clock.

A dying girl was recovering.

It was the resurrection of the dead; it was a miracle!

He had not yet examined her; he could not yet know the real condition of her lesions. But he had seen with his own eyes a functional improvement which was in itself a miracle. How simple, how private, it had been! The crowd at the Grotto was not even aware that it had happened. . . .

At half-past seven, he started for the hospital, tense and on fire with curiosity.

The sun had vanished behind the hilltops. In the early-evening quiet, the patients on stretchers or in little carts were being taken back to the hospital; they were singing hymns and Aves. Some patients were walking, their faces radiant with joy. They were surrounded by relatives and friends. Even strangers accompanied them, drawn by the power of the miraculous. These few were the select, the blessed, upon whom the compassionate Virgin had bestowed her healing glance. But even the poor cancerous wretches returning to the hospital wards to lie there in continued suffering had a look of happiness on their faces.

They had not lost their conviction that Jesus would come down from Heaven to cure them.

One question alone filled Lerrac's mind: had the incurable Marie Ferrand been cured?

Opening the door of the ward of the Immaculate Conception, he hastened across the room to her bedside. With mute astonishment, he stood and gazed. The change was overpowering.

Marie Ferrand, in a white jacket, was sitting up in bed. Though her face was still gray and emaciated, it was alight with life; her eyes shone; a faint color tinged her cheeks. The lines at the corners of her mouth, etched there by years of suffering, still showed. But such an indescribable serenity emanated from her person that it seemed to illuminate the whole sad ward with joy.

"Doctor," she said, "I am completely cured. I feel very weak, but I think I could even walk."

Lerrac put his hand on her wrist. The pulse beat was calm and regular, eighty times a minute. Yet a few short hours ago it had been so accelerated, so fluttering, that he could hardly count it. Her respiration had also become completely normal; her chest rose and fell with slow regularity.

Confusion flooded Lerrac's mind. Was this merely an apparent cure, an extraordinary functional improvement, the result of the violent stimulus of autosuggestion? Or had the lesions really healed? Was this a rare, but accepted phenomenon in nature, or was it a new fact, an astounding, unacceptable event—a miracle?

Voyage to Lourdes, by Alexis Carrel

WALTER REED

"It was a grand coöperative fight ... fought by a strange crew ..."

In this selection from Microbe Hunters, *Paul de Kruif tells the story of the conquest of yellow fever. He writes with his accustomed wry approach to his characters. They are never posed heroically on his pages. They stumble through errors and oversights, and reach their goal more by persistence than brilliance. But his pungent style cannot conceal de Kruif's admiration for these men. To risk one's life on a battlefield in wartime is one thing—to risk it in a laboratory is another. The kind of devotion to mankind that makes a man deliberately subject himself to infection by disease in order to prove its source and eventually effect its cure comes as close to true selfless heroism as anything known to man. . . .*

EVERYBODY IS agreed that Walter Reed—head of the Yellow Fever Commission—was a courteous man and a blameless one, that he was a mild man and a logical: there is not one particle of doubt he had to risk human lives; animals simply will not catch yellow fever!

Then it is certain that the ex-lumberjack, James Carroll, was perfectly ready to let go his own life to prove Reed's point, and he was not too sentimental about the lives of others when *he* needed to prove a point—which might and might not be what you would call a major point.

All Cubans (who were on the spot and ought to know) are agreed that those American soldiers who volunteered for the fate of guinea-pigs were brave beyond imagining. All Americans who were then in Cuba are sure that those Spanish immigrants who volunteered for the fate of guinea-pigs were not brave, but money-loving—for didn't each one of them get two hundred dollars?

Of course you might protest that fate hit Jesse Lazear a hard knock —but it was his own fault: why didn't he brush that mosquito off the back of his hand instead of letting her drink her fill? Then, too, fate has been kind to his memory; the United States Government named a Battery in Baltimore Harbor in his honor! And that same government has been more than kind to his wife: the widow Lazear gets a pension of fifteen hundred dollars a year! You see, there are no arguments—and that makes it fun to tell this story of yellow fever. And aside from the pleasure, it has to be told: this history is absolutely necessary to the book of Microbe Hunters. It vindicates Pasteur! At last Pasteur, from his handsome tomb in that basement in Paris, can tell the world: "I told you so!" Because, in 1926, there is hardly enough of the poison of yellow fever left in the world to put on the points of six pins; in a few years there may not be a single speck of that virus left on earth—it will be as completely extinct as the dinosaurs—unless there is a catch in the fine gruesome experiments of Reed and his Spanish immigrants and American soldiers.

It was a grand coöperative fight, that scotching of the yellow jack. It was fought by a strange crew, and the fight was begun by a curious old man, with enviable mutton chop whiskers—his name was Doctor Carlos Finlay—who made an amazingly right guess, who was a terrible muddler at experiments, who was considered by all good Cubans and wise doctors to be a Theorizing Old Fool. What a crazy crank is Finlay, said everybody.

For everybody knew just how to fight that most panic-striking plague, yellow fever; everybody had a different idea of just how to combat it. You should fumigate silks and satins and possessions of folks before they *left* yellow fever towns—no! that is not enough: you should burn them. You should bury, burn, and utterly destroy these silks and satins and possessions before they *come into* yellow fever towns. It was wise not to shake hands with friends whose families were dying of yellow fever; it was perfectly safe to shake hands with them. It was best to burn down houses where yellow fever had lurked —no! it was enough to smoke them out with sulphur. But there was one thing nearly everybody in North, Central, and South America had been agreed upon for nearly two hundred years, and that was this: when folks of a town began to turn yellow and hiccup and vomit black, by scores, by hundreds, every day—the only thing to do was to get up and get out of that town. Because the yellow murderer had a way of crawling through walls and slithering along the ground and popping around corners—it could even pass through fires!—it could die and rise from the dead, that yellow murderer; and after everybody (including the very best physicians) had fought it by doing as many contrary things as they could think of as frankly as they could do them—the yellow jack kept on killing, until suddenly it got fed up with killing. In North America that always came with the frosts in the fall.

This was the state of scientific knowledge about yellow fever up to the year 1900. But from between his mutton chop whiskers Carlos Finlay of Habana howled in a scornful wilderness: "You are all wrong —yellow fever is caused by a mosquito!"

II

There was a bad state of affairs in San Cristobal de Habana in Cuba in 1900. The yellow jack had killed thousands more American soldiers than the bullets of the Spaniards had killed. And it wasn't like most diseases, which considerately pounce upon poor dirty people—it had killed more than one third of the officers of General Leonard Wood's staff, and staff officers—as all soldiers know—are the cleanest of all officers and the best protected. General Wood had thundered orders; Habana had been scrubbed; happy dirty Cubans had been made into unhappy clean Cubans—"No stone had been left unturned"—in vain! There was more yellow fever in Habana than there had been in twenty years!

Cablegrams from Habana to Washington, and on June 25th of 1900 Major Walter Reed came to Quemados in Cuba with orders to "give special attention to questions relating to the cause and prevention of yellow fever." It was a big order. Considering who the man Walter Reed was, it was altogether too big an order. Pasteur had tried it! Of course, in certain ways—though you would say they had nothing to do with hunting microbes—Walter Reed had qualifications. He was the best of soldiers; fourteen years and more he had served on the western plains and mountains; he had been a brave angel flying through blizzards to the bedsides of sick settlers—he had shunned the dangers of beer and bottle-pool in the officers' mess and resisted the seductions of poker. He had a strong moral nature. He was gentle. But it will take a genius to dig out this microbe of the yellow jack, you say—and are geniuses gentle? Just the same, you will see that this job needed particularly a strong moral nature, and then, besides, since 1891 Walter Reed *had* been doing a bit of microbe hunting. He had done some odd jobs of searching at the very best medical school under the most eminent professor of microbe hunting in America—and that professor had known Robert Koch, intimately.

So Walter Reed came to Quemados, and as he went into the yellow fever hospital there, more than enough young American soldiers passed him, going out, on their backs, feet first. There were going to be plenty of cases to work on all right—fatal cases! Dr. James Carroll was with Walter Reed, and he was not what you would call gentle, but you will see in a moment what a soldier-searcher James Carroll was. And Reed found Jesse Lazear waiting for him—Lazear was a European-trained microbe hunter, aged thirty-four, with a wife and two babies in the States, and with doom in his eyes. Finally there was Aristides Agramonte (who was a Cuban)—it was to be his job to cut up the dead bodies, and very well he did that job, though he never became famous because he had had yellow fever already and so ran no risks. These four were the Yellow Fever Commission.

The first thing the Commission did was to fail to find any microbe whatever in the first eighteen cases of yellow fever that they probed into. There were many severe cases in those eighteen; there were four of those eighteen cases who died: there was not one of those eighteen cases that they didn't claw through from stem to gudgeon, so to speak, drawing blood, making cultures, cutting up the dead ones, making endless careful cultures—and not one bacillus did they find. All the time—it was July and the very worst time for yellow fever—the soldiers were coming out of the hospital of Las Animas feet first. The Commission failed absolutely to find any cause, but that failure put them on the right track. That is one of the humors of microbe hunting— the way men make their finds! Theobald Smith found out about those ticks because he had faith in certain farmers; Ronald Ross found out the doings of those gray mosquitoes because Patrick Manson told him to; Grassi discovered the zanzarone carrying malaria because he was patriotic. And now Walter Reed had failed in the very first part— and anybody would say it was the most important part—of his work. What to do? There was nothing to do. And so Reed had time to hear the voice of that Theorizing Old Fool, Dr. Carlos Finlay, of Habana, shouting: "Yellow fever is caused by a *mosquito!*"

The Commission went to call on Dr. Finlay, and that old gentleman—everybody had laughed at him, nobody had listened to him— was very glad to explain his fool theory to the Commission. He told them the ingenious but vague reasons why he thought it was mosquitoes carried yellow fever; he showed them records of those awful experiments, which would convince nobody; he gave them some little black eggs shaped like cigars and said: "Those are the eggs of the criminal!" And Walter Reed took those eggs, and gave them to Lazear, who had been in Italy and knew a thing or two about mosquitoes, and Lazear put the eggs into a warm place to hatch into wigglers, which presently wiggled themselves into extremely pretty mosquitoes, with silver markings on their backs—markings that looked like a lyre. Now Walter Reed had failed, but you have to give him credit for being a sharp-eyed man with plenty of common sense—and then too, as you will see, he was extraordinarily lucky. While he was failing to find bacilli, even in the dreadful cases, with bloodshot eyes and chests yellow as gold, with hiccups and with those prophetic retchings—while he was failing, Walter Reed noticed that the nurses who handled those cases, were soiled by those cases, never got yellow fever! They were non-immunes too, those nurses, but they didn't get yellow fever.

"If this disease were caused by a bacillus, like cholera, or plague, some of those nurses certainly should get it," argued Walter Reed to his Commission.

Then all kinds of strange tricks of yellow fever struck Walter Reed. He watched cases of the disease pop up most weirdly in Quemados. A man in a house in 102 Real Street came down with it; then it jumped around the corner to 20 General Lee Street, and from there it hopped across the road—and not one of these families had anything to do with each other, hadn't seen each other, even!

"That smells like something carrying the disease through the air to those houses," said Reed. There were various other exceedingly strange things about yellow fever—they had been discovered by an American, Carter. A man came down with yellow fever in a house. For two or three weeks nothing more happened—the man might die, he might have got better and gone away, but at the end of that two weeks, bang! a bunch of other cases broke out in that house. "That two weeks makes it look as if the virus were taking time to grow in some insect," said Reed, to his Commission, who thought it was silly, but they were soldiers.

"So we will try Finlay's notion about mosquitoes," said Walter Reed, for all of the just-mentioned reasons, but particularly because there was nothing else for the Commission to do.

That was easy to say, but how to go on with it? Everybody knew perfectly well that you cannot give yellow fever to any animal—not even to a monkey or an ape. To make any kind of experiment to prove mosquitoes carry yellow fever you *must* have experimental animals, and that meant nothing more nor less than human animals. But give human beings yellow fever! In some epidemics—there were records of them!—eighty-five men out of a hundred died of it; in some, fifty out of every hundred—almost never less than twenty out of every hundred. It would be murder! But that is where the strong moral nature of Walter Reed came to help him. Here was a blameless man, a Christian man, and a man—though he was mild—who was mad to help his fellow men. And if you could *prove* that yellow fever was *only* carried by mosquitoes!

So, on one hot night after a day among dying men at Pinar del Rio, he faced his Commission: "If the members of the Commission take the risk first—if they let themselves be bitten by mosquitoes that have fed on yellow fever cases, that will set an example to American soldiers, and then—" Reed looked at Lazear, and then at James Carroll.

"I am ready to take a bite," said Jesse Lazear, who had a wife and two small children.

"You can count on me, sir," said James Carroll, whose total assets were his searcher's brain, and his miserable pay as an assistant-surgeon in the army. (His liabilities were a wife and five children.)

III

Then Walter Reed (he had been called home to Washington to make a report on work done in the Spanish War) gave elaborate instructions to Carroll and Lazear and Agramonte. They were secret instructions, and savage instructions, when you consider the mild man he was. It was an immoral business—it was a breach of discipline in its way, for Walter Reed then had no permission from the high military authorities to start it. So Reed left for Washington, and Lazear and Carroll set off on the wildest, most daring journey any two microbe hunters had ever taken. Lazear? You could not see the doom in his eyes—the gleam of the searcher outshone it. Carroll? That was a soldier who cared neither for death nor courts-martial—Carroll was a microbe hunter of the great line.

Lazear went down between the rows of beds on which lay men, doomed men with faces yellow as the leaves of autumn, delirious men with bloodshot eyes. He bit those men with his silver-striped she-mosquitoes; carefully he carried these blood-filled beasts back to their glass homes, in which were little saucers of water and little lumps of sugar. Here the she-mosquitoes digested their meal of yellow fever blood, and buzzed a little, and waited for the test.

"We should remember malaria," Reed had told Lazear and Carroll. "In that disease it takes two or three weeks for the mosquito to become dangerous—maybe it's the same here."

But look at the bold face of Jesse Lazear, and tell me if that was a patient man! Not he. Somehow he collected seven volunteers, who so far as I can find have remained nameless, since the test was done in dark secrecy. To these seven men—whom for all I know he may have shanghaied—but first of all to himself, Lazear applied those mosquitoes who a few days before had fed on men who now were dead.

But alas, they all stayed as fit as fiddles, and that discouraged Lazear.

But there was James Carroll. For years he had been the righthand man of Walter Reed. He had come into the army as a buck private and had been a corporal and a sergeant for years—obeying orders was burned into his very bones—and Major Reed had said: "Try mosquitoes!" What is more, what Major Reed thought was right, James Carroll thought was right, too, and Major Reed thought there was something in the notion of that Old Theorizing Fool. But in the army, thoughts are secondary—Major Reed had left them saying: "Try mosquitoes!"

So James Carroll reminded the discouraged Lazear: "I am ready!" He told Lazear to bring out the most dangerous mosquito in his collection—not one that had bitten only a single case, but he must use a mosquito that had bitten many cases—and they must be bad cases—of yellow fever. That mosquito must be as dangerous as possible! On the twenty-seventh of August, Jesse Lazear picked out what he thought to be his champion mosquito, and this creature, which had fed on four cases of yellow fever, two of them severe ones, settled down on the arm of James Carroll.

That soldier watched her while she felt around with her stinger. What did he think as he watched her swell into a bright balloon with his blood? Nobody knows. But he could think, what everybody knows: "I am forty-six years old, and in yellow fever the older the fewer —get better." He was forty-six years old. He had a wife and five children, but that evening James Carroll wrote to Walter Reed: "If there is anything in the mosquito theory, I should get a good dose of yellow fever!" He did.

Two days later he felt tired and didn't want to visit patients in the yellow fever ward. Two days after that he was really sick: "I must have malaria!" he cried, and went to the laboratory under his own power, to squint at his own blood under the microscope. But no malaria. That night his eyes were bloodshot, his face a dusky red. The next morning Lazear packed Carroll off to the yellow fever wards, and there he lay, near to death for days and days. There was one minute when he thought his heart had stopped . . . and that, as you will see, was a bad minute for Assistant-Surgeon Carroll.

He always said those were the proudest days of his life. "I was the first case to come down with yellow fever after the experimental bite of a mosquito!" said Carroll.

Then there was that American private soldier they called "X.Y."— these outlaw searchers called him "X.Y.," though he was really William Dean, of Grand Rapids, Michigan. While James Carroll was having his first headaches, they bit this X.Y. with four mosquitoes—the one that nearly killed Carroll, and then three other silver-striped beauties besides, who had fed on six men that were fairly sick, and four men that were very sick with yellow fever and two men that died.

Now everything was fine with the experiments of Quemados. Eight men had been bitten, it is true, and were fit as fiddles—but the last two, James Carroll and X.Y., they were real experimental guinea-pigs, those two, they had both got yellow fever—and James Carroll's heart had nearly stopped, but now they were both getting better, and Carroll was on the heights, writing to Walter Reed, waiting proudly for his chief to come back—to show him the records. Only Jesse Lazear was a little cynical about these two cases, because Lazear was a fine experimenter, a tight one, a man who had to have every condition just so, like a real searcher—and, thought Lazear, "It is too bad, seeing the nerve of Carroll and X.Y.—but both of them exposed themselves in dangerous zones once or twice, before they came down. It wasn't an absolutely perfect experiment—it isn't sure that *my* mosquitoes gave them yellow fever!" So Lazear was skeptical, but orders were orders, and every afternoon he went to those rows of beds at Las Animas, in the room with the faint strange smell, and here he turned his test-tubes upside-down on the arms of boys with bloodshot eyes, and let his she-mosquitoes suck their fill. But September 13th was a bad day, it was an unlucky day for Jesse Lazear, for while he was at this silly job of feeding his mosquitoes, a stray mosquito settled down on the back of his hand. "Oh! that's nothing!" he thought. "That wouldn't be the right kind of mosquito anyway!" he muttered, and he let the mosquito drink her fill—though, mind you, she was a stray beast that lived in this ward where men were dying!

That was September 13th.

"On the evening of September 18th Dr. Lazear complained of feeling out of sorts, and had a chill at 8 P.M.," says a hospital record at Las Animas.

"September 19: Twelve o'clock noon," goes on that laconic record, "temperature 102.4 degrees, pulse 112. Eyes injected, face suffused." (That means bloodshot and red) ". . . 6 P.M. temperature 103.8 degrees, pulse 106. Jaundice appeared on the third day. The subsequent history of this case was one of progressive and fatal yellow fever" (and the record softens a little), "the death of our lamented colleague having occurred on the evening of September 25, 1900."

IV

Then Reed came back to Cuba, and Carroll met him with enthusiasm, and Walter Reed was sad for Lazear, but very happy about those two successful cases of Carroll and X.Y.—and then, and then (brushing aside tears for Lazear) even in that there was the Hand of God, there was something for Science: "As Dr. Lazear was bitten by a mosquito while present in the wards of a yellow fever hospital," wrote

Walter Reed, "one must, at least, admit the possibility of this insect's contamination by a previous bite of a yellow fever patient. This case of accidental infection therefore *cannot fail to be of interest.*"

"Now it is my turn to take the bite!" said Walter Reed, but he was fifty years old, and they persuaded him not to. "But we *must* prove it!" he insisted, so gently, that, hearing his musical voice and looking at his chin that did not stick out like the chin of a he-man, you might think Walter Reed was wavering (after all, here was one man dead out of three).

"But we must prove it," said that soft voice, and Reed went to General Leonard Wood, and told him the exciting events that had happened. Who could be less of a mollycoddle than this Wood? And he gave Walter Reed permission to go as far as he liked. He gave him money to build a camp of seven tents and two little houses—to say nothing of a flagpole—but what was best of all, Wood gave him money to buy men, who would get handsomely paid for taking a sure one chance out of five of never having a chance to spend that money! So Walter Reed said: "Thank you, General," and one mile from Quemados they pitched seven tents and raised a flagpole, and flew an American flag and called that place Camp Lazear (three cheers for Lazear!), and you will see what glorious things occurred there.

Now, nothing is more sure than this: that every man of the great line of microbe hunters is different from every other man of them, but every man Jack of them has one thing in common: they are original. They were all original, excepting Walter Reed—who you cannot say would be shot for his originality, seeing that this business of mosquitoes and various bugs and ticks carrying diseases was very much in the air in those last ten years of the nineteenth century. It was natural for a man to think of that! But he was by all odds the most moral of the great line of microbe hunters—aside from being a very thorough clean-cut experimenter—and now that Walter Reed's moral nature told him: "You must kill men to save them!" he set out to plan a series of air-tight tests—never was there a good man who thought of more hellish and dastardly tests!

And he was exact. Every man about to be bit by a mosquito must stay locked up for days and days and weeks, in that sun-baked Camp Lazear—to keep him away from all danger of accidental contact with yellow fever. There would be no catch in these experiments! And then Walter Reed let it be known, to the American soldiers in Cuba, that there was another war on, a war for the saving of men—were there men who would volunteer? Before the ink was dry on the announcements Private Kissenger of Ohio stepped into his office, and with him came John J. Moran, who wasn't even a soldier—he was a civilian clerk in the office of General Fitzhugh Lee. "You can try it on us, sir!" they told him.

Walter Reed was a thoroughly conscientious man. "But, men, do you realize the danger?" And he told them of the headaches and the hiccups and the black vomit—and he told them of fearful epidemics in which not a man had lived to carry news or tell the horrors.

"We know," said Private Kissenger and John J. Moran of Ohio, "we volunteer solely for the cause of humanity and in the interest of science."

Then Walter Reed told them of the generosity of General Wood. A handsome sum of money they would get—two hundred, maybe three hundred dollars, if the silver-striped she-mosquitoes did things to them that would give them one chance out of five not to spend that money.

"The one condition on which we volunteer, sir," said Private Kissenger and civilian clerk John J. Moran of Ohio, "is that we get no compensation for it."

To the tip of his cap went the hand of Walter Reed (who was a major): "Gentlemen, I salute you!" And that day Kissenger and John J. Moran went into the preparatory quarantine, that would make them first-class, unquestionable guinea-pigs, above suspicion and beyond reproach. On the 5th of December Kissenger furnished nice full meals for five mosquitoes—two of them had bitten fatal cases fifteen days and nineteen days before. Presto! Five days later he had the devil of a backache, two days more and he was turning yellow—it was a perfect case, and in his quarters Walter Reed thanked God, for Kissenger got better! Then great days came to Reed and Carroll and Agramonte —for, if they weren't exactly overrun with young Americans who were ready to throw away their lives in the interest of science—and for humanity still there were ignorant people, just come to Cuba from Spain, who could very well use two hundred dollars. There were five of these mercenary fellows—whom I shall simply have to call "Spanish immigrants," or I could call them Man 1, 2, 3, and 4—just as microbe hunters often mark animals: "Rabbit 1, 2, 3, and 4—" anyway they were bitten, carefully, by mosquitoes who, when you take averages, were much more dangerous than machine gun bullets. They earned their two hundred dollars—for four out of five of them had nice typical (doctors would look scientific and call them beautiful) cases of yellow fever! It was a triumph! It was sure! Not one of these men had been anywhere near yellow fever—like so many mice they had been kept in their screened tents at Quemados. If they hadn't been ignorant immigrants—hardly more intelligent than animals, you might say—they might have been bored, because nothing had happened to them excepting—the stabs of silver-striped she-mosquitoes.

"Rejoice with me, sweetheart," Walter Reed wrote to his wife, "as, aside from the antitoxin of diphtheria and Koch's discovery of the tubercle bacillus, it will be regarded as the most important piece of work, scientifically, during the nineteenth century."

Walter Reed was so thorough that you can call him original, as original as any of the microbe hunters of the great line—for he was certainly original in his thoroughness. He might have called it a day —you would swear he was tempted to call it a day: eight men had got yellow fever from mosquito bites, and only one—what amazing luck!—had died.

"But can yellow fever be carried in any other way?" asked Reed.

Everybody believed that clothing and bedding and possessions of yellow fever victims were deadly—millions of dollars' worth of clothing and bedding had been destroyed; the Surgeon-General believed it; every eminent physician in America, North, South and Central (excepting that old fool Finlay) believed it. "But can it?" asked Reed, and while he was being so joyfully successful with Kissenger and Spaniards 1, 2, 3, and 4, carpenters came, and built two ugly little houses in Camp Lazear. House No. 1 was the nastier of these two little houses. It was fourteen feet by twenty, it had two doors cleverly arranged one back of the other so no mosquitoes could get into it, it had two windows looking south—they were on the same side as the door, so no draft could blow through that little house. Then it was furnished with a nice stove, to keep the temperature well above ninety, and there were tubs of water in the house—to keep the air as chokey as the hold of a ship in the tropics. So you see it was an uninhabitable little house—under the best of conditions—but now, on the thirtieth of November in 1900, sweating soldiers carried several tightly nailed suspicious-looking boxes, that came from the yellow fever wards of Las Animas—to make the house altogether cursed.

That night, of the thirtieth of November, Walter Reed and James Carroll were the witnesses of a miracle of bravery, for into this House No. 1 walked a young American doctor named Cooke, and two American soldiers, whose names—where are their monuments?—were Folk and Jernegan.

Those three men opened the tightly nailed, suspicious-looking boxes. They opened those boxes inside that house, in air already too sticky for proper breathing.

Phew! There were cursings, there were holdings of noses.

But they went on opening those boxes, and out of them Cooke and Folk and Jernegan took pillows, soiled with the black vomit of men dead of yellow fever; out of them they took sheets and blankets, dirty with the discharges of dying men past helping themselves. They beat those pillows and shook those sheets and blankets—"you must see the yellow fever poison is well spread around that room!" Walter Reed had told them. Then Cooke and Folk and Jernegan made up their little army cots with those pillows and blankets and sheets. They undressed. They lay down on those filthy beds. They tried to sleep—in that room fouler than the dankest of medieval dungeons. And Walter Reed and James Carroll guarded that little house, so tenderly, to see no mosquito got into it, and Folk and Cooke and Jernegan had the very best of food, you may be sure.

Night after night those three lay in that house, wondering perhaps about the welfare of the souls of their predecessors in those sheets and blankets. They lay there, wondering whether anything else besides mosquitoes (though mosquitoes hadn't even been proved to carry it then!) carried yellow fever. Then Walter Reed, who was a moral man and a thorough man, and James Carroll, who was a grim man, came to make their test a little more thorough. More boxes came to them from Las Animas—and when Cooke and Jernegan and Folk unpacked them, they had to rush out of their little house, it was so dreadful.

But they went back in, and they went to sleep.

For twenty nights—where are their monuments?—these three men stayed there, and then they were quarantined in a nice airy tent, to wait for their attack of yellow fever. But they gained weight. They felt fit as fiddles. They made vast jokes about their dirty house and their perilous sheets and blankets. They were happy as so many schoolboys when they heard Kissenger and those Spaniards (1, 2, 3, and 4) had really got the yellow jack after the mosquito bites. What a marvelous proof, you will say, but what a dastardly experiment—but for the insanely scientific Walter Reed that most dastardly experiment was not marvelous enough! Three more American boys went in there, and for twenty nights slept in new unspeakable sheets and blankets— with this little refinement of the experiment: they slept in the very pajamas in which yellow fever victims had died. And then for twenty more nights three other American lads went into House No. 1, and slept that way—with this additional little refinement of the experiment: they slept on pillows covered with towels soaked with the blood of men whom the yellow jack had killed.

But they all stayed fit as fiddles! Not a soul of these nine men had so much as a touch of yellow fever! How wonderful is science, thought Walter Reed. "So," he wrote, "the bubble of the belief that clothing can transmit yellow fever was pricked by the first touch of human experimentation." Walter Reed was right. It is true, science is wonderful. But science is cruel, microbe hunting can be heartless, and that relentless devil that was the experimenter in Walter Reed kept asking: "But is your experiment really sound?" None of those men who slept in House No. 1 got yellow fever, that is true—but how do you know they were *susceptible* to yellow fever? Maybe they were naturally immune! Then Reed and Carroll, who had already asked as much of Folk and Jernegan as any captain has ever asked of any soldier—so it was that Reed and Carroll now shot virulent yellow fever blood under the skin of Jernegan, so it was they bit Folk with mosquitoes who had fed on fatal cases of yellow fever. They both came down with wracking pains and flushed faces and bloodshot eyes. They both came through their Valley of the Shadow. "Thank God," murmured Reed—but especially Walter Reed thanked God he had proved those two boys were not immune during those twenty hot stinking nights in House No. 1.

For these deeds Warren Gladsden Jernegan and Levi E. Folk were generously rewarded with a purse of three hundred dollars—which in those days was a lot of money.

While these tests were going on John J. Moran, that civilian clerk from Ohio, whom Walter Reed had paid the honor of a salute, was a very disappointed man. He had absolutely refused to be paid; he had volunteered in "the interest of science and for the cause of humanity," he had been bitten by those silver-striped Stegomyia mosquitoes (the bug experts just then thought this was the proper name for that mosquito)—he had been stabbed several times by several choice poisonous ones, but he hadn't come down with yellow fever, alas, he stayed fit as a fiddle. What to do with John J. Moran?

"I have it!" said Walter Reed. "This to do with John J. Moran!"

So there was built, close by that detestable little House No. 1, another little house, called House No. 2. That was a comfortable house! It had windows on the side opposite to its door, so that a fine trade wind played through it. It was cool. It had a nice clean cot in it, with steam-disinfected bedding. It would have been an excellent house for a consumptive to get better in. It was a thoroughly sanitary little house. Half way across the inside of it was a screen, from top to bottom, a fine-meshed screen that the tiniest mosquito found it impossible to fly through. At 12 o'clock noon on the twenty-first of December in 1900, this John J. Moran (who was a hog for these tests) "clad only in a nightshirt and fresh from a bath," walked into this healthy little house. Five minutes before Reed and Carroll had opened a glass jar in that room, and out of that jar flew fifteen she-mosquitoes, thirsty for blood, whining for a meal of blood, and each and every one of those fifteen mosquitoes, had fed, on various days before—on the blood of yellow-faced boys in the hospital of Las Animas.

Clad only in a nightshirt and fresh from a bath, Moran—who knows of him now?—walked into the healthy little room and lay down on his clean cot. In a minute that damned buzzing started round his head, in two minutes he was bitten, in the thirty minutes he lay there he was stabbed seven times—without even the satisfaction of smashing those mosquitoes. You remember Mr. Sola, whom Grassi tortured— he probably had his worried moments—but all Mr. Sola had to look forward to was a little attack of malaria and a good dose of curative quinine to get him out of it. But Moran? But John J. Moran was a hog for such tests! He was back there at four-thirty the same afternoon, to be bitten again, and once more the next day—to satisfy the rest of the hungry she-mosquitoes who hadn't found him the first day. In the other room of this house, with only a fine-meshed but perfect wire screen between them and Moran—and the mosquitoes—lay two other boys, and those two boys slept in that house safely for eighteen nights.

But Moran?

On Christmas morning of 1900, there was a fine present waiting for him—in his head, how that thumped—in his eyes, how red they were and how the light hurt them—in his bones, how tired they were! A nasty knock those mosquitoes had hit him and he came within a hair of dying but (thank God! murmured Walter Reed) he was saved, this Moran, to live the rest of his life in an obscurity he didn't deserve. So Moran had his wish—in the interest of science, and for humanity! So he, with Folk and Jernegan and Cooke and all those others proved that the dirty pest hole of a house (with no mosquitoes) was safe; and that the clean house (but with mosquitoes) was dangerous, so dangerous! So at last Walter Reed had every answer to his diabolical questions, and he wrote, in that old-fashioned prose of his: "The essential factor in the infection of a building with yellow fever is the presence therein of mosquitoes that have bitten cases of yellow fever."

It was so simple. It was true. That was all. That was that. And Walter Reed wrote to his wife:

"The prayer that has been mine for twenty years, that I might be permitted in some way or at some time to do something to alleviate human suffering has been granted! A thousand Happy New Years. . . . Hark, there go the twenty-four buglers in concert, all sounding taps for the old year!"

They were sounding taps, were those buglers, for the searcher that was Jesse Lazear, and for the scourge of yellow fever that could now be wiped from the earth.

Microbe Hunters, by Paul de Kruif

ALBERT SCHWEITZER

"... I quietly began my work. My search was over."

There is no doubt that Albert Schweitzer comes as close to being a true 'Renaissance Man' as anyone now living. Philosopher, clergyman, organist, scholar and physician for the last forty years, he has devoted himself to native medicine, deep in the African jungles —a life which as a truly practicing Christian he felt compelled to follow.

Schweitzer planned his life as though it were a campaign and in truth that is what it has been—a campaign against ignorance and against disease . . . a campaign against bigotry and prejudice. More than any other man of the twentieth century, Schweitzer is a symbol of faith in action—of a Christian who does, not just prescribes. In the piece that follows, Schweitzer writes of his decision to go to Africa to begin his dedication in the service of medicine and of God.

On October 13th, 1905, a Friday, I dropped into a letter box in the Avenue de la Grande Armée in Paris, letters to my parents and to some of my most intimate acquaintances, telling them that at the beginning of the winter term I should enter myself as a medical student, in order to go later on to Equatorial Africa as a doctor. In one of them I sent in the resignation of my post as principal of the Theological College of St. Thomas', because of the claim on my time that my intended course of study would make.

The plan which I meant now to put into execution had been in my mind for a long time, having been conceived so long ago as my student days. It struck me as incomprehensible that I should be allowed to lead such a happy life, while I saw so many people around me wrestling with care and suffering. Even at school I had felt stirred whenever I got a glimpse of the miserable home surroundings of some of my schoolfellows and compared them with the absolutely ideal conditions in which we children of the parsonage at Günsbach lived. While at the university and enjoying the happiness of being able to study and even to produce some results in science and art, I could not help thinking continually of others who were denied that happiness by their material circumstances or their health. Then one brilliant summer morning at Günsbach, during the Whitsuntide holidays—it was in 1896—there came to me, as I awoke, the thought that I must not accept this happiness as a matter of course, but must give something in return for it. Proceeding to think the matter out at once with calm deliberation, while the birds were singing outside, I settled with myself before I got up, that I would consider myself justified in living until I was thirty for science and art, in order to devote myself from that time forward to the direct service of humanity. Many a time already had I tried to settle what meaning lay hidden for me in the saying of Jesus! "Whosoever would save his life shall lose it, and whosoever shall lose his life for My sake and the Gospels shall save it." Now the answer was found. In addition to the outward, I now had inward happiness.

What would be the character of the activities thus planned for the future was not yet clear to me. I left it to circumstances to guide me. One thing only was certain, that it must be directly human service, however inconspicuous the sphere of it. . . . What I wanted was an absolutely personal and independent activity. Although I was resolved to put my services at the disposal of some organization, if it should be really necessary, I nevertheless never gave up the hope of finding a sphere of activity to which I could devote myself as an individual and as wholly free. That this longing of mine found fulfillment I have always regarded as a signal instance of the mercy which has again and again been vouchsafed to me.

One morning in the autumn of 1904 I found on my writing table in the college one of the green-covered magazines in which the Paris Missionary Society reported every month on its activities. A certain Miss Scherdlin used to put them there knowing that I was specially interested in this society on account of the impression made on me by the letters of one of its earliest missionaries, Casalis by name, when my father read them aloud at his missionary services during my childhood. That evening, in the very act of putting it aside that I might go on with my work, I mechanically opened this magazine, which had been laid on my table during my absence. As I did so, my eye caught the title of an article: *Les besoins de la Mission du Congo* ("The needs of the Congo Mission").

It was by Alfred Boegner, the president of the Paris Missionary Society, an Alsatian, and contained a complaint that the mission had not enough workers to carry on its work in the Gaboon, the northern province of the Congo Colony. The writer expressed his hope that his appeal would bring some of those "on whom the Master's eyes already rested" to a decision to offer themselves for this urgent work. The conclusion ran: "Men and women who can reply simply to the Master's call, 'Lord, I am coming,' those are the people whom the Church needs." Having finished the article, I quietly began my work. My search was over.

My thirtieth birthday, a few months later, I spent like the man in the parable who "desiring to build a tower, first counts the cost whether he have wherewith to complete it." The result was that I resolved to realize my plan of direct human service in Equatorial Africa.

With the exception of one trustworthy friend no one knew of my intention. When it became known through the letters I had sent from Paris, I had hard battles to fight with my relations and friends. Almost more than with my contemplated new start itself they reproached me with not having shown them so much confidence as to discuss it with them first. With this side issue they tormented me beyond measure during those difficult weeks. That theological friends should outdo the others in their protests struck me as all the more preposterous, because they had, no doubt, all preached a fine sermon—perhaps a very fine one—showing how St. Paul, as he has recorded in his letter to the Galatians, "conferred not with flesh and blood" beforehand about what he meant to do for Jesus.

My relatives and my friends all joined in expostulating with me on the folly of my enterprise. I was a man, they said, who was burying the talent entrusted to him and wanted to trade with false currency. Work among savages I ought to leave to those who would not thereby be compelled to leave gifts and acquirements in science and art unused. . . . What seemed to my friends the most irrational thing in my plan was that I wanted to go to Africa, not as a missionary, but as a doctor, and thus when already thirty years of age burdened myself as a beginning with a long period of laborious study. And that this study would mean for me a tremendous effort, I had no manner of doubt. I did, in truth, look forward to the next few years with dread. But the reasons which determined me to follow the way of service I had chosen, as a doctor, weighed so heavily that other considerations were as dust in the balance.

I wanted to be a doctor that I might be able to work without having to talk. For years I had been giving myself out in words and it was with joy that I had followed the calling of theological teacher and of preacher. But this new form of activity I could not represent to myself as being talking about the religion of love, but only as an actual putting it into practice. Medical knowledge made it possible for me to carry out my intention in the best and most complete way, wherever the path of service might lead me. In view of the plan for Equatorial

Africa, the acquisition of such knowledge was especially indicated because in the district to which I thought of going, a doctor was, according to the missionaries' reports, the most needed of all needed things. They were always complaining in their magazine that the natives who visited them in physical suffering could not be given the help they desired. To become one day the doctor whom these poor creatures needed, it was worth while, so I judged, to become a medical student. Whenever I was inclined to feel that the years I should have to sacrifice were too long, I reminded myself that Hamilcar and Hannibal had prepared for their march on Rome by their slow and tedious conquest of Spain. . . . My medical course made such demands on me that I had neither time nor strength to concern myself about what was to happen afterwards.

Out of My Life and Thought, by Albert Schweitzer

III. A TIME FOR ACTION

Action is eloquence.

WILLIAM SHAKESPEARE

Coriolanus, Act III, Scene 2

PATRICK HENRY

"The question ... is one of
awful moment to this country."

If ever there was a legislator who was at the same time truly a man of action, Patrick Henry was that man. The son of a Scottish immigrant he found his field in law and government. He was an outstanding and vivid speaker in a time when the art of oratory was at its most resplendent—and his popular following in his state of Virginia rivaled that of George Washington. For more than ten years, he had spoken out in the House of Burgesses as the leader of the insurgents, damning the British for their arbitrary and unfair taxes. When the royal governor dissolved the legislature in 1775 it met again to debate the passage of a resolution defying the British and denying their power. The house wavered. It was a big step. Then Patrick Henry rose to address his fellows with this, one of the most brilliant and moving speeches in the annals of American history. It was all that was necessary—the resolution passed, and, as far as Virginia was concerned, the die was cast.

Mr. President:—

No man thinks more highly than I do of the patriotism, as well as abilities, of the very worthy gentlemen who have just addressed the house. But different men often see the same subject in different lights; and, therefore, I hope it will not be thought disrespectful to those gentlemen, if, entertaining as I do opinions of a character very opposite to theirs, I shall speak forth my sentiments freely, and without reserve. This is no time for ceremony. The question before the house is one of awful moment to this country. For my own part, I consider it as nothing less than a question of freedom or slavery. And in proportion to the magnitude of the subject ought to be the freedom of the debate. It is only in this way that we can hope to arrive at truth and fulfill the great responsibility which we hold to God and our country. Should I keep back my opinions at such a time, through fear of giving offense, I should consider myself as guilty of treason towards my country, and of an act of disloyalty toward the Majesty of Heaven, which I revere above all earthly kings.

Mr. President, it is natural to man to indulge in the illusions of hope. We are apt to shut our eyes against a painful truth, and listen to the song of that siren till she transforms us into beasts. Is this the part of wise men, engaged in a great and arduous struggle for liberty? Are we disposed to be of the number of those who having eyes see not, and having ears hear not, the things which so nearly concern their temporal salvation? For my part, whatever anguish of spirit it may cost, I am willing to know the whole truth; to know the worst and to provide for it.

I have but one lamp by which my feet are guided, and that is the lamp of experience. I know of no way of judging of the future but by the past. And judging by the past, I wish to know what there has been in the conduct of the British ministry for the last ten years, to justify those hopes with which gentlemen have been pleased to solace themselves and the house? Is it that insidious smile with which our petition has been lately received? Trust it not, sir: it will prove a snare to your feet. Suffer not yourselves to be betrayed with a kiss. Ask yourselves how this gracious reception of our petition comports with those warlike preparations which cover our waters and darken our land. Are fleets and armies necessary to a work of love and reconciliation? Have we shown ourselves so unwilling to be reconciled that force must be called in to win back our love? Let us not deceive ourselves, sir. These are the implements of war and subjugation—the last arguments to which kings resort. I ask gentlemen, sir, What means this martial array, if its purpose be not to force us to submission? Can gentlemen assign any other possible motive for it? Has Great Britain any enemy in this quarter of the world, to call for all this accumulation of navies and armies? No, sir, she has none. They are meant for us: they can be meant for no other. They are sent over to bind and rivet upon us those chains which the British ministry have been so long forging. And what have we to oppose to them? Shall we try argument? Sir, we have been trying that for the last ten years. Have we anything new to offer upon the subject? Nothing. We have held the subject up in every light of which it is capable; but it has been all in vain. Shall we resort to entreaty and humble supplication? What terms shall we find which have not been already exhausted? Let us not, I beseech you, sir, deceive ourselves longer.

Sir, we have done everything that could be done to avert the storm which is now coming on. We have petitioned; we have remonstrated; we have supplicated; we have prostrated ourselves before the throne, and have implored its interposition to arrest the tyrannical hands of the ministry and Parliament. Our petitions have been slighted; our remonstrances have produced additional violence and insult; our supplications have been disregarded; and we have been spurned with contempt from the foot of the throne! In vain, after these things, may we indulge the fond hope of peace and reconciliation. There is no longer any room for hope. If we wish to be free, if we mean to preserve inviolate those inestimable privileges for which we have been so long contending, if we mean not basely to abandon the noble struggle in which we have been so long engaged, and which we have pledged ourselves never to abandon until the glorious object of our contest shall be obtained—we must fight! I repeat it, sir, we must fight! An appeal to arms and to the God of Hosts is all that is left us!

They tell us, sir, that we are weak—unable to cope with so formidable an adversary. But when shall we be stronger? Will it be the next week, or the next year? Will it be when we are totally disarmed, and when a British guard shall be stationed in every house? Shall we gather strength by irresolution and inaction? Shall we acquire the means of effectual resistance by lying supinely on our backs, and hugging the delusive phantom of hope until our enemies shall have bound us hand and foot? Sir, we are not weak, if we make a proper use of those means which the God of nature hath placed in our power. Three millions of people, armed in the holy cause of liberty, and in such a country as that which we possess, are invincible by any force which our enemy can send against us. Besides, sir, we shall not fight our battles alone. There is a just God who presides over the destinies of nations, and who will raise up friends to fight our battles for us. The battle, sir, is not to the strong alone; it is to the vigilant, the active, the brave. Besides, sir, we have no election. If we were base enough to desire it, it is now too late to retire from the contest. There is no retreat but in submission and slavery! Our chains are forged! their clanking may be heard on the plains of Boston! The war is inevitable—and let it come! I repeat it, sir, let it come!

It is in vain, sir, to extenuate the matter. Gentlemen may cry, Peace, Peace—but there is no peace. The war is actually begun! The next gale that sweeps from the north will bring to our ears the clash of resounding arms! Our brethren are already in the field! Why stand we here idle? What is it that gentlemen wish? What would they have? Is life so dear, or peace so sweet, as to be purchased at the price of chains and slavery? Forbid it, Almighty God! I know not what course others may take; but as for me, give me liberty or give me death!

Speech Before the Virginia House of Burgesses, by Patrick Henry

JACQUES-YVES COUSTEAU

"The sky was no longer our business."

There is probably no area of endeavor in which the scientist and the sportsman come so close to being one and the same man as in that of the modern professional skin diver. Jacques-Yves Cousteau is an explorer searching one of the last two great uncharted regions. By the middle of the twentieth century, the frontiers of earth have all but disappeared and man has begun increasingly to look upward to space . . . and down into the mysterious seas. Here, below the surfaces which we have travelled for so many centuries is a new and different world—nearly as strange to us as the moon will seem, when we eventually land upon it.

Cousteau is the father of the new sport-science of undersea archaeology. His discovery of a pre-Christian wineship in the Mediterranean near Marseille has been called "the most important since Pompeii." The work is exciting, arduous and extremely dangerous. Far beneath the surface the men must fight themselves—fight the weird compelling fantasies that carbon monoxide poisoning throws into their minds. Sometimes they come perilously close to losing the battle, as in the deep caves of Vaucluse, near Avignon in south-central France, where Cousteau and his partner, Dumas, stayed down too long. . . .

OUR WORST experience in five thousand dives did not come in the sea but in an inland water cave, the famous Fountain of Vaucluse near Avignon. The renowned spring is a quiet pool in a crater under a six-hundred-foot limestone cliff above the River Sorgue. A trickle flows from it the year round, until March comes; then the Fountain of Vaucluse erupts in a rage of water which swells the Sorgue to flood. It pumps furiously for five weeks, then subsides. The phenomenon has occurred every year of recorded history.

The fountain has evoked the fancy of poets since the Middle Ages. Petrarch wrote sonnets to Laura by the Fountain of Vaucluse in the fourteenth century. Frédéric Mistral, our Provençal poet, was another admirer of the spring. Generations of hydrologists have leaned over the fountain, evolving dozens of theories. They have measured the rainfall on the plateau above, mapped the potholes in it, analyzed the water, and determined that it is an invariable fifty-five degrees Fahrenheit the year round. But no one knew what happened to discharge the amazing flood.

One principle of intermittent natural fountains is that of an underground siphon, which taps a pool of water lying higher inside the hill than the water level of the surface pool. Simple overflows of the inner pool by heavy rain seeping through the porous limestone, did not explain Vaucluse, because it did not entirely respond to rainfall. There was either a huge inner reservoir or a series of inner caverns and a system of siphons. Scientific theories had no more validity than Mistral's explanation: "One day the fairy of the Fountain changed herself into a beautiful maiden and took an old strolling minstrel by the hand and led him down through Vaucluse's waters to an underground prairie, where seven huge diamonds plugged seven holes. 'See these diamonds?' said the fairy. 'When I lift the seventh, the fountain rises to the roots of the fig tree that drinks only once a year.' " Mistral's theory, as a matter of fact, possessed one more piece of tangible evidence than the scientific guesses. There is a rachitic hundred-year-old fig tree hooked on the vertical wall at the waterline of the annual flood. Its roots are watered but once a year.

A retired Army officer, Commandant Brunet, who had settled in the nearby village of Apt, became an addict of the Fountain as had Petrarch six hundred years before. The Commandant suggested that the Undersea Research Group dive into the Fountain and learn the secret of the mechanism. In 1946 the Navy gave us permission to try. We journeyed to Vaucluse on the 24th of August, when the spring was quiescent. There seemed to be no point in entering a violent flood, if its source might be discovered when the fountain was quiet.

The arrival of uniformed naval officers and sailors in trucks loaded with diving equipment, set off a commotion in Vaucluse. We were overwhelmed by boys, vying for the privilege of carrying our air cylinders, portable decompression chamber, aqualungs and diving dresses up the wooded trail to the Fountain. Half the town, led by Mayor Garcin, dropped work and accompanied us. They told us about the formidable dive into the Fountain made by Señor Negri in 1936. What a bold type was this Señor Negri! He had descended in a diving suit with a microphone inside the helmet through which he broadcast a running account of his incredible rigors as he plunged one hundred and twenty feet to the inferior elbow of a siphon.

We had predicated our tactical planning on the physical features described by pioneer divers. Dumas and I were to form the first *cordée*—we used the mountain climber's term because we were to be tied together by a thirty-foot cord attached to our belts. Negri's measurements determined the length of our guide rope—four hundred feet —and the weights we carried on our belts, which were unusually heavy to allow us to penetrate the tunnel he had described and to plant ourselves against currents inside the siphon.

What we could not know until we had gone inside the Fountain was that Negri was overimaginative. The topography of the cavern was completely unlike his description. That misinformation was not all of the burden we carried into the Fountain: the new air compressor with which we filled the breathing cylinders had prepared a fantastic fate for us.

We adjusted our eyes to the gloom of the crater. Mayor Garcin had lent us a Canadian canoe, which was floated over the throat of the Fountain, to anchor the guide rope. There was a heavy pig-iron weight on the end of the rope, which we wanted lowered beforehand as far as it would go down. The underwater entry was partially blocked by a huge stone buttress, but we managed to lower the pig iron fifty-five feet. Chief Petty Officer Jean Pinard volunteered to dive without a protective suit to attempt to roll the pig iron down as far as it was possible. Pinard returned lobster-red with cold and reported he had shoved the weight down to ninety feet. He did not suspect that he had been down further than Negri.

I donned my constant-volume diving dress over long woolens, under the eyes of an appreciative audience perched around the rocky lip of the crater. My wife was among them, not liking this venture at all. Dumas wore an Italian Navy frogman outfit. We were loaded like donkeys. Each wore a three-cylinder lung, rubber foot fins, heavy dagger and two large waterproof flashlights, one in hand and one on the belt. Over my left arm was coiled three hundred feet of line in three pieces. Dumas carried an emergency micro-aqualung on his belt, a depth gauge and a *piolet*, the Alpinist's ice axe. There were rock slopes to be negotiated: with our heavy ballast we might need the *piolet*.

The surface commander was the late Lieutenant Maurice Fargues, our resourceful equipment officer. He was to keep his hand on the guide line as we transported the pig iron down with us. The guide rope was our only communication with the surface. We had memorized a signal code. One tug from below requested Fargues to tighten the rope to clear snags. Three tugs means pay out more line. Six tugs was the emergency signal for Fargues to haul us up as quickly as possible.

When the *cordée* reached Negri's siphon, we planned to station the pig iron, and attach to it one of the lengths of rope I carried over my arm. As we climbed on into the siphon, I would unreel this line behind me. We believed that our goal would be found up a long sloping arm of the siphon, in an air cave, where in some manner unknown the annual outburst of Vaucluse was launched.

Embarrassed by our pendant gadgetry and requiring the support of our comrades, we waded into the pool. We looked around for the last time. I saw the reassuring silhouette of Fargues and the crowd jutting around the amphitheater. In their forefront was a young *abbé*, who had come no doubt to be of service in a certain eventuality.

As we submerged, the water liberated us from weight. We stayed motionless in the pool for a minute to test our ballast and communications system. Under my flexible helmet I had a special mouthpiece which allowed me to articulate under water. Dumas had no speaking facility, but could answer me with nods and gestures.

I turned face down and plunged through the dark door. I rapidly passed the buttress into the shaft, unworried about Dumas's keeping pace on the thirty-foot cord at my waist. He can outswim me any time. Our dive was a trial run: we were the first *cordée* of a series. We intended to waste no time on details of topography but proceed directly to the pig iron and take it on to the elbow of Negri's siphon, from which we would quickly take up a new thread into the secret of the Fountain. In retrospect I can also find that my subconscious mechanism was anxious to conclude the first dive as soon as possible.

I glanced back and saw Didi gliding easily through the door against a faint green haze. The sky was no longer our business. We belonged now to a world where no light had ever struck. I could not see my flashlight beam beneath me in the frightening dark—the water had no suspended motes to reflect light. A disc of light blinked on and off in the darkness, when my flashlight beam hit rock. I went head down with tigerish speed, sinking by my overballast, unmindful of Dumas. Suddenly I was held by the belt and stones rattled past me. Heavier borne than I, Dumas was trying to brake his fall with his feet. His suit was filling with water. Big limestone blocks came loose and rumbled down around me. A stone bounced off my shoulder. I remotely realized I should try to think. I could not think.

Ninety feet down I found the pig iron standing on a ledge. It did not appear in the torch beam as an object from the world above, but as something germane to this place. Dimly I recalled that I must do something about the pig iron. I shoved it down the slope. It roared down with Dumas's stones. During this blurred effort I did not notice that I lost the lines coiled on my arm. I did not know that I had failed to give Fargues three tugs on the line to pay out the weight. I had forgotten Fargues, and everything behind. The tunnel broke into a sharper decline. I circled my right hand continuously, playing the torch in spirals on the clean and polished walls. I was traveling at two knots. I was in the Paris subway. I met nobody. There was nobody in the Metro, not a single rock bass. No fish at all.

At that time of year our ears are well trained to pressure after a summer's diving. *Why did my ears ache so?* Something was happening. The light no longer ran around the tunnel walls. The beam spread on a flat bottom, covered with pebbles. It was earth, not rock, the detritus of the chasm. I could find no walls. I was on the floor of a vast drowned cave. My head ached. I was drained of initiative.

I returned to our purpose, to learn the geography of the immensity that had no visible roof or walls, but rolled away down at a forty-five-degree incline. I could not surface without searching the ceiling for the hole that led up to the inner cavern of our theory.

I was attached to something, I remembered. The flashlight picked out a rope which curled off to a strange form floating supine above the pebbles. Dumas hung there in his cumbersome equipment, holding his torch like a ridiculous glowworm. Only his arms were moving. He was sleepily trying to tie his *piolet* to the pig-iron line. His black frogman suit was filling with water. He struggled weakly to inflate it with compressed air. I swam to him and looked at his depth gauge. It read one hundred and fifty feet. The dial was flooded. We were deeper than that. We were at least two hundred feet down, four hundred feet away from the surface at the bottom of a crooked slanting tunnel.

We had rapture of the depths, but not the familiar drunkenness. We felt heavy and anxious, instead of exuberant. Dumas was stricken worse than I. This is what I thought: *I shouldn't feel this way in this depth. . . . I can't go back until I learn where we are. Why don't I feel a current? The pig-iron line is our only way home. What if we lose it? Where is the rope I had on my arm?* I was able in that instant to recall that I had lost the line somewhere above. I took Dumas's hand and closed it around the guide line. "Stay here," I shouted. "I'll find the shaft." Dumas understood me to mean I had no air and needed the safety aqualung. I sent the beam of the flashlight around in search of the roof of the cave. I found no ceiling.

Dumas was passing under heavy narcosis. He thought I was the one in danger. He fumbled to release the emergency lung. As he tugged hopelessly at his belt, he scudded across the drowned shingle and abandoned the guide line to the surface. The rope dissolved in the dark. I was swimming above, mulishly seeking for a wall or a ceiling, when I felt his weight tugging me back like a drifting anchor, restraining my search.

Above us somewhere were seventy fathoms of tunnel and crumbling rock. My weakened brain found the power to conjure up our fate. When our air ran out we would grope along the ceiling and suffocate in dulled agony. I shook off this thought and swam down to the ebbing glow of Dumas's flashlight.

He had lost the better part of his consciousness. When I touched him, he grabbed my wrist with awful strength and hauled me toward him for a final experience of life, an embrace that would take me with him. I twisted out of his hold and backed off. I examined Dumas with the torch. I saw his protruded eyes rolling inside the mask.

The cave was quiet between my gasping breaths. I marshaled all my remaining brain power to consider the situation. Fortunately there was no current to carry Dumas away from the pig iron. If there had been the least current we would have been lost. *The pig iron must be near.* I looked for that rusted metal block, more precious than gold. And suddenly there was the stolid and reassuring pig iron. Its line flew away into the dark, toward the hope of life.

In his stupor, Didi lost control of his jaws and his mouthpiece slipped from his teeth. He swallowed water and took some in his lungs before he somehow got the grip back into his mouth. Now, with the guide line beckoning, I realized that I could not swim to the surface, carrying the inert Dumas, who weighed at least twenty-five pounds in his waterlogged suit. I was in a state of exhaustion from the mysterious effect of the cave. We had not exercised strenuously, yet Dumas was helpless and I was becoming idiotic.

I would climb the rope, dragging Dumas with me. I grasped the pig-iron rope and started up, hand over hand, with Dumas drifting below, along the smooth vertical rock.

My first three hand holds on the line were interpreted correctly by Fargues as the signal to pay out more rope. He did so, with a will. I regarded with utter dismay the phenomena of the rope slackening and made superhuman efforts to climb it. Fargues smartly fed me rope when he felt my traction. It took an eternal minute for me to form the tactic that I should continue to haul down rope, until the end of it came into Fargues's hand. He would never let that go. I hauled rope in dull glee.

Four hundred feet of rope passed through my hands and curled into the cavern. And a knot came into my hands. Fargues was giving us more rope to penetrate the ultimate gallery of Vaucluse. He had efficiently tied on another length to encourage us to pass deeper.

I dropped the rope like an enemy. I would have to climb the tunnel slope like an Alpinist. Foot by foot I climbed the fingerholds of rock, stopping when I lost my respiratory rhythm by exertion and was near to fainting. I drove myself on, and felt that I was making progress. I reached for a good hand hold, standing on the tips of my fins. The crag eluded my fingers and I was dragged down by the weight of Dumas.

The shock turned my mind to the rope again and I received a last-minute remembrance of our signals: six tugs meant pull everything up. I grabbed the line and jerked it, confident that I could count to six. The line was slacked and snagged on obstacles in the four hundred feet to Maurice Fargues. *Fargues, do you not understand my situation?* I was at the end of my strength. Dumas was hanging on me.

Why doesn't Dumas understand how bad he is for me? Dumas, you will die, anyway. Maybe you are already gone. Didi, I hate to do it, but you are dead and you will not let me live. Go away, Didi. I reached for my belt dagger and prepared to cut the cord to Dumas.

Even in my incompetence there was something that held the knife in its holster. *Before I cut you off, Didi, I will try again to reach Fargues.* I took the line and repeated the distress signal, again and again. *Didi, I am doing all a man can do. I am dying too.*

On shore, Fargues stood in perplexed concentration. The first *cordée* had not been down for the full period of the plan, but the strange pattern of our signals disturbed him. His hard but sensitive hand on the rope had felt no clear signals since the episode a few minutes back when suddenly we wanted lots of rope. He had given it to us, eagerly adding another length. *They must have found something tremendous down there,* thought Fargues. He was eager to penetrate the mystery himself on a later dive. Yet he was uneasy about the lifelessness of the rope in the last few minutes. He frowned and fingered the rope like a pulse, and waited.

Up from the lag of rope, four hundred feet across the friction of rocks, and through the surface, a faint vibration tickled Fargues's finger. He reacted by standing and grumbling, half to himself, half to the cave watchers, "*Qu'est-ce que je risque? De me faire engueuler?*" (What do I risk? A bawling out?) With a set face he hauled the pig iron in.

I felt the rope tighten. I jerked my hand off the dagger and hung on. Dumas's air cylinders rang on the rocks as we were borne swiftly up. A hundred feet above I saw a faint triangle of green light, where hope lay. In less than a minute Fargues pulled us out into the pool and leaped in the water after the senseless Dumas. Tailliez and Pinard waded in after me. I gathered what strength I had left to control my emotions, not to break down. I managed to walk out of the pool. Dumas lay on his stomach and vomited. Our friends stripped off our rubber suits. I warmed myself around a flaming caldron of gasoline. Fargues and the doctor worked over Dumas. In five minutes he was on his feet, standing by the fire. I handed him a bottle of brandy. He took a drink and said, "I'm going down again." I wondered where Simone was.

The Mayor said, "When your air bubbles stopped coming to the surface, your wife ran down the hill. She said she could not stand it." Poor Simone had raced to a café in Vaucluse and ordered the most powerful spirit in the house. A rumor monger raced through the village, yelling that one of the divers was drowned. Simone cried, "Which one? What color was his mask?"

"Red," said the harbinger.

Simone gasped with relief—my mask was blue. Then she thought of Didi of the red mask and her joy collapsed. She returned distractedly up the trail to the Fountain. There stood Didi, a miracle to her.

Dumas's recuperative powers put the color back on him and his mind cleared. He wanted to know why we had been drugged in the cavern. In the afternoon another *cordée*, Tailliez and Guy Morandière, prepared to dive, without the junk we had carried. They wore only long underwear and light ballast, which rendered them slightly buoyant. They planned to go to the cavern and reconnoiter for the passage which led to the secret of Vaucluse. Having found it they would immediately return and sketch the layout for the third *cordée*, which would make the final plunge.

From the diving logs of Captain Tailliez and Morandière, I am able to recount their experience, which was almost as appalling as ours. Certainly it took greater courage than ours to enter the Fountain from which we had been luckily saved. In their familiarization period just under the surface of the pool, Morandière felt intense cold. They entered the tunnel abreast, roped together. Second *cordée* tactics were to swim down side by side along the ceiling.

When they encountered humps sticking down from the roof, they were to duck under and return to follow closely the ceiling contour. Each hump they met promised to level off beyond, but never did. They went down and down. Our only depth gauge had been ruined, but the veteran Tailliez had a sharp physiological sense of depth. At an estimated one hundred and twenty feet he halted the march so they might study their subjective sensations. Tailliez felt the first inviting throbs of rapture of the depths. He knew that to be impossible at a mere twenty fathoms. However, the symptoms were pronounced.

He hooted to Morandière that they should turn back. Morandière maneuvered himself and the rope to facilitate Tailliez's turnabout. As he did so, he heard that Tailliez's respiratory rhythm was disorderly, and faced his partner so that Tailliez could see him give six pulls on the pig-iron rope. Unable to exchange words under water, the team had to depend on errant flashlight beams and understanding, to accomplish the turn. Morandière stationed himself below Tailliez to conduct the Captain to the surface. Tailliez construed these activities to mean that Morandière was in trouble. Both men were slipping into the blank rapture that had almost finished the first *cordée*. Tailliez carefully climbed the guide line. The rope behind drifted aimlessly in the water and a loop hung around his shoulders. Tailliez felt he had to sever the rope before it entangled him. He whipped out his dagger and cut it away. Morandière, swimming freely below him, was afraid his mate was passing out. The confused second *cordée* ascended to the green hall light of the Fountain. Morandière closed in, took Tailliez's feet and gave him a strong boost through the narrow door. The effort upset Morandière's breathing cycle.

We saw Tailliez emerge in his white underwear, Morandière following through the underwater door. Tailliez broke the surface, found a footing and walked out of the water, erect and wild-eyed. In his right hand he held his dagger, upside down. His fingers were bitten to the bone by the blade and blood flowed down his sodden woolens. He did not feel it.

We resolved to call it a day with a shallow plunge to map the entrance of the Fountain. We made sure that Didi, in his anger against the cave, could not slip down to the drowned cavern that had nearly been our tomb. Fargues lashed a one hundred and fifty foot line to Dumas's waist and took Didi's dagger so he couldn't cut himself loose and go down further. The final reconnaissance of the entrance shaft passed without incident.

It was an emotional day. That evening in Vaucluse the first and second *cordées* made a subjective comparison of cognac narcosis and rapture of the Fountain. None of us could relax, thinking of the enigmatic stupor that had overtaken us. We knew the berserk intoxication of *l'ivresse des grandes profondeurs* at two hundred and twenty feet in the sea, but why did this clear, lifeless limestone water cheat a man's mind in a different way?

Simone, Didi and I drove back to Toulon that night, thinking hard, despite fatigue and headache. Long silences were spaced by occasional suggestions. Didi said, "Narcotic effects aren't the only cause of diving accidents. There are social and subjective fears, the air you breathe . . ." I jumped at the idea. "The air you breathe!" I said. "Let's run a lab test on the air left in the lungs."

The next morning we sampled the cylinders. The analysis showed 1/2000 of carbon monoxide. At a depth of one hundred and sixty feet the effect of carbon monoxide is sixfold. The amount we were breathing may kill a man in twenty minutes. We started our new

Diesel-powered free-piston air compressor. We saw the compressor sucking in its own exhaust fumes. We had all been breathing lethal doses of carbon monoxide.

Further expeditions were made to the caves of Chartreux and Estramar which taught us much about the problems of cave diving. But we still had not gone through a siphon or the mechanism that shot water earthward. In 1948, while most of us were away on the *Bathyscaphe* expedition, three members of the Group finally achieved the goal, Lieutenant Jean Alinat, Dr. F. Devilla and CPO Jean Pinard, this time assisted by the Army Corps of Engineers. The spring of Vitarelles near Gramat was the object of their large cave expedition.

Vitarelles is a subterranean spring. The surface of the water is three hundred and ninety feet down. The engineers carried out a full-scale dry-cave operation before the divers reached the water. First the soldiers descended an air shaft two hundred and seventy feet deep, lowering pontoons, duckboards, aqualungs, constant-volume suits, lines, electric-lighting equipment, and food. From this landing they conveyed the equipment down another hole, narrow and almost vertical, one hundred and twenty feet to an underground chamber. From this base they were required to lay duckboards and pack the gear sixteen hundred feet through partially flooded galleries, including a dangerous cramped passage thirty feet long. Only then did they reach the surface of the spring, into which the divers were to continue for hundreds of feet more. The engineers established a pontoon pier in the pool, with diving ladders, and the sailors prepared to dive.

Alinat's plan was to send divers down one at a time, on safety ropes of progressively greater lengths. Using measuring lines, flashlights, compasses, depth gauges and sketch blocks, the divers mapped the water tunnel, each one advancing further than the man before. The scheme worked smoothly, and the chart moved league-by-league into the void. The culminating tenth dive was made by Alinat on the 29th of October, 1948.

The diver before him had reached the entrance to a siphon. Alinat went down, fastened to a four-hundred-foot safety line, and rapidly swam to the limit of the chart. The gallery rose at a twenty-degree angle. Alinat swam into the narrow tunnel. He passed uphill through forty feet of rather turbid water in a darkness pierced only by his narrow flashlight beam. He felt his head part a gentle tissue and water resistance ceased. Through his mask, now blurred like a windshield in rain, he saw that his head was in air. He was in a sealed clay vault one hundred and fifty feet long. He removed his mouthpiece and mask and breathed natural air. When water flows, even in a sealed pocket beneath the earth, there is air.

He climbed out on a slippery strand that ranged down one side of the long room. He was the first living thing in the vault of water, earth and air, where no sun had ever brought the gift of life. He walked along the shore, measuring and sketching, elated with the victory of our campaigns against the fountains.

At the far end, Alinat received a bitter revelation. Plain under the clear water was the aperture of another siphon. The mechanism of Vitarelles held further secrets. Alinat sat down and thought of the cost of penetrating the new labyrinth. The divers would have to transport equipment nearly four hundred feet under water to set up an advanced camp in the clay room, before they could plunge into the second siphon.

Alinat finished his sketch and walked back to the entrance, imprinting rubber frog tracks on the hidden beach. He spit in the mask and sloshed it in the water. He molded the mask over his face and inserted the mouth grip. He slipped into the water, turned up his flukes and sailed head down through the current of the first siphon. In a few minutes his exhalations sputtered out on the surface. Nothingness was restored in the cave. The tracks of man vanished into darkness.

The Silent World, by Jacques-Yves Cousteau

JOHN WILKES BOOTH

"... He would snatch victory at this last moment."

John Wilkes Booth thought of himself as a Brutus striking down an intolerable tyrant . . . and in a twisted way he was right. But far from bringing about the results he had envisaged, Booth's act led inevitably to chaos. He lost his own life and the cause in which he believed suffered immeasurably. Nothing Booth could have done could have hurt the South more. The compassionate Lincoln was replaced by a weaker man who could not hold back the vindictive onslaught of the northern extremists. With Lincoln gone, the William Lloyd Garrisons, the Horace Greeleys and the Charles Sumners made the South suffer moral penance in flesh and goods for thirty years. The wounds they inflicted have still not healed. And much, if not all, of this was the result of the act of one deranged 26-year-old actor. . . .

Here is the core of that sickening tragedy taken from Philip Van Doren Stern's fictionalized biography that startlingly recreates that ugly 14th day of April, 1865. . . .

BOOTH OPENED his trunk and took out of it a single-barreled deringer pistol. He pulled back the hammer and snapped the trigger to make certain that it was in perfect working order. Then he loaded the barrel carefully and placed a percussion cap under the hammer. His fingers closed around the tiny wooden stock, and the weapon, which was only six inches long, lay in his hand completely concealed. He would have only one shot, one chance. If the gun misfired he would be forced to use his knife, but his mind shrank from the thought of having to plunge its blade into the back of the unsuspecting man who would be sitting in the box. The pistol was so much more remote, so much more impersonal in its action, and, above all, if he succeeded with it, he would not have to touch the body of the man he was going to kill.

He took out a false beard and some material he could use for disguising himself. He had already scornfully rejected the idea of entering the theater in disguise, since he wanted to be identified as the slayer of his country's enemy, but he saw no reason why he should not employ such a device if he needed it during his flight afterwards.

He lay down on the bed. The dark little room was close and stuffy. The furniture and carpet had a smell of ancient dust about them that even the fresh air of springtime coming through the open window could not dispel. He could hear the street sounds that always seem to be unduly loud at night, and, as he looked at the ceiling, he could see vague shadows move across it.

What I am going to do now, he thought, will break my life sharply into halves that can never be joined together again. From now on I shall have to be another person, a fugitive who can never return to this land. . . .

He had to go out now—outside on the streets. He felt lonely and afraid, like a small boy who realizes that he is going away from home for the first time to be among people who are hostile and strange. . . .

He took the little deringer in his hand. The feel of it gave him strength. The simple pressure of his finger on the trigger would send thunder crashing into the world to obliterate the monster Lincoln. This one small weapon might have a greater effect than all the huge mortars, howitzers, and cannon that had been fired during the last four years. His single shot would start their mighty voices roaring again. . . . He would snatch victory at this last moment. . . . He heard the people of the South acclaiming him. . . . No actor in all the world's history had ever had such an ovation.

And yet he might fail. He might be stopped before he reached Lincoln's side. Someone in the box might strike up his hand. And how could he be certain that the pistol would fire? He began to walk up and down the room with the deringer in his hand, his finger held loosely over the trigger.

The fate of a nation depends on the functioning of this bit of steel and wood, on the fallibility of this tiny percussion cap, he thought. He examined the little weapon carefully. Single-shot pistols were sometimes uncertain in their action, and wartime percussion caps had often been known to fail. He would surely not have time to pull out another pistol if the first one misfired.

He went to the window and looked out at the street with these disturbing thoughts running through his mind. Here within the confines of this skull, he said to himself, looking out on the world through these eyes, is the being that is John Wilkes Booth. From the center of this being, within a few hours now, destiny will go forth at my bidding to change the fate of nations and alter the history of mankind. In one brief instant I shall strike down the colossus that bestrides this world and shatter his image into nothingness. His name and mine will forever be associated.

He could see himself standing in the box, holding the pistol to Lincoln's head. The report of the shot would freeze the play into sudden silence, and then his moment would come. Tyranny. Tyranny. What could he say about tyranny? "Liberty! Freedom! Tyranny is dead! Run hence, proclaim, cry it about the streets." How had they phrased this in Latin when Brutus struck great Caesar down? *Libertas. Tyr—tyrannis.* . . . He knew no Latin. *Tyrannis.* . . . And then it came to him suddenly: *Sic semper tyrannis!* "Thus always to tyrants." That was the motto of Virginia, the capital State of the Confederacy. *Sic semper tyrannis!* It was the very phrase he needed. He mouthed it over, rolling the r's under his tongue.

The bells of the city began to strike eight o'clock. The metallic clangor of their tongues rolled through the dark streets. He slipped the pistol into his pocket and armed himself with several heavy revolvers and a knife.

The curtain at Ford's Theater had already been raised. . . . Booth's horse clattered down the narrow alley that led to the open space in back of the theater. Negro women, sitting on the steps of their shanties, ceased talking when they heard the horse approach. It was completely dark except for the light of a single lamp over the stage entrance at the far end of the alley. No one was in sight near the theater. Booth dismounted and led his horse to the doorway. He stepped inside, holding the reins over his arm. A man was standing in the passageway near the door.

"Tell Ned Spangler to come out here for a minute, will you?" Booth asked quietly.

The man recognized him and sauntered off in search of Spangler. Booth examined the mare's saddle-girth. He made sure that the deringer was in his pocket, and he loosened his bowie knife in its sheath. Then he looked up at the narrow slit of sky where the stars were shining between scattered clouds. Rain would be fatal. It would turn the clay roads of Southern Maryland into a morass of sticky, impassable mud.

There were so many things beyond his control, he thought, so many things that could defeat him. Courage, even reckless courage, was not enough. The little gods of chance that can cause a pistol to misfire, or a blundering guard to get in the way, must withhold their spitefulness now, or he would fail and be lost.

The Negro women began to talk again. He could hear the soft murmur of their voices coming from the darkness beyond the circle of light around the stage door. He patted the smooth flank of his mare, and she turned her head inquiringly to look at him. . . .

Then Spangler came out of the doorway, cursing angrily.

"Damn it! I can't be ordered out here like this, Mr. Booth," the man was saying. "I've got to be on the stage. They'll be changing sets in a few minutes. I can't stand here holding a horse."

"Then get someone who can," Booth told him peremptorily. "I have business here that can't wait. But be sure the horse is held here for me."

He thrust the reins into Spangler's unwilling hands and asked him if the President had arrived. The man nodded sullenly. Booth swung around and entered the theater.

"May I cross the stage now?" he whispered to one of the actors standing inside.

"No. The dairy scene has just gone on, and the stage is open all the way back. You can't get across. Go down underneath."

Booth stood for a few minutes in the wings, looking at the brilliantly lighted stage. The actors moved about busily, eager to catch a laugh from the audience seated in the black void beyond the footlights. Tall piles of scenery were stacked around him, and he could smell the familiar odor of paint, hot gaslight, and freshly cut lumber.

The sight of the play being enacted before him gave him new courage. What he had to do seemed very simple now. He had only to walk on to play his part as he had done a thousand times before. He had killed dozens of men with sword and pistol—on the stage. He had made all sorts of desperate gestures—on the stage. What he was about to do now could not be so very different. He had only to wait for his cue: *Don't know the manners of good society, eh?*" And there was plenty of time, plenty of time before he would be called upon to act. He would have a chance to reinforce himself with brandy as he always did before undertaking the performance of a new and difficult part.

He went down the stairs to the understage passage and walked through, groping in the darkness. He could hear the shuffling of feet on the boards overhead, and the players' voices came to him as disembodied sounds, permeating the blackness with the strange senseless quality of words chattered in delirium. Words like these were too dangerously close to the echoes of sounds that sometimes rose up from the depths of his own mind, terrifying him with their insistent urging, their dark summoning. . . . He was glad when he got beyond their reach to the open street in front of the theater.

The sidewalk was brightly illuminated. Two soldiers were sitting on the wooden carriage platform under a flaring gas lantern. The downward rays of the lamp threw their features into strong relief, making their eyes seem like black holes, and drawing heavy lines of shadow across their mouths. They stopped talking and stared at Booth.

Immediately he sensed danger. Perhaps these men were special guards detailed to the theater. The War Department might have learned something. . . . Could these soldiers have been sent here to watch the theater? And then he realized why they were looking at him. Why, of course! He was John Wilkes Booth, the famous actor. What could be more natural than for these yokels to gape at a celebrity? He turned away, stroking his mustache impressively. He had forgotten his own fame.

He looked at the clock in the lobby. It was still early. He stood and watched the scene on the sidewalk. Some curiosity-seekers, attracted by the advertised presence of the President as the guest of honor, were gazing at the playbills posted in front of the house. "Benefit and last night of Miss Laura Keene, the distinguished Manageress, Authoress and Actress . . . in Tom Taylor's celebrated eccentric comedy, as originally produced in America by Miss Keene, and performed by her upwards of one thousand nights, entitled *Our American Cousin.*" . . .

He paced up and down on the sidewalk. By God, at this moment he should be on the stage! Never had he felt the vast surge of energy so tremendous within him. He could move an audience to tears, to shouts, to wild salvos of applause. It was a pity that he had to wait until after ten o'clock. He wished that he could leap upon the stage now, to stand defiant before the footlights, bringing the flaming spirit of war and vengeance to these Yankees who were sitting in the theater, smug with the thought that victory was already theirs. But they would never forget this coming moment, never forget this single figure who would fling the cry "Unconquered!" in their faces while they sat helpless in the very heart of their own Northern citadel. . . .

He looked at the lobby clock that was marking away the minutes to ten o'clock. They would be talking about him tomorrow . . . his name would be on the lips of every cracker-barrel commentator in the country. They would all have a new factor to contend with in their discussions of the problems of war and peace.

He turned away . . . to look down the street toward Pennsylvania Avenue. Someone in uniform was approaching, beckoning to him as he came. Booth . . . put his hand in the pocket where he had placed his pistol. The man in uniform entered the circle of lamplight, calling out a hearty greeting to Booth. It was Captain Williams of the Washington police force, a man whom Booth knew well.

"What's the matter, Wilkes?" he said, surprised by the startled expression on Booth's face. "You look as if you expected me to arrest you. And I must say that you seem to be prepared to make a desperate stand."

Booth laughed nervously and held out his hand to his friend.

"I thought you might want to step in somewhere for a drink with me," Williams said. "I have a wonderful little story to tell you about a certain lady who is playing right now in a theater not a million miles away from here."

Booth smiled at him, and clasped his shoulder with a show of good nature. "It breaks my heart to turn down an invitation like that, Captain, but Keene will be on the stage in a minute and I promised to look in on her performance tonight."

Williams lingered a moment, trying to persuade Booth to come with him. Finally, he went on his way, and Booth's tensed muscles relaxed. What terrible coincidence had caused this man to cross his tracks at this crucial instant? And was it coincidence? He looked again at the two soldiers sitting on the carriage platform. They were no longer paying any attention to him, he noticed with relief. . . . He looked up at the lobby clock. The minute hand had crept forward to five minutes to ten. Paine and Herold should be riding toward Lafayette Square now. . . .

Buckingham, the theater's tall lanky doorkeeper, was standing with his back to the lobby. His arm barred the entrance way. Booth touched his hand lightly. Buckingham turned around, scowling.

"I guess you don't need a ticket from me, do you?" Booth asked pleasantly. The doorkeeper's long homely face cracked into a wide grin.

"No, sir, I should say not. Fact is you couldn't buy a ticket here if you tried to. Courtesy of the house, sir." He bowed sweepingly. "Go right in." He was proud of his acquaintance with this young star who was so democratic in his relationships with the theater's people.

He lowered his arm and stepped back, still grinning good-naturedly. Booth entered the theater. The house was well filled with an audience in which blue army uniforms predominated. The stage lights filtered back into the auditorium with a soft glow that emphasized the white shoulders of women and brought out the metallic gleam of epaulets and army insignia on the men.

The dairy set, which was used for the first scene of the third act, was on the stage, but the scene still had some time to run. Booth walked to the rear row of seats and stood behind it. The state box was brightly lighted by one of the two big chandeliers that hung over the stage, but it was difficult to see inside the box. Flags and lace curtains concealed the opening. He could just make out the forms of

an army officer and a young girl in evening dress, and he could see a
rather stout woman who was probably Mrs. Lincoln. Lincoln himself
was hidden from the audience by the front wall of the box. Evidently the armchair had not been moved.

Booth walked over to look into the boxes on the other side of the
stage. They were all empty. This was so unusual that it frightened
him for a moment. Could there be some purpose in not selling any
of the seats in the other boxes? Then he realized that this had probably been done for the protection of the President, and the idea gave
him a certain grim pleasure. It was a fortunate thing, after all, since
no one could look directly across the stage into the rear part of the
state box where Lincoln was seated.

Booth walked across the theater again and went up the dress-circle
stairs. As he reached the top, his eyes immediately sought the little
white door leading into Lincoln's box. He expected to find a guard
seated at the entrance. A chair was standing there beside the door,
half-hidden in the darkness, but it was empty and no one was near it.
The guard had evidently wandered off in search of a better seat from
which to watch the performance. All the little gods of chance were
with him now, he felt, and they had even given him this unforeseen
opportunity of entering the box without being challenged.

He went down the stairs, exulting. Surely destiny was on his side!
Second by second the clocks of the world were eating away the life of
the man he was going to kill. Paine and Herold were moving toward
the Seward residence, and somewhere in the dimly lighted corridors
of the Kirkwood House, Atzerodt was lying in wait for Johnson. He
could only hope that someone was on the train with Grant. . . . In
less than ten minutes the fatal second scene of the third act would be
on. Booth decided that he needed a drink. . . .

The far end of the long bar was still covered with glasses left by
the theatergoers during the last intermission. Taltavul was leisurely
putting the glassware on a tray. He walked forward and greeted Booth
cordially.

"What'll it be this evening?" he asked, wiping the surface of the
bar in front of Booth with a beer-stained rag.

"Same as usual, Peter. The brandy bottle and a glass of water."

"Quite an honor having the President next door," Taltavul com-
mented cheerfully. "I wish he'd come oftener. It's good for business.
There's a fine crowd there tonight." He pushed a bottle of brandy
toward Booth and filled a glass with water.

Booth indicated that he was glad the President's visit was good for
business.

"Well, to tell the truth, I can't complain about business anyway,"

Taltavul said, wringing out the wet rag. He leaned on the bar and thrust his grizzled face toward Booth. "Business has been very good. Yes, sir, very good. This celebration, you know. . . ." He winked solemnly. "A lot of liquor went down the nation's gullet when Richmond fell."

Booth finished two glasses of brandy and then stepped back to see the clock at the front of the bar. Seven minutes after. They would be changing scenes in a few minutes now. Just time for another drink. He filled his glass again. This was the last drink he would ever be able to take in the city of Washington. He lifted the glass in a silent toast to the Confederacy. So many people were counting on him . . . so much human happiness depended on his success . . . the South . . . the old South—God bless her!

Taltavul was still talking about the celebration. Booth realized that he was asking him a question.

"Sorry, Peter," he said. "I didn't hear you. What did you say?"

"Thinking about the ladies again, eh, Mr. Booth?" Taltavul chuckled. "Well, I can't blame you. I do myself sometimes. I was just asking you, did you think they would hold a big parade—you know, bring all the soldiers here to march down the Avenue, maybe?"

"Undoubtedly . . . undoubtedly." Booth took up the water glass and drank from it, staring at the barkeeper over its rim. Victory, victory, victory—all these filthy little shopkeepers were thinking of nothing but victory and their own profits.

"God, wouldn't that be magnificent?" Taltavul said gleefully. "All them soldier boys brought here to Washington, and every one of 'em thirsty."

Booth put some money down on the wet bar. Taltavul started to make change, but his customer had already left the saloon, humming a tune as he went.

The air outside was cool and fresh. Most of the loiterers had gone, but Gifford was waiting. He seemed surprised to see Booth come out of Taltavul's saloon, but he immediately collared him and tried to engage him in conversation again. Booth felt that it was impossible even to attempt to be polite to the man now—he had to get rid of him quickly. The play inside was moving on, line by line, to the moment when his cue would be spoken. He had to be in the theater before then, and he could allow nothing to stop him.

Gifford was standing in the lobby entrance, blocking his way. Booth interrupted his flow of meaningless words and asked him abruptly: "Can you see the time on the lobby clock?"

Gifford turned to look, and Booth took advantage of his movement to slip past him.

"Ten minutes after ten," Gifford announced in a loud voice. "What's your hurry?" he asked in surprise. "Miss Keene won't be on for at least five minutes yet."

Booth felt Gifford's hand touch his arm. This restraining gesture drove him to such fury that the thought of knocking the man down occurred to him. Then he controlled himself, and in a normal voice said: "I want to find a comfortable seat somewhere—if there is one." He paused, using up some of his time which had now become precious. "You can understand that, can't you?" he said, smiling ingratiatingly. "I don't often have the privilege of seeing a play from the front of the house, you know."

Gifford grinned sympathetically and released his arm. Booth went through the lobby. . . . He watched the actors wearily, waiting for his moment to come. The play moved on with deadly slowness. I am tired of the life of the theater, he thought. I have had enough of being Macbeth, Hamlet, Brutus, Pescara, and all the others who strut the stage for an hour, mouthing another man's words. I have become death's emissary in order to rid myself of the many ghosts I have caused to walk the earth again, speaking through my voice, living in my body. Away with them! They are as insubstantial as everything else in this world that I have dreamed. I lent them reality for a moment, as I lend it now to the people here around me. . . .

He knew then he must go up the stairs to the dress circle. He turned to the left of the orchestra pit, and with slow deliberate steps began the ascent. He could see the image of the lobby clock before him as he went, and it seemed to him that his own feet were keeping time with the monotonous beat of its heavy pendulum. As he stepped on to the dress-circle floor he saw Harry Hawk appear on the stage to play Asa Trenchard's part.

"Ah, Mr. Trenchard, we were just talking of your archery powers," Mrs. Montchessington said in a voice that seemed even louder and more raucous than usual.

He could hear Asa Trenchard answer in the drawling Yankee tones that reminded him of Lincoln's homely accents. "Wal, I guess shooting with bows and arrows is just about like most things in life. All you've got to do is keep the sun out of your eyes, look straight—pull strong—calculate the distance, and you're sure to hit the mark in most things as well as shooting."

Well spoken, Harry! Good advice even if you don't realize what your words suggest at this moment, Booth thought. He leaned against the back wall of the theater and looked around the house. The guard's chair at the entrance to the President's box was still vacant.

The play dragged on, its unreal comedy lines drawing unreal laughter from the audience. Like puppets pulled with strings the actors moved and gesticulated before the absurdly painted flat with its two huge vases and its writhing, tangled mass of drapery. Booth waited motionless, patient—although consumed with a vast impatience—his eyes intent upon the President's box. He saw Lincoln's hand reach out and place itself on the box-rail. His own hands were hot with sweat, and he kept digging his fingers into his palms.

Now the moment was very near. Mrs. Montchessington was learning that Asa Trenchard was not the millionaire she had imagined him to be. "No heir to the fortune, Mr. Trenchard?"

"Oh, no."

Augusta cried out: "What, no fortune?"

"Nary red," Trenchard told her cheerfully, "it all comes to their barking up the wrong tree about the old man's property."

These were the lines that came just before his cue. In a few seconds Harry Hawk would be alone upon the stage. Booth unhurriedly began his progress across the back of the dress circle. His feet made no sound on the carpeted floor, and he glided along the wall, hands outstretched, feeling his way in the semidarkness. His black-clad, high-booted figure moved stealthily toward the door that led to the President's box. Asa Trenchard's sallies filled the house with laughter as he went. (A droll fellow, this Yankee, he'll put the English snobs in their places before he's through.) Down the steps now, the white door beckoning. Booth's face was rigid as his jaw muscles clenched, and his eyes stared into the darkness ahead of him. Step by step, nearer and nearer—the door was close to him now. He seized the knob and pushed his knee against the panel.

A man seated near the box entrance suddenly rose and approached him. Booth's hand reached under his coat for his knife. Then he realized what he was doing, and he turned, ready to placate this inquisitive stranger. He drew out his cardcase and showed the man one of Senator Hale's calling cards. The man backed away, apologizing.

Now the way is clear. Trenchard's remarks sweep the house with laughter again. The door swings open, and Booth is inside the passageway at last. He closes the door behind him and stands there with his hand on the knob, his heart pounding, and his breath coming in short spasmodic gasps. There is no light inside the narrow passage, and he is alone in utter darkness. He feels for the wooden bar he had left in the corner behind the door, and his fingers close around its smooth square sides—only a moment's work to slip it in place, clos-

ing the only entrance to the box against all intruders. Quickly, quickly
now. There is no time to be lost. That fellow outside the door has
made him lose precious seconds. The voices on the stage muffled and
far away, have been speaking, and he listens to them carefully for his
first cue.

"Augusta, dear, to your room."

"Yes, Ma. The nasty beast!"

"I am aware, Mr. Trenchard, that you are not used to the manners
of good society—"

The words send a sudden quiver through him. He knows that he
will hear them again, and then he will have to act. Mechanically he
moves toward the second door. The hole he had cut in the panel
gleams in the darkness—a single malignant eye, unblinking and steady,
drawing him toward it. He peers into the box—the high back of the
armchair is in front of him, and he can see a dark head rising above it.
Mrs. Lincoln is leaning toward her husband, speaking to him. Beyond
them the lights from the stage shine through the lace curtains that
hang like a mist in the background.

It is time for the two women to leave the stage now, and Booth
listens for Asa Trenchard's words which will tell him when they are
gone.

Now the final summons is about to be spoken. The Yankee voice
gives him the words: *"Don't know the manners of good society, eh?"*

There can be no hesitation. This is the moment! His final cue has
been spoken, and he must make his entrance. His pistol is ready in
his hand. His breath rushes into his lungs—can they hear the terrible
sound of it? His left hand turns the doorknob—the door opens, letting
in the light—his feet move silently on the carpet. . . . The people
in the box are all watching the stage. They do not notice him. He
steps forward, raising his hand with the deringer in it. He holds it
close to that hated head. There must be no chance of missing. Now!
Now! Asa Trenchard's voice still drawls on: "Well, I guess I know
enough to turn you inside out, you sockdologizing old man-trap—"

And then the report, sharp and loud—the pistol almost seemed to
go off by itself, kicking his hand upward. *"Sic semper tyrannis!"* he
cries. He has done it! He has done it! He has killed Lincoln! The
man in the chair never moves. He sits there, his head sagging forward,
white smoke billowing around him. Mrs. Lincoln's face, upturned
and startled, looks into Booth's for an instant. The officer at the other
end of the box is standing up, and Booth sees him coming toward
him. He drops his empty pistol and draws his knife. The officer lunges
at him. Booth slashes quickly with the dagger. He feels the blade tear
through cloth and flesh. The man clutches for an instant at his own

arm, but he makes another attempt to seize Booth, snatching at his coat-tails as he turns toward the edge of the box. The knife jabs back again and Booth is free. Over the box-rail now to the stage, the light burning in his eyes, and a tearing sound as he jumps—one of his spurs has caught in the flag draping the box, and he is thrown off balance. He lands on the stage heavily, all his weight on his left foot. It crumples under him, and he sprawls on the floor, half unconscious from the terrible stab of pain.

He gets up and almost falls again. Harry Hawk has stopped speaking and is looking at him wonderingly. Booth is up now, and he begins to run across the stage, forcing himself to bear the pain that is crippling him. The lines he had intended to speak at this supreme moment are forgotten; he struggles desperately to reach the protection of the wings. The audience, puzzled by what has happened, and thinking that perhaps it is all part of the play, watches him in silence.

Then there comes a scream from the President's box. A man sitting in the front row of the orchestra scrambles up on the stage and runs after Booth. Laura Keene comes out from the wings. Booth rushes past her, nearly colliding with a young actor who is just behind her. The audience begins to shout. Mrs. Lincoln is still screaming.

Booth runs with uncertain steps into the long passage that leads to the stage door. Someone tries to bar his way. He strikes with his knife, and the man scuttles out of his path. He is at the stage door now, tugging frantically at its handle. He hears the heavy tread of a running man behind him. The door opens with a rush of cool night air, and the quiet darkness of the theater alley lies before him.

A boy is lying on a bench near the stage door idly holding the mare's reins. He tries to get up, but Booth pushes him violently away and strikes at him with the handle of his knife. The horse shies. Booth seizes the reins, and the frightened animal stands still long enough to permit him to get his foot into the stirrup. As he springs up to mount the horse, the weight of his body on his injured foot sends another paralyzing wave of pain through him. He manages to scramble into the saddle, clutching in agony at the pommel. The horse starts off with a clatter of hoofs, tossing its head at this sudden strange treatment. The man who has followed him out of the theater tries to grasp the reins, but the horse is too quick for him. Booth kicks her side with his right foot and heads her down the alley, which lies muddy and deserted in the darkness.

The Man Who Killed Lincoln, by Philip Van Doren Stern

FRANCISCO PIZARRO

"He did not know the character of the Spaniard."

They were called Conquistadors—*a word so grand and so chivalric in its sound that it has never needed translation. History has drawn of them some noble portraits—civilizers, saviors of the soul of the infidels. Novelists have placed them on horseback, in gleaming steel armor, black eyes searching the distant horizon—symbols of honor in an age of chivalry. Yet in reality, they were only the jackals who followed in the wake of the discoverer, hungry for nothing but gold and the power it would bring them. They killed and pillaged until they could find nothing more—and then they turned on each other.*

The history of the Conquistadors *becomes, at times, almost unbelievably bloody. Francisco Pizarro, illegitimate son of a Spanish nobleman, was a good soldier, a brave man and a resourceful explorer. And like so many of his compatriots he was ruthless to a point of inhumanity. W. H. Prescott wrote* The Conquest of Peru *in 1847, but even today there exists no better portrait than the one he drew of the men who conquered and raped a continent in this bloody opening of a new era.*

The clouds of the evening had passed away, and the sun rose bright on the [that] morning, the most memorable epoch in the annals of Peru. It was Saturday, the sixteenth of November, 1532. The loud cry of the trumpet called the Spaniards to arms with the first streak of dawn; and Pizarro, briefly acquainting them with the plan of the assault, made the necessary dispositions.

The *plaza* was defended on its three sides by low ranges of buildings, consisting of spacious halls with wide doors or vomitories opening into the square. In these halls he stationed his cavalry in two divisions, one under his brother Hernando, the other under De Soto. The infantry he placed in another of the buildings, reserving twenty chosen men to act with himself as occasion might require. Pedro de Candia, with a few soldiers and the artillery—comprehending under this imposing name two small pieces of ordnance, called falconets— he established in the fortress.

All received orders to wait at their posts till the arrival of the Inca. After his entrance into the great square, they were still to remain under cover, withdrawn from observation, till the signal was given by the discharge of a gun, when they were to cry their war cries, to rush out in a body from their covert, and, putting the Peruvians to the sword, bear off the person of the Inca.

The arrangement of the immense halls, opening on a level with the *plaza*, seemed to be contrived on purpose for a *coup de théâtre*. Pizarro particularly inculcated order and implicit obedience, that in the hurry of the moment there should be no confusion. Everything depended on their acting with concert, coolness, and celerity.

The chief next saw that their arms were in good order; and that the breastplates of their horses were garnished with bells, to add by their noise to the consternation of the Indians. Refreshments were, also, liberally provided, that the troops should be in condition for the conflict.

These arrangements being completed, mass was performed with great solemnity by the ecclesiastics who attended the expedition; the God of battles was invoked to spread his shield over the soldiers who were fighting to extend the empire of the Cross; and all joined with enthusiasm in the chant, *"Exsurge, Domine,"* "Rise, O Lord! and judge thine own cause." One might have supposed them a company of martyrs, about to lay down their lives in defense of their faith, instead of a licentious band of adventurers, meditating one of the most atrocious acts of perfidy on the record of history! Yet, whatever were the vices of the Castilian cavalier, hypocrisy was not among the number.

He felt that he was battling for the Cross, and under this conviction, exalted as it was at such a moment as this into the predominant impulse, he was blind to the baser motives which mingled with the enterprise. With feelings thus kindled to a flame of religious ardor, the soldiers of Pizarro looked forward with renovated spirits to the coming conflict; and the chieftain saw with satisfaction, that in the hour of trial his men would be true to their leader and themselves.

It was late in the day before any movement was visible in the Peruvian camp, where much preparation was making to approach the Christian quarters with due state and ceremony. A message was received from Atahuallpa, informing the Spanish commander that he should come with his warriors fully armed, in the same manner as the Spaniards had come to his quarters the night preceding. This was not an agreeable intimation to Pizarro, though he had no reason, probably, to expect the contrary. But to object might imply distrust, or, perhaps, disclose, in some measure, his own designs. He expressed his satisfaction, therefore, at the intelligence, assuring the Inca, that, come as he would, he would be received by him as a friend and brother.

It was noon before the Indian procession was on its march, when it was seen occupying the great causeway for a long extent. In front came a large body of attendants, whose office seemed to be to sweep away every particle of rubbish from the road. High above the crowd appeared the Inca, borne on the shoulders of his principal nobles, while others of the same rank marched by the sides of his litter, displaying such a dazzling show of ornaments on their persons, that, in the language of one of the Conquerors, "they blazed like the sun." But the greater part of the Inca's forces mustered along the fields that lined the road, and were spread over the broad meadows as far as the eye could reach.

When the royal procession had arrived within half a mile of the city, it came to a halt; and Pizarro saw with surprise that Atahuallpa was preparing to pitch his tents, as if to encamp there. A messenger soon after arrived, informing the Spaniards that the Inca would occupy his present station the ensuing night, and enter the city on the following morning.

This intelligence greatly disturbed Pizarro, who had shared in the general impatience of his men at the tardy movements of the Peruvians. The troops had been under arms since daylight, the cavalry mounted, and the infantry at their post, waiting in silence the coming of the Inca. A profound stillness reigned throughout the town, broken only at intervals by the cry of the sentinel from the summit of the fortress, as he proclaimed the movements of the Indian army.

Nothing, Pizarro well knew, was so trying to the soldier as prolonged suspense, in a critical situation like the present; and he feared lest his ardor might evaporate, and be succeeded by that nervous feeling natural to the bravest soul at such a crisis, and which, if not fear, is near akin to it. He returned an answer, therefore, to Atahuallpa, deprecating his change of purpose; and adding that he had provided everything for his entertainment, and expected him that night to sup with him.

This message turned the Inca from his purpose; and, striking his tents again, he resumed his march, first advising the general that he should leave the greater part of his warriors behind, and enter the place with only a few of them, and without arms, as he preferred to pass the night at Caxamalca. At the same time he ordered accommodations to be provided for himself and his retinue in one of the large stone buildings, called, from a serpent sculptured on the walls, "The House of the Serpent." No tidings could have been more grateful to the Spanish. It seemed as if the Indian monarch was eager to rush into the snare that had been spread for him! The fanatical cavalier could not fail to discern in it the immediate finger of Providence.

It is difficult to account for this wavering conduct of Atahuallpa, so different from the bold and decided character which history ascribes to him. There is no doubt that he made his visit to the white men in perfect good faith; though Pizarro was probably right in conjecturing that this amiable disposition stood on a very precarious footing.

There is as little reason to suppose that he distrusted the sincerity of the strangers; or he would not thus unnecessarily have proposed to visit them unarmed. His original purpose of coming with all his force was doubtless to display his royal state, and perhaps, also, to show greater respect for the Spaniards; but when he consented to accept their hospitality, and pass the night in their quarters, he was willing to dispense with a great part of his armed soldiery, and visit them in a manner that implied entire confidence in their good faith.

He was too absolute in his own empire easily to suspect; and he probably could not comprehend the audacity with which a few men, like those now assembled in Caxamalca, meditated an assault on a powerful monarch in the midst of his victorious army. He did not know the character of the Spaniard.

It was not long before sunset, when the van of the royal procession entered the gates of the city. First came some hundreds of the menials, employed to clear the path from every obstacle, and singing songs of triumph as they came, "which, in our ears," says one of the Conquerors, "sounded like the songs of hell"! Then followed other bodies of different ranks, and dressed in different liveries. Some wore a showy stuff, checkered white and red, like the squares of a chessboard. Others were clad in pure white, bearing hammers or maces of silver or copper; and the guards, together with those in immediate attendance on the prince, were distinguished by a rich azure livery, and a profusion of gay ornaments, while the large pendants attached to the ears indicated the Peruvian noble.

Elevated high above his vassals came the Inca Atahuallpa, borne on a sedan or open litter, on which was a sort of throne made of massive gold of inestimable value. The palanquin was lined with the richly colored plumes of tropical birds, and studded with shining plates of gold and silver. The monarch's attire was much richer than on the preceding evening. Round his neck was suspended a collar of emeralds of uncommon size and brilliancy. His short hair was decorated with golden ornaments, and the imperial *borla* encircled his temples. The bearing of the Inca was sedate and dignified; and from his lofty station he looked down on the multitudes below with an air of composure, like one accustomed to command.

As the leading files of the procession entered the great square, larger, says an old chronicler, than any square in Spain, they opened to the right and left for the royal retinue to pass. Everything was conducted with admirable order. The monarch was permitted to traverse the *plaza* in silence, and not a Spaniard was to be seen. When some five or six thousand of his people had entered the place, Atahuallpa halted, and, turning round with an inquiring look, demanded, "Where are the strangers?"

At this moment Fray Vicente de Valverde, a Dominican friar, Pizarro's chaplain, and afterward Bishop of Cuzco, came forward with his breviary, or, as other accounts say, a Bible, in one hand, and a crucifix in the other, and, approaching the Inca, told him, that he came by order of his commander to expound to him the doctrines of the true faith, for which purpose the Spaniards had come from a great distance to his country. The friar then explained, as clearly as he could, the mysterious doctrine of the Trinity, and, ascending high in his account, began with the creation of man, thence passed to his fall, to his subsequent redemption by Jesus Christ, to the crucifixion, and the ascension, when the Saviour left the Apostle Peter as his Vicegerent upon earth.

This power had been transmitted to the successors of the Apostle, good and wise men, who, under the title of Popes, held authority over all powers and potentates on earth.

One of the last of these Popes had commissioned the Spanish emperor, the most mighty monarch in the world, to conquer and convert the natives in this western hemisphere; and his general, Francisco Pizarro, had now come to execute this important mission. The friar concluded with beseeching the Peruvian monarch to receive him kindly; to abjure the errors of his own faith, and embrace that of the Christians now proffered to him, the only one by which he could hope for salvation; and, furthermore, to acknowledge himself a tributary of the Emperor Charles the Fifth, who, in that event, would aid and protect him as his loyal vassal.

Whether Atahuallpa possessed himself of every link in the curious chain of argument by which the monk connected Pizarro with St. Peter, may be doubted. It is certain, however, that he must have had very incorrect notions of the Trinity, if, as Garcilasso states, the interpreter Felipillo explained it by saying, that "the Christians believed in three Gods and one God, and that made four." But there is no doubt he perfectly comprehended that the drift of the discourse was to persuade him to resign his scepter and acknowledge the supremacy of another.

The eyes of the Indian monarch flashed fire, and his dark brow grew darker as he replied—"I will be no man's tributary. I am greater than any prince upon earth. Your emperor may be a great prince; I do not doubt it, when I see that he has sent his subjects so far across the waters; and I am willing to hold him as a brother. As for the Pope of whom you speak, he must be crazy to talk of giving away countries which do not belong to him. For my faith," he continued, "I will not change it. Your own God, as you say, was put to death by the very men whom he created. But mine," he concluded, pointing to his Deity —then, alas! sinking in glory behind the mountain—"my God still lives in the heavens, and looks down on his children."

He then demanded Valverde by what authority he had said these things. The friar pointed to the book which he held, as his authority. Atahuallpa, taking it, turned over the pages a moment, then, as the insult he had received probably flashed across his mind, he threw it down with vehemence, and exclaimed—"Tell your comrades that they shall give me an account of their doings in my land. I will not go from here, till they have made me full satisfaction for all the wrongs they have committed."

The friar, greatly scandalized by the indignity offered to the sacred volume, stayed only to pick it up, and, hastening to Pizarro, informed him of what had been done, exclaiming, at the same time—"Do you not see, that, while we stand here wasting our breath in talking with this dog, full of pride as he is, the fields are filling with Indians? Set on, at once; I absolve you." Pizarro saw that the hour had come. He waved a white scarf in the air, the appointed signal. The fatal gun was fired from the fortress.

Then, springing into the square, the Spanish captain and his followers shouted the old war cry of "St. Jago and at them."

It was answered by the battle cry of every Spaniard in the city, as, rushing from the avenues of the great halls in which they were concealed, they poured into the *plaza*, horse and foot, each in his own dark column, and threw themselves into the midst of the Indian crowd. The latter, taken by surprise, stunned by the report of artillery and muskets, the echoes of which reverberated like thunder from the surrounding buildings, and blinded by the smoke which rolled in sulphurous volumes along the square, were seized with a panic.

They knew not whither to fly for refuge from the coming rain. Nobles and commoners—all were trampled down under the fierce charge of the cavalry, who dealt their blows, right and left, without sparing; while their swords, flashing through the thick gloom, carried dismay into the hearts of the wretched natives, who now, for the first time, saw the horse and his rider in all their terrors.

They made no resistance—as, indeed, they had no weapons with which to make it. Every avenue to escape was closed, for the entrance to the square was choked up with the dead bodies of men who had perished in vain efforts to fly; and, such was the agony of the survivors under the terrible pressure of their assailants, that a large body of Indians, by their convulsive struggles, burst through the wall of stone and dried clay which formed part of the boundary of the *plaza!* It fell, leaving an opening of more than a hundred paces, through which multitudes now found their way into the country, still hotly pursued by the cavalry, who, leaping the fallen rubbish, hung on the rear of the fugitives, striking them down in all directions.

Meanwhile the fight, or rather massacre, continued hot around the Inca, whose person was the great object of the assault. His faithful nobles, rallying about him, threw themselves in the way of the assailants, and strove, by tearing them from their saddles, or, at least, by offering their own bosoms as a mark for their vengeance, to shield their beloved master. It is said by some authorities, that they carried weapons concealed under their clothes. If so, it availed them little, as it is not pretended that they used them. But the most timid animal will defend itself when at bay. That they did not so in the present instance is proof that they had no weapons to use. Yet they still continued to force back the cavaliers, clinging to their horses with dying grasp, and, as one was cut down, another taking the place of his fallen comrade with a loyalty truly affecting.

The Indian monarch, stunned and bewildered, saw his faithful subjects falling round him without fully comprehending his situation. The litter on which he rode heaved to and fro, as the mighty press swayed backwards and forwards; and he gazed on the overwhelming ruin, like some forlorn mariner, who, tossed about in his bark by the furious elements, sees the lightning's flash and hears the thunder bursting around him with the consciousness that he can do nothing to avert his fate. At length, weary with the work of destruction, the Spaniards, as the shades of evening grew deeper, felt afraid that the royal prize might, after all, elude them; and some of the cavaliers made a desperate attempt to end the affray at once by taking Atahuallpa's life. But Pizarro, who was nearest his person, called out with stentorian voice, "Let no one, who values his life, strike at the Inca"; and, stretching out his arm to shield him, received a wound on the hand from one of his own men—the only wound received by a Spaniard in the action.

The struggle now became fiercer than ever round the royal litter. It reeled more and more, and at length, several of the nobles who supported it having been slain, it was overturned, and the Indian prince would have come with violence to the ground, had not his fall been broken by the efforts of Pizarro and some other of the cavaliers, who caught him in their arms. The imperial *borla* was instantly snatched from his temples by a soldier named Estete, and the unhappy monarch, strongly secured, was removed to a neighboring building, where he was carefully guarded.

All attempt at resistance now ceased. The fate of the Inca soon spread over town and country. The charm which might have held the Peruvians together was dissolved. Every man thought only of his own safety. Even the soldiery encamped on the adjacent fields took the alarm, and, learning the fatal tidings, were seen flying in every direction before their pursuers, who in the heat of triumph showed no touch of mercy. At length night, more pitiful than man, threw her friendly mantle over the fugitives, and the scattered troops of Pizarro rallied once more at the sound of the trumpet in the bloody square of Caxamalca.

The Conquest of Peru, by W. H. Prescott

ENOS ABIJAH MILLS

"Blind on the summit of the Continental Divide."

A forester and naturalist, Enos A. Mills worked for many years in the U. S. Forest Service. He was one of those responsible for the creation of Glacier National Park and Rocky Mountain National Park. The recorded accomplishments of his life are not particularly remarkable or newsworthy. This story, however, is one of the most fascinating tales of individual fortitude and perseverance we have ever read. Mills was a State Snow Observer, whose job was to estimate the summer's water supply in the valleys and on the plains by estimating how much snow there was on the mountain peaks. His job was a lonely one—and one which took him high into the deserted mountain ranges of the Rockies. Here is a picture of resourcefulness and courage in the face of unarming death. In many ways it can teach a lesson to all of us.

As I CLIMBED up out of the dwarfed woods at timberline in the Rocky Mountains, and started across the treeless white summit, the terrific sun glare on the snow warned me of the danger of snow-blindness. I had lost my snow glasses. But the wild attractions of the heights caused me to forget the care of my eyes and I lingered to look down into canyons. A number of mountain sheep also interested me. Then for half an hour I circled a confiding flock of ptarmigan and took picture after picture.

Through the clear air the sunlight poured with burning intensity. I was 12,000 feet above the sea. Around me there was not a dark crag nor even a tree to absorb the excess of light. A wilderness of high, rugged peaks stood about—splendid sunlit mountains of snow. To east and west they faced winter's noonday sun with great shadows flowing from their shoulders.

As I started to hurry on across the pass, I began to experience the scorching pains that go with seared, sunburnt eyes—snow-blindness. Unfortunately, I had failed to take even the precaution of blackening my face, which would have dulled the glare. At the summit my eyes became so painful that I could endure the light only a few seconds at a time. Occasionally I sat down and closed them for a minute or two. Finally, while doing this, the lids adhered to the balls and the eyes swelled so that I could not open them.

Blind on the summit of the Continental Divide! I made a grab for my useful staff which I had left standing beside me in the snow. In the fraction of a second that elapsed between thinking of the staff and finding it, my brain awoke to the seriousness of the situation. To the nearest trees it was more than a mile, and the nearest house was many miles away across ridges of rough mountains. I had matches and a hatchet, but no provisions. Still, while well aware of my peril, I was only moderately excited, feeling no terror. Less startling incidents have shocked me more; narrow escapes from street automobiles have terrified me.

It had been a wondrous morning. The day cleared after a heavy fall of fluffy snow. I had snowshoed up the slope through a ragged, snow-carpeted spruce forest, whose shadows wrought splendid black-and-white effects upon the shining floor. There were thousands of towering, slender spruces, each brilliantly laden with snow flowers, standing soft, white, and motionless in the sunlight. While I was looking at one of these artistically decorated trees, a mass of snow dropped upon me from its top, throwing me headlong and causing me to lose my precious eye-protecting snow glasses. But now I was blind.

With staff in hand, I stood for a minute or two planning the best manner in which to get along without eyes. My faculties were intensely awake. Serious situations in the wilds had more than once before this stimulated them to do their best. Temporary blindness is a good stimulus for the imagination and the memory—in fact, it is good educational training for all the senses. However perilous my predicament during a mountain trip, the possibility of a fatal ending never even occurred to me. Looking back now, I cannot but wonder at my matter-of-fact attitude concerning the perils in which that snow-blindness placed me.

I had planned to cross the pass and descend into a trail at timberline. The appearance of the slope down which I was to travel was distinctly in my mind from my impressions, just before darkness settled over me.

Off I slowly started. I guided myself with information from feet and staff, feeling my way with the staff so as not to step off a cliff or walk overboard into a canyon. In imagination I pictured myself following the shadow of a staff-bearing and slouch-hatted form. Did mountain sheep, curious and slightly suspicious, linger on crags to watch my slow and hesitating advance? Across the snow did the shadow of a soaring eagle coast and circle?

I must have wandered far from the direct course to timberline. Again and again I swung my staff to right and left, hoping to strike a tree. I had traveled more than twice as long as it should have taken to reach timberline before I stood face to face with a low-growing tree that bristled up through the deep snow. But had I come out at the point for which I aimed—at the trail? This was the vital question.

The deep snow buried all trail blazes. Making my way from tree to tree I thrust an arm deep into the snow and felt of the bark, searching for a trail blaze. At last I found a blaze and going on a few steps I dug down again into the snow and examined a tree which I felt should mark the trail. This, too, was blazed.

Feeling certain that I was on the trail, I went down the mountain through the forest for some minutes without searching for another blaze. When I did examine a number of trees not another blaze could I find. The topography since entering the forest and the size and character of the trees were such that I felt I was on familiar ground. But going on a few steps I came out on the edge of an unknown rocky cliff. I was now lost as well as blind.

During the hours I had wandered in reaching timberline, I had had a vague feeling that I might be traveling in a circle, and might return to trees on the western slope of the Divide up which I had climbed. When I walked out on the edge of the cliff the feeling that I had doubled to the western slope became insistent. If true, this was most serious. To reach the nearest house on the west side of the range would be extremely difficult, even though I should discover just where I was. But I believed I was somewhere on the eastern slope.

I tried to figure out the course I had taken. Had I, in descending from the heights, gone too far to the right or to the left? Though fairly well acquainted with the country along this timberline, I was unable to recall a rocky cliff at this point. My staff found no bottom and warned me that I was at a jumping-off place.

Increasing coolness indicated that night was upon me. But darkness did not matter; my light had failed at noon. Going back along my trail a short distance I avoided the cliff and started on through the night down a rocky, forested, and snow-covered slope. I planned to get into the bottom of a canyon and follow downstream. Every few steps I shouted, hoping to attract the attention of a possible prospector, miner, or woodchopper. No voice answered. The many echoes, however, gave me an idea of the topography—of the mountain ridges and canyons before me. I listened intently after each shout and noticed the direction from which the reply came—its intensity and the cross echoes—and concluded that I was going down into the head of a deep, forest-walled canyon, and, I hoped, traveling eastward.

For points of the compass I appealed to the trees, hoping through my knowledge of woodcraft to orient myself. In the study of tree distribution I had learned that the altitude might often be approximated and the points of the compass determined by noting the characteristic kinds of trees.

Canyons of east-and-west trend in this locality carried mostly limber pines on the wall that faces south and mostly Engelmann spruces on the wall that faces the north. Believing that I was traveling eastward, I turned to my right, climbed out of the canyon, and examined a number of trees along the slope. Most of these were Engelmann spruces. The slope probably faced north. Turning about, I descended this slope and ascended the opposite one. The trees on this were mostly limber pines. Hurrah! Limber pines are abundant only on southern slopes. With limber pines on my left and Engelmann spruces on my right, I was now satisfied that I was traveling eastward and must be on the eastern side of the range.

To put a final check upon this—for a blind or lost man sometimes manages to do exactly the opposite of what he thinks he is doing—I examined lichen growths on the rocks and moss growths on the trees. In the deep canyon I dug down into the snow and examined the faces of low-lying boulders. With the greatest care I felt the lichen growth on the rocks. These verified the information that I had from the trees —but none too well. Then I felt over the moss growth, both long and short, on the trunks and lower limbs of trees, but this testimony was not absolutely convincing. The moss growth was so nearly even all the way around the trunk that I concluded that the surrounding topography must be such as to admit the light freely from all quarters, and also that the wall or slope on my right must be either a gentle one or else a low one and somewhat broken. I climbed to make sure. In a few minutes I was on a terrace—as I expected. Possibly back on the right lay a basin that might be tributary to this canyon. The reports made by the echoes of my shoutings said that this was true. A few minutes of travel down the canyon and I came to the expected incoming stream, which made its swift presence heard beneath its cover of ice and snow.

A short distance farther down the canyon I examined a number of trees that stood in thick growth on the lower part of what I thought was the southern slope. Here the character of the moss and lichens and their abundant growth on the northerly sides of the trees verified the testimony of the tree distribution and of previous moss and lichen growths. I was satisfied as to the points of the compass. I was on the eastern side of the Continental Divide, traveling eastward.

After three or four hours of slow descending I reached the bottom.

Steep walls rose on both right and left. The enormous rock masses and the entanglements of fallen and leaning trees made progress difficult. Feeling that if I continued in the bottom of the canyon I might come to a precipitous place down which I would be unable to descend, I tried to walk along one of the side walls, and thus keep above the bottom. But the walls were too steep and I got into trouble.

Out on a narrow ledge I walked. The snow gave way beneath me and down I went over the ledge. As I struck, feet foremost, one snowshoe sank deeply. I wondered, as I wiggled out, if I had landed on another ledge. I had. Not desiring to have more tumbles, I tried to climb back up on the ledge from which I had fallen, but I could not do it. The ledge was broad and short and there appeared to be no safe way off. As I explored again my staff encountered the top of a dead tree that leaned against the ledge. Breaking a number of dead limbs off, I threw them overboard. Listening as they struck the snow below, I concluded that it could not be more than thirty feet to the bottom.

I let go my staff and dropped it after the limbs. Then, without taking off snowshoes, I let myself down the limbless trunk. I could hear water running beneath the ice and snow. I recovered my staff and resumed the journey.

In time the canyon widened a little and traveling became easier. I had just paused to give a shout when a rumbling and crashing high up the right-hand slope told me that a snowslide was plunging down. Whether it would land in the canyon before me or behind me or on top of me could not be guessed. The awful smashing and crashing and roar proclaimed it of enormous size and indicated that trees and rocky debris were being swept onward with it. During the few seconds that I stood awaiting my fate, thought after thought raced through my brain as I recorded the ever-varying crashes and thunders of the wild, irresistible slide.

With terrific crash and roar the snowslide swept into the canyon a short distance in front of me. I was knocked down by the outrush or concussion of air and for several minutes was nearly smothered with the whirling, settling snow dust and rock powder which fell thickly all around. The air cleared and I went on.

I had gone only a dozen steps when I came upon the enormous wreckage brought down by the slide. Snow, earthy matter, rocks, and splintered trees were flung in fierce confusion together. For three or four hundred feet this accumulation filled the canyon from wall to wall and was fifty or sixty feet high. The slide wreckage smashed the ice and dammed the stream. As I started to climb across this snowy debris a shattered place in the ice beneath gave way and dropped me into the water, but my long staff caught and by clinging to it I saved myself from going in above my hips. My snowshoes caught in the shattered ice, and while I tried to get my feet free a mass of snow fell upon me and nearly broke my hold. Shaking off the snow, I put forth all my strength and finally pulled my feet free of the ice and crawled out upon the debris. This was a close call and at last I was thoroughly frightened.

As the wreckage was a mixture of broken trees, stones, and snow, I could not use my snowshoes; so I took them off to carry them until I was over the debris. Once across, I planned to pause and build a fire to dry my icy clothes.

With difficulty I worked my way up and across the debris. Much of the snow was compressed almost to ice by the force of contact, and in this icy cement many kinds of wreckage were set in wild disorder. While descending a steep place in this mass, carrying snowshoes under one arm, my footing gave way and I fell. I suffered no injury but I lost one of the snowshoes. For an hour or longer I searched for it but I did not find it.

The night was intensely cold and, in the search, my feet became almost frozen. In order to rub them I was about to take off my shoes when I came upon something warm. It proved to be a dead mountain sheep with one horn broken off. As I sat with my feet beneath its warm carcass and my hands upon it, I thought how but a few minutes before the animal had been alive on the heights with all its ever wide-awake senses vigilant for its preservation; yet I, wandering blindly, had escaped with my life when the snowslide swept into the canyon. The night was calm, but of zero temperature or lower. It probably was crystal clear. As I sat warming my hands and feet on the proud master of the crags I imagined the bright, clear sky crowded thick with stars. I pictured to myself the dark slope down which the slide had come. It appeared to reach up close to the frosty stars.

But the lost snowshoe must be found; wallowing through the deep mountain snow with only one snowshoe would be almost hopeless. I had vainly searched the surface and lower wreckage projections, but made one more search. This proved successful. The shoe had slid for a short distance, struck an obstacle, bounced upward over smashed logs, and lay about four feet above the general surface. A few minutes and I was beyond the snowslide wreckage. Again on snowshoes, staff in hand, I continued feeling my way down the mountain.

My ice-stiffened trousers and chilled limbs were not good traveling companions, and at the first cliff that I encountered I stopped to make a fire. I gathered two or three armfuls of dead limbs, with the aid of my hatchet, and soon had a lively blaze going. But the heat increased the pain in my eyes; so with clothes only partly dried I went on. Repeatedly through the night I applied snow to my eyes, trying to subdue the fiery torment.

From timberline I had traveled downward through a green forest mostly of Engelmann spruce with a scattering of fir and limber pine. I frequently felt of the tree trunks. But a short time after leaving my campfire I came to the edge of an extensive region that had been burned over. For more than an hour I traveled through dead standing trees, on many of which only the bark had been burned away; on others the fire had burned more deeply.

Pausing on the way down, I thrust my staff into the snow and leaned against a tree to hold snow against my burning eyes. While I was doing this two owls hooted happily to each other, and I listened to their contented calls with satisfaction.

Hearing the pleasant, low call of a chickadee, I listened. Apparently he was dreaming and talking in his sleep. The dream must have been a happy one, for every note was cheerful. Realizing that he probably was in an abandoned woodpecker nesting hole, I tapped on the dead tree against which I was leaning. This was followed by a chorus of lively, surprised chirpings, and one, two, three!—then several—chickadees flew out of a hole a few inches above my head. Sorry to have disturbed them, I went on.

At last I felt the morning sun in my face. With increased light my eyes became extremely painful. For a time I relaxed upon the snow, finding it difficult to believe that I had been traveling all night in complete darkness. While lying here I caught the scent of smoke. There was no mistaking it. It was the smoke of burning aspen, a wood much burned in the cookstoves of mountain people. Eagerly I rose to find it. I shouted again and again but there was no response.

Down the mountainside I went, hour after hour. My ears caught the chirp of birds and the fall of icicles which ordinarily I would hardly have heard. My nose was constantly and keenly analyzing the air. With touch and clasp I kept in contact with the trees. Again my nostrils picked up aspen smoke. This time it was much stronger. Perhaps I was near a house! But the whirling air currents gave me no clue as to the direction from which the smoke came, and only echoes responded to my call.

All my senses worked willingly in seeking wireless news to substitute for the eyes. My nose readily detected odors and smoke. My ears were more vigilant and more sensitive than usual. My fingers, too, were responsive from the instant that my eyes failed. Delightfully eager they were, as I felt the snow-buried trees, hoping with touch to discover possible trail blazes. My feet also were quickly, steadily alert to translate the topography.

Occasionally a cloud shadow passed over. In imagination I often pictured the appearance of these clouds against the blue sky and tried to estimate the size of each by the number of seconds its shadow took to drift across me.

Mid-afternoon, or later, my nose suddenly detected the odor of an ancient corral. This was a sign of civilization. A few minutes later my staff came in contact with the corner of a cabin. I shouted, "Hello!" but heard no answer. I continued feeling until I came to the door and found that a board was nailed across it. The cabin was locked and deserted! I broke in the door.

In the cabin I found a stove and wood. As soon as I had a fire going I dropped snow upon the stove and steamed my painful eyes. After two hours or more of this steaming they became more comfortable. Two strenuous days and one toilsome night had made me extremely drowsy. Sitting down upon the floor near the stove, I leaned against the wall and fell asleep. But the fire burned itself out. In the night I awoke nearly frozen and unable to rise. Fortunately, I had on mittens; otherwise my fingers probably would have frozen. By rubbing my hands together, then rubbing my arms and legs, I finally managed to limber myself, and though unable to rise, I succeeded in starting a new fire. It was more than an hour before I ceased shivering; then, as the room began to warm, my legs came back to life, and again I could walk.

I was hungry. This was my first thought of food since becoming blind. If there was anything to eat in the cabin, I failed to find it. Searching my pockets, I found a dozen or more raisins and with these I broke my sixty-hour fast. Then I had another sleep, and it must have been near noon when I awakened. Again I steamed the eye pain into partial submission.

Going to the door, I stood and listened. A campbird only a few feet away spoke gently and confidingly. Then a crested jay called impatiently. The campbird alighted on my shoulder. I tried to explain to the birds that there was nothing to eat. The prospector who had lived in this cabin evidently had been friendly with the bird neighbors.

Again I could smell the smoke of aspen wood. Several shouts evoked echoes—nothing more. I stood listening and wondering whether to stay in the cabin or to venture forth and try to follow the snow-filled roadway that must lead down through the woods from the cabin. Wherever this open way led I could follow. But, of course, I must take care not to lose it.

In the nature of things I felt that I must be three or four miles to the south of the trail which I had planned to follow down the mountain. I wished I might see my long and crooked line of foot-marks in the snow from the summit to timberline.

Hearing the open water in rapids close to the cabin, I went out to try for a drink. I advanced slowly, blind-man fashion, feeling the way with my long staff. As I neared the rapids, a water ouzel, which prob-ably had lunched in the open water, sang with all his might. I stood still as he repeated his liquid, hopeful song. On the spot I shook off procrastination and decided to try to find a place where someone lived.

After writing a note explaining why I had smashed in the door and used so much wood, I readjusted my snowshoes and started down through the woods. I suppose it must have been late afternoon.

I found an open way that had been made into a road. The woods were thick and the open roadway readily guided me. Feeling and thrusting with my staff, I walked for some time at normal pace.

For a short distance the road ran through dense woods. Several times I paused to touch the trees on each side with my hands. When I emerged from the woods, the pungent aspen smoke said that I must at last be near a human habitation. In fear of passing it, I stopped to use my ears. As I stood listening, a little girl gently, curiously, asked:

"Are you going to stay here tonight?"

The Adventures of a Nature Guide, by Enos A. Mills

THE LIGHT BRIGADE

"C'est magnifique, mais ce n'est pas la guerre."

In the opening pages of her magnificent book, The Reason Why, Cecil Woodham-Smith describes the future Lord Cardigan by saying, "He was, alas, unusually stupid; in fact, as Greville pronounced later, an ass. The melancholy truth was that his glorious golden head had nothing in it." This was the man destined to lead the Light Brigade to its infamous, glorious annihilation at Balaclava in the Crimea.

The seeds of disaster had all been planted long before the day of that frightful charge. The Brigade was commanded by general officers who had bought their original commissions, and had paid handsomely for every advance in rank. None of them, with exception of Lord Raglan, had any previous experience under fire. Worst of all, Lord Cardigan and his immediate superior, Lord Lucan, were brothers-in-law who despised each other so violently that they spoke only at times of military necessity.

This, then, was the situation on that fateful day of October 25, 1854. . . .

WITH A SIGH of relief the watchers saw him (Nolan) arrive safely, gallop furiously across the plain, and, with his horse trembling, sweating, and blown from the wild descent, hand the order to Lord Lucan sitting in the saddle between his two brigades. Lucan opened and read it.

The order appeared to him to be utterly obscure. Lord Raglan and General Airey had forgotten that they were looking down from six hundred feet. Not only could they survey the whole action, but the inequalities of the plain disappeared when viewed from above. Lucan from his position could see nothing; inequalities of the ground concealed the activity round the redoubts, no single enemy soldier was in sight; nor had he any picture of the movements of the enemy in his mind's eye, because he had unaccountably neglected to take any steps to acquaint himself with the Russian dispositions. He should, after receiving the third order, have made it his business to make some form of reconnaissance; he should, when he found he could see nothing from his position, have shifted his ground—but he did not.

He read the order "carefully," with the fussy deliberateness which maddened his staff, while Nolan quivered with impatience at his side. It seemed to Lord Lucan that the order was not only obscure but absurd: artillery was to be attacked by cavalry; infantry support was not mentioned; it was elementary that cavalry charging artillery in such circumstances must be annihilated. In his own account of these fatal moments Lucan says that he "hesitated and urged the uselessness of such an attack and the dangers attending it"; but Nolan, almost insane with impatience, cut him short and "in a most authoritative tone" repeated the final message he had been given on the heights: "Lord Raglan's orders are that the cavalry are to attack immediately."

For such a tone to be used by an aide-de-camp to a lieutenant-general was unheard of; moreover, Lord Lucan was perfectly aware that Nolan detested him and habitually abused him. It would have been asking a very great deal of any man to keep his temper in such circumstances, and Lord Lucan's temper was violent. He could see nothing, "neither enemy nor guns being in sight," he wrote, nor did he in the least understand what the order meant. He turned angrily on Nolan, "Attack, sir? Attack what? What guns, sir?"

The crucial moment had arrived. Nolan threw back his head, and, "in a most disrespectful and significant manner," flung out his arm and, with a furious gesture, pointed, not to the Causeway Heights and the redoubts with the captured British guns, but to the end of the North Valley, where the Russian cavalry routed by the Heavy Brigade were now established with their guns in front of them. "There, my lord, is your enemy, there are your guns," he said, and with those words and that gesture the doom of the Light Brigade was sealed.

What did Nolan mean? It has been maintained that his gesture was merely a taunt, that he had no intention of indicating any direction, and that Lord Lucan, carried away by rage, read a meaning into his outflung arm which was never there.

The truth will never be known, because a few minutes later Nolan was killed, but his behaviour in that short interval indicates that he did believe the attack was to be down the North Valley and on those guns with which the Russian cavalry routed by the Heavy Brigade had been allowed to retire.

It is not difficult to account for such a mistake. Nolan, the cavalry enthusiast and a cavalry commander of talent, was well aware that a magnificent opportunity had been lost when the Light Brigade failed to pursue after the charge of the Heavies. It was, indeed, the outstanding, the flagrant error of the day, and he must have watched with fury and despair as the routed Russians were suffered to withdraw in safety with the much-desired trophies, their guns. When he received the fourth order, he was almost off his head with excitement and impatience, and he misread it. He leapt to the joyful conclusion that at last vengeance was to be taken on those Russians who had been suffered to escape.

And so he plunged down the heights and with a contemptuous gesture, scorning the man who in his opinion was responsible for the wretched mishandling of the cavalry, he pointed down the North Valley. "There, my lord, is your enemy; there are your guns."

Lord Lucan felt himself to be in a hideous dilemma. His resentment against Lord Raglan was indescribable; the orders he had received during the battle had been, in his opinion, not only idiotic and ambiguous, but insulting. He had been treated, he wrote later, like a subaltern. He had been peremptorily ordered out of his first position—the excellent position chosen in conjunction with Sir Colin Campbell—consequently after the charge of the Heavies there had been no pursuit. He had received without explanation a vague order to wait for infantry. What infantry? Now came this latest order to take his division and charge to certain death. Throughout the campaign he had had bitter experience of orders from Lord Raglan, and now he foresaw ruin; but he was helpless. The Queen's Regulations laid down that "all orders sent by aides-de-camp . . . are to be obeyed with the same readiness, as if delivered personally by the general officers to whom such aides are attached." The Duke of Wellington himself had laid this down. Had Lord Lucan refused to execute an order brought by a member of the headquarters staff and delivered with every assumption of authority he would, in his own words, have had no choice but "to blow his brains out."

Nolan's manner had been so obviously insolent that observers thought he would be placed under arrest. Lord Lucan, however, merely shrugged his shoulders, and turning his back on Nolan, trotted off, alone, to where Lord Cardigan was sitting in front of the Light Brigade.

Nolan then rode over to his friend Captain Morris, who was sitting in his saddle in front of the 17th Lancers—the same Captain Morris who had urged Lord Cardigan to pursue earlier in the day—and received permission to ride beside him in the charge.

There was now a pause of several minutes, and it is almost impossible to believe that Nolan, sitting beside his close friend and sympathiser, did not disclose the objective of the charge. If Nolan had believed the attack was to be on the Causeway Heights and the redoubts, he must surely have told Captain Morris. Morris, however, who survived the charge though desperately wounded, believed the attack was to be on the guns at the end of the North Valley.

Meanwhile Lord Lucan, almost for the first time, was speaking directly and personally to Lord Cardigan. Had the two men not detested each other so bitterly, had they been able to examine the order together and discuss its meaning, the Light Brigade might have been saved. Alas, thirty years of hatred could not be bridged; each, however, observed perfect military courtesy. Holding the order in his hand, Lord Lucan informed Lord Cardigan of the contents and ordered him to advance down the North Valley with the Light Brigade, while he himself followed in support with the Heavy Brigade.

Lord Cardigan now took an astonishing step. Much as he hated the man before him, rigid as were his ideas of military etiquette, he remonstrated with his superior officer. Bringing down his sword in salute, he said, "Certainly, sir; but allow me to point out to you that the Russians have a battery in the valley on our front, and batteries and riflemen on both sides."

Lord Lucan once more shrugged his shoulders. "I know it," he said, "but Lord Raglan will have it. We have no choice but to obey." Lord Cardigan made no further comment, but saluted again; Lord Lucan then instructed him to "advance very steadily and keep his men well in hand." Lord Cardigan saluted once more, wheeled his horse, and rode over to his second-in-command, Lord George Paget, remarking aloud to himself as he did so, "Well, here goes the last of the Brudenells."

Most of the officers and men of the Light Brigade were lounging by their horses, the officers eating biscuits and hard-boiled eggs and drinking rum and water from their flasks. One or two of the men had lighted pipes, and were told to put them out at once, and not disgrace their regiments by smoking in the presence of the enemy. Lord George Paget, who had just lighted a cigar, felt embarrassed. Was he setting a bad example? Ought he to throw away his excellent cigar, a rarity in Balaclava? While he was debating the point, Lord Cardigan rode up and said, "Lord George, we are ordered to make an attack to the front. You will take command of the second line, and I expect your best support—mind, your best support." Cardigan, who was very much excited, repeated the last sentence twice very loudly, and Lord George, rather irritated, replied as loudly, "You shall have it, my lord." It was the first intimation Lord George had had of an intended attack; he thought it was permissible to keep his cigar, and noticed that it lasted him until he got to the guns.

Lord Cardigan now hastened at a gallop back to his troops and drew the Brigade up in two lines: the first the 13th Light Dragoons, 11th Hussars, and the 17th Lancers; the second the 4th Light Dragoons and the main body of the 8th Hussars. A troop of the 8th Hussars, under Captain Duberly, had been detached to act as escort to Lord Raglan.

At the last moment Lord Lucan irritatingly interfered and ordered the 11th Hussars to fall back in support of the first line, so that there were now three lines, with the 13th Light Dragoons and the 17th Lancers leading. Lord Lucan's interference was made more annoying by the fact that he gave the order, not to Cardigan, but directly to Colonel Douglas, who commanded the 11th. Moreover, the 11th was Cardigan's own regiment, of which he was inordinately proud, and the 11th was taken out of the first line, while the 17th Lancers, Lucan's old regiment, remained.

Lord Cardigan meanwhile had placed himself quite alone, about two lengths in front of his staff and five lengths in advance of his front line. He now drew his sword and raised it, a single trumpet sounded, and without any signs of excitement and in a quiet voice he gave the orders, "The Brigade will advance. Walk, march, trot," and the three lines of the Light Brigade began to move, followed after a few minutes' interval by the Heavy Brigade, led by Lord Lucan. The troop of Horse Artillery was left behind because part of the valley was ploughed.

The North Valley was about a mile and a quarter long and a little less than a mile wide. On the Fedioukine Hills, which enclosed the valley to the north, were drawn up eight battalions of infantry, four squadrons of cavalry, and fourteen guns; on the Causeway Heights to the south were the bulk of the eleven battalions, with thirty guns and a field battery which had captured the redoubts earlier in the day; at the end of the valley, facing the Light Brigade, the mass of the Russian cavalry which had been defeated by the Heavy Brigade was drawn up in three lines, with twelve guns unlimbered before them, strengthened by six additional squadrons of Lancers, three on each flank. The Light Brigade was not merely to run a gauntlet of fire: it was advancing into a deadly three-sided trap, from which there was no escape.

The Brigade was not up to strength, cholera and dysentery having taken their toll—the five regiments present could muster only about seven hundred of all ranks, and both regiments in the first line, the 17th Lancers and the 13th Light Dragoons, were led by captains, Captain Morris and Captain Oldham respectively.

Nevertheless, the Brigade made a brave show as they trotted across the short turf. They were the finest light horsemen in Europe, drilled and disciplined to perfection, bold by nature, filled with British self-confidence, burning to show the "damned Heavies" what the Light Brigade could do.

As the Brigade moved, a sudden silence fell over the battlefield: by chance for a moment gun and rifle fire ceased, and the watchers on the heights felt the pause was sinister. More than half a century afterwards old men recalled that as the Light Brigade moved to its doom a strange hush fell, and it became so quiet that the jingle of bits and accoutrements could be clearly heard.

The Brigade advanced with beautiful precision, Lord Cardigan riding alone at their head, a brilliant and gallant figure. It was his great day: he was performing the task for which he was supremely well fitted, no power of reflection or intelligence was asked of him, dauntless physical courage was the only requirement, and he had, as Lord Raglan said truly, "the heart of a lion." He rode quietly at a trot, stiff and upright in the saddle, never once looking back: a cavalry commander about to lead a charge must keep strictly looking forward; if he looks back, his men will receive an impression of uncertainty.

He wore the gorgeous uniform of the 11th Hussars and, living as he did on his yacht, he had been able to preserve it in pristine splendour. The bright sunlight lit up the brilliance of cherry colour and royal blue, the richness of fur and plume and lace; instead of wearing his gold-laced pelisse dangling from his shoulders, he had put it on as a coat, and his figure, slender as a young man's, in spite of his fifty-seven years, was outlined in a blaze of gold. He rode his favourite charger, Ronald, "a thoroughbred chestnut of great beauty," and as he led his Brigade steadily down the valley towards the guns, he was, as his aide-de-camp Sir George Wombwell wrote, "the very incarnation of bravery."

Before the Light Brigade had advanced fifty yards, the hush came to an end: the Russian guns crashed out, and great clouds of smoke rose at the end of the valley. A moment later an extraordinary and inexplicable incident took place. The advance was proceeding at a steady trot when suddenly Nolan, riding beside his friend Captain Morris in the first line, urged on his horse and began to gallop diagonally across the front. Morris thought that Nolan was losing his head with excitement, and, knowing that a mile and a quarter must be traversed before the guns were reached, shouted, "That won't do, Nolan! We've a long way to go and must be steady." Nolan took no notice; galloping madly ahead and to the right, he crossed in front of Lord Cardigan—an unprecedented breach of military etiquette—and, turning in his saddle, shouted and waved his sword as if he would address the Brigade, but the guns were firing with great crashes, and not a word could be heard. Had he suddenly realised that his interpretation of the order had been wrong, and that in his impetuosity he had directed the Light Brigade to certain death? No one will ever know, because at that moment a Russian shell burst on the right of Lord Cardigan, and a fragment tore its way into Nolan's breast, exposing his heart. The sword fell from his hand, but his right arm was still erect, and his body remained rigid in the saddle. His horse wheeled and began to gallop back through the advancing Brigade, and then from the body there burst a strange and appalling cry, a shriek so unearthly as to freeze the blood of all who heard him. The terrified horse carried the body, still shrieking, through the 4th Light Dragoons, and then at last Nolan fell from the saddle, dead.

Lord Cardigan, looking strictly straight ahead and not aware of Nolan's death, was transported with fury. It was his impression that Nolan had been trying to take the command of the Brigade away from him, to lead the charge himself; and so intense was his rage that when he was asked what he thought about as he advanced towards the guns, he replied that his mind was entirely occupied with anger against Nolan.

The first few hundred yards of the advance of the Light Brigade covered the same ground, whether the attack was to be on the guns on the Causeway Heights or the guns at the end of the valley. The Russians assumed that the redoubts were to be charged, and the watchers on the heights saw the Russian infantry retire first from redoubt No. 3 and then from No. 2 and form hollow squares to receive the expected charge; but the Light Brigade, incredibly, made no attempt to wheel. With a gasp of horror, the watchers saw the lines of horsemen continue straight on down the North Valley.

The Russian artillery and riflemen on the Fedioukine Hills and the slopes of the Causeway Heights were absolutely taken by surprise; it was not possible to believe that this small force trotting down the North Valley in such beautiful order intended to attempt an attack on the battery at the end of the valley, intended, utterly helpless as it was, to expose itself to a cross-fire, of the most frightful and deadly kind, to which it had no possibility of replying. There was again a moment's pause, and then from the Fedioukine Hills on one side and the Causeway Heights on the other, battalion upon battalion of riflemen, battery upon battery of guns, poured down fire on the Light Brigade.

When advancing cavalry are caught in a withering fire and are too courageous to think of retreat, it is their instinct to quicken their pace, to gallop forward as fast as individual horses will carry them and get to grips with the enemy as soon as possible. But Lord Cardigan tightly restrained the pace of the Light Brigade: the line was to advance with parade-ground perfection. The inner squadron of the 17th Lancers broke into a canter, Captain White, its leader, being, he said, "frankly anxious to get out of such a murderous fire and into the guns as being the lesser of two evils," and he shot forward, level with his brigadier. Lord Cardigan checked him instantly; lowering his sword and laying it across Captain White's breast, he told him sharply not to ride level with his commanding officer and not to force the pace. Private Wightman of the 17th Lancers, riding behind, heard his stern, hoarse voice rising above the din of the guns "Steady, steady, the 17th Lancers." Otherwise during the whole course of the charge Lord Cardigan neither spoke nor made any sign.

All he could see at the end of the valley as he rode was a white bank of smoke, through which from time to time flashed great tongues of flame marking the position of the guns. He chose one which seemed to be about the centre of the battery and rode steadily for it, neither turning in his saddle nor moving his head. Erect, rigid, and dauntless, his bearing contributed enormously to the steadiness, the astonishing discipline which earned the Charge of the Light Brigade immortality.

And now the watchers on the heights saw that the lines of horsemen, like toys down on the plain, were expanding and contracting with strange mechanical precision. Death was coming fast, and the Light Brigade was meeting death in perfect order; as a man or horse dropped, the riders on each side of him opened out; as soon as they had ridden clear, the ranks closed again. Orderly, as if on the parade ground, the Light Brigade rode on, but its numbers grew every moment smaller and smaller as they moved down the valley. Those on the heights who could understand what that regular mechanical movement meant in terms of discipline and courage were intolerably moved, and one old soldier burst into tears. It was at this moment that Bosquet, the French general, observed, "C'est magnifique mais ce n'est pas la guerre."

The fire grew fiercer; the first line was now within range of the guns at the end of the valley, as well as the fire pouring from both flanks. Round shot, grape, and shells began to mow men down not singly, but by groups; the pace quickened and quickened again—the men could no longer be restrained, and the trot became a canter.

The Heavy Brigade were being left behind; slower in any case than the Light Cavalry, they were wearied by their earlier action, and as the pace of the Light Brigade quickened, the gap began to widen rapidly. At this moment the Heavy Brigade came under the withering cross-fire which had just torn the Light Brigade to pieces. Lord Lucan, leading the Brigade, was wounded in the leg and his horse hit in two places; one of his aides was killed, and two of his staff wounded. Looking back, he saw that his two leading regiments—the Greys and the Royals—were sustaining heavy casualties. In the Royals twenty-one men had already fallen. Lord Lucan's indifference under fire was remarkable: it was on this occasion that an officer described as "one of his most steady haters" admitted, "Yes, damn him, he's brave," but he felt himself once more in a dilemma. Should he continue to advance and destroy the Heavy Brigade, or should he halt and leave the Light Brigade to its fate without support? He turned to Lord William Paulet, who was riding at his side and had just had his forage cap torn off his head by a musket ball. "They have sacrificed the Light Brigade: they shall not the Heavy, if I can help it," he said. Ordering the halt to be sounded, he retired the Brigade out of range and waited, having decided in his own words that "the only use to which the Heavy Brigade could be turned was to protect the Light Cavalry against pursuit on their return."

With sadness and horror the Heavy Brigade watched the Light Brigade go on alone down the valley and vanish in smoke. Help now came from the French. As a result of General Canrobert's earlier order the Chasseurs d'Afrique were drawn up beneath the heights. Originally raised as irregular cavalry, this force, which had a record of extraordinary distinction, now consisted of French troopers, mounted on Algerian horses.

Their commander, General Morris, had seen the Light Brigade fail to wheel, and advance down the valley to certain doom with stupefied horror. Nothing could be done for them, but he determined to aid the survivors. He ordered the Chasseurs d'Afrique to charge the batteries and infantry battalions on the Fedioukine Hills. Galloping as if by a miracle over broken and scrubby ground in a loose formation learned in their campaigns in the Atlas mountains of Morocco, they attacked with brilliant success. Both Russian artillery and infantry were forced to retreat, and at a cost of only thirty-eight casualties— ten killed and twenty-eight wounded—the fire from the Fedioukine Hills was silenced. Such remnants of the Light Brigade as might return would now endure fire only on one flank, from the Causeway Heights.

The first line of the Light Brigade was now more than halfway down the valley, and casualties were so heavy that the squadrons could no longer keep their entity: formation was lost and the front line broke into a gallop, the regiments racing each other as they rode down to death. "Come on," yelled a trooper of the 13th to his comrades, "come on. Don't let those b——s of the 17th get in front of us." The men, no longer to be restrained, began to shoot forward in front of their officers, and Lord Cardigan was forced to increase his pace or be overwhelmed. The gallop became headlong, the troopers cheering and yelling; their blood was up, and they were on fire to get at the enemy. Hell for leather, with whistling bullets and crashing shells taking their toll every moment, cheers changing to death cries, horses falling with a scream, the first line of the Light Brigade—17th Lancers and 13th Light Dragoons—raced down the valley to the guns. Close behind them came the second line. Lord George Paget, remembering Lord Cardigan's stern admonition, "Your best support—mind, your best support," had increased the pace of his regiment, the 4th Light Dragoons, and caught up the 11th Hussars. The 8th Hussars, sternly kept in hand by their commanding officer, Colonel Shewell, advanced at a steady trot, and refused to increase their pace. The second line therefore consisted of the 4th Light Dragoons and the 11th Hussars, with the 8th Hussars to the right rear.

As they, too, plunged into the inferno of fire, and as batteries and massed riflemen on each flank began to tear gaps in their ranks and trooper after trooper came crashing to the ground, they had a new and horrible difficulty to face. The ground was strewn with casualties of the first line—not only dead men and dead horses, but horses and men not yet dead, able to crawl, to scream, to writhe. They had perpetually to avoid riding over men they knew, while riderless horses, some unhurt, some horribly injured, tried to force their way into the ranks. Troop horses in battle, as long as they feel the hand of their rider and his weight on their backs, are, even when wounded, singularly free from fear. When Lord George Paget's charger was hit, he was astonished to find the horse showed no sign of panic. But, once deprived of his rider, the troop horse becomes crazed with terror. He does not gallop out of the action and seek safety: trained to range himself in line, he seeks the companionship of other horses, and, mad with fear, eyeballs protruding, he attempts to attach himself to some leader or to force himself into the ranks of the nearest squadrons. Lord George, riding in advance of the second line, found himself actually in danger. The poor brutes made dashes at him, trying to gallop with him. At one moment he was riding in the midst of seven riderless horses, who cringed and pushed against him as round shot and bullets came by, covering him with blood from their wounds, and so nearly unhorsing him that he was forced to use his sword to free himself.

And all the time, through the cheers, the groans, the ping of bullets whizzing through the air, the whirr and crash of shells, the earth-shaking thunder of galloping horses' hooves, when men were not merely falling one by one but being swept away in groups, words of command rang out as on the parade ground, "Close in to your centre. Back the right flank! Keep up, Private Smith. Left squadron, keep back. Look to your dressing." Until at last, as the ranks grew thinner and thinner, only one command was heard: "Close in! Close in! Close in to the centre! Close in! Close in!"

Eight minutes had now passed since the advance began, and Lord Cardigan, with the survivors of the first line hard on his heels, galloping furiously but steadily, was within a few yards of the battery. The troopers could see the faces of the gunners, and Lord Cardigan selected the particular space between two guns where he intended to enter. One thought, wrote a survivor, was in all their minds: they were nearly out of it at last, and close on the accursed guns, and Lord Cardigan, still sitting rigid in his saddle, "steady as a church," waved his sword over his head. At that moment there was a roar, the earth trembled, huge flashes of flame shot out, and the smoke became so dense that darkness seemed to fall. The Russian gunners had fired a salvo from their twelve guns into the first line of the Light Brigade at a distance of eighty yards. The first line ceased to exist. To the second line, riding behind, it was as if the line had simply dissolved. Lord Cardigan's charger Ronald was blown sideways by the blast, a torrent of flame seemed to belch down his right side, and for a moment he thought he had lost a leg. He was, he estimated, only two or three lengths from the mouths of the guns. Then, wrenching Ronald's head round, he drove into the smoke and, charging into the space he had previously selected, was the first man into the battery. And now the Heavy Brigade, watching in an agony of anxiety and impatience, became aware of a sudden and sinister silence. No roars, no great flashes of flame came from the guns—all was strangely, menacingly quiet. Nothing could be seen: the pall of smoke hung like a curtain over the end of the valley; only from time to time through their glasses the watchers saw riderless horses gallop out and men stagger into sight to fall prostrate among the corpses of their comrades littering the ground.

Fifty men only, blinded and stunned, had survived from the first line. Private Wightman of the 17th Lancers felt the frightful crash, saw his captain fall dead; then his horse made a "tremendous leap into the air," though what he jumped at Wightman never knew—the pall of smoke was so dense that he could not see his arm before him—but suddenly he was in the battery, and in the darkness there were sounds of fighting and slaughter. The scene was extraordinary: smoke so obscured the sun that it was barely twilight, and in the gloom the British troopers, maddened with excitement, cut and thrust and hacked like demons, while the Russian gunners with superb courage fought to remove the guns.

While the struggle went on in the battery, another action was taking place outside. Twenty survivors of the 17th Lancers—the regiment was reduced to thirty-seven men—riding behind Captain Morris had outflanked the battery on the left, and, emerging from the smoke, suddenly found themselves confronted with a solid mass of Russian cavalry drawn up behind the guns. Turning in his saddle, Morris shouted, "Now, remember what I have told you, men, and keep together," and without a moment's hesitation charged. Rushing himself upon the Russian officer in command, he engaged him in single combat and ran him through the body. The Russians again received the charge halted, allowed the handful of British to penetrate their ranks, broke, and retreated in disorder, pursued by the 17th. Within a few seconds an overwhelming body of Cossacks came up, the 17th were forced to retreat in their turn, and, fighting like madmen, every trooper encircled by a swarm of Cossacks, they tumbled back in confusion towards the guns. Morris was left behind unconscious with his skull cut open in two places.

Meanwhile in those few minutes the situation in the battery had completely changed. In the midst of the struggle for the guns, Colonel Mayow, the Brigade major, looked up and saw a body of Russian cavalry preparing to descend in such force that the men fighting in the battery must inevitably be overwhelmed. Shouting, "Seventeenth! Seventeenth! this way! this way!" he collected the remaining survivors of the 17th and all that was left of the 13th Light Dragoons—some twelve men—and, placing himself at their head, charged out of the battery, driving the Russians before him until he was some five hundred yards away.

At this moment the second line swept down. The 11th Hussars outflanked the battery, as the 17th had done; the 8th Hussars had not yet come up, but the 4th Light Dragoons under Lord George Paget crashed into the battery. So great was the smoke and the confusion that Lord George did not see the battery until his regiment was on top of it. As they rode headlong down, one of his officers gave a "View halloo," and suddenly they were in and fighting among the guns. The Russian gunners, with great courage, persisted in their attempt to take the guns away, and the 4th Light Dragoons, mad with excitement, fell on them with savage frenzy. A cut-and-thrust, hand-to-hand combat raged, in which the British fought like tigers, one officer tearing at the Russians with his bare hands and wielding his sword in a delirium of slaughter. After the battle this officer's reaction was so great that he sat down and burst into tears. Brave as the Russians were, they were forced to give way; the Russian gunners were slaughtered, and the 4th Light Dragoon secured absolute mastery of every gun.

While this fierce and bloody combat was being waged, Colonel Douglas, outflanking the battery with the 11th Hussars, had charged a body of Lancers on the left with considerable success, only to find himself confronted with the main body of the Russian cavalry, and infantry in such strength that he felt he was confronted by the whole Russian army. He had hastily to retreat with a large Russian force following in pursuit.

Meanwhile the 4th Light Dragoons, having silenced the guns, had pressed on out of the battery and beyond it. Lord George had, he said, an idea that somewhere ahead was Lord Cardigan, and Lord Cardigan's admonition enjoining his best support was "always ringing in his ears." As they advanced, they collided with the 11th in their retreat, and the two groups, numbering not more than seventy men, joined together. Their situation was desperate. Advancing on them were enormous masses of Russian cavalry—the leading horsemen were actually within a few hundred yards; but Lord George noticed the great mass was strangely disorderly in its movements and displayed the hesitation and bewilderment the Russian cavalry had shown when advancing on the Heavy Brigade in the morning. Reining in his horse, Lord George shouted at the top of his voice, "Halt front; if you don't front, my boys, we are done." The 11th checked, and, with admirable steadiness, the whole group "halted and fronted as if they had been on parade." So for a few minutes the handful of British cavalry faced the advancing army. The movement had barely been completed when a trooper shouted, "They are attacking us, my lord, in our rear," and, looking round, Lord George saw, only five hundred yards away, a formidable body of Russian Lancers formed up in the direct line of retreat. Lord George turned to his major: "We are in a desperate scrape; what the devil shall we do? Has anyone seen Lord Cardigan?"

When Lord Cardigan dashed into the battery he had, by a miracle, passed through the gap between the two guns unhurt, and in a few seconds was clear—the first man into the battery and the first man out. Behind him, under the pall of smoke, in murk and gloom, a savage combat was taking place, but Lord Cardigan neither turned back nor paused. In his opinion, he said later, it was "no part of a general's duty to fight the enemy among private soldiers"; he galloped on, until suddenly he was clear of the smoke, and before him, less than one hundred yards away, he saw halted a great mass of Russian cavalry. His charger was wild with excitement, and before he could be checked Lord Cardigan had been carried to within twenty yards of the Russians. For a moment they stared at each other, the Russians utterly astonished by the sudden apparition of this solitary horseman, gorgeous and glittering with gold. By an amazing coincidence, one of the officers, Prince Radzivil, recognised Lord Cardigan—they had met in London at dinners and balls—and the Prince detached a troop of Cossacks with instructions to capture him alive. To this coincidence Lord Cardigan probably owed his life. The Cossacks approached him, but did not attempt to cut him down; and after a short encounter in which he received a slight wound on the thigh, he evaded them by wheeling his horse, galloped back through the guns again, and came out almost where, only a few minutes earlier, he had dashed in.

By this time the fight in the guns was over, and the battery, still veiled with smoke, was a hideous, confused mass of dead and dying. The second line had swept on, and Lord George Paget and Colonel Douglas, with their handful of survivors, were now halted, with the Russian army both in front of them and behind them, asking, "Where is Lord Cardigan?"

Lord Cardigan, however, looking up the valley over the scene of the charge, could see no sign of his Brigade. The valley was strewn with dead and dying; small groups of men wounded or unhorsed were struggling towards the British lines; both his aides-de-camp had vanished; he had ridden never once looking back, and had no idea of what the fate of his Brigade had been. Nor had he any feeling of responsibility— in his own words, having "led the Brigade and launched them with due impetus, he considered his duty was done." The idea of trying to find out what had happened to his men or of rallying the survivors never crossed his mind. With extraordinary indifference to danger he had led the Light Brigade down the valley as if he were leading a charge in a review in Hyde Park, and he now continued to behave as if he were in a review in Hyde Park. He had, however, he wrote, some apprehension that for a general his isolated position was unusual, and he avoided any undignified appearance of haste by riding back very slowly, most of the time at a walk. By another miracle he was untouched by the fire from the Causeway Heights, which, although the batteries on the Fedioukine Hills had been silenced by the French, was still raking the unfortunate survivors of the charge in the valley. As he rode he continued to brood on Nolan's behaviour, and on nothing else. The marvellous ride, the dauntless valour of the Light Brigade and their frightful destruction, his own miraculous escape from death, made no impression on his mind; Nolan's insubordination occupied him exclusively, and when he reached the point where the Heavy Brigade was halted, he rode up to General Scarlett and immediately broke into accusations of Nolan, furiously complaining of Nolan's insubordination, his ride across the front of the Brigade, his attempt to assume command, and, Lord Cardigan finished contemptuously, "Imagine the fellow screaming like a woman when he was hit." General

Scarlett checked him: "Say no more, my lord; you have just ridden over Captain Nolan's dead body."

Meanwhile the seventy survivors of the 4th Light Dragoons and 11th Hussars under Lord George Paget, unaware that their general had retired from the field, were preparing to sell their lives dearly. There seemed little hope for them: they were a rabble, their horses worn out, many men wounded. Nevertheless, wheeling about, and jamming spurs into the exhausted horses, they charged the body of Russian Lancers who barred their retreat, "as fast," wrote Lord George Paget, "as our poor tired horses could carry us." As the British approached, the Russians, who had been in close column across their path, threw back their right, thus presenting a sloping front, and, with the air of uncertainty Lord George had noticed earlier, stopped—did nothing. The British, at a distance of a horse's length only, were allowed to "shuffle and edge away," brushing along the Russian front and parrying thrusts from Russian lances. Lord George said his sword crossed the end of lances three or four times, but all the Russians did was to jab at him. It seems probable that the Russians, having witnessed the destruction of the main body of the Light Brigade, were not greatly concerned with the handfuls of survivors. So, without the loss of a single man, "and how I know not," wrote Lord George, the survivors of the 4th Light Dragoons and the 11th Hussars escaped once more, and began the painful retreat back up the valley.

One other small body of survivors had also been fighting beyond the guns. The 8th Hussars, restrained with an iron hand by their commanding officer, Colonel Shewell, had reached the battery in beautiful formation to find the 4th Light Dragoons had done their work and the guns were silenced. Colonel Shewell then led his men through the battery and halted on the other side, enquiring, like Lord George Paget, "Where is Lord Cardigan?" For about three minutes the 8th Hussars waited, then on the skyline appeared lances. The fifteen men of the 17th Lancers, who with the few survivors of the 13th Light Dragoons had charged out of the battery before the second line attacked, were now retreating, with a large Russian force in pursuit. Colonel Mayow, their leader, galloped up to Colonel Shewell. "Where is Lord Cardigan?" he asked. At that moment Colonel Shewell turned his head and saw that he, too, was not only menaced in front: at his rear a large force of Russian cavalry had suddenly come up, and was preparing to cut off his retreat and the retreat of any other survivors of the Light Brigade who might still be alive beyond the guns. A stern, pious man, by no means popular with his troops, Colonel Shewell had the harsh courage of Cromwell's Bible soldiers. Assuming command, he wheeled the little force into line and gave the order to charge. He himself, discarding his sword—he was a poor swordsman —gripped his reins in both hands, put down his head, and rushed like a thunderbolt at the Russian commanding officer. The Russian stood his ground, but his horse flinched. Shewell burst through the gap and was carried through the ranks to the other side. Riding for their lives, his seventy-odd troopers dashed after him. The Russians were thrown into confusion and withdrew, and the way was clear.

But what was to be done next? Colonel Shewell paused. No supports were coming up, Lord Cardigan was not to be seen; there was nothing for it but retreat, and, just ahead of Lord George Paget and Colonel Douglas with the 4th Light Dragoons and the 11th Hussars, the other survivors of the Light Brigade began slowly and painfully to trail back up the valley.

Confusion was utter. No one knew what had taken place, who was alive, or who was dead; no control existed; no one gave orders; no one knew what to do next. At the time when the survivors of the Light Brigade had begun to trail up the valley, Captain Lockwood, one of Lord Cardigan's three aides-de-camp, suddenly rode up to Lord Lucan.

"My lord, can you tell me where is Lord Cardigan?" he asked. Lord Lucan replied that Lord Cardigan had gone by some time ago, upon which Captain Lockwood, misunderstanding him, turned his horse's head, rode down into the valley, and was never seen again.

The retreat, wrote Robert Portal, was worse than the advance. Men and horses were utterly exhausted and almost none was unhurt. Troopers who had become attached to their horses refused to leave them behind, and wounded and bleeding men staggered along, dragging with them wounded and bleeding beasts. Horses able to move were given up to wounded men; Major de Salis of the 8th Hussars retreated on foot, leading his horse with a wounded trooper in the saddle. All formation had been lost, and it was a rabble who limped painfully along. Mrs. Duberly on the heights saw scattered groups of men appearing at the end of the valley. "What can those skirmishers be doing?" she asked. "Good God! It is the Light Brigade!" The pace was heartbreakingly slow; most survivors were on foot; little groups of men dragged along step by step, leaning on each other. At first Russian Lancers made harassing attacks, swooping down, cutting off stragglers, and taking prisoners, but when the retreating force came under fire from the Causeway Heights the Russians sustained casualties from their own guns and were withdrawn. Nearly a mile had to be covered, every step under fire; but the fire came from one side only, and the straggling trail of men offered no such target as the brilliant squadrons in parade order which had earlier swept down the valley. The wreckage of men and horses was piteous. "What a scene of havoc was this last mile—strewn with the dead and dying and all friends!" wrote Lord George Paget. Men recognised their comrades, "some running, some limping, some crawling," saw horses in the trappings of their regiments "in every position of agony struggling to get up, then floundering back again on their mutilated riders." So, painfully, step by step, under heavy fire, the exhausted, bleeding remnants of the Light Brigade dragged themselves back to safety. As each group stumbled in, it was greeted with ringing cheers. Men ran down to meet their comrades and wrung them by the hand, as if they had struggled back from the depths of hell itself.

One of the last to return was Lord George Paget, and as he toiled up the slope he was greeted by Lord Cardigan, "riding composedly from the opposite direction." Lord George was extremely angry with Lord Cardigan; later he wrote an official complaint of his conduct. He considered it was Lord Cardigan's "bounden duty," after strictly enjoining that Lord George should give his best support—"your best support, mind"—to "see him out of it"; instead of which Lord Cardigan had disappeared, leaving his brigade to its fate. "Halloa, Lord Cardigan! were you not there?" he said. "Oh, wasn't I, though!" replied Lord Cardigan. "Here, Jenyns, did you not see me at the guns?" Captain Jenyns, one of the few survivors of the 13th Light Dragoons, answered that he had: he had been very near Lord Cardigan at the time when he entered the battery.

Out of this conversation, and a feeling that Lord Cardigan's desertion of his Brigade could not be reconciled with heroism, grew a legend that Lord Cardigan never had taken part in the charge. During his lifetime he was haunted by the whisper, and as late as 1909 Wilfrid Scawen Blunt was told positively that "Cardigan was not in the charge at all, being all the time on board his yacht, and only arrived on the field of battle as his regiment was on its way back from the Valley of Death."

When the last survivors had trailed in, the remnants of the Light Brigade re-formed on a slope looking southward over Balaclava. The charge had lasted twenty minutes from the moment the trumpet sounded the advance to the return of the last survivor. Lord Cardigan rode forward. "Men, it is a mad-brained trick, but it is no fault of mine," he said in his loud, hoarse voice. A voice answered, "Never mind, my lord; we are ready to go again," and the roll call began, punctuated by the melancholy sound of pistol shots as the farriers went round despatching ruined horses.

Some 700 horsemen had charged down the valley, and 195 had returned. The 17th Lancers were reduced to thirty-seven troopers, the 13th Light Dragoons could muster only two officers and eight mounted men; 500 horses had been killed.

The Reason Why, by Cecil Woodham-Smith

"No trouble or expense must be spared to obtain them."

In 1771, a young member of the colonial militia opened the London Bookstore in Boston. One of the rewards from the otherwise generally unprofitable business of bookselling is time and opportunity to read. Henry Knox was not a man to waste time. He read avidly in the fields of military strategy and tactics, and studied everything he could find on modern uses of artillery. There is little doubt that his choice of reading matter was a calculated one—for he had seen the Boston Massacre of 1770. More than most people, he realized that the conflict between the colonies and the crown might burst into flame at any time.

Knox studied his lessons well. In 1776, after the Battle of Bunker Hill and the defense of Boston, he was made a Brigadier General—at the age of 27. As Washington's close friend and artillery advisor he took part in most of the war's major battles and later became America's first Secretary of War.

The year 1776 was a time for valor. It was a year when necessity made the impossible possible . . . the year in which a few backwoods colonies began their fight for freedom from the strongest power in the world. Henry Knox, the bookseller, was a man of action. . . .

BY THE TIME Washington took command of the American Army at Cambridge in July, 1775, his troops had dug fortifications on the hilltops ringing Boston. The British, who had occupied the city for over a year, were pinned down but could not be starved out as long as their navy kept the port open. The Americans lacked siege guns and trained storm troops. On the other hand, General Gage, the British commander, had been made cautious by the mauling his infantry had received on the Concord expedition and at Bunker Hill.

American artillery could threaten British shipping only on one of the two heights situated at opposite tips of the crescent formed by the American lines: Bunker Hill, north of Boston, and Dorchester Heights, across the bay to the southeast. Bunker Hill had been won by the British and neither side was yet ready to fight for Dorchester Heights—the British because of Gage's reluctance to risk the loss of more troops difficult to replace; the Americans because they lacked the artillery to take advantage of the superior location once it had been occupied.

The military situation had reached a frustrating stalemate. In keeping secret his shortage of arms and powder, Washington had divested himself of an ostensible reason, in the eyes of his men and the Continental Congress, for not taking Boston. His troops, after all, outnumbered the British better than two to one. The inactivity was fomenting low morale and wholesale desertions. In a few months, the year's enlistment period would be up for Washington's army and the straws in the wind were enough to inform him that there would be few soldiers who would remain for a second hitch. Supplied with artillery, he could quickly place the guns within effective range of the British land defenses and naval vessels and drive Gage out of Boston.

Where were enough artillery pieces to be obtained? Even if they could be spared from defense points elsewhere in the colonies, the logistical problem of transporting them in time and in sufficient number to be worthwhile could not be overcome.

Washington's answer came from one of the few men he had come to like, trust and respect since the general's arrival in Cambridge: Henry Knox, a civilian volunteer, a bookseller. . . .

To Washington, artillery was the all-important element. He was impressed by Knox's perpetual optimism in the face of a gloomy predicament and by the large man's resourcefulness in ideas. Nor did Knox let the general down. One day he suggested to Washington that the cannon captured at Fort Ticonderoga the previous May might be sledded and floated the 300 miles to Cambridge that winter and be available for use against the British the next year, 1776. Washington at once endorsed the proposal, adding that "no trouble or expense must be spared to obtain them."

Knox, then 25 years old, left for New York in late November, taking with him his brother William. They took a boat up the Hudson to Albany. . . . He and William reached Ticonderoga four days later, riding on rutted, frozen roads to Fort George, at the southern end of Lake George, and by boat to Fort Ticonderoga.

Ticonderoga stood where Lake George empties into Lake Champlain. . . . Ethan Allen was encouraged by the colonists to take it to protect their rear from an attack by a Canadian force. In executing this assignment Allen's forces, with Benedict Arnold, had also captured guns and boats at nearby Crown Point.

Much of the captured artillery at Ticonderoga was too worn to be of use, but 78 pieces were salvageable, ranging from 4-pound to 24-pound guns, as well as six mortars, three howitzers, 30,000 flints, and tons of muskets and cannon balls. A rare prize, indeed, if the ponderous equipment could be dragged over the Berkshires and across the length of Massachusetts before a spring thaw sabotaged the effort.

Knox at once dismantled nearly sixty cannon and lowered them from their lofty wall emplacements to the ground where they were carted across a swampy, wooded peninsula by the colonist garrison and loaded into three boats: a scow, known as a "gondola," a bateau, which to French Canadians and Louisianians meant a flat-bottomed boat with tapered ends, and what Knox in his diary called a *pettiauger*.

Leaving William in charge of the heavily-laden craft, Henry hurried ahead in a lighter, faster bateau, in order to get together all the oxen, horses and sleds necessary for the next part of the trip back to Boston.

Navigating 33-mile Lake George with this priceless cargo was a breath-taking enterprise. The lake, which at its widest is only three miles across, was forming ice on either side a mile from shore. A favorable wind died almost immediately. The scow ran on a sunken rock and William managed to free it only to have the unmanageable craft go aground in earnest at Sabbath Day Point, not halfway down the lake. The damage this time was so substantial that the guns had to be unloaded from the scow and some added to the other boats, already low in the water from their loads of lead, brass and iron. Eventually, the guns arrived at Fort George without a loss.

Henry and his crew had been fed and warmed their first night on the lake by friendly Indians at Sabbath Day Point, but the next day they ran into a headwind which forced them to row desperately for ten hours to make Fort George.

Hurrying on alone by land in the attempt to beat the arrival of heavy snow or to take advantage of any normal snowfall, Knox arrived at Stillwater, two-thirds the distance between Fort George (now the village of Lake George) and Albany, to obtain animals and sleds from Squire Charles Palmer, whose assistance in the matter had been assured. Returning to Fort George, thus supplied in part, Knox had an additional 42 heavy sleds made and finally collected eighty oxen for the big pull south to Albany. Schuyler, meanwhile, had dispatched men and horses from Albany and Saratoga to help Knox through the foothills of the Adirondacks. . . .

In following the rude woodland roads south to Albany he believed he would have to cross the unreliably frozen Hudson four times, al-

though actually he had to cross it but once and the Mohawk once.
At Albany, a thaw for a time prevented his crossing to the east side at
all. Where open water confronted the teamsters, it was necessary to
load sleds, guns and horses into scows for the crossing. Where the ice
was too thin to support the train but too thick to permit boat passage,
Knox was helpless. He frequently had to cut holes in the river's ice in
order for the overflow of water to freeze and add to the ice's
thickness. . . .

The first cannon, a brass 24-pounder, reached Albany on January
4, 1776, somewhat behind Knox's schedule. Within three days the
remainder of the guns had entered Albany for the final crossing of the
Hudson. . . .

Eventually the freeze arrived and Knox's artillery train streamed
across the Hudson. Continuing south, Knox arrived at Claverack,
where a broken sleigh detained him for two days. The need for plenty
of able-bodied help in case of a mishap prompted Knox's policy of
delaying the entire column if but one of its components got into
trouble.

At Claverack, Knox took the hazardous military trail used by only
a few others, which headed east over the Berkshires, through Great
Barrington, Otis and to Springfield on what is now Route 23, a treacherous road for motorists even today. Using eighty oxen again in place
of horses, Knox wrote, "We reached No. 1 [referring to Monterey,
Mass.] after having climbed mountains from which we might almost
have seen all the Kingdoms of the Earth."

Plunging into a twelve-mile stretch called "Greenwoods," made
dreary and forbidding by dense evergreen forests, Knox passed
through what is now East Otis and reached Blandford, where more
trouble awaited him. The descent of Glasgow (now Westfield)
Mountain had to be made. It required three hours of arguments by
Knox to assure the Hudson Valley teamsters that the treacherous trip
down could be made without danger from runaway, weighted sleds
plummeting downhill upon them. Knox supervised the precautionary
measures taken, such as drag chains, poles thrust under runners, and
check ropes anchored to one tree after another. . . .

At Springfield there was the broad Connecticut River to cross. The
ice held, but on the far side the "noble train of artillery" bogged down
in the mud of a sudden thaw. Knox paid off the drivers from New
York State there and hired native teamsters. When the ground froze
again he pushed on. At Framingham, he temporarily deposited most
of the heavier pieces in order to rush the more portable cannon to
Washington at Cambridge.

Back in camp, Knox learned that the colonists had accidentally acquired plenty of ammunition to fit his guns, thanks to an American warship which had captured the British supply brigantine, *Nancy*, and had salvaged her cargo of powder and shot.

Knox's artillery began a bombardment of Boston on March 2, 1776, and Washington moved men into Dorchester Heights in preparation for cannon installations there. The British didn't wait for these to materialize. General Howe (Gage had been recalled some months before) made halfhearted plans for taking the heights and then decided instead to evacuate the city. He threatened to burn Boston if his embarkation was molested by Knox's artillery and, on this unpleasant note, took his departure practically undisturbed. This was on March 17, which is observed annually in Massachusetts by a proclamation by the governor.

Knox's own modest estimate of his remarkable achievement in those desperate winter months of 1775–76 is possibly reflected accurately in the simple memorandum of expenses he submitted at the conclusion of the arduous venture: "For expenditures in a journey from the camp round Boston to New York, Albany, and Ticonderoga, and from thence, with 55 pieces of iron and brass ordnance, 1 barrel of flints, and 23 boxes of lead, back to camp (including expenses of self, brother, and servant), £520.15.8¾."

By standards of military supply in any age, this amount (some $1,458.20 in modern currency) charged the Continental Congress in exchange for Boston, must represent a model instance of government spending.

Big Guns for Washington, by Clay Perry

AARON BURR

"He may thank me. I made him a great man."

American history presents Aaron Burr as a scalawag—which, indeed, he was. He was a man whose ambition and drive for personal prestige was such that morality had no meaning for him. Yet he was also an extremely charming gentleman, an able executive, and a consummate politician. Although he was never a popular figure and was generally distrusted, he came to within one vote of becoming the third President of the United States. It was only after thirty-five deadlocked ballots in the House of Representatives that the office finally went to Mr. Jefferson.

Here is Burr, the Vice President of his young country, coldly preparing to fight—and murder—a political enemy, Alexander Hamilton. It is followed by excerpts from Hamilton's papers covering the same last few days. The contrast we get between these two men is astounding.

EARLY IN June Mr. Burr called together the Little Band to consider a delicate question. They had fought and bled for him, these disciples. Henceforth he would attend to such matters in person. Let them choose which of the two enemies should be the first to face his pistols.

They voted. Mr. Hamilton had won his last election.

"In the name of God. Amen.

"I, Alexander Hamilton," having written his Last Will and Testament, was burning the midnight oil before the shrine of a double immortality. At his library desk on the tenth night of June, 1804, he was fully confident that his next darkness would be the eternal one. Consequently he was performing the gruesome rites of embalming both his Christian soul and his patriotic integrity. Tomorrow morning, thought Mr. Hamilton, he must die that something bigger than himself might live. All this he was explaining as he wrote his Remarks "On My Expected Interview with Colonel Burr."

A man intensely religious, Mr. Hamilton allowed the Friday at Calvary to stand him as model. He would go unresisting to his Cross, for "I have resolved . . . to reserve and throw away my first fire." He would pray forgiveness of his executioner, hoping that Aaron Burr "by his future conduct may show himself worthy of all the confidence and esteem, and prove an ornament and a blessing to the country." He would die serene in the knowledge of serving a higher cause which had "imposed on me, as I thought, a peculiar necessity . . . in these crises of our public affairs which seem likely to happen."

Unnecessary, he felt, to define "these crises." The words would be well understood by men still plotting a northern confederacy. Mr. Hamilton had been planning a trip to Boston, where he would meet the conspirators and attempt to argue them out of their folly. He felt that his death would dissuade them more certainly. He would suffer in haste, lest the country repent in leisure. His blood, shed by Aaron Burr, would prevent bloodshed in battles in case the Northern Confederacy became a reality. At least the converse was true. By declining the duel he, as Commanding General of the American Army, would forfeit "the ability to be in future useful whether in resisting mischief or effecting good." Sweet and fitting to die for one's country, and Mr. Hamilton wanted to leave no posthumous doubt as to his motives. That night he wrote a letter which, on its receipt, would come as a voice from the grave to the rebels of New England.

I will here express but one sentiment, which is, that dismemberment of our empire will be a clear sacrifice of great positive advantages, without any counterbalancing good; administering no relief to our real disease which is *Democracy*, the poison of which by subdivision will only be more concentrated in each part, and consequently the more virulent . . . God bless you!

A. H.

Mr. Hamilton did not want to die. He had already done everything within the code of officer and gentleman to evade that fatal duty. On the morning of June 18 Billy Van Ness had come into the Wall Street office with a newspaper clipping and a curt note from Colonel Burr. The first was the printed letter from Charles Cooper to Philip Schuyler which ended, "I could detail to you a still more despicable opinion which General Hamilton has expressed of Mr. Burr."

"You must perceive, sir," wrote the Colonel, "the necessity of a prompt and unqualified acknowledgment or denial."

Mr. Hamilton's reply was neither prompt nor unqualified. The matter, he told Billy, "required some consideration." Nine days and as many letters passed back and forth while he sought to put aside the bitter cup.

'Tis evident [he answered the first note] that the phrase "still more despicable" admits of infinite shades, from very light to very dark. How am I to judge of the degrees intended? . . . How could you be sure that even this opinion had exceeded the bounds which you would yourself deem admissible between political opponents?

The Colonel would not be placated.

The common sense of mankind [he retorted] affixes to the epithet adopted by Doctor Cooper the idea of dishonor. It has been publicly applied to me under the sanction of your name. The question is not whether he understood the meaning of the word, or used it according to syntax and with grammatical accuracy, but whether you authorized this application.

At that Mr. Hamilton shifted his ground. "The conversation to which Doctor Cooper alluded turned wholly on political topics and did not attribute to Colonel Burr any instance of dishonorable conduct, nor relate to his private character."

He was, returned the Colonel,

greatly surprised at receiving a letter which he considered as evasive and which, in manner, he deemed not altogether decorous. . . . He feels as a gentleman should when his honor is impeached or assailed; and, without sensations of hostility or wishes of revenge, he is determined to vindicate that honor at such hazards as the nature of the case demands.

Mr. Hamilton's own honor forbade him any further retreat. "My religious and moral principles are strongly opposed to the practice of dueling," but he appointed Judge Nathaniel Pendleton to make the necessary arrangements. He only asked a ten-day truce in order to settle some cases before the Circuit Court.

Mr. Burr readily assented and in the interim came an attempted rescue. A Hamilton colleague, Samuel Bradhurst, heard of the affair and decided upon heroic measures. Aware of Burr's marksmanship —"There was hardly ever a man could fire so true"—Bradhurst would take no chance on pistols. Presumably a nimble bladesman, he would provoke a challenge, choose swords and carve up the Colonel for carrion. The first phase of the plan proved highly successful. Bradhurst had no trouble inducing Mr. Burr to a duel, but retired wounded from the field trailing more blood than glory.

Mr. Hamilton might recognize the incident as his last hope of reprieve. He was, as afterward described by John Randolph, "a sinking fox, pressed by a vigorous old hound, where no shift is permitted to avail him." And, foxlike, he expected no mercy of the pursuer. There were reports, soon to be loosed, that the Vice President spent many hours in his garden at pistol practice. Hamilton's own son told later how Burr would fire shot after shot at a target as fast as accomplices could reload and hand him the pistols. A neighbor at Richmond Hill claimed to have seen the Colonel in a strange pantomime. He would pace off a distance, mutter something to himself, then whirl and shoot at a target.

Whether he heard these tales or whether he believed with Charles Biddle that "Burr had no need to practice," Mr. Hamilton this night in his library was not allowing himself to hope. On July fourth he and Burr attended the Society of Cincinnati banquet, where men would remember with what tenderness the Colonel listened to Hamilton's solo of their old war song, "The Drum." They had long been friendly enemies in the political cockpit. Burr, it seems, might gladly have accepted the near-apologies except for his obligations to the Little Band. As a sportsman he must have preferred matching shots with the pugnacious De Witt Clinton. But the Colonel also had a duty to perform.

Too good a soldier to fear death, Mr. Hamilton was too thoughtful a gentleman not to dread it. "My wife and children are extremely dear to me . . ." he wrote that night. "I feel a sense of obligation towards my creditors." He was fast paying off the debts accumulated during the years of public office; it pained him that this last service must be at the sacrifice of private duty. Still it was ever a soldier's lot to be married only to his country's cause. He took paper and wrote——

My Beloved Eliza:
    . . . God's will be done! . . . Adieu my darling, darling wife. . . .

It was nearly dawn when he had finished.

The same dawn lighted Billy Van Ness into the Richmond Hill library where he found the Vice President, stripped to shirt sleeves and stockinged feet, "in a very sound sleep" on the couch. Roused from his slumber Mr. Burr attired himself for the day's work. He had lately read how an English girl, shot in the breast, had been saved by the ball's striking a silk handkerchief carried in her bodice. As a friend of science, Mr. Burr thought the experiment worth repeating, so he donned this morning a black bombazine coat, woofed in ribbed silk and said to be tailored especially for the occasion. On the library table lay his will, "the six blue boxes" of love letters and two other epistles written the previous night to his daughter and her husband. They dealt at length with the settlement of his estate, arranged an honorarium for Peggy, the cook, and Leonora, the mistress; not forgetting the Little Band. "Give each of them . . . some small token in remembrance of me." And finally,

"If it should be my lot to fall . . . yet I shall live in you and in your son."

John Swartwout arrived, then Matthew Davis, Marinus Willett and a few others. Billy would act as his hero's second. Davis and Willett were permitted to go along so they might hide in the bushes and observe unseen. Swartwout was delegated to remain behind and to be ready to spread the tidings, sad or glad, among the anxious absentees.

His toilet complete, Mr. Burr and his friends walked downhill to the wharf and stepped into the waiting barge. In one hand Billy Van Ness carried the pistol case; in the other, though the day promised to be fair, he bore an umbrella. The Jersey shore across the river was a high wall of summer woodlands, broken here and there by the roll of a lawn sloping down to the water front. Three miles diagonally upstream from Richmond Hill reared the craggy heights of Weehawken. Only at low tide was there a landing place among the rocks at its base. This morning as their prow grounded in the sand, Billy raised his umbrella and sheltered his principal's head. The laws of New York and New Jersey both forbade dueling, though the edict was never enforced. As part of the ritual gentlemen liked to go covered to their crime.

It was just six-thirty, the men remembered, when they disembarked and began climbing the path that was marked by the feet of many duelists. They spoke in whispers lest they arouse one whom they called "the Captain," a kindly old hermit who lived in a cottage at the hilltop. It hugely annoyed this good man that his retreat should be made a communal slaughterground. More than once he had outraged the stilted dignity of these affairs by planting himself between the opponents and scolding them off the premises. Whereupon all would repair to a tavern half a mile down the beach and regale themselves into maudlin friendship with the aid of the innkeeper's wine. But this morning the Captain's sleep was undisturbed. Twenty feet above the water line Mr. Burr and Billy came to the field of honor—a shelf of level land scarcely eleven paces long, hemmed in on three sides by rocks and canopied by overhanging foliage and wild flowers.

Heated by the climb, Billy removed his coat and aided his master in trampling down the undergrowth to clear a space for the hostilities. The task quickly accomplished, they waited. From where he stood Colonel Burr watched the gleaming reach of the river as it flowed

past Richmond Hill and into the harbor beyond. Dawn was up out
of the bay, laying its tranquil splendor on the sleeping city and countryside. Aaron Burr may never cease scoffing at the inanities of organized religion, but he knew what it was to stand humbly before Nature.
On one occasion when he had time to record it, he expressed the
pantheism which was his only faith, wishing for the grandchild that
he might "initiate his young mind and introduce him to the gods."

"I passed," he wrote, "some hours on deck admiring the brilliancy
of the stars, following their majestic course through infinite space and
tracing the hand of Omnipotence. Presumptuous aim! Yet there is a
charm in such contemplation."

This morning there were other thoughts to move him. The Hudson's tide flowed between shores of memory. In the highland where
it rose had taken place his foray against Tryon, the only victorious
campaign in a life which panted for military fame. Off Paramus he
had taken as bride the one woman he could constantly love. Where
the River straddled Manhattan Island he had single handed saved a
brigade which had been lost by George Washington. And further off
was the panorama of New York harbor which he had first viewed from
the masthead. . . .

It lacked a few minutes of seven o'clock when Colonel Burr saw
another craft beaching among the rocks. Three men alighted. He knew
that Mr. Hamilton, besides a second, had brought a surgeon.

The seven o'clock sun of July 11 hangs high over Manhattan on a
horizontal line with the crest of Weehawken. It sends up a blinding
glare from the river to one who faces eastward. It warms the back of
one who faces westward in a silken coat. Aaron Burr's left side and
shoulder were drenched in sunlight. His right made a slender profile
in the direction of the cocked pistol that Alexander Hamilton had
raised "to try the light." It was the Colonel's third trip to the field of
honor, and the first on which he enjoyed an even chance of living to
remember it. Against John Church his gun was jammed. Against Samuel Bradhurst he was handicapped by an unfamiliar weapon. But today
the odds were with him. Hamilton won at the drawing of lots and had
chosen to face into the glare of sun and water. The cavity of rocks in
which he stood was hardly four feet wide and made a perfect background with himself as target. "[I] was sure," thought Aaron Burr,
"of being able to kill him," and he listened to Judge Pendleton
stolidly explaining the rules.

". . . shall loudly and distinctly give the word 'Present'—If one of
the parties fires and the other hath not fired, the opposite shall say

one, two, three, fire, and he shall then fire or lose his shot. A snap or a flash is a fire.

"The gentlemen . . . ready?"

Mr. Burr measured the distance and noted that his adversary "caught my eye and quailed under it."

"Stop," said Hamilton, "in certain states of light one requires glasses."

The Colonel did not know what shaft of light had come from heaven to reprieve Mr. Hamilton from suicide. "He looked," thought Burr with growing contempt, "like a convicted felon . . . oppressed with the horrors of conscious guilt." Testing the light again, Mr. Hamilton placed the spectacles on his nose, "and repeated the experiment several times."

"Ready," he said.

Aaron Burr nodded assent, toeing the sod which was loose with scattered pebbles.

"Present!"

He pulled hard on the trigger. The recoil of the heavy gun threw him momentarily off balance. His foot slid with a rolling stone. He staggered so that Billy thought he was hit. Mr. Burr heard two reports and a hissing sigh of foliage overhead. A clipped branch dropped beside him. He could not see through the smoke of his fuming weapon. He had missed the flick of impact as his ball struck a searing pain through the ribs below Mr. Hamilton's right nipple, lifting the body on its toes and spinning it in rhythmic agony as it sunk to the ground. But through the haze Mr. Burr received a message of victory. He heard a voice cry:

"I am a dead man," and then Billy Van Ness was there with the umbrella urging him downhill to the boat, while the surgeon came running up.

"This is a mortal wound, Doctor," cried Hamilton.

"He may thank me," was the Colonel's considered opinion. "I made him a great man."

Aaron Burr: Proud Pretender, by Holmes Alexander

ALEXANDER HAMILTON

"... I have resolved ... to reserve and throw away my first fire ..."

Alexander Hamilton's star had risen fast. Overcoming his illegitimacy and his West Indian birth, he had served as Washington's secretary and aide-de-camp in the Revolution while still in his early twenties. As a member of the Continental Congress he was a power not only in his state of New York, but in the whole country. He was influential in drafting the new Constitution, and then in getting it ratified and at thirty-two became the first U. S. Secretary of the Treasury. At the time of the duel with Burr he was one of the best-known figures in the country.

If Hamilton's personality did not command love, it most certainly did respect. Although many people, including those of his own party, disagreed with his policies, they never doubted his honesty. The fact that he was killed in a duel in which he played the part of the injuring party is doubly ironic, for Hamilton, the peace-loving man, was not prone to use slander as a weapon.

Here, in his last papers, his will and his final letters to his wife is a prelude to the tragic finale.

ON MY EXPECTED interview with Col. Burr, I think it proper to make some remarks explanatory of my conduct, motives, and views. I was certainly desirous of avoiding this interview for the most cogent reasons:

(1) My religious and moral principles are strongly opposed to the practice of duelling, and it would ever give me pain to be obliged to shed the blood of a fellow-creature in a private combat forbidden by the laws.

(2) My wife and children are extremely dear to me, and my life is of the utmost importance to them in various views.

(3) I feel a sense of obligation towards my creditors; who, in case of accident to me by the forced sale of my property, may be in some

degree sufferers. I did not think myself at liberty as a man of probity lightly to expose them to this hazard.

(4) I am conscious of no *ill will* to Col. Burr, distinct from political opposition, which, as I trust, has proceeded from pure and upright motives.

Lastly, I shall hazard much and can possibly gain nothing by the issue of the interview.

But it was, as I conceive, impossible for me to avoid it. There were *intrinsic* difficulties in the thing and *artificial* embarrassments, from the manner of proceeding on the part of Col. Burr.

Intrinsic, because it is not to be denied that my animadversions on the political principles, character, and views of Col. Burr have been extremely severe; and on different occasions I, in common with many others, have made very unfavorable criticisms on particular instances of the private conduct of this gentleman. In proportion as these impressions were entertained with sincerity and uttered with motives and for purposes which might appear to me commendable, would be the difficulty (until they could be removed by evidence of their being erroneous) of explanation or apology. The disavowal required of me by Col. Burr in a general and indefinite form was out of my power, if it had really been proper for me to submit to be questioned, but I was sincerely of opinion that this could not be, and in this opinion I was confirmed by that of a very moderate and judicious friend whom I consulted. Besides that, Col. Burr appeared to me to assume, in the first instance, a tone unnecessarily peremptory and menacing, and, in the second, positively offensive. Yet I wished, as far as might be practicable, to leave a door open to accommodation. This, I think, will be inferred from the written communication made by me and by my directions, and would be confirmed by the conversations between Mr. Van Ness and myself which arose out of the subject. I am not sure whether, under all the circumstances, I did not go further in the attempt to accommodate than a punctilious delicacy will justify. If so, I hope the motives I have stated will excuse me. It is not my design, by what I have said, to affix any odium on the conduct of Col. Burr in this case. He doubtless has heard of animadversions of mine which bore very hard upon him, and it is probable that as usual they were accompanied with some falsehoods. He may have supposed himself under a necessity of acting as he has done. I hope the grounds of his proceeding have been such as ought to satisfy his own conscience. I trust, at the same time, that the world will do me the justice to believe that I have not censured him on light grounds nor from unworthy inducements. I certainly have had strong reasons for what I have said, though it is possible that in some particulars I may have been influenced by misconstruction or misinformation. It is also my ardent wish that I may have been more mistaken than I think I have been; and that he, by his future conduct, may show himself worthy of all confidence and esteem and prove an ornament and a blessing to the country. As well, because it is possible that I may have injured Col. Burr, however convinced myself that my opinions and declarations have been well-founded, as from my general principles and temper in relation to similar affairs, I have resolved, if our interview is conducted in the usual manner, and it pleases God to give me the opportunity, to *reserve* and *throw away* my first fire, and I *have thoughts* even of *reserving* my second fire, and thus giving a double opportunity to Col. Burr to pause and reflect. It is not, however, my intention to enter into any explanations on the ground. Apology from principle, I hope, rather than pride, is out of the question. To those who, with me, abhorring the practice of duelling, may think that I ought on no account to have added to the number of bad examples, I answer that my *relative* situation, as well in public as private, enforcing all the considerations which constitute what men of the world denominate honor, imposed on me (as I thought) a peculiar necessity not to decline the call. The ability to be in future useful, whether in resisting mischief or in effecting good, in those crises of our public affairs which seem likely to happen, would probably be inseparable from a conformity with public prejudice in this particular.

A. H.

July 9, 1804

LAST WILL AND TESTAMENT OF
ALEXANDER HAMILTON

In the name of God, Amen.

I, ALEXANDER HAMILTON, of the City of New York, counsellor at law, do make this my last will and testament, as follows:

First, I appoint John B. Church, Nicholas Fish, and Nathaniel Pendleton, of the city aforesaid, esquires, to be executors and trustees of this my will; and I devise to them, their heirs and assigns, as joint tenants, and not as tenants in common, all my estate, real and personal, whatsoever, and wheresoever, upon trust, at their discretion to sell and dispose of the same at such time and times, in such manner, and upon such terms as they the survivors and survivor shall think fit; and out of the proceeds to pay all the debts which I shall owe at the time of my decease; in whole, if the fund shall be sufficient; proportionably, if it shall be insufficient; and the residue, if any there shall be, to pay and deliver to my excellent and dear wife, Elizabeth Hamilton.

Though, if it should please God to spare my life, I may look for a considerable surplus out of my present property; yet if He should speedily call me to the eternal world, a forced sale, as is usual, may possibly render it insufficient to satisfy my debts. I pray God that something may remain for the maintenance and education of my dear wife and children. But should it on the contrary happen that there is not enough for the payment of my debts, I entreat my dear children, if they or any of them shall ever be able, to make up the deficiency. I without hesitation commit to their delicacy a wish which is dictated by my own.—Though conscious that I have too far sacrificed the interests of my family to public avocations, and on this account have the less claim to burthen my children, yet I trust in their magnanimity to appreciate, as they ought, this my request. In so unfavorable an event of things, the support of their dear mother, with the most respectful and tender attention, is a duty all the sacredness of which they will feel. Probably her own patrimonial resources will preserve her from indigence. But in all situations they are charged to bear in mind that she has been to them the most devoted and best of mothers.

In testimony whereof, I have hereunto subscribed my hand, the ninth day of July, in the year of our Lord one thousand eight hundred and four.

ALEXANDER HAMILTON.

Signed, sealed, published, and declared, as and for his last will and testament in our presence, who have subscribed our names in his presence, the words *John B. Church* being above interlined.

DOMINICK F. BLAKE.

GRAHAM NEWELL.

THEO. B. VALLEAU.

July 10, 1804

To Elizabeth Hamilton.

This letter, my dear Eliza, will not be delivered to you, unless I shall first have terminated my earthly career, to begin, as I humbly hope, from redeeming grace and divine mercy, a happy immortality. If it had been possible for me to have avoided the interview, my love for you and my precious children would have been alone a decisive motive. But it was not possible, without sacrifices which would have rendered me unworthy of your esteem. I need not tell you of the pangs I feel from the idea of quitting you, and exposing you to the anguish I know you would feel. Nor could I dwell on the topic, lest it should unman me. The consolations of religion, my beloved, can alone support you; and these you have a right to enjoy. Fly to the bosom of your God, and be comforted. With my last idea I shall cherish the sweet hope of meeting you in a better world. Adieu, best of wives—best of women. Embrace all my darling children for me.

Tuesday evening, 10 o'clock, 1804

To Elizabeth Hamilton.

. . . The scruples of a Christian have determined me to expose my own life to any extent, rather than subject myself to the guilt of taking the life of another. This much increases my hazards, and redoubles my pangs for you. But you had rather I should die innocent than live guilty. Heaven can preserve me, and I humbly hope will; but, in the contrary event, I charge you to remember that you are a Christian. God's will be done! The will of a merciful God must be good. Once more,

Adieu, my darling, darling wife.

Private Papers of Alexander Hamilton

BOOKER T. WASHINGTON

"It seemed to me to be the largest and most beautiful building I had ever seen."

A pioneer needs faith as well as vision. He must believe in the destiny of his cause. He must also work to support his faith and realize his vision. Booker T. Washington understood this better than most men . . . he understood that no work is too menial or too exacting if it is work with a purpose.

Washington's later life was as filled with honors as his early life was devoid of comforts. Harvard made him an honorary Master of Arts and Dartmouth a Doctor of Laws. His Tuskegee Institute grew from a single shack to an establishment with more than forty buildings housing hundreds of students learning trades and skills, providing opportunities for study never before offered to Negroes. At his death in 1915, he was everywhere acknowledged as the foremost Negro educator in the country. He was a successful man in the eyes of the world and in terms of his own vision.

Few men have ever travelled so long a road from the dreams of their youth. . . .

ONE DAY, while at work in the coal-mine, I happened to overhear two miners talking about a great school for coloured people somewhere in Virginia. This was the first time that I had ever heard anything about any kind of school or college that was more pretentious than the little coloured school in our town.

In the darkness of the mine I noiselessly crept as close as I could to the two men who were talking. I heard one tell the other that not only was the school established for the members of my race, but that opportunities were provided by which poor but worthy students could work out all or a part of the cost of board, and at the same time be taught some trade or industry.

As they went on describing the school, it seemed to me that it must be the greatest place on earth, and not even Heaven presented more attractions for me at that time than did the Hampton Normal and

Agricultural Institute in Virginia, about which these men were talking. I resolved at once to go to that school, although I had no idea where it was, or how many miles away, or how I was going to reach it; I remembered only that I was on fire constantly with one ambition, and that was to go to Hampton. This thought was with me day and night.

After hearing of the Hampton Institute, I continued to work for a few months longer in the coal-mine. While at work there, I heard of a vacant position in the household of General Lewis Ruffner, the owner of the salt-furnace and coal-mine. Mrs. Viola Ruffner, the wife of General Ruffner, was a "Yankee" woman from Vermont. Mrs. Ruffner had a reputation all through the vicinity for being very strict with her servants, and especially with the boys who tried to serve her. Few of them had remained with her more than two or three weeks. They all left with the same excuse: she was too strict. I decided, however, that I would rather try Mrs. Ruffner's house than remain in the coal-mine, and so my mother applied to her for the vacant position. I was hired at a salary of $5 per month.

I had heard so much about Mrs. Ruffner's severity that I was almost afraid to see her, and trembled when I went into her presence. I had not lived with her many weeks, however, before I began to understand her. I soon began to learn that, first of all, she wanted everything kept clean about her, that she wanted things done promptly and systematically, and that at the bottom of everything she wanted absolute honesty and frankness. Nothing must be sloven or slipshod; every door, every fence, must be kept in repair.

I cannot now recall how long I lived with Mrs. Ruffner before going to Hampton, but I think it must have been a year and a half. At any rate, I here repeat what I have said more than once before, that the lessons that I learned in the home of Mrs. Ruffner were as valuable to me as any education I have ever gotten anywhere since. Even to this day I never see bits of paper scattered around a house or in the street that I do not want to pick them up at once. I never see a filthy yard that I do not want to clean it, a paling off of a fence that I do not want to put it on, an unpainted or unwhitewashed house that I do not want to paint or whitewash it, or a button off one's clothes, or a grease-spot on them or on a floor, that I do not want to call attention to it.

From fearing Mrs. Ruffner I soon learned to look upon her as one of my best friends. When she found that she could trust me she did so implicitly. During the one or two winters that I was with her she gave me an opportunity to go to school for an hour in the day during a portion of the winter months, but most of my studying was done at night, sometimes alone, sometimes under some one whom I could hire to teach me. Mrs. Ruffner always encouraged and sympathized with me in all my efforts to get an education. It was while living with her that I began to get together my first library. I secured a dry-goods box, knocked out one side of it, put some shelves in it, and began putting into it every kind of book that I could get my hands upon, and called it my "library."

Notwithstanding my success at Mrs. Ruffner's I did not give up the idea of going to the Hampton Institute. In the fall of 1872 I determined to make an effort to get there, although, as I have stated, I had no definite idea of the direction in which Hampton was, or of what it would cost to go there. I do not think that any one thoroughly sympathized with me in my ambition to go to Hampton unless it was my mother, and she was troubled with a grave fear that I was starting out on a "wild-goose chase." At any rate, I got only a half-hearted consent from her that I might start. The small amount of money that I had earned had been consumed by my stepfather and the remainder of the family, with the exception of a very few dollars, and so I had very little with which to buy clothes and pay my travelling expenses. My brother John helped me all that he could, but of course that was not a great deal, for his work was in the coal-mine, where he did not earn much, and most of what he did earn went in the direction of paying the household expenses.

Perhaps the thing that touched and pleased me most in connection with my starting for Hampton was the interest that many of the older coloured people took in the matter. They had spent the best days of their lives in slavery, and hardly expected to live to see the time when they would see a member of their race leave home to attend a boarding-school. Some of these older people would give me a nickel, others a quarter, or a handkerchief.

Finally the great day came, and I started for Hampton. I had only a small, cheap satchel that contained what few articles of clothing I could get. My mother at the time was rather weak and broken in health. I hardly expected to see her again, and thus our parting was all the more sad. She, however, was very brave through it all. At that time there were no through trains connecting that part of West Virginia with eastern Virginia. Trains ran only a portion of the way, and the remainder of the distance was travelled by stage-coaches.

The distance from Malden to Hampton is about five hundred miles. I had not been away from home many hours before it began to grow painfully evident that I did not have enough money to pay my fare to Hampton. One experience I shall long remember. I had been travelling over the mountains most of the afternoon in an old-fashioned stage-coach, when, late in the evening, the coach stopped for the night at a common, unpainted house called a hotel. All the other passengers except myself were whites. In my ignorance I supposed that the little hotel existed for the purpose of accommodating the passengers who travelled on the stage-coach. The difference that the colour of one's skin would make I had not thought anything about. After all the other passengers had been shown rooms and were getting ready for supper, I shyly presented myself before the man at the desk. It is true I had practically no money in my pocket with which to pay for bed or food, but I had hoped in some way to beg my way into the good graces of the landlord, for at that season in the mountains of Virginia the weather was cold, and I wanted to get indoors for the night. Without asking as to whether I had any money, the man at the desk firmly refused to even consider the matter of providing me with food or lodging. This was my first experience in finding out what the colour of my skin meant. In some way I managed to keep warm by walking about, and so got through the night. My whole soul was so bent upon reaching Hampton that I did not have time to cherish any bitterness toward the hotel-keeper.

By walking, begging rides both in wagons and in the cars, in some way, after a number of days, I reached the city of Richmond, Virginia, about eighty-two miles from Hampton. When I reached there, tired, hungry, and dirty, it was late in the night. I had never been in a large city, and this rather added to my misery. When I reached Richmond, I was completely out of money. I had not a single acquaintance in the place, and, being unused to city ways, I did not know where to go. I applied at several places for lodging, but they all wanted money, and that was what I did not have. Knowing nothing else better to do, I walked the streets. In doing this I passed by many foodstands where fried chicken and half-moon apple pies were piled high and made to present a most tempting appearance. At that time it seemed to me that I would have promised all that I expected to possess in the future to have gotten hold of one of those chicken legs or one of those pies. But I could not get either of these, nor anything else to eat.

I must have walked the streets till after midnight. At last I became so exhausted that I could walk no longer. I was tired, I was hungry, I was everything but discouraged. Just about the time when I reached extreme physical exhaustion, I came upon a portion of a street where the board sidewalk was considerably elevated. I waited for a few minutes, till I was sure that no passers-by could see me, and then crept under the sidewalk and lay for the night upon the ground, with my satchel of clothing for a pillow. Nearly all night I could hear the tramp of feet over my head. The next morning I found myself somewhat refreshed, but I was extremely hungry, because it had been a long time since I had had sufficient food. As soon as it became light enough for me to see my surroundings I noticed that I was near a large ship, and that this ship seemed to be unloading a cargo of pig iron. I went at once to the vessel and asked the captain to permit me to help unload the vessel in order to get money for food. The captain, a white man, who seemed to be kind-hearted, consented. I worked long enough to earn money for my breakfast, and it seems to me, as I remember it now, to have been about the best breakfast that I have ever eaten.

My work pleased the captain so well that he told me if I desired I could continue working for a small amount per day. This I was very glad to do. I continued working on this vessel for a number of days. After buying food with the small wages I received there was not much left to add to the amount I must get to pay my way to Hampton. In order to economize in every way possible, so as to be sure to reach Hampton in a reasonable time, I continued to sleep under the same sidewalk that gave me shelter the first night I was in Richmond. Many years after that the coloured citizens of Richmond very kindly tendered me a reception at which there must have been two thousand people present. This reception was held not far from the spot where I slept the first night I spent in that city, and I must confess that my mind was more upon the sidewalk that first gave me shelter than upon the reception, agreeable and cordial as it was.

When I had saved what I considered enough money with which to reach Hampton, I thanked the captain of the vessel for his kindness, and started again. Without any unusual occurrence I reached Hampton, with a surplus of exactly fifty cents with which to begin my education. To me it had been a long, eventful journey; but the first sight of the large, three-story, brick school building seemed to have rewarded me for all that I had undergone in order to reach the place. If the people who gave the money to provide that building could appreciate the influence the sight of it had upon me, as well as upon thousands of other youths, they would feel all the more encouraged to make such gifts. It seemed to me to be the largest and most beautiful building I had ever seen. The sight of it seemed to give me new life. I felt that a new kind of existence had now begun—that life would now have a new meaning. I felt that I had reached the promised land, and I resolved to let no obstacle prevent me from putting forth the highest effort to fit myself to accomplish the most good in the world.

As soon as possible after reaching the grounds of the Hampton Institute, I presented myself before the head teacher for assignment to a class. Having been so long without proper food, a bath and change of clothing, I did not, of course, make a very favourable impression upon her, and I could see at once that there were doubts in her mind about the wisdom of admitting me as a student. I felt that I could hardly blame her if she got the idea that I was a worthless loafer or tramp. For some time she did not refuse to admit me, neither did she decide in my favour, and I continued to linger about her, and to impress her in all the ways I could with my worthiness. In the meantime I saw her admitting other students, and that added greatly to my discomfort, for I felt, deep down in my heart, that I could do as well as they, if I could only get a chance to show what was in me.

After some hours had passed, the head teacher said to me: "The adjoining recitation-room needs sweeping. Take the broom and sweep it."

It occurred to me at once that here was my chance. Never did I receive an order with more delight. I knew that I could sweep, for Mrs. Ruffner had thoroughly taught me how to do that when I lived with her.

I swept the recitation-room three times. Then I got a dusting-cloth and I dusted it four times. All the woodwork around the walls, every bench, table, and desk, I went over four times with my dusting-cloth. Besides, every piece of furniture had been moved and every closet and corner in the room had been thoroughly cleaned. I had the feeling that in a large measure my future depended upon the impression I made upon the teacher in the cleaning of that room. When I was through, I reported to the head teacher. She was a "Yankee" woman who knew just where to look for dirt. She went into the room and inspected the floor and closets; then she took her handkerchief and rubbed it on the woodwork about the walls, and over the table and benches. When she was unable to find one bit of dirt on the floor, or a particle of dust on any of the furniture, she quietly remarked, "I guess you will do to enter this institution."

I was one of the happiest souls on earth. The sweeping of that room was my college examination, and never did any youth pass an examination for entrance into Harvard or Yale that gave him more genuine satisfaction. I have passed several examinations since then, but I have always felt that this was the best one I ever passed. . . .

Up from Slavery, by Booker T. Washington

IV. THE MOMENT OF TRIUMPH

. . . the harder the conflict,

the more glorious their triumph.

THOMAS PAINE
The American Crisis No. 1

ABRAHAM LINCOLN

"I think the time has come now."

No President of the United States, and, indeed, few men in the history of the world, have been so thoroughly analyzed, studied and discussed. He was a fascinating figure—profound, brooding, complicated. And yet, to many of those who knew him, Lincoln seemed basically a simple man who possessed the genius of reasonableness. He was a moderate in a world of extremes—a man whose genius it was to pick a sure path through the peaks and valleys of temporary excesses. Here is an incident which typifies Lincoln's steady strength as well as any in his life. Feeling for and against the expected proclamation freeing the slaves was running high. New rumors and dire predictions appeared almost daily. Yet Lincoln waited. He would not be forced to act hastily, either by his own emotions or by the threats of others.

Carl Sandburg's picture of Lincoln as he faced the moment of decision is surely one of the finest passages in his monumental biography.

TWO PLANS the President struggled with incessantly, like an engineer wrestling to put bridges over a swollen river during a flood rush. One of these was to make practical the colonization of Negroes to be freed. The other was gradual compensated abolishment. He wrote in one message, "Any member of Congress, with the census tables and treasury reports before him, can readily see for himself how very soon the current expenditures of this war would purchase at fair valuation, all the slaves in any named State." He pointed to Kentucky as a State that recently through legal process had become the owner of slaves, and she sold none but liberated all.

The President asked, and Congress passed, an act recognizing the Negro republics of Hayti and Liberia. . . . Congress revised the war regulations so as to forbid any officer of the army or the navy to use his forces to capture and return fugitive slaves. Another act provided that such officers could not hear evidence and try cases as to whether a runaway slave should be returned on the claim of an owner. A treaty was negotiated with Great Britain for suppression of the African slave trade. By another act of Congress all slaves in Territories of the United States were declared free. Along with the purchase and emancipation of slaves in the District of Columbia came further legislation for the education of Negro children; and Negroes were made admissible as mail-carriers.

These acts of Congress were capped by the Confiscation Act, which the President signed in July of '62. Slaves of persons convicted of treason or rebellion should be made free, this act declared, and furthermore, slaves of rebels who escaped into Union Army lines, or slaves whose masters had run away, or slaves found by the Union Army in places formerly occupied by rebel forces, should all be designated as prisoners of war and set free. Other bills provided that slaves entering Union Army lines could be put to work and earn their freedom; the President could enroll and employ Negroes for camp labor and military service, while the wives, mothers, and children of such Negro slaves, if they were the property of armed "rebels," should be set free; the President was authorized "to employ as many persons of African descent as he may deem necessary and proper for the suppression of this rebellion, and for this purpose he may organize and use them in such manner as he may judge best for the public welfare."

Lincoln at first intended to veto the Confiscation Act and have it reframed. Instead he signed it, and returned it with his intended veto message attached, for future record. "It is startling to say that Congress can free a slave within a State," ran part of this veto message, "and yet if it were said that the ownership of the slave had first been transferred to the nation, and that Congress had then liberated him, the difficulty would at once vanish." The slaves of a traitor were forfeited to the Government, which raised the question: "Shall they be made free, or sold to new masters?" He could see no objection to Congress' deciding in advance that they should be free.

Thus far all laws passed by Congress fully protected the ownership of slaves held by men loyal to the Union, or men not partaking in the rebellion. Not many were there of such Unionist slaveowners. All other owners of slaves were under the threat of confiscation of their property if and when the Union armies reached their plantations.

In the midst of these zigzags of public policy, the editors of *Harper's Weekly* saw the President as following a midway path, giving in to neither of the extremists. An editorial in May set forth: "In the President of the United States Providence has vouchsafed a leader whose moral perceptions are blinded neither by sophistry nor enthusiasm— who knows that permanent results must grow, and can not be prematurely seized—a man who, whatever he has not, has that inestimable common sense which is the last best gift of Heaven to all who are clothed with great authority."

By the use of "political mesmerism" the President could be reached, said Henry Ward Beecher. As though Beecher was close to the people and Lincoln far aloof and out of touch, Beecher wrote in the *Independent*: "What the people see, the President will see. What the people taste, will repeat itself on the President's tongue." He would politically mesmerize Lincoln into a somnolent state of obedience to God's decree written in heavenly light: "universal emancipation."

Months earlier, as far back as December, 1861, Lincoln spoke to Senator Sumner about sending a message on emancipation to Congress. Sumner said that would be glorious. Lincoln reminded him: "Don't say a word about that. I know very well that the name connected with this act will never be forgotten."

But the armies were slow. The North got no grip on the South to warrant action. The President waited.

The idea of emancipation as a war measure, a military necessity, began developing. Even the Copperhead Democrats would have added difficulty arguing against emancipation if it could be shown as necessary to win the war. This looked promising. However, when Senator James Harlan and others one day urged the President to free and arm the slaves, he told them: "Gentlemen, I have put thousands of muskets into the hands of loyal citizens of Tennessee, Kentucky, and western North Carolina. They said they could defend themselves if they had guns. I have given them the guns. Now these men do not believe in mustering in the Negro. If I do it these thousands of muskets will be turned against us. We should lose more than we should gain."

The Senators argued that Europe would intervene unless the slaves were freed. It might even be that England and France would get the South to free its slaves in exchange for recognition. When the Senators ran out of arguments, Lincoln said, as Harlan heard him: "Gentlemen, I can't do it. I can't see it as you do. You may be right and I may be wrong. But I'll tell you what I can do. I can resign in favor of Mr. Hamlin. Perhaps Mr. Hamlin could do it." The Senators were thunderstruck, said that the President from where he stood could see the whole horizon; he must do what he thought right; whatever else, he must not resign.

In the labyrinth of viewpoints in which Lincoln found himself, encircled by groups trying to infiltrate him with their special ideas, he sent a telegram to Leonard Swett at Bloomington, Illinois, asking him to come to Washington at once. Swett got on a train, traveled two days, arrived in Washington, and went at once, without breakfast, to the White House. The two met, old partners in trying law cases, sleeping in the same bed in zero weather at taverns on the old Eighth Circuit.

Lincoln invited Swett into the Cabinet room, asked about old friends in Illinois, pulled up a chair to a cabinet, and out of a drawer took a letter. This he read to Swett, who sat in quiet. The letter was from William Lloyd Garrison, one of the more patient and considerate of the uncompromising abolitionists. Unless some step was taken, Garrison urged, to cut out by the roots the institution of slavery, the North would be disappointed, the moral wrong at the bottom of the war not touched, and the war long in continuation.

Then, putting this letter back with no comment, Lincoln took out another. This was from Garrett Davis, Senator from Kentucky, showing the delicate balance of forces at war, reasoning that radical action as to slavery would throw the Border State people toward the Confederacy. Laying this letter back with no comment, Lincoln took out one from a Swiss statesman who told of European nations looking for a pretext to intervene in America. Emancipation measures would be taken in Europe as the equivalent of stirring up slave insurrections. From the earliest times in history any interference with the enemy's slaves had been regarded as a cruel expedient; it was not done.

After putting away this letter, Lincoln turned to Swett and began a discussion of emancipation in all its phases. He turned it inside out and outside in. He reasoned as though he did not care about convincing Swett, but as though he needed to think out loud in the presence of an old-timer he knew and could trust. Swett watched the mental operations of his friend until after an hour they came to an end. The President asked for no comment, hoped that Swett would get home safely, sent his best wishes to acquaintances, and the interview, as such, was closed. Thus Swett related it.

John W. Crisfield, once a fellow member of Congress with Lincoln, and now a member of a House committee to report on gradual compensated emancipation, came to Lincoln's office in July of '62 and, according to Lamon, they exchanged remarks.

"Well, Crisfield, how are you getting along with your report? Have you written it yet?"

"No."

"You had better come to an agreement. Niggers will never be cheaper."

On July 22, 1862, as the McClellan campaign for Richmond was fading in mist, mud, and disaster, Lincoln called his Cabinet for a meeting. And as he told it himself at a later time to the painter Frank B. Carpenter, it was a notable day.

"Things had gone on from bad to worse," said Lincoln, "until I felt that we had reached the end of our rope on the plan of operations we had been pursuing; that we had about played our last card, and must change our tactics, or lose the game. I now determined upon the adoption of the emancipation policy, and without consultation with or the knowledge of the Cabinet, I prepared the original draft of the proclamation, and after much anxious thought, called a Cabinet meeting upon the subject. I said to the Cabinet that I had resolved upon this step, and had not called them together to ask their advice, but to lay the subject matter of a proclamation before them, suggestions as to which would be in order, after they had heard it read. Secretary Chase wished the language stronger in reference to the arming of the blacks. Mr. Blair deprecated the policy, on the ground that it would cost the administration the fall elections.

"Nothing, however, was offered that I had not already fully anticipated and settled in my own mind, until Secretary Seward spoke. He said in substance, 'Mr. President, I approve of the proclamation, but I question the expediency of its issue at this juncture. The depression of the public mind, consequent upon our repeated reverses, is so great that I fear the effect of so important a step. It may be viewed as the last measure of an exhausted government, a cry for help; the government stretching forth its hands to Ethiopia, instead of Ethiopia stretching forth her hands to the government.' His idea was that it would be considered our last *shriek*, on the retreat. 'Now,' continued Mr. Seward, 'while I approve the measure, I suggest, sir, that you postpone its issue, until you can give it to the country supported by military success, instead of issuing it, as would be the case now, upon the greatest disasters of the war.' The wisdom of the view of the Secretary of State struck me with very great force. It was an aspect of the case that, in all my thought upon the subject, I had entirely overlooked.

"The result was that I put the draft of the proclamation aside. . . . From time to time I added or changed a line, touching it up here and there, anxiously awaiting the progress of events. Well, the next news we had was of Pope's disaster, at Bull Run. Things looked darker than ever. Finally, came the week of the battle of Antietam. I determined to wait no longer. The news came, I think, on Wednesday, that the advantage was on our side. I was then staying at the Soldiers' Home [three miles out of Washington]. Here I finished writing the second draft of the preliminary proclamation, came up on Saturday; called the Cabinet together to hear it, and it was published the following Monday."

Vice-President Hamlin told of his call to notify the President that he was going home in a few days. And the President laughed an order "to sit in that chair and afterward ride with me to supper." They rode horseback to the Soldiers' Home, after supper took chairs in the library, Lincoln having carefully closed the doors to the room. "Now listen while I read this paper," said Lincoln. "We will correct it together as I go on." Then he read the Emancipation Proclamation, and Hamlin approved.

Welles and Chase wrote in their diaries of what happened at the Cabinet meeting on September 22, 1862, and the final discussion of the Emancipation Proclamation before its going out for the round world to read and think about. The President mentioned in opening the Cabinet meeting that Artemus Ward had sent him a book with a chapter in it titled "High-Handed Outrage at Utica." The President said he would read this chapter, which he thought very funny. He read:

In the Faul of 1856, I showed my show in Utiky, a trooly grate sitty in the State of New York.

The people gave me a cordyal recepshun. The press was loud in her prases.

1 day as I was givin a descripshun of my Beests and Snaiks in my usual flowry stile what was my skorn & disgust to see a big burly feller walk up to the cage containin my wax figgers of the Lord's Last Supper, and cease Judas Iscarrot by the feet and drag him out on the ground. He then commenced fur to pound him as hard as he cood.

"What under the son are you abowt?" cried I.

Sez he, "What did you bring this pussylanermus cuss here fur?" & he hit the wax figger another tremenjis blow on the hed.

Sez I, "You egrejus ass, that air's a wax figger—a representashun of the false 'Postle."

Sez he, "That's all very well fur you to say, but I tell you, old man, that Judas Iscarrot can't show hisself in Utiky with impunerty by a darn site!" with which observashun he kaved in Judassis hed. The young man belonged to 1 of the first famerlies in Utiky. I sood him, and the Joory brawt in a verdick of Arson in the 3d degree.

Lincoln seemed to enjoy this clownery. So did other members of the Cabinet, though Seward laughed for fun while Chase smiled rather conventionally. Stanton was the exception. Stanton sat glum and glowering.

Then, as though he had purposely relaxed himself and others for the high tension of the business at hand, Lincoln took a grave tone, spoke with a solemn deliberation. He reminded them of the Emancipation

Proclamation they had considered two months before. Ever since then his mind had been occupied with it. "I have thought all along that the time for acting on it might probably come. I think the time has come now. I wish it was a better time. I wish that we were in a better condition. The action of the army against the rebels has not been quite what I should have best liked. But they have been driven out of Maryland, and Pennsylvania is no longer in danger of invasion. When the rebel army was at Frederick, I determined, as soon as it should be driven out of Maryland, to issue a proclamation of emancipation, such as I thought most likely to be useful. I said nothing to anyone; but I made the promise to myself and [hesitating a little, Chase noted]—to my Maker. The rebel army is now driven out, and I am going to fulfill that promise.

"I have got you together to hear what I have written down. I do not wish your advice about the main matter; for that I have determined for myself. This I say without intending anything but respect for any one of you. But I already know the views of each on this question. They have been heretofore expressed, and I have considered them as thoroughly and carefully as I can. What I have written is that which my reflections have determined me to say. If there is anything in the expressions I use, or in any other minor matter, which any one of you thinks had best be changed, I shall be glad to receive the suggestions.

"One other observation I will make. I know very well that many others might, in this matter as in others, do better than I can; and if I was satisfied that the public confidence was more fully possessed by any one of them than by me, and knew of any constitutional way in which he could be put in my place, he should have it. I would gladly yield it to him. But though I believe that I have not so much of the confidence of the people as I had, some time since, I do not know that, all things considered, any person has more; and, however this may be, there is no way in which I can have any other man put where I am. I am here. I must do the best I can, and bear the responsibility of taking the course which I feel I ought to take."

Lincoln read the proclamation, commenting as he went along, as though he had considered it in all its lights. It began with saying the war would go on for the Union, that the efforts would go on for buying and setting free the slaves of the Border States, and the colonizing of them; that on January 1, 1863, all slaves in States or parts of States in rebellion against the United States "shall be then, thenceforward, and forever free," and the Federal Government would "recognize the freedom of such persons." It was a preliminary proclamation, to be followed by a final one on next New Year's Day.

Seward suggested adding the words "and maintain" after the word "recognize." Chase joined Seward in this, and it was done. Blair said he was for the principle involved, but the result of the proclamation would be to send the Border States into the arms of the secessionists as soon as it was read in those States; also it would give a club to hostile political elements in the North. Seward made another minor suggestion, that colonization should be only with the consent of the colonists; Negroes were to be sent out of the country only as they were willing to go. Lincoln put that in quickly. Then he asked Seward why he had not proposed both of his important changes at once. Seward hedged.

And Lincoln said Seward reminded him of a hired man out West who came to the farmer one afternoon with news that one of a yoke of oxen had dropped dead. And after hesitating and waiting a while, the hired man said the other ox in the team had dropped dead too. The farmer asked, "Why didn't you tell me at once that both oxen were dead?" "Because," said the hired man, "I didn't want to hurt you by telling you too much at one time."

Two days later, September 24, 1862, on a Monday morning, this preliminary Emancipation Proclamation was published, for the country and the world to read. The President held that to have issued it six months earlier would have been too soon. What he called "public sentiment" would not have stood for it. "A man watches his pear-tree day after day, impatient for the ripening of the fruit. Let him attempt to *force* the process and he may spoil both fruit and tree. But let him patiently *wait*, and the ripe pear at length falls into his lap. . . . I have done what no man could have helped doing, standing in my place." . . .

"What I did, I did after a very full deliberation. . . . I can only trust in God I have made no mistake. I shall make no attempt on this occasion to sustain what I have done or said by any comment. It is now for the country and the world to pass judgment, and, maybe, take action upon it." He was "environed with difficulties," he soberly wished the crowd to know. "Yet they are scarcely as great as the difficulties of those who upon the battle-field are endeavoring to purchase with their blood and their lives the future happiness and prosperity of this country." He wanted those soldiers with him. He was privately wondering how many of them now were stronger for him.

Abraham Lincoln: The War Years, by Carl Sandburg

THE WRIGHT BROTHERS

"... I look with amazement upon our audacity ..."

Man must have always envied the birds. The flight of a hawk, of a seagull, of an eagle is a beautiful free thing—and for thousands of years, man has tried to imitate it. Great geniuses like Leonardo da Vinci and mad visionaries like Francesco de Lana planned machines to win the sky; but it remained for two practical mechanics, proprietors of a bicycle shop in Dayton, Ohio, to be the first to succeed. Wilbur and Orville Wright had a dream. In this account in Orville's own words their dream becomes reality.

I TOOK A position at one of the wings, intending to help balance the machine as it ran down the track, but when the restraining wire was slipped, the machine started off so quickly I could stay with it only a few feet. After a 35- to 40-foot run, it lifted from the rail.

But it was allowed to turn up too much. It climbed a few feet, stalled, and then settled to the ground near the foot of the hill, 105 feet below. My stop-watch showed that it had been in the air just three and a half seconds. In landing, the left wing touched first. The machine swung around, dug the skids into the sand and broke one of them. Several other parts were also broken, but the damage to the machine was not serious. While the tests had shown nothing as to whether the power of the motor was sufficient to keep the machine up, since the landing was made many feet below the starting point, the experiment had demonstrated that the method adopted for launching the machine was a safe and practical one. On the whole, we were much pleased.

Two days were consumed in making repairs, and the machine was not ready again till late in the afternoon of the 16th. While we had it out on the track in front of the building, making the final adjustments, a stranger came along. After looking at the machine a few seconds, he inquired what it was. When we told him it was a flying-machine he asked whether we intended to fly it. We said we did, as soon as we had a suitable wind. He looked at it several minutes longer and then, wishing to be courteous, remarked that it looked as if it would fly, if it had a "suitable wind." We were much amused, for, no doubt, he had in mind the recent 75-mile gale when he repeated our words, "a suitable wind"!

During the night of December 16th a strong cold wind blew from the north. When we arose on the morning of the 17th, the puddles of water which had been standing about the camp since the recent rains were covered with ice. The wind had a velocity of 10 to 12 meters per second (22 to 27 miles an hour). We thought it would die down before long, and so remained indoors the early part of the morning. But when ten o'clock arrived, and the wind was as brisk as ever, we decided that we had better get the machine out and attempt a flight. We hung out the signal for the men of the Life-Saving Station. We thought that by facing the flyer into a strong wind, there ought to be no trouble in launching it from the level ground about camp. We realized the difficulties of flying in so high a wind, but estimated that the added dangers in flight would be partly compensated for by the slower speed in landing.

We laid the track on a smooth stretch of ground about one hundred feet west of the new building. The biting cold wind made work difficult, and we had to warm up frequently in our living room, where we had a good fire in an improvised stove made of a large carbide can. By the time all was ready, J. T. Daniels, W. S. Dough and E. D. Etheridge, members of the Kill Devil Life-Saving Station; W. C. Brinkley of Manteo; and Johnny Moore, a boy from Nag's Head, had arrived.

We had a "Richard" hand anemometer with which we measured the velocity of the wind. Measurements made just before starting the first flight showed velocities of 11 to 12 meters per second, or 24 to 27 miles per hour. Measurements made just before the last flight gave between 9 and 10 meters per second. One made just afterwards showed a little over 8 meters. The records of the Government Weather Bureau at Kitty Hawk gave the velocity of the wind between the hours of 10:30 and twelve o'clock, the time during which the four flights were made, as averaging 27 miles at the time of the first flight and 24 miles at the time of the last.

With all the knowledge and skill acquired in thousands of flights in the last ten years, I would hardly think today of making my first flight on a strange machine in a 27-mile wind, even if I knew that the machine had already been flown and was safe. After these years of experience, I look with amazement upon our audacity in attempting flights with a new and untried machine under such circumstances. Yet faith in our calculations and the design of the first machine, based upon our tables of air pressures, obtained by months of careful laboratory work, and confidence in our system of control developed by three years of actual experience in balancing gliders in the air, had convinced us that the machine was capable of lifting and maintaining itself in the air, and that, with a little practice, it could be safely flown.

Wilbur having used his turn in the unsuccessful attempt on the 14th, the right to the first trial now belonged to me. After running the motor a few minutes to heat it up, I released the wire that held the machine to the track, and the machine started forward into the wind. Wilbur ran at the side of the machine, holding the wing to balance it on the track. Unlike the start on the 14th, made in a calm, the machine, facing a 27-mile wind, started very slowly. Wilbur was able to stay with it till it lifted from the track after a 40-foot run. One of the Life-Saving men snapped the camera for us, taking a picture just as the machine had reached the end of the track and had risen to a height of about two feet. The slow forward speed of the machine over the ground is clearly shown in the picture by Wilbur's attitude. He stayed along beside the machine without any effort.

The course of the flight up and down was exceedingly erratic, partly due to the irregularity of the air and partly to lack of experience in handling this machine. The control of the front rudder was difficult on account of its being balanced too near the center. This gave it a tendency to turn itself when started, so that it turned too far on one side and then too far on the other. As a result, the machine would rise suddenly to about ten feet, and then as suddenly dart for the ground. A sudden dart when a little over a hundred feet from the end of the track, or a little over 120 feet from the point at which we rose into the air, ended the flight. As the velocity of the wind was over 35 feet per second and the speed of the machine over the ground against this wind ten feet per second, the speed of the machine relative to the air was over 45 feet per second, and the length of the flight was equivalent to a flight of 540 feet made in calm air.

This flight lasted only 12 seconds, but it was nevertheless the first in the history of the world in which a machine carrying a man had raised itself by its own power into the air in full flight, had sailed forward without reduction of speed, and had finally landed at a point as high as that from which it started. A surprising thing about the flights was that each brother wore, as usual, a stiff white starched collar and a necktie.

With the assistance of our visitors we carried the machine back to the track and prepared for another flight. The wind, however, had chilled us all through, so that before attempting a second flight, we all went to the building again to warm up. Johnny Moore, seeing under the table a box filled with eggs, asked one of the Station men where we got so many of them. The people of the neighborhood eke out a bare existence by catching fish during the short fishing season, and their supplies of other articles of food are limited. He probably had never seen so many eggs at one time in his whole life.

The one addressed jokingly asked him whether he hadn't noticed the small hen running about the outside of the building. "That chicken lays eight to ten eggs a day!" Moore, having just seen a piece of machinery lift itself from the ground and fly, a thing at that time considered as impossible as perpetual motion, was ready to believe nearly anything. But after going out and having a good look at the wonderful fowl, he returned with the remark, "It's only a common-looking chicken!"

At twenty minutes after eleven Wilbur started on the second flight. The course of this flight was much like that of the first, very much up and down. The speed over the ground was somewhat faster than that of the first flight, due to the lesser wind. The duration of the flight was less than a second longer than the first, but the distance covered was about 75 feet greater.

Twenty minutes later, the third flight started. This one was steadier than the first one an hour before. I was proceeding along pretty well when a sudden gust from the right lifted the machine up twelve to fifteen feet and turned it up sidewise in an alarming manner. It began a lively sidling off to the left. I warped the wings to try to recover the lateral balance and at the same time pointed the machine down to reach the ground as quickly as possible. The lateral control was more effective than I had imagined and before I reached the ground the right wing was lower than the left and struck first. The time of this flight was fifteen seconds and the distance over the ground a little over 200 feet.

Wilbur started the fourth and last flight at just twelve o'clock. The first few hundred feet were up and down, as before, but by the time three hundred feet had been covered, the machine was under much better control. The course for the next four or five hundred feet had but little undulation. However, when out about eight hundred feet the machine began pitching again, and in one of its darts downward, struck the ground. The distance over the ground was measured, and found to be 852 feet; the time of the flight 59 seconds. The frame supporting the front rudder was badly broken, but the main part of the machine was not injured at all. We estimated that the machine could be put in condition for flight again in a day or two.

While we were standing about discussing this last flight, a sudden strong gust of wind struck the machine and began to turn it over.

Everybody made a rush for it. Wilbur, who was at one end, seized it in front. Mr. Daniels and I, who were behind, tried to stop it by holding to the rear uprights.

All our efforts were in vain. The machine rolled over and over. Daniels, who had retained his grip, was carried along with it, and was thrown about, head over heels, inside of the machine. Fortunately, he was not seriously injured, though badly bruised in falling about against the motor, chain guides, etc. The ribs in the surfaces of the machine were broken, the motor injured and the chain guides badly bent, so that all possibility of further flights with it for that year were at an end.

The Wright Brothers, by Fred C. Kelly

ENRICO CARUSO

"His voice was like a shower of stars ..."

Caruso's life was a parade of triumphs. Born to poverty-stricken parents and forced by his circumstances to start work in a factory at the age of ten, his amazing natural voice could not be hidden. By the time he was 22 in 1895 he had made his Italian debut. This fabulous success was followed by his debut in London in 1902, and at the Metropolitan in New York in 1903. His success everywhere was phenomenal. He was the idol of the musical world—sought after, pampered, praised and worshipped.

On Christmas Eve of 1920, while singing the part of Eleazar in La Juive, a blood vessel ruptured in his throat, and Caruso's career was finished. He returned the following spring to his native Naples —a famous, rich yet dispirited old man. Caruso's life without music was a dreary day-to-day existence. . . .

In her biography of her husband Dorothy Caruso tells the sad, yet supremely beautiful story, of Caruso's last great triumph.

We were all to sail on the *President Wilson*. . . . Thirty-eight trunks were already locked and labeled; only the music trunk remained open. We were taking Gloria's crib, pen, collapsible gocarts—there were also boxes of zwieback, cartons of cereal and dozens of bottles of Walker-Gordon milk.

While I was telephoning the order for the milk Enrico came in. "When I was a baby I had not special milk," he said.

"What did you have—did your mother nurse you?"

"No, my mother had no more milk—she had twenty-one children. Twenty boys and one girl—too many. I am number nineteen boy. A lady who was a countess was kind to my mother. Her baby died and she was sad and did not come to see my mother so often. So my mother went to her and said, 'I have no milk for little Enrico. Will you give him?' And so she gave me. I think that is the reason for me to be different from my family."

The day before sailing we went out for our last drive. Enrico said we would stop at one place to pay a bill—"I not want to leave owing someone, so we go there first."

I didn't know we were going to the office of the doctor who had taken the X-rays. He was out, but his young assistant, whom we had never seen before, received us.

We had already said good-by and were at the door when the young man stopped us. "By the way, Mr. Caruso, your rib has already grown half an inch." My heart turned over.

"My *rib?*"

There was no way to stop what followed. The young doctor brought Enrico the X-ray plates and showed him where four inches of his rib had been removed.

The door closed behind us. Enrico stood motionless in the corridor and stared at me. "Doro! My rib is gone!"

I took his arm and we walked to the car.

"Do you mind if we go home?" he said. "I do not feel to drive today."

On the way home . . . he simply said nothing at all. Nor could I find anything to say—he was beyond consolation.

When we reached the apartment he went directly to the studio, where Fucito was packing the scores. "Do not work any more, Fucito," he said, "I have decided not to take with me my music."

I watched him from the door. He walked slowly to the piano and with a gentle gesture closed the lid. . . .

After a few days of rest in Naples we sailed across the bay to Sorrento, where we took a floor in the Hotel Vittoria. It was perfect for Enrico, as all the rooms opened on a long covered terrace above the Mediterranean. . . . The salon was somewhat formal, with Louis XVI furniture and a great gilt piano. I began by disliking this room, but when Enrico told me why it pleased him I liked it too—"All these chairs so stiff and hard will permit people who come to see us to remain not long."

Our meals were served on the terrace and it was there he taught little Gloria her first steps and her first Italian words. All the week he slept and rested, and then one morning he felt strong enough to walk in the hotel gardens and visit the town. We walked very slowly across the sunlit *piazza*. He hadn't walked so far since his illness, and I found many pretexts to stop and rest along the way. Dr. Stella had warned me that he must put no strain on his weak heart, that he must never overtire himself. Above all he advised me to conceal this fact from him, since to worry about it might only retard his progress. . . .

The population treated him with the loving reverence they might have shown to a great cardinal who had come home after a voyage. He was welcomed with smiles and little words of greeting; children shyly offered him wild flowers and refused his pennies. No one stared, or asked him questions, or tried to shake his hand. . . .

The weeks drifted by—lovely days of quiet pleasures, hot sunshine and long sweet moonlit nights. Then in July a group of Enrico's New York friends arrived, announcing that they were going to stay several weeks in order to be near him. He was sorry they had come to disturb our peace, but at the same time glad to see familiar faces. Little by little they broke down our restful routine, persuaded him to go on excursions with them. . . . I didn't quite know what to do, since I dared not tell them about his heart. Sometimes I would say that I was too tired to go and he also would refuse; but afterward they would describe the fun he had missed. . . .

As they knew that he intended to make an offering of thanks for his recovery to the Church of the Madonna of Pompeii, they proposed to go with us and afterward take us to lunch and visit the ruins. . . .

The road from Sorrento to Pompeii twisted between walls too high to see over and too low to give shade. . . . When we reached the church Enrico told them to wait on the steps for the other car while he and I went inside.

We walked up the long aisle toward the altar. A priest rose from his knees to greet Enrico and they went together into the sacristy. When he rejoined me he was smiling cheerfully. "*Ecco*—I thanked my Madonna."

. . . . As usual the news of our plans had run ahead of us and when we arrived at the entrance to the ruins a group of officials was waiting to welcome us. After the handshaking, congratulations and long speeches, the committee told us that . . . Hirohito, the Crown Prince of Japan, had also chosen this day to visit Pompeii. . . . We came upon Hirohito and his party at the new excavation pit. The future Emperor of Japan had a skinny neck, wore thick spectacles and made jerky little bows at us; he didn't smile or offer to shake hands. We watched the workmen surprisingly unearth a statue and a bronze bowl. Enrico whispered, "They put in last night." . . .

Our cars were waiting for us at the gate and beside them stood a young man. He stepped forward and said, "Signor Caruso, if I come to Sorrento will you give me an audition and tell me what you think of my voice?" I think I have never seen an expression as pitiful as Enrico's when he answered, "You want to sing? Yes, I will hear you. Come tomorrow morning." The boy, enraptured, said he would come at eleven. "Bring some music with you," Enrico called from the car.

. . . That night I sat for a long time on the terrace, looking at the lights of Naples and dreading the morning.

I dressed before Enrico wakened. When he came out on the terrace he was paler than usual but said he had slept. "I go on no more excursions—it is enough," he said. We drank our coffee and waited for the boy.

I felt a shock when I saw that he had brought with him the score of *Martha* . . . one of Enrico's best-loved operas.

"What voice you have—baritone?"

"No, Signor Caruso, tenor."

"So—you sing my part. Well, we try."

We went into the salon and Enrico seated himself at the piano. "I know not to accompany—just some chords," he said. Neither his voice nor his eyes had any expression. I thought, "This is too horrible. How will he be able to stand it?"

"I will try to sing '*M'appari*'," the boy said, and Enrico struck a chord.

From the first note I knew that the boy had no voice. Enrico stopped him, told him not to be nervous and to begin again. I went to my room to wait.

I heard them talking. The boy began again. I heard Enrico say, "No, no." There was a moment of silence.

And then I heard a voice! I ran to the salon. There stood Enrico, singing as he had never sung before. His voice was like a shower of stars, more beautiful than it had ever been. As he finished the song he flung out his arms. His face was transfigured. "Doro, I can sing! I can sing! I have not lost my voice. I can sing!"

Music had come back into our lives. All that day, with an enthusiasm I had never heard from him before, Enrico talked of singing— not as hard work, a trust and a responsibility, but as a source of life and happiness.

That evening I sent Gloria's phonograph down to the hotel terrace and after dinner Enrico gave a concert of his records. . . . As that voice poured through the evening air people came silently from the salons and gardens to listen. He made little comments on his singing and hummed happily as he chose his songs. At midnight he sent Mario to fetch waltz and tango records, told everyone to dance and said good night.

In our room I watched him as he lay reading the newspaper and noticed that his eyes weren't following the printed lines. "Are you all right, Rico?" "Oh, yes," he answered, but he gave a little sigh. "I think on the time when Gloria will reach to the door handle. You know I don't mind to die, only I hate not to see our little girl grow up."

The doctor beside me lifted his wrist to count the pulse. I heard the wall clock striking nine and the sound of water being poured into a glass. He opened his eyes and looked at me.

"Doro—I—am—thirsty—" He gave a little cough. "Doro—they—hurt—me—again." He began to gasp for air.

"Don't be afraid, Rico darling—everything is all right."

"Doro—I—can't—get—my—breath—"

I saw his eyes close and his hand drop. I hid my face and thought, "At last Enrico is well." I wanted to go out in the sunshine but I knew I could not because no one would understand. From far away came sounds of weeping and two nuns entered, murmuring prayers. I rose from my knees and walked out of the door without looking back.

Enrico Caruso: His Life and Death, by Dorothy Caruso

JOHN BROWN

"In Cleveland fourteen hundred people are praying together in a black-draped hall."

Wendell Phillips, the Massachusetts reformer, said of John Brown that he "had letters of marque from God." To the abolitionists he was a fiery symbol of the right of their cause—an avenging angel fighting in the service of the Lord. To the South and to many northern moderates he was an instigator of insurrection and a murderer—a vicious and bloody criminal.

Whatever else he may have been, John Brown was certainly a fanatic—a rock-hard figure to stand beside the prophets, a man who never doubted that he was God's strong hand in a holy battle against slavery. At Pottawatomie, in Kansas, without a qualm he massacred five men in cold blood—retribution for five killed in his holy war. At Harper's Ferry he fought his last fight. His band was overwhelmed by federal troops, two of his sons were killed, and he was wounded. Proud and defiant to the end, he was tried for murder and conspiracy, found guilty, and hanged. . . .

But John Brown, the zealot . . . John Brown, the avenger . . . John Brown, whose slashing, violent life had proved so bloody—and so futile—found in death his moment of triumph. He became a martyr, the symbol around which the anti-slavery element rallied. His soul went marching on.

God's Angry Man, from which the following section is taken, is not in a strict sense biography. Erlich has interpolated conversations and hypothesized emotions where the record is incomplete. But the book is an overpoweringly strong and vivid portrait of an almost legendary modern crusader.

"A NOTORIOUS Kansas horsethief," said Stephen A. Douglas; "a criminal who will rightly suffer on the gallows for his crimes."

"John the Just!" exclaimed Louisa Alcott.

Old Brown will be executed for treason to a state, reflected Abraham Lincoln. We cannot object, even though he agreed with us in thinking slavery wrong. That cannot excuse violence, bloodshed, treason. It can avail him nothing that he thinks himself right.

"They are leading John Brown to execution in Virginia," breathed Henry Wadsworth Longfellow to his diary. "It will be a great day in our history: the date of a new Revolution—quite as much needed as the old one. This is sowing the wind to reap the whirlwind, *which will come soon.*"

In town halls and churches from Maine to the Territories men gathered agitated, held meetings.

In New York, a vast one: "Be it resolved . . . that we regard the recent outrage at Harper's Ferry as a crime, not only against the state of Virginia, but against the Union itself. . . ." An ex-Governor spoke; the Mayor presided. There were three overflow meetings in the streets. Emergency police forces kept a difficult order.

In Boston, a vast one. When the doors of the hall were opened men and women were swept in, some without touching the ground with their feet. Wendell Phillips was a brand of passion. Garrison spoke; Ralph Waldo Emerson: ". . . The new saint, than whom none purer or more brave was ever led by love of man into conflict and death . . . who will make the gallows glorious like the cross. . . ."

In the Virginia Legislature: "The South must stand forth as one man and say to fanaticism in her own language—whenever you advance a hostile foot upon our soil, we will welcome you with bloody hands to hospitable graves!"

"The Ferry raid presses on the approaching conflict," said Horace Greeley; "and I think the end of slavery in the Union is ten years nearer than it seemed a few weeks ago."

Governor Wise was at his desk in the Virginia capital; harassed, distraught. Daily by the hundreds the communications poured in upon the Richmond desk—warnings, counsels, threats.

"Pardon the old man, it is expedient, do not make a martyr."

"Hang the old man, give us our revenge."

"Take his life—and we will take yours."

"Declare him insane, shut him up as one does a mad dog."

Desperately Henry Wise sought in himself the right way. The days were clutchings at his brain, sleepless he tossed through the nights. He was at once febrile and strong-willed, mercurial and stubborn; these inflooding exhortations swept him this way and that, but let him once make up his mind and nothing would turn him from it. Desperately, for his conscience's sake and the continuing life of his beloved Southland, Henry Wise sought in himself.

Suddenly he decided.

First: *John Brown was not insane.* Whatever the dark record of his heritage might be, the old man himself had escaped the taint. True, he was too fiercely exalted to be of "normal" mind, he was a fanatic certainly; but equally certain it was that he must be counted responsibly intelligent. Henry Wise had talked with the old man, he remembered the startling interview in the paymaster's office just after the raid ("No man sent me here. It was by my own prompting and that of my Maker"); he had read and been profoundly moved despite himself by the letters from the Charlestown jail: no madman had ever talked and written thus. Now Henry Wise entered in his notebook: "I *know* that he is sane; and remarkably sane, if quick and clear perception, if assumed rational premises, and consecutive reasoning from them, if cautious tact in avoiding disclosures and in covering conclusions and inferences, if memory and conception and practical sense, if composure and self-possession are evidence of a sound state of mind. He is a fanatic, but a man of courage, fortitude and supreme honor; a bundle of the best nerves I ever saw cut and thrust and bleeding and in bonds. He is responsible for his act. *I will take no smallest step to have Old Brown pardoned on grounds of insanity.*"

Second: He, Governor Wise, would not be swayed by appeals to expediency. (". . . To hang a fanatic is to make a martyr of him," had warned a Southern editorial; "and fledge another brood of the same sort. Better send these creatures to the penitentiary and so make them felons. Monsters are hydra-headed, decapitation only quickens vitality and power of reproduction." And again: "Dare you do a bold thing, my friend?" had written Fernando Wood, New York's proslaver mayor. "Have you nerve enough to send him to States Prison instead of hanging him? No Southern man could go further than myself in defence of Southern rights, but yet were I Governor of Virginia, Brown *should not be hung.* And in such a course my conduct would be governed by sound policy. The South will gain by showing that it can be magnanimous to a fanatic in its power. The man is the crazed tool of Abolitionist scoundrels. *Do not make him a martyr. . . .*")

Governor Wise's answer went out: "I have duly received and weighed every word of your letter. Now, listen to me, for my mind is inflexibly made up. . . . These men have been scrupulously afforded a fair trial, with every opportunity of defence for crimes which were openly perpetrated before the eyes of hundreds and as openly confessed. The crimes deliberately done by them are of the deepest and darkest kind which can be committed against our people. Brown the leader has been legally and fairly tried and convicted, and admits the humanity of his treatment as a prisoner, the truth of the indictment, and the truthfulness of the witnesses against him. He has been allowed excess of counsel, and freedom of speech beyond any prisoner known to me in our trials. It was impossible not to convict him. He is sentenced to be hanged—the sentence of a mild code humanely adjudged and requiring no duty from me except to see that it be executed. I have to sign no death warrant. If the Executive interposes at all, it is to pardon. And to pardon him I have received petitions, prayers, threats, from almost every state in the Union. By honest patriotic men like yourself I am warned that hanging will make him a martyr. You ask: Have you nerve enough to send Brown to States Prison for life instead of hanging him? Yes—if I didn't think he *ought to be hung*. I could do it without the quiver of a muscle against a universal clamor for his life. But is it wisely said to a State that she had better spare a murderer, a traitor, because public sentiment elsewhere will glorify the criminal with martyrdom? I say to you firmly that I have precisely the nerve enough to let him be executed. He shall be executed as the law sentences him, and his body shall await the resurrection without a grave in our soil. I have shown him all the mercy which humanity can claim. . . . Yours truly, Henry Wise."

But still the communications poured in. Letters, telegrams, threats, warnings. Damn Judge Parker, the Governor groaned, why had he let the old man live so long, given him a whole month? The very thing Wise had feared had come to pass—the countryside, the whole nation was seething with a huge ferment. And Wise cursed himself too: why had he not proclaimed martial-law after the raid, and executed the traitor under a court-martial! A panic began to grip the Governor.

"I have seen between 30 & 36 men," wrote T. A. B. from Ohio; "all armed with Colts Six Shooters & a species of home made Bowie knife, well calculated to do Exicution. They will cross the river near Cisterville with 200 others and arrive Dec 1 for Ferry rescue. . . ."

From Cleveland the United States marshal forwarded a letter: ". . . and they have 9000 desperate men, and boast that he will not be hanged."

Philadelphia reported: "5000 men armed with Pikes rifles and four cannon."

Detroit warned: "8000 men . . . Dec 1 . . . new style carbines . . . 10 shots a minute at the jail guards."

Governor Henry Wise marked these communications: "Contemptible Nonsense." Governor Henry Wise wired to President Buchanan of the United States: "I have reliable information . . . convinced that attempt will be made to rescue prisoners. . . . Places in Maryland,

Ohio and Pa. occupied as depots and rendezvous by desperadoes. . . . We are kept in continual apprehension of outrages from fire and rapine on our borders."

Two days later Colonel Robert E. Lee, United States Army, arrived in Charlestown with three hundred artillerymen from Fort Monroe. A thousand militiamen from neighboring towns bivouacked about Charlestown. Four hundred men from Richmond and Petersburg were ordered in, with cannon. Proud serious-faced lads arrived from Lexington, cadets of the Virginia Military Institute, under a Professor T. J. Jackson. Charlestown was like a town besieged. Troops were quartered in the churches, the schools. In the court-house the guns were stacked outside the counsels' railing, and knapsacks and canteens were piled upon the bench. Even the graveyards knew the hobbed boots and the clangor of steel. Mounted patrols ranged every precinct of the county. Sentries were stationed a full mile beyond the town; it took an hour and forty minutes to post the guard.

Night after night mysterious fires licked at the winter sky. The barns of three Charlestown citizens were burned down; the three citizens had been on the jury which had doomed an old man to the gallows. The fires continued throughout November. There were strange rifleshots outside the windows of prominent townsmen. Mayor Green ordered all strangers to leave Charlestown, under pain of arrest. (Young Hoyt was among these; he had failed, the old man had stood against his purpose like stone, but the lawyer-stripling left with a strange sense of fulfillment, with "I am worth infinitely more . . ." echoing in him, like an exultation.) And now the little town was a single throbbing body of dread. There were frantic rumors of invasion, sudden alarms shuddering through from house to house. The troops would fall hastily into line, the cavalry would go rushing with cries and ringing hoofs through the cold dark of the night.

(The South's very heart was beating in that little town. The dread, vague, almost nameless, the ominous sense of some vast fate beyond this special moment, hung dark, hung over the Tennessee mountains, over the red baked fields of Georgia and the cotton lands leaning hotly close upon the waters of the Gulf. That mad thrust of an old man and some boys was like a knife unsheathed, the knife of the North thrusting for the Southland's heart, murderously singing: blood, frenzy, insurrection. Twenty-two evil little creatures had stolen down into their land; they were as a snarl and a threatening footfall—a beast which was half a nation crouched ravenous and waiting.

Men of the South, be ready, let us be ready, let us fight for our land and our life and the ways of our fathers!)

The gallows-day was approaching. Governor Wise sent orders to Major-General W. B. Taliaferro: "Keep full guard on the line of frontier from Martinsburg to Harper's Ferry, on the day of Dec 2d. Warn inhabitants to arm and keep guard and patrol on that day and for days beforehand. Prevent all strangers and especially parties of strangers from proceeding to Charlestown on Dec 2d. Station guard at Ferry sufficient to control crowds on the cars from East and West. Be prepared, if situation requires, to tear up railroad tracks. Let mounted men guard outposts. Two companies to keep crowd clear of outer line of military. Form two concentric squares around gallows. Have extra strong guard at jail and for escort to execution. Let no crowd be near enough to the prisoner to hear any speech he may attempt. Allow no more visitors to be admitted to jail. . . ."

And in the Charlestown lock-up, full in the midst of the dread and the rage, the old man with the flowing white beard and the sabre cuts calmly spoke and wrote, and the words went out. (A hundred reporters sent him living and etched into millions of wide-flung homes. Now he was doing this, saying that; yesterday he had written his will: could the rights of his stricken family be respected in regard to all his property not of a warlike nature?—today he was requesting a plain pine coffin for the last rest of his body.) And the nation listened.

"I am only walking now as God foreordained I should walk. All our actions, even the follies leading to this disaster were decreed to happen ages before this world was made. . . . And God will not forget the work of his hands."

"Let them hang me. I forgive them, and may God forgive them. For they know not what they do."

Calm little words. And the nation listening (on the 28th of November 1859 a brief obscure note in the newspapers says that Washington Irving is dead), the nation a vast gripped gaze; with here grief, and there a fury of hatred, but wonderment everywhere (across the Atlantic waters Victor Hugo is saying: "The eyes of Europe are fixed on America. The hanging of John Brown will open a latent fissure that will finally split the Union asunder. . . . You preserve your shame but you kill your glory"), wonderment everywhere and an inner searching. For those little words speak deep beyond themselves, they seem in a torn bewildered land to hold some serene yet passionate mystery of faith: *I, John Brown, will go without fear, with a great shining peace in my heart; I will show men how to die for truth.* Calm little words, inescapable, like fingers pointing; little ghosts of words haunting the thoughts of men: *Where do you stand? what do you believe? We can no longer go as fools in a blind wilderness. This*

people in our midst, this dark prostrate soul will shape our life or our
death. Americans, brothers, which way are your eyes turned?

Darkly on the horizon creep the deep low sounds; louder, faintly
louder; as creep the sullen mutterings of a distant storm.

The voices of grief and revulsion rise, from the North, the South,
from the farthest West in the land of the brothers tragically cloven.

And in the sky there are portents, and signs like flames.

*   *   *

Mary Brown, after receiving the plea to remain away from the
Charlestown jail and "not to go wild; out of pity to me," did not
return to her mountain home. "I'll abide my husband's mind," she
said; but she stayed in Philadelphia, with the McKims, and waited;
waited with desolate patience for the word that in the end she knew
would come. It came. "Mary, if you are equal to the undertaking of
seeing me before I suffer; if you can afford to meet the expence &
trouble of coming on here to gather up the bones of our beloved sons
& of your husband; and the Virginia people will suffer you to do so;
I am entirely willing."

She showed the word to McKim. The Abolitionist said that she
must write at once to Governor Wise, she must get his permission.
She flushed. "I don't think I can do this . . . good enough," she said.
Of course not, answered McKim gently; she was under a terrible
strain; might he tend to the request for her? She could approve it.

"Governor Henry Wise: . . . and I beg for the mortal remains of
my husband and sons . . . for decent and tender interment among
their kindred . . . Mary Brown."

Would this do? McKim asked, gentler still. Yes, it would do, she
said; and wept softly; and soon was calm again.

In Charlestown, Major-General Taliaferro, commanding the Commonwealth's troops, received a telegraphed order: "Sir: when John
Brown is executed on Friday the 2d proximo, you will place his mortal
remains under strict guard and protect them from all mutilation. Place
them in a plain coffin and have them taken to Harper's Ferry, there
to await the orders of Mrs. Mary Brown who has a duplicate of this
order. You will also allow the bodies of her sons, who fell at Harper's
Ferry, to be disinterred and taken by her or her agent or order. Re-
spectfully, Henry Wise."

(Close by the waters of the Shenandoah, Oliver Brown lay in an
unmarked grave, together with eight of his comrades. It would be beyond her heart's strength to look upon him, for identification. . . .

The remains of Watson Brown had been taken to a Virginia college
for preservation as an anatomical specimen.)

Mary Brown left for Harper's Ferry with the McKims and Hector
Tyndale, a young Philadelphia lawyer. They arrived on the night of
November 30th; they stayed at the Wager House. Only Mary Brown
would be permitted to go on to Charlestown, the others would have to
remain at the Ferry. (Her friends were virtually prisoners; eyes
watched them ceaselessly. Once as they took a turn about the streets
to ease the sickening strain of waiting, a mocking bullet whined high
above them in the air. Twenty-six months later, on February 7th,
1862, a Major H. Tyndale, commanding the Twenty-eighth Pennsylvania Infantry, would, under superior military orders, burn the arsenal
town of Harper's Ferry. A squat stone engine-house—where once, on a
morning of white ravelling mists and a hush over the shining rivers, a
cracked voice had called "Calm, men; sell your life dear, sell it dear!"
and blue-tunicked Marines had come swarming with bayonets and
sledges—the engine-house would stand through the flames.) Now, on
this first day of December, Mary Brown left her friends at the Ferry
hostelry, and stepped heavily into the waiting carriage. She was dark-
veiled. A captain of militia sat beside her. The carriage, with nine
cavalrymen riding as an escort, wheeled off into the cold gray day,
swiftly along the Charlestown road.

And while these things were going on and the gallows-time approached, a little inner world settled deeper into its final peace. The
old man was "dayly & hourly striving to gather up what little I may
from the wreck." He sat writing, writing, all through the days, and
far into the nights, until his eyes would fail. Jesus Christ, he told himself, had taken from him the sword of blood, and had placed in his
hands another—the "words, words" he had despised so long were now
become his very strength. Aye, he would speak to the heart of his
land (only yesterday he had read in the newspapers what Emerson
had said: The slaveholder believes while he chains and chops John
Brown that he is getting rid of his tormentor. Does he not see that
the air this man breathes is Liberty? that it will be breathed by thousands and millions?) So the letters, even as his days forever diminished, went out steadily, to relatives, to friends, to public-men, to
strangers.

"I have been *whiped* as the saying is; but I am sure I can recover
all the lost capital occasioned by this disaster; by only hanging a few
minutes by the neck. . . . I cannot remember a night so dark as to
have hindered the coming of day, nor a storm so furious or dreadful
as to prevent the return of warm sunshine and a cloudless sky. . . .

May God for Christ's sake ever make his face to shine on you all. . . ."

"I have asked to be spared from having any mock; or *hypocritical prayers* made over me when I am publicly murdered: & that my only religious attendants be poor *little, dirty, ragged, bareheaded, & barefooted Slave boys*; & Girls, led by some old grey headed slave Mother. . . ."

"It affords me some satisfaction to feel conscious of having tried to better the condition of those who are on the under-hill side, and I am now in hopes of being able to meet the consequences without a murmur. . . . Did not Jesus of Nazareth suffer death on the cross as a fellon? Think too of the crushed Millions who have no comforters. *I charge you all* never to forget the griefs of the poor that cry & of those that have none to help them. . . . Farewell. Farewell."

Often, Avis the jailer, reading in accordance with his duty these letters of his homeland's enemy, would look forth unseeing through tear-filled eyes.

And now, on this deepening afternoon, the last before the hanging, Avis the jailer stood before the old man, and said:

"Captain Brown. Your wife is here."

*   *   *

Mrs. Avis, a tall faded woman, led Mary Brown into a private room of the prison structure.

"I must ask you to take your coat off, Mrs. Brown," she said, hesitantly, not meeting the other's eyes. "Those are my orders."

She began to run her moist fingers through the garments of Mary Brown; then slowly over the soft heavy body.

"How is my husband's health?" trembled Mary Brown, all unheeding, as in a dream.

"His wounds are healing nicely."

When the searching was over, the jailer's wife stood there, fumbling her keys in the big moist hands. "You . . . mustn't think . . . we're glad," she said.

"Can I go in to see him now?" asked Mary Brown faintly.

"Come."

Avis was waiting in the corridor. He led Mary Brown to the cell-door. He unlocked it.

John Brown was standing half-shrouded in the darkness by the further wall, beneath the barred window. A taper was burning on the table. The iron door clicked shut behind her; the footsteps faded. . . . She moved toward him. He took two steps forward, the chains clanking.

"Oh, John."

"Mary."

They stood clinging to each other, weeping. A minute passed; two; they clung weeping.

But soon they were quiet. They sat by the table, and quietly talked; a gaunt bowed man, in carpet slippers and seedy black trousers, with a white beard falling away from his breast; a pale heavy woman, dressed in black.

"I'm glad you came, Mary."

"John . . . it's a hard lot."

"Be cheerful, Mary. We must all bear it in the best manner we can. I think it's all for the best."

"Our poor children."

"Aye . . . aye." They sat. His bony hand stole across the table, found hers. Through the hands their hearts flowed, they clung in their hearts. "But we'll not be separated forever, wife. We'll come together in another house."

Then anxiously he asked: "Tell me, Mary, do you blame me? Have I given you too much to bear?"

"I have no blame, John."

"No," he said, and his eyes shone. "Our sacrifices are not at all too great."

He began to talk about the Elba home. Had the crops matured well this season? How were all those yet living? Was Martha carrying her baby well? Once suddenly he groaned, "Our poor shattered children." But this did not last; he went on quietly. God, he said, would be a husband to the widow, he would be a father to the fatherless. . . .

". . . And now, Mary, let me say a little about educating our young daughters. I know it doesn't become me to dictate in this matter. I have little right to meddle now in your worldly affairs—I have done so poorly in them. But still, you know, Mary, don't you, I have not lost interest in my daughters." So let them be told that he wished them educated for a plain life. He did not at all mean an education as miserable as he or she had got; he meant enough of the learning of schools to enable them to transact the common business as well as the common duties. Let his daughters be useful though poor, let them know the music of the washtub and the needle before the music of the piano. Aye, he wished them to be "matter of fact women."

She nodded brokenly as he spoke. Her eyes went again and again to the chains that galled his ankles beneath the heavy white-wool socks.

"They say it'll be tomorrow, John. Will it be tomorrow, John?"

"I'm peaceful, Mary. I've had a long life."

Footsteps sounded harsh along the corridor. . . . The militia captain called through the bars: "You will have to leave soon, Mrs. Brown. Your carriage goes back in half an hour."

"Why?" the old man said. "Surely my wife will be allowed to stay this night!"

"No. Mrs. Brown must return to the Ferry."

The old man leaped up, went clanking half in a limp to the bars; one of his slippers fell from his foot. "But you can't do this. It's a little thing. Why, tomorrow we'll be apart."

"I'm sorry. My orders won't allow it."

The old man stood there, quivering in a sudden rage. His hands gripped the bars, they were white circling gnarls of bone. "Orders!" he cried with scorn and pleading. "Orders on this night!"

Mary Brown went to him. She put her hand on his arm. "Don't, John," she said. He glared at her. Then he dropped his hands from the bars. He turned; stooped to pick up the slipper; and limped weakly back to his bench by the table.

"I ask nothing of you, sir. I beg nothing from the state of Virginia. Carry out your orders. I'm content."

The officer went silently away. . . .

"I want to read this to you, Mary, before you go. It's my last will. I wrote it this morning. . . . Listen with care, Mary. I wish it carried out, exactly. . . ."

I give to my son John Brown Jr. my Surveyors Compass & other surveyors articles if found also my old Granite Monument now at North Elba . . . Said stone Monument to remain however at North Elba, so long as any of my children or my wife; may remain there; as residents.

He gave her a slip of paper. "This is what I wish carven on the two sides of the stone, Mary," he said. "I have left blank the day of birth of our Watson and Oliver. I have marked their deaths, but you will remember better than I their day of birth. . . ." Then he went on reading the will:

I give to my Son Jason my Silver Watch with my name egraved on iner case. . . .

I give to my son Owen Brown my double Spry or opera Glass & my Rifle Gun (if found). It is Globe Sighted & new. I give also to the same Son Fifty Dollars in consideration of his terrible sufferings in Kansas: & his crippled condition from his childhood. . . .

"Do you hear, Mary? Is this clear?"

"Yes, husband." She was silently weeping, with upturned face.

I give to my Daughter Ruth Thompson my large old Bible containing family record. . . .

I give to each of my GrandChildren that may be living when my

Father's Estate is settled: as good a copy of the Bible as can be pur-chased at a cost of $3, Three Dollars each . . . all the Bibles to be purchased at one and the same time for Cash on best terms. . . .

The voice went on: *I give . . . I desire . . . It is my will. . . .*

"Do you hear, Mary?"

"Yes, John. Yes."

And now it was the time for them to separate. He held her hands, and said, "Mary . . . I hope you will always live in Essex County. . . . Get, if you can, all our remaining children together. . . . Impress right principles, Mary . . . to each succeeding generation."

He bent; their lips touched, trembled together.

"Now go, Mary. . . . God will be with us. . . . Good-bye. Good-bye."

"Oh John. . . . Good-bye."

Mary Brown began the long dark ride back to Harper's Ferry. There she would wait through the night; tomorrow she would take up the body.

John Brown sat writing his last letters. When he had finished these, he read a little in his Bible. . . . Then he slept.

*   *   *

As I now begin what is probably the last letter I shall ever write to any of you; I conclude to write to you all at the same time. . . . I am waiting the hour of my public *murder* with great composure of mind, & cheerfulness: feeling the strongest assurance that in no other possi-ble way could I be used to so much advance the cause of God; & of humanity: & that nothing that either I or all my family have sacrificed or suffered: will be lost. The reflection that a *wise & merciful, as well as just & holy God:* rules not only the affairs of *this world;* but of all worlds; is a rock to set our feet upon; under all circumstances: *even* those more severely *trying ones:* into which our own follies; & rongs have placed us. . . . I am endeavouring to 'return' like a 'poor Prodi-gal' *as I am,* to my Father: against whom I have *always* sined: *in the hope;* that he may kindly, & forgivingly 'meet me: though a *verry great way off.'* . . . Oh do not trust your eternal all uppon the boisterous Ocean, without *even* a *Helm;* or *Compass* to *aid* you in steering. . . . My dear young children will you listen to the last poor admonition of one who can only love you? Oh be determined at once to give your whole hearts to God; & let *nothing* shake; or alter; that resolution. You need have no fear of *regreting* it. Do not be vain; and thoughtless: but *sober minded.* And let me entreat you all to love the *whole rem-nant* of our once great family: 'with a pure *heart fervently.'* Try to *build again:* your broken walls: & to make *the utmost* of every *stone*

that is left. Nothing can so tend to make life a blessing as the consciousness that you *love: & are beloved*: & 'love ye the stranger' *still.*
. . . Be faithful until death. From the exercise of habitual love to man: *it cannot* be very *hard*: to *learn to love* his *maker.* . . .

John Rogers wrote to his children, 'Abhor the arrant whore of Rome.' John Brown writes to his children to abhor with *undiing hatred*, also: that 'sum of all vilainies'; Slavery. . . . And now dearly beloved Farewell: 'be of good cheer' and God Allmighty bless, save, comfort, guide, & keep; you, to 'the end.'

Your Affectionate Husband & Father
John Brown

*   *   *

They led John Brown out to the porch of the jail. (Inside, the young fellows whom he had brought to the threshold of death—Emperor Green, huge, ebon-glistening, with dumb anguished eyes; proud Copeland the Oberlin student, slender and straight as a javelin; black-bearded Stevens, former army-deserter; the Quaker boy Edwin Coppoc, now suddenly weeping; slim dark John Cook, the husband of the "lark"—they stood by the bars, listening to the fading footsteps, hearing still the echo of his "Good-bye, my men. God save you all." Only one he had not bidden farewell. Hazlett; who had been captured in the Pennsylvania hills and extradited to Virginia—illegally, for there was no proof that he had been among the raiders. To the very end the old man and his comrades would not recognize him, in the hope of cheating the gibbet of his young life. "I do not know him," they said again and again as they were questioned. But Hazlett too would go to his death. They would all go.) They led John Brown out to the porch of the jail. An officer, a sheriff, and Avis the jailer, led the way. The old man limped in the midst of the four guards, with his seedy black trousers and the white-wool socks showing above the loose carpet-slippers; his arms were pinioned close to his body. The air was sharp and pure; the morning sun flooded the street. Soldiers. Soldiers. Bayonets gleaming. Cannon grimly trained. Tramping feet. "I had no idea," the old man said, "that they would consider my death so important."

In the road, between files of militia, was a big open wagon with a team of white horses. A pine coffin was in the back. The old man as he went down the steps of the porch handed a small paper to the officer. Then he climbed into the wagon, helped by the sheriff; and sat down upon the coffin. Avis sat by him. The sheriff, an undertaker, and the driver, were up on the front seat. The officer in silence read the scrawl:

"I John Brown am now quite *certain* that the crimes of this *guilty land*: will never be purged away; but with Blood. I had *as I now think*: vainly flattered myself that without *very much* bloodshed; it might be done."

The scaffold rose against the morning sky. It was well beyond the town; in a field of forty acres, on a hillock yet in grass despite the winter. Fifteen hundred troops were massed about in a great hollow square. From the ends of the field, howitzers were trained to sweep every approach.

(Behind the gibbet, standing in line with Company "F" of the Richmond militia, was a young actor. John Wilkes Booth.)

The wagon, with its escort of cavalry and marching men, came wheeling slowly around the bend of the road. The old man on the coffin beheld the vast swept Shenandoah sky; the white clouds low over the northern woods; and looming far off to the east and the south the misty Blue Ridge Mountains.

"This *is* a beautiful country," he said. "I never had the pleasure of really seeing it before."

The wagon drew up on the rise; creaked into the troop-square; halted. A command rang out; the files veered in a swift and precise evolution; a bristling passageway was formed from the wagon to the gallows. The old man climbed down, unassisted. He walked without an order to the structure; went slowly up the ten steps to the platform. There he stood—a little bowed, the white beard ruffled in the wind— looking out to the low surrounding hills where the people would be gathered to watch Avis and the sheriff ascend the platform.

The old man shook his jailer's hand. "I have no words to thank you for your kindness," he said. "Farewell."

He shook the sheriff's hand. "Farewell," he said.

The sheriff drew a white cowl over John Brown's head. He adjusted the thin tarred rope about his neck.

"I can't see, gentlemen; you must lead me."

They placed John Brown on the drop.

The troops of the escort deployed into their places. The minutes went by; the troops wheeled, marched, countermarched. Twelve eternal minutes went by; the muskets rattled, the ground shook beneath the tramping feet. John Brown, soldier of the Lord, stood still and erect.

"Do you want a signal before I spring her?" whispered the sheriff.

"It does not matter. Only do not keep me waiting too long."

The maneuver was ended, the last Virginia soldier was in his place.

A hush now hung . . . the fields, the sky, the men were hushed. . . .

Colonel Preston of Virginia raised his hand. The sheriff gripped tighter his hatchet. He stood forth, poising himself. His arm heaved, steel gleamed in an arc, the trap crashed, the rope spun through, the rope jerked and shivered . . . shivered . . . shivered. . . .

Silence.

Clear, calm, Colonel Preston's voice now rose: "So *perish all such enemies of Virginia! All such enemies of the Union! All such foes of the human race!*"

*   *   *

John Brown's body hung on the gibbet for thirty-seven minutes. . . .

Then the Charlestown surgeons came forward. The body was slowly swinging with the wind. They put their arms around the body to hold it steady; they held their ears at the breast to listen to the heart. They pronounced the body dead.

Then the military surgeons listened at the breast.

Verified. John Brown's body was dead.

(In distant Albany they are firing a dirge of one hundred guns.)

The simple pine coffin was placed on a special train of two cars. Fifteen Virginia citizens volunteered as a bodyguard to see that no harm befell the body on its return to Mary Brown. They brought the coffin to her in Harper's Ferry, late on the winter afternoon. By nightfall Mary and John Brown were started on the long journey back to the Elba mountains; the train moaned northward through the darkness.

(In Cleveland, fourteen hundred people are praying together in a black-draped hall.)

The next day, Friday, at noon, the funeral train reached Philadelphia. A great crowd was waiting at the station. Hundreds of Negroes were there—and scores of those hostile ones who yesterday had tried to break up a meeting of sympathy. The mayor of the city had called out two hundred policemen. Now he forbade the brief resting of the body at an undertaker's; ordered the body to be forwarded out of Philadelphia at once, he could not have this disorder in his city. As a feint an empty hearse was driven away from the station; the coffin was secretly placed in a furniture car and borne to the Walnut Street wharf. A boat slipped out, crept up along the coast towards New York. The next day Mary Brown followed, by train, with McKim.

No, she said when she arrived in New York; would they please not ask for public ceremonies. She wanted her husband to come home quietly. So they rested over the Sabbath; and John Brown's body lay at an undertaker's. The face did not have the pallor of death; the rope had left it faintly flushed. He lay as a person in a quiet sleep.

(In Rochester, Syracuse, Fitchburg, the church bells are tolling. In Plymouth and New Bedford, in Concord, in Manchester, tolling, tolling.)

On Monday the journey home began again. Wendell Phillips the orator was now by the side of Mary Brown. Night came; the train reached the town of Rutland, Vermont. A heavy snow was falling; the bells rang out on the dark windy night. Early the next morning sleighs were waiting for the funeral party; the storm had hours ago stopped, but the drifts were high. Thirty men and four women were waiting, with boots and snowshoes; they would walk a distance through the snow, for his memory. The procession started, the men and women moved slowly and silently ahead of the horses pulling the three big sleighs. Bells sounded again, bells were like silver on the pure shining air. Soon they came to a bridge arching a frozen stream. The townspeople formed themselves into a double line along the sides of the bridge. The men uncovered their heads. The sleighs glided through the silent lanes. In the cold faint distance the bells were ringing. . . .

Just before dark descended they came to Westport, New York. They were now within thirty miles of Elba; but the road wound over a mountain almost impassable, it would take the whole of the next day to cover it. So once more the party rested; and John Brown's body lay in the village court-house, and six young men sat till dawn as a guard of honor.

Again the retinue of mourners started, in carriages now, for a heavy night rain had washed the snows. Hours ago a village lad had started off over the mountain on a swift horse, to tell John Brown's people that he would soon be home.

All that day they slowly climbed the wild winding pass to the summit; and as slowly descended into the valley beyond. The sun was going down when they reached the handful of poor dwellings which formed the town of North Elba; it was night as they came out of the last forest depth, into a dark clearing. They saw lights flickering down the slope towards them. Some Negro neighbors were coming to guide them, with lanterns.

The carriages drew up before the low huddled house. McKim gave Mary Brown his hands. She stepped heavily down. At once from the doorway there came a sharp broken cry . . . and Annie Brown was locked convulsively weeping in her mother's embrace. Then Sarah came, and little Nell; and inside there sounded the wailing of the girls who were widows.

The next afternoon the small bare parlor was crowded. The Brown family; McKim, Wendell Phillips, a Reverend Young; the handful of neighbors, whites and Negroes. The coffin was on a table near the open door. The face was exposed, the sun was on it. He lay as in a quiet sleep.

"Almighty and merciful God. Thou art speaking to us in the great and solemn circumstances which have brought us here together. Before Jesus Christ, the Saviour of Man, may we consecrate ourselves anew to the work of truth and love for which our brother laid down his life. May we consecrate ourselves to the outcast and the oppressed, to the humble and the least of our fellow-men. Father in Heaven, in imitation of the self-forgetting and sacrifice of the departed, we supplicate Thy special blessing upon God's despised ones. . . . We ask this in the name of Jesus Christ. Amen."

Now let John Brown's neighbors come forward, those who wished it, and look this last time upon him.

One by one they came forward. The Negroes were weeping.

Then John Brown's people stood close by his body, by the face as in a quiet sleep. And Wendell Phillips said:

"God bless this roof. Make it bless us. . . . We dare not say bless you, children of this home. For you stand nearer to one whose lips God touched, and we rather bend for your blessing. God make us worthier of him whose dust we lay among these hills. . . . He sleeps in the blessings of the crushed and the poor, and men believe more firmly in love, now that such a man has lived. . . ."

The short procession from the house to the grave began. Four of the Negroes bore the coffin. Mary Brown followed, supported by Wendell Phillips. Then Oliver's Martha, leaning on the arm of McKim, and little Nell clutching his hand. . . . Bella walking by the Reverend Young. . . . Salmon Brown, Sarah, Annie. . . . Ruth and Hen Thompson. . . . Hen's aged father and mother, parents of Will and Dauphin Thompson lying in Virginia. . . . The friends, the neighbors.

They buried him by the great boulder—at the foot of the letters J. B. which once he had graven in the rock to show Mary Brown where she should put him when he returned. As they lowered the body into the winter earth, old Epps the Negro, his son and two daughters, sang *Blow Ye the Trumpet, Blow!*—the hymn which John Brown had sung at night to his children, carrying them in his arms before they went to sleep. . . . And now it was done.

Night came on. The grave lay hushed in the silence of the mountains.

God's Angry Man, by Leonard Ehrlich

ENRICO FERMI

"The Italian Navigator has reached the New World."

The atomic theory was first postulated twenty-four hundred years ago by Democritus; but it wasn't until the beginning of the nineteenth century that John Dalton, an English physicist, revived it, making it a part of the base-knowledge of modern physics. During the nineteenth and early twentieth centuries, theories tested in the laboratories in Germany, England and America became facts until in the 1930's Einstein's equation stating the equivalence of mass and energy was proven. It took the impetus of impending war to drive the theoretical uses of this monstrous potential energy into the state in which they could actually be harnessed . . . and then unleashed.

The race for the construction of the atomic bomb was a quiet one. Not more than a handful of men throughout the world knew of its existence. Yet it was one of the most exciting—and most important—races ever run in the history of man. Enrico Fermi was an Italian, winner of the Nobel Prize for his work in physics. He was also a man who loved freedom and who abhorred the Fascist regime in his native land. Without him—and without Einstein—another refugee from totalitarian despotism—it is doubtful that this race of death—and life—would have ended as it did.

MEANWHILE HERBERT ANDERSON and his group at the Met. Lab. had also been building small piles and gathering information for a larger pile from their behavior. The best place Compton had been able to find for work on the pile was a squash court under the West Stands of Stagg Field, the University of Chicago stadium. President Hutchins had banned football from the Chicago campus, and Stagg Field was used for odd purposes. To the west, on Ellis Avenue, the stadium is closed by a tall gray-stone structure in the guise of a medieval castle. Through a heavy portal is the entrance to the space beneath the West

Stands. The Squash Court was part of this space. It was 30 feet wide, twice as long, and over 26 feet high.

The physicists would have liked more space, but places better suited for the pile, which Professor Compton had hoped he could have, had been requisitioned by the expanding armed forces stationed in Chicago. The physicists were to be contented with the Squash Court, and there Herbert Anderson had started assembling piles. They were still "small piles," because material flowed to the West Stands at a very slow, if steady, pace. As each new shipment of crates arrived, Herbert's spirits rose. He loved working and was of impatient temperament. His slender, almost delicate, body had unsuspected resilience and endurance. He could work at all hours and drive his associates to work along with his same intensity and enthusiasm.

A shipment of crates arrived at the West Stands on a Saturday afternoon, when the hired men who normally unpack them were not working. A university professor, older by several years than Herbert, gave a look at the crates and said lightly: "Those fellows will unpack them Monday morning."

"Those fellows, Hell! We'll do them now," flared up Herbert, who had never felt inhibited in the presence of older men, higher up in the academic hierarchy. The professor took off his coat, and the two of them started wrenching at the crates.

Profanity was freely used at the Met. Lab. It relieved the tension built up by having to work against time. Would Germany get atomic weapons before the United States developed them? Would these weapons come in time to help win the war? These unanswered questions constantly present in the minds of the leaders in the project pressed them to work faster and faster, to be tense, and to swear.

Success was assured by the spring. A small pile assembled in the Squash Court showed that all conditions—purity of materials, distribution of uranium in the graphite lattice—were such that a pile of critical size would chain-react.

"It could be May, or early June at latest," Enrico told me, as we recently reminisced about the times of the Met. Lab. "I remember I talked about that experiment on the Indiana dunes, and it was the first time I saw the dunes. You were still in Leonia. I went with a group from the Met. Lab. I liked the dunes: it was a clear day, with no fog to dim colors. . . ."

"I don't want to hear about the dunes," I said. "Tell me about that experiment."

"I like to swim in the lake. . . ." Enrico paid no attention to my remark. I knew that he enjoyed a good swim, and I could well imagine

him challenging a group of younger people, swimming farther and for
a longer time than any of them, then emerging on the shore with a
triumphant grin.

"Tell me about that experiment," I insisted.

"We came out of the water, and we walked along the beach."

I began to feel impatient. He did not have to mention the walk.
He always walks after swimming, dripping wet, water streaming from
his hair. In 1942 there was certainly much more hair on his head to
shed water, not just the little fringe on the sides and on the back that
there is now, and it was much darker.

". . . and I talked about the experiment with Professor Stearns. The
two of us walked ahead of the others on the beach. I remember
our efforts to speak in such a way that the others would not understand. . . ."

"Why? Didn't everyone at the Met. Lab. know that you were building piles?"

"They knew we built piles. They did not know that at last we had
the certainty that a pile would work. The fact that a chain reaction
was feasible remained classified material for a while. I could talk freely
with Stearns because he was one of the leaders."

"If you were sure a larger pile would work, why didn't you start it
at once?"

"We did not have enough materials, neither uranium nor graphite.
Procurement of uranium metal was always an obstacle. It hampered
progress."

While waiting for more materials, Herbert Anderson went to the
Goodyear Tire and Rubber Company to place an order for a square
balloon. The Goodyear people had never heard of square balloons,
they did not think they could fly. At first they threw suspicious glances
at Herbert. The young man, however, seemed to be in full possession
of his wits. He talked earnestly, had figured out precise specifications,
and knew exactly what he wanted. The Goodyear people promised
to make a square balloon of rubberized cloth. They delivered it a
couple of months later to the Squash Court. It came neatly folded,
but, once unfolded, it was a huge thing that reached from floor to
ceiling.

The Squash Court ceiling could not be pushed up as the physicists
would have liked. They had calculated that their final pile ought to
chain-react somewhat before it reached the ceiling. But not much margin was left, and calculations are never to be trusted entirely. Some
impurities might go unnoticed, some unforeseen factor might upset
theory. The critical size of the pile might not be reached at the ceiling.
Since the physicists were compelled to stay within that very concrete

limit, they thought of improving the performance of the pile by means other than size.

The experiment at Columbia with a canned pile had indicated that such an aim might be attained by removing the air from the pores of the graphite. To can as large a pile as they were to build now would be impracticable, but they could assemble it inside a square balloon and pump the air from it if necessary.

The Squash Court was not large. When the scientists opened the balloon and tried to haul it into place, they could not see its top from the floor. There was a movable elevator in the room, some sort of scaffolding on wheels that could raise a platform. Fermi climbed onto it, let himself be hoisted to a height that gave him a good view of the entire balloon, and from there he gave orders:

"All hands stand by!"

"Now haul the rope and heave her!"

"More to the right!"

"Brace the tackles to the left!"

To the people below he seemed an admiral on his bridge, and "Admiral" they called him for a while.

When the balloon was secured on five sides, with the flap that formed the sixth left down, the group began to assemble the pile inside it. Not all the material had arrived, but they trusted that it would come in time.

From the numerous experiments they had performed so far, they had an idea of what the pile should be, but they had not worked out the details, there were no drawings nor blueprints and no time to spare to make them. They planned their pile even as they built it. They were to give it the shape of a sphere of about 26 feet in diameter, supported by a square frame, hence the square balloon.

The pile supports consisted of blocks of wood. As a block was put in place inside the balloon, the size and shape of the next were figured. Between the Squash Court and the nearby carpenter's shop there was a steady flow of boys, who fetched finished blocks and brought specifications for more on bits of paper.

When the physicists started handling graphite bricks, everything became black. The walls of the Squash Court were black to start with. Now a huge black wall of graphite was going up fast. Graphite powder covered the floor and made it black and as slippery as a dance floor. Black figures skidded on it, figures in overalls and goggles under a layer of graphite dust. There was one woman among them, Leona Woods; she could not be distinguished from the men, and she got her share of cussing from the bosses.

The carpenters and the machinists who executed orders with no knowledge of their purpose and the high-school boys who helped lay bricks for the pile must have wondered at the black scene. Had they been aware that the ultimate result would be an atomic bomb, they might have renamed the court Pluto's Workshop or Hell's Kitchen.

To solve difficulties as one meets them is much faster than to try to foresee them all in detail. As the pile grew, measurements were taken and further construction adapted to results.

The pile never reached the ceiling. It was planned as a sphere 26 feet in diameter, but the last layers were never put into place. The sphere remained flattened at the top. To make a vacuum proved unnecessary, and the balloon was never sealed. The critical size of the pile was attained sooner than was anticipated.

Only six weeks had passed from the laying of the first graphite brick, and it was the morning of December 2.

Herbert Anderson was sleepy and grouchy. He had been up until two in the morning to give the pile its finishing touches. Had he pulled a control rod during the night, he could have operated the pile and have been the first man to achieve a chain reaction, at least in a material, mechanical sense. He had a moral duty not to pull that rod, despite the strong temptation. It would not be fair to Fermi. Fermi was the leader. He had directed research and worked out theories. His were the basic ideas. His were the privilege and the responsibility of conducting the final experiment and controlling the chain reaction.

"So the show was all Enrico's, and he had gone to bed early the night before," Herbert told me years later, and a bit of regret still lingered in his voice.

Walter Zinn also could have produced a chain reaction during the night. He, too, had been up and at work. But he did not care whether he operated the pile or not; he did not care in the least. It was not his job.

His task had been to smooth out difficulties during the pile construction. He had been some sort of general contractor: he had placed orders for material and made sure that they were delivered in time; he had supervised the machine shops where graphite was milled; he had spurred others to work faster, longer, more efficiently. He had become angry, had shouted, and had reached his goal. In six weeks the pile was assembled, and now he viewed it with relaxed nerves and with that vague feeling of emptiness, of slight disorientation, which never fails to follow completion of a purposeful task.

There is no record of what were the feelings of the three young men who crouched on top of the pile, under the ceiling of the square balloon. They were called the "suicide squad." It was a joke, but perhaps they were asking themselves whether the joke held some truth.

They were like firemen alerted to the possibility of a fire, ready to extinguish it. If something unexpected were to happen, if the pile should get out of control, they would "extinguish" it by flooding it with a cadmium solution. Cadmium absorbs neutrons and prevents a chain reaction.

A sense of apprehension was in the air. Everyone felt it, but outwardly, at least, they were all calm and composed. . . .

They all [the witnesses] climbed onto the balcony at the north end of the Squash Court; all, except the three boys perched on top of the pile and except a young physicist, George Weil, who stood alone on the floor by a cadmium rod that he was to pull out of the pile when so instructed.

And so the show began.

There was utter silence in the audience, and only Fermi spoke. His gray eyes betrayed his intense thinking, and his hands moved along with his thoughts.

"The pile is not performing now because inside it there are rods of cadmium which absorb neutrons. One single rod is sufficient to prevent a chain reaction. So our first step will be to pull out of the pile all control rods, but the one that George Weil will man." As he spoke others acted. Each chore had been assigned in advance and rehearsed. So Fermi went on speaking, and his hands pointed out the things he mentioned.

"This rod, that we have pulled out with the others, is automatically controlled. Should the intensity of the reaction become greater than a pre-set limit, this rod would go back inside the pile by itself.

"This pen will trace a line indicating the intensity of the radiation. When the pile chain-reacts, the pen will trace a line that will go up and up and that will not tend to level off. In other words, it will be an exponential line.

"Presently we shall begin our experiment. George will pull out his rod a little at a time. We shall take measurements and verify that the pile will keep on acting as we have calculated.

"Weil will first set the rod at thirteen feet. This means that thirteen feet of the rod will still be inside the pile. The counters will click faster and the pen will move up to this point, and then its trace will level off. Go ahead, George!"

Eyes turned to the graph pen. Breathing was suspended. Fermi grinned with confidence. The counters stepped up their clicking; the pen went up and then stopped where Fermi had said it would. Greenewalt gasped audibly. Fermi continued to grin.

He gave more orders. Each time Weil pulled the rod out some

more, the counters increased the rate of their clicking, the pen raised to the point that Fermi predicted, then it leveled off.

The morning went by. Fermi was conscious that a new experiment of this kind, carried out in the heart of a big city, might become a potential hazard unless all precautions were taken to make sure that at all times the operation of the pile conformed closely with the results of the calculations. In his mind he was sure that if George Weil's rod had been pulled out all at once, the pile would have started reacting at a leisurely rate and could have been stopped at will by reinserting one of the rods. He chose, however, to take his time and be certain that no unforeseen phenomenon would disturb the experiment.

It is impossible to say how great a danger this unforeseen element constituted or what consequences it might have brought about. According to the theory, an explosion was out of the question. The release of lethal amounts of radiation through an uncontrolled reaction was improbable. Yet the men in the Squash Court were working with the unknown. They could not claim to know the answers to all the questions that were in their minds. Caution was welcome. Caution was essential. It would have been reckless to dispense with caution.

So it was lunch time, and, although nobody else had given signs of being hungry, Fermi, who is a man of habits, pronounced the now historical sentence:

"Let's go to lunch."

After lunch they all resumed their places . . . but again the experiment proceeded by small steps, until it was 3:20.

Once more Fermi said to Weil:

"Pull it out another foot"; but this time he added, turning to the anxious group in the balcony: "This will do it. Now the pile will chain-react."

The counters stepped up; the pen started its upward rise. It showed no tendency to level off. A chain reaction was taking place in the pile.

In the back of everyone's mind was one unavoidable question: "When do we become scared?"

Under the ceiling of the balloon the suicide squad was alert, ready with their liquid cadmium: this was the moment. But nothing much happened. The group watched the recording instruments for 28 minutes. The pile behaved as it should, as they all had hoped it would, as they had feared it would not.

The rest of the story is well known. Eugene Wigner, the Hungarian-born physicist who in 1939 with Szilard and Einstein had alerted President Roosevelt to the importance of uranium fission, presented Fermi with a bottle of Chianti. According to an improbable legend, Wigner had concealed the bottle behind his back during the entire experiment.

All those present drank. From paper cups, in silence, with no toast. Then all signed the straw cover on the bottle of Chianti. It is the only record of the persons in the Squash Court on that day.

The group broke up. Some stayed to round up their measurements and put in order the data gathered from their instruments. Others went to duties elsewhere. Arthur Compton placed a long-distance call to Mr. Conant of the Office of Scientific Research and Development at Harvard.

"The Italian Navigator has reached the New World," said Compton as soon as he got Conant on the line.

"And how did he find the natives?"

"Very friendly."

Here the official story ends. . . .

Atoms in the Family, by Laura Fermi

BABE RUTH

"The roaring tribute of the unbelieving fans was a gratifying sound."

There has never been a figure in sports who soared so high or fell so far as did the Bambino, Babe Ruth. He was the Sultan of Swat, the chief executioner in the fabled Yankee "Murderer's Row." On the field he was the terror of the opposing pitching staffs—off the field he was a high-living, free-spending playboy, thinking only of today and letting tomorrow take care of itself. And when the Babe began to lose his powers—his miraculous eyesight, his tremendous strength and coordination—the bottom dropped out of his life. Here is a portrait by Robert Slevin of the Babe in his last days. . . .

WHEN BABE RUTH quit the Yanks after the 1934 season following a managerial showdown with Owner Jake Ruppert, in which the colonel blandly affirmed his satisfaction with Joe McCarthy, the question was: what of the Babe's future in baseball?

At this time, the National League's Boston Braves were a limp assortment of players built around the big bat of Center Fielder Wally Berger. In 1934 they finished fourth, as high as they'd finished since 1916, when they came in third; and they gave no indication of improving. Boston fans were avoiding Braves Field.

Owner Emil Fuchs, to whom the tinkle of the cash register was as cathedral chimes, thought Ruth might be a way to woo his patrons. With a glittering bait of meaningless titles, he approached the Babe.

In February of 1935, the Babe signed as vice president, assistant manager and part-time outfielder. Apparently everyone but Ruth knew it was a farcical attempt to capitalize on his drawing power. Manager McKechnie, on the most uncomfortable spot in baseball, wisely said nothing and opened the season with the Bam in left field.

Forty, corpulent and slowed to a gentle trot, Ruth—except for flashes of his old form—was a travesty of his once great self. His eyes were failing, and base hits were few and far between. Boston pitchers, hard-working men, watched fly balls fall for base hits and screamed like wounded animals. Berger wore himself out trying to cover two-thirds of the outfield.

But the fans turned out, and Judge Fuchs bought a bottle of black ink. A small bottle.

On Saturday, May 25, the Braves rolled into Forbes Field to display their new gate attraction to Pittsburgh patrons. Batting less than .200, but with three homers to his credit, Ruth heard more jeers than cheers from fans whose short memory is a gay feature of the American scene.

The pitching that day wasn't the strongest he'd ever faced, for the Pirate flingers had seen their best days with other clubs—Lucas with the Reds, Bush with the Cubs and Waite Hoyt as a Yankee team-mate. Perhaps it was a combination of soft pitching, anger at the fans and resentment at his employers that worked on the once great star. Whatever it was, for that one day the Babe forgot his aching legs, wiped the film from his eyes and plucked a day from the past.

He strode to the plate in the first inning with Bill Urbanski on and the venerable Red Lucas pitching for Pittsburgh. Red, with somewhat less respect than he should have shown, served up a fat pitch; Ruth leaned his weight on it, and the ball disappeared into the stands. The startled Lucas yielded another hit and also left the field.

In the third the big fellow came up with Les Mallon on and the ex-Cub work horse, Guy Bush, working for the Pirates. Bush, unperturbed by the fate of his predecessor, wound up and fired away. The Bam wound up and whacked the ball on top of the right field stands and trotted around the bases. The roaring tribute of the unbelieving fans was a gratifying sound.

In the fifth inning the situation was the same, with Mallon waiting on base for a lift home. It was a moral victory for the Pittsburgh hurler that he held the Babe to a single, although he did drive in his fifth run.

By the time the seventh had rolled around, the Braves were behind in spite of Ruth's heroic stickwork. Bush fired one down the middle. The Babe brought his bat around from behind his left ear and sent a towering shot high over the wall into Schenley Park for the longest drive they had ever seen in Pittsburgh. The shattered Bush was led away and given a hot shower to soothe his nerves, Waite Hoyt finishing for the Bucs.

Ruth, with three homers, a single and six runs batted in, quit in the seventh; the fans rose and gave him an ovation that stopped the game.

Eight days later, on June 2, bone-weary and embittered, baseball's greatest player retired from the game.

The Babe Bows Out, by Robert L. Slevin

WINSTON CHURCHILL

"Facts are better than dreams."

It is sometimes difficult to believe that Winston Churchill, so much the contemporary figure, was active in politics before the beginning of the century. He first entered Parliament in 1901, and by 1906 he had become a member of the Cabinet. Conservative, then a Liberal, then Conservative again, he wielded a tremendous influence while both in and out of the Government for the next 33 years. He had not held a Cabinet post in ten years when, after the outbreak of war in 1939, Neville Chamberlain was forced to appoint him—as his own party's most vocal and persuasive opponent of appeasement—to the post of First Lord of the Admiralty. It was from this post that he took over the reins of government which he was to hold throughout the war.

A politician who is also a statesman, a Prime Minister who is also a writer, is a rare and remarkable combination. Here is Churchill, the statesman, at his moment of triumph in 1940—in the words of Churchill, the gifted writer and historian—proud, disdainful and mocking, yet strong and surprisingly humble.

THE MANY disappointments and disasters of the brief campaign in Norway caused profound perturbation at home, and the currents of passion mounted even in the breasts of some of those who had been most slothful and purblind in the years before the war. . . . The House was filled with members in a high state of irritation and distress. Mr. Chamberlain's opening statement did not stem the hostile tide. . . . One speaker after another from both sides of the House attacked the Government and especially its chief with unusual bitterness and vehemence, and found themselves sustained by growing applause from all quarters. Mr. Amery quoted amid ringing cheers Cromwell's imperious words to the Long Parliament: "You have sat too long here for any good you have been doing. Depart, I say, and let us have done with you. In the name of God, go!" These were terrible words. . . .

I had volunteered to wind up the debate, which was no more than my duty, not only in loyalty to the chief under whom I served, but also because of the exceptionally prominent part I had played in the use of our inadequate forces during our forlorn attempt to succor Norway. I did my very best to regain control of the House for the Government in the teeth of continuous interruption, coming chiefly from the Labour Opposition benches. I did this with good heart when I thought of their mistaken and dangerous pacifism in former years. . . . When they broke in upon me, I retorted upon them and defied them, and several times the clamor was such that I could not make myself heard. Yet all the time it was clear that their anger was not directed against me, but at the Prime Minister, whom I was defending to the utmost of my ability and without regard for any other considerations. When I sat down at eleven o'clock, the House divided . . . there was no doubt . . . both the debate and the division were a violent manifestation of want of confidence in Mr. Chamberlain and his Administration.

. . . I learned that Mr. Chamberlain was resolved upon the formation of a National Government and, if he could not be the head, he would give way to anyone commanding his confidence who could. Thus, by the afternoon, I became aware that I might well be called upon to take the lead. The prospect neither excited nor alarmed me. I thought it would be by far the best plan. I was content to let events unfold. . . .

The morning of the tenth of May dawned, and with it came tremendous news. Boxes with telegrams poured in from the Admiralty, the War Office and the Foreign Office. The Germans had struck their long-awaited blow. Holland and Belgium were both invaded. Their frontiers had been crossed at numerous points. The whole movement of the German Army upon the invasion of the Low Countries and of France had begun. . . .

In the splintering crash of this vast battle, the quiet conversations we had had in Downing Street faded or fell back in one's mind. However, I remember being told that Mr. Chamberlain had gone, or was going, to see the King, and this was naturally to be expected. Presently a message arrived summoning me to the Palace at six o'clock. It only takes two minutes to drive there from the Admiralty along the Mall. . . .

I was taken immediately to the King. His Majesty received me most graciously and bade me sit down. He looked at me searchingly and quizzically for some moments, and then said: "I suppose you don't know why I have sent for you?" Adopting his mood, I replied: "Sir, I simply couldn't imagine why." He laughed and said: "I want to ask you to form a Government." I said I would certainly do so. . . .

I told the King that I would immediately send for the leaders of the Labour and Liberal Parties, that I proposed to form a War Cabinet of five or six Ministers, and that I hoped to let him have at least five names before midnight. . . .

Thus, then, on the night of the tenth of May, at the outset of this mighty battle, I acquired the chief power in the State, which henceforth I wielded in ever-growing measure for five years and three months of world war, at the end of which time, all our enemies having surrendered unconditionally, or being about to do so, I was immediately dismissed by the British electorate from all further conduct of their affairs.

During these last crowded days of the political crisis, my pulse had not quickened at any moment. I took it all as it came. But I cannot conceal from the reader of this truthful account that as I went to bed at about 3 A.M. I was conscious of a profound sense of relief. At last I had the authority to give directions over the whole scene. I felt as if I were walking with Destiny, and that all my past life had been but a preparation for this hour and for this trial. Eleven years in the political wilderness had freed me from ordinary party antagonisms. My warnings over the last six years had been so numerous, so detailed, and were now so terribly vindicated, that no one could gainsay me. I could not be reproached either for making the war or for want of preparation for it. I thought I knew a good deal about it all, and I was sure I should not fail. Therefore, although impatient for the morning, I slept soundly and had no need for cheering dreams. Facts are better than dreams.

The Gathering Storm, by Winston Churchill

SAMUEL TAYLOR COLERIDGE

"... in a profound sleep ..."

O*ver this strange little tale quoted from Coleridge's literary reminiscences there hangs an odd air of tragedy. It was in this year of 1797, when the poet was just 25 years old, that his life-long addiction to drugs began. He says here that he had taken "an anodyne" which had been prescribed for a slight indisposition. It is more than possible that the "indisposition" had been caused by the hangover-reaction from a previous dosage. For the anodyne Coleridge took was laudanum, a derivative of opium and a poison which was to become one of his greatest necessities as he grew older—until finally it led him to virtual self-imprisonment under the care of a doctor for the last eighteen years of his life. Yet here, this deceptive drug was responsible for the vision that became Coleridge's masterpiece —Kubla Khan. . . .*

IN THE SUMMER of the year 1797 the author, then in ill health, had retired to a lonely farmhouse between Porlock and Linton, on the Exmoor confines of Somerset and Devonshire. In consequence of a slight indisposition, an anodyne had been prescribed, from the effects of which he fell asleep in his chair at the moment that he was reading the following sentence, or words of the same substance, in "Purchas's Pilgrimage": "Here the Khan Kubla commanded a palace to be built, and a stately garden thereunto. And thus ten miles of fertile ground were inclosed with a wall." The author continued for about three hours in a profound sleep, at least of the external senses, during which time he had the most vivid confidence, that he could not have composed less than from two to three hundred lines; if that indeed can be called composition in which all the images rose up before him as things, with a parallel production of the correspondent expressions, without any sensation or consciousness of effort. On awakening, he appeared to himself to have a distinct recollection of the whole, and taking his pen, ink and paper, instantly and eagerly wrote down the lines that are here preserved. At this moment he was unfortunately called out by a person on business from Porlock, and detained by him above an hour, and on his return to his room, found, to his no small surprise and mortification, that though he still retained some vague and dim recollection of the general purport of the vision, yet, with the exception of some eight or ten scattered lines and images, all the rest had passed away like the images on the surface of a stream into which a stone has been cast. . . .

Kubla Khan

In Xanadu did Kubla Khan
A stately pleasure-dome decree:
Where Alph, the sacred river, ran
Through caverns measureless to man
Down to a sunless sea.
So twice five miles of fertile ground
With walls and towers were girdled round:
And there were gardens bright with sinuous rills,
Where blossomed many an incense-bearing tree;
And here were forests ancient as the hills,
Enfolding sunny spots of greenery.

But oh! that deep romantic chasm which slanted
Down the green hill athwart a cedarn cover!
A savage place! as holy and enchanted
As e'er beneath a waning moon was haunted
By woman wailing for her demon-lover!
And from this chasm, with ceaseless turmoil seething,
As if this earth in fast thick pants was breathing,
A mighty fountain momently was forced:
Amid whose swift half-intermitted burst
Huge fragments vaulted like rebounding hail,
Or chaffy grain beneath the thresher's flail:
And 'mid these dancing rocks at once and ever
It flung up momently the sacred river.
Five miles meandering with a mazy motion
Through wood and dale the sacred river ran,
Then reached the caverns measureless to man,
And sank in tumult to a lifeless ocean:
And 'mid this tumult Kubla heard from far
Ancestral voices prophesying war!
The shadow of the dome of pleasure
Floated midway on the waves;
Where was heard the mingled measure

From the fountain and the caves.
It was a miracle of rare device,
A sunny pleasure-dome with caves of ice!
A damsel with a dulcimer
In a vision once I saw:
It was an Abyssinian maid,
And on her dulcimer she played,
Singing on Mount Abora.
Could I revive within me
Her symphony and song,
To such a deep delight 'twould win me,
That with music loud and long,
I would build that dome in air.
That sunny dome! those caves of ice!
And all who heard should see them there,
And all should cry, Beware! Beware!
His flashing eyes, his floating hair!
Weave a circle round him thrice,
And close your eyes with holy dread,
For he on honey-dew hath fed,
And drunk the milk of Paradise.

Literary Reminiscences, of Samuel Taylor Coleridge

ANTOINE DE SAINT-EXUPÉRY

"Had I been afraid? I couldn't say. I had witnessed a strange sight."

The forces of nature—the massive pressures that create hurricanes and cyclones, earthquakes and monsoons—make all the destructive devices man has invented look like firecrackers compared with an artillery barrage. This is the story of the triumph of one man over the elements—the story of a man who, in effect, wrestled with a cyclone and defeated it by staying alive.

Antoine de Saint-Exupéry was a rebel. Against the wishes of his family he became a pilot, and, after flying commercial routes in Europe and Africa, established an air-mail route in South America. It is of a mail flight over the Andes that he writes here. The wind is a real enemy—it is brought to life by his pen, taking on almost human aspect—a foe to be fought and defeated. Saint-Exupéry's style is so vivid that although the book was written in French it does not suffer from English translation. There should be few who on reading this find themselves unshaken and unaffected at the end.

THE CYCLONE of which I am about to speak was, physically, much the most brutal and overwhelming experience I ever underwent; and yet beyond a certain point I do not know how to convey its violence except by piling one adjective on another, so that in the end I should convey no impression at all—unless perhaps that of an embarrassing taste for exaggeration.

It took me some time to grasp the fundamental reason for this powerlessness, which is simply that I should be trying to describe a catastrophe that never took place. The reason why writers fail when they attempt to evoke horror is that horror is something invented after the fact, when one is re-creating the experience over again in the memory. Horror does not manifest itself in the world of reality. And so, in beginning my story of a revolt of the elements which I myself lived through, I have no feeling that I shall write something which you will find dramatic.

I had taken off from the field at Trelew and was flying down to Comodoro-Rivadavia, in the Patagonian Argentine. Here the crust of the earth is as dented as an old boiler. The high-pressure regions over the Pacific send the winds past a gap in the Andes into a corridor fifty miles wide, through which they rush to the Atlantic in a strangled and accelerated buffeting that scrapes the surface of everything in their path. The sole vegetation visible in this barren landscape is a plantation of oil derricks looking like the aftereffects of a forest fire. Towering over the round hills on which the winds have left a residue of stony gravel, there rises a chain of prow-shaped, saw-toothed, razor-edged mountains stripped by the elements down to the bare rock.

For three months of the year the speed of these winds at ground level is up to a hundred miles an hour. We who flew the route knew that, once we had crossed the marshes of Trelew and had reached the threshold of the zone they swept, we should recognize the winds from afar by a gray-blue tint in the atmosphere, at the sight of which we would tighten our belts and shoulder straps in preparation for what was coming. From then on we had an hour of stiff fighting and of stumbling again and again into invisible ditches of air. This was manual labor, and our muscles felt it pretty much as if we had been carrying a longshoreman's load. But it lasted only an hour. Our machines stood up under it. We had no fear of wings suddenly dropping off. Visibility was generally good, and not a problem. This section of the line was a stint, yes; it was certainly not a drama.

But on this particular day I did not like the color of the sky.

The sky was blue. Pure blue. Too pure. A hard blue sky that shone over the scraped and barren world while the fleshless vertebrae of the mountain chain flashed in the sunlight. Not a cloud. The blue sky glittered like a new-honed knife. I felt in advance the vague distaste that accompanies the prospect of physical exertion. The purity of the sky upset me. Give me a good black storm in which the enemy is plainly visible. I can measure its extent and prepare myself for its attack. I can get my hands on my adversary. But when you are flying very high in clear weather, the shock of a blue storm is as disturbing as if something collapsed that had been holding up your ship in the air. It is the only time when a pilot feels that there is a gulf beneath his ship.

Another thing bothered me. I could see on a level with the mountain peaks not a haze, not a mist, not a sandy fog, but a sort of ash-colored streamer in the sky. I did not like the look of that scarf of filings scraped off the surface of the earth and borne out to sea by the wind. I tightened my leather harness as far as it would go, and I steered the ship with one hand while with the other I hung onto the *longéron* that ran alongside my seat. I was still flying in remarkably calm air.

Very soon came a slight tremor. As every pilot knows, there are secret little quiverings that foretell your real storm. No rolling, no pitching. No swing to speak of. The flight continues horizontal and rectilinear. But you have felt a warning drum on the wings of your plane, little intermittent rappings scarcely audible and infinitely brief, little cracklings from time to time as if there were traces of gunpowder in the air.

And then everything round me blew up.

Concerning the next couple of minutes I have nothing to say. All that I can find in my memory is a few rudimentary notions, fragments of thoughts, direct observations. I cannot compose them into a dramatic recital because there was no drama. The best I can do is to line them up in a kind of chronological order.

In the first place, I was standing still. Having banked right in order to correct a sudden drift, I saw the landscape freeze abruptly where it was and remain jiggling on the same spot. I was making no headway. My wings had ceased to nibble into the outline of the earth. I could see the earth buckle, pivot—but it stayed put. The plane was skidding as if on a toothless cogwheel.

Meanwhile I had the absurd feeling that I had exposed myself completely to the enemy. All those peaks, those crests, those teeth that were cutting into the wind and unleashing its gusts in my direction, seemed to me so many guns pointed straight at my defenseless person. I was slow to think; but the thought did come to me that I ought to give up altitude and make for one of the neighboring valleys, where I might take shelter against a mountainside. As a matter of fact, whether I liked it or not I was being helplessly sucked down toward the earth.

Trapped this way in the first breaking waves of a cyclone about which I learned, twenty minutes later, that at sea level it was blowing at the fantastic rate of one hundred and fifty miles an hour, I certainly had no impression of tragedy. Now, as I write, if I shut my eyes, if I forget the plane and the flight and try to express the plain truth about what was happening to me, I find that I felt weighed down; I felt like a porter carrying a slippery load, grabbing one object in a jerky movement that sent another slithering down, so that, overcome by exasperation, the porter is tempted to let the whole load drop. There is a kind of law of the shortest distance to the image, a psychological law by which the event to which one is subjected is visualized in a symbol that represents its swiftest summing up: I was

a man who, carrying a pile of plates, had slipped on a waxed floor
and let his scaffolding of porcelain crash.

I found myself imprisoned in a valley. My discomfort was not less;
it was greater. I grant you that a down current has never killed anybody, that the expression "flattened out by a down current" belongs
to journalism and not to the language of flyers. How could air possibly
pierce the ground? But here I was in a valley at the wheel of a ship
that was three-quarters out of my control. Ahead of me a rocky prow
swung to left and right, rose suddenly high in the air for a second
like a wave over my head, and then plunged down below my horizon.

Horizon? There was no longer a horizon. I was in the wings of a
theater cluttered up with bits of scenery. Vertical, oblique, horizontal,
all of plane geometry was awhirl. A hundred transversal valleys were
muddled in a jumble of perspectives. Whenever I seemed about to
take my bearings, a new eruption would swing me round in a circle
or send me tumbling wing over wing and I would have to try all over
again to get clear of all this rubbish. Two ideas came into my mind.
One was a discovery: for the first time I understood the cause of
certain accidents in the mountains when no fog was present to explain them. For a single second, in a waltzing landscape like this, the
flyer had been unable to distinguish between vertical mountainsides
and horizontal planes. The other idea was a fixation: the sea is flat;
I shall not hook anything out at sea.

I banked—or should I use that word to indicate a vague and stubborn jockeying through the east-west valleys? Still nothing pathetic to
report. I was wrestling with chaos, was wearing myself out in a battle
with chaos, struggling to keep in the air a gigantic house of cards
that kept collapsing despite all I could do. Scarcely the faintest twinge
of fear went through me when one of the walls of my prison rose
suddenly like a tidal wave over my head. My heart hardly skipped a
beat when I was tripped up by one of the whirling eddies of air that
the sharp ridge darted into my ship. If I felt anything unmistakably
in the haze of confused feelings and notions that came over me each
time one of these powder magazines blew up, it was a feeling of
respect. I respected that sharp-toothed ridge. I respected that peak.
I respected that dome. I respected that transversal valley opening out
into my valley and about to toss me, God knew how violently, as
soon as its torrent of wind flowed into the one on which I was being
borne along.

What I was struggling against, I discovered, was not the wind but
the ridge itself, the crest, the rocky peak. Despite my distance from
it, it was the wall of rock I was fighting with. By some trick of invisible prolongation, by the play of a secret set of muscles, this was

what was pummeling me. It was against this that I was butting my head. Before me on the right I recognized the peak of Salamanca, a perfect cone which, I knew, dominated the sea. It cheered me to think I was about to escape out to sea. But first I should have to wrestle with the gale off that peak, try to avoid its down-crushing blow. The peak of Salamanca was a giant. I was filled with respect for the peak of Salamanca.

There had been granted me one second of respite. Two seconds. Something was collecting itself into a knot, coiling itself up, growing taut. I sat amazed. I opened astonished eyes. My whole plane seemed to be shivering, spreading outward, swelling up. Horizontal and stationary it was, yet lifted, before I knew it, fifteen hundred feet straight into the air in a kind of apotheosis. I who for forty minutes had not been able to climb higher than two hundred feet off the ground was suddenly able to look down on the enemy. The plane quivered as if in boiling water. I could see the wide waters of the ocean. The valley opened out into this ocean, this salvation. And at that very moment, without any warning whatever, half a mile for Salamanca, I was suddenly struck straight in the midriff by the gale off that peak and sent hurtling out to sea.

There I was, throttle wide open, facing the coast. At right angles to the coast and facing it. A lot had happened in a single minute. In the first place, I had not flown out to sea. I had been spat out to sea by a monstrous cough, vomited out of my valley as from the mouth of a howitzer. When, what seemed to me instantly, I banked in order to put myself where I wanted to be in respect of the coast line, I saw that the coast line was a mere blur, a characterless strip of blue; and I was five miles out to sea. The mountain range stood up like a crenelated fortress against the pure sky while the cyclone crushed me down to the surface of the waters. How hard that wind was blowing I found out as soon as I tried to climb, as soon as I became conscious of my disastrous mistake: throttle wide open, engines running at my maximum, which was one hundred and fifty miles an hour, my plane hanging sixty feet over the water, I was unable to budge. When a wind like this one attacks a tropical forest, it swirls through the branches like a flame, twists them into corkscrews, and uproots giant trees as if they were radishes. Here, bounding off the mountain range, it was leveling out the sea.

Hanging on with all the power in my engines, face to the coast, face to that wind where each gap in the teeth of the range sent forth a stream of air like a long reptile, I felt as if I were clinging to the tip of a monstrous whip that was cracking over the sea.

In this latitude the South American continent is narrow and the

Andes are not far from the Atlantic. I was struggling not merely against the whirling winds that blew off the east-coast range, but more likely also against a whole sky blown down upon me off the peaks of the Andean chain. For the first time in four years of airline flying I began to worry about the strength of my wings. Also, I was fearful of bumping the sea—not because of the down currents, which, at sea level, would necessarily provide me with a horizontal air mattress, but because of the helplessly acrobatic positions in which this wind was buffeting me. Each time that I was tossed I became afraid that I might be unable to straighten out. Besides, there was a chance that I should find myself out of fuel and simply drown. I kept expecting the gasoline pumps to stop priming; and, indeed, the plane was so violently shaken up that in the half-filled tanks as well as in the gas lines the gasoline was sloshing round, not coming through, and the engines, instead of their steady roar, were sputtering in a sort of dot-and-dash series of uncertain growls.

I hung on, meanwhile, to the controls of my heavy transport plane, my attention monopolized by the physical struggle and my mind occupied by the very simplest thoughts. I was feeling practically nothing as I stared down at the imprint made by the wind on the sea. I saw a series of great white puddles, each perhaps eight hundred yards in extent. They were running toward me at a speed of one hundred and fifty miles an hour where the down-surging wind spouts broke against the surface of the sea in a succession of horizontal explosions. The sea was white and it was green—white with the whiteness of crushed sugar and green in puddles the color of emeralds. In this tumult one wave was indistinguishable from another. Torrents of air were pouring down upon the sea. The winds were sweeping past in giant gusts as when, before the autumn harvests, they blow a great flowing change of color over a wheat field. Now and again the water went incongruously transparent between the white pools, and I could see a green and black sea bottom. And then the great glass of the sea would be shattered anew into a thousand glittering fragments.

It seemed hopeless. In twenty minutes of struggle I had not moved forward a hundred yards. What was more, with flying as hard as it was out here five miles from the coast, I wondered how I could possibly buck the winds along the shore, assuming I was able to fight my way in. I was a perfect target for the enemy there on shore. Fear, however, was out of the question. I was incapable of thinking. I was emptied of everything except the vision of a very simple act. I must straighten out. Straighten out. Straighten out.

There were moments of respite, nevertheless. I dare say those moments themselves were equal to the worst storms I had hitherto met, but by comparison with the cyclone they were moments of relaxation. The urgency of fighting off the wind was not quite so great. And I could tell when these intervals were coming. It was not I who moved toward those zones of relative calm, those almost green oases clearly painted on the sea, but they that flowed toward me. I could read clearly in the waters the advertisement of a habitable province. And with each interval of repose the power to feel and to think was restored to me. Then, in those moments, I began to feel I was doomed. Then was the time that little by little I began to tremble for myself. So much so that each time I saw the unfurling of a new wave of the white offensive I was seized by a brief spasm of panic which lasted until the exact instant when, on the edge of that bubbling caldron, I bumped into the invisible wall of wind. That restored me to numbness again.

Up! I wanted to be higher up. The next time I saw one of those green zones of calm it seemed to me deeper than before, and I began to be hopeful of getting out. If I could climb high enough, I thought, I would find other currents in which I could make some headway. I took advantage of the truce to essay a swift climb. It was hard. The enemy had not weakened. Three hundred feet. Six hundred feet. If I could get up to three thousand feet I was safe, I said to myself. But there on the horizon I saw again that white pack unleashed in my direction. I gave it up. I did not want them at my throat again: I did not want to be caught off balance. But it was too late. The first blow sent me rolling over and over, and the sky became a slippery dome on which I could not find a footing.

One has a pair of hands and they obey. How are one's orders transmitted to one's hands?

I had made a discovery that horrified me: my hands were numb. My hands were dead. They sent me no message. Probably they had been numb a long time and I had not noticed it. The pity was that I had noticed it, had raised the question. That was serious.

Lashed by the wind, the wings of the plane had been dragging and jerking at the cables by which they were controlled from the wheel, and the wheel in my hands had not ceased jerking a single second. I had been gripping the wheel with all my might for forty minutes, fearful lest the strain snap the cables. So desperate had been my grip that now I could not feel my hands.

What a discovery! My hands were not my own. I looked at them and decided to lift a finger: it obeyed me. I looked away and issued the same order: now I could not feel whether the finger had obeyed or not. No message had reached me. I thought: "Suppose my hands were to open. How would I know it?" I swung my head round and looked again: my hands were still locked round the wheel. Nevertheless, I was afraid. How can a man tell the difference between the sight of a hand opening and the decision to open that hand, when there is no longer an exchange of sensations between the hand and the brain? How can one tell the difference between an image and an act of the will? Better stop thinking of the picture of open hands. Hands live a life of their own. Better not offer them this monstrous temptation. And I began to chant a silly litany which went on uninterruptedly until this flight was over. A single thought. A single image. A single phrase tirelessly chanted over and over again: "I shut my hands. I shut my hands. I shut my hands." All of me was condensed into that phrase and for me the white sea, the whirling eddies, the saw-toothed range ceased to exist. There was only "I shut my hands." There was no danger, no cyclone, no land unattained. Somewhere there was a pair of rubber hands which, once they let go the wheel, could not possibly come alive in time to recover from the tumbling drop into the sea.

I had no thoughts. I had no feelings except the feeling of being emptied out. My strength was draining out of me and so was my impulse to go on fighting. The engines continued their dot-and-dash sputterings, their little crashing noises that were like the intermittent cracklings of a ripping canvas. Whenever they were silent longer than a second I felt as if a heart had stopped beating. There, that's the end! No, they've started up again.

The thermometer on the wing, I happened to see, stood at twenty below zero, but I was bathed in sweat from head to foot. My face was running with perspiration. What a dance! Later I was to discover that my storage batteries had been jerked out of their steel flanges and hurtled up through the roof of the plane. I did not know then, either, that the ribs on my wings had come unglued and that certain of my steel cables had been sawed down to the last thread. And I continued to feel strength and will oozing out of me. Any minute now I should be overcome by the indifference born of utter weariness and by the mortal yearning to take my rest.

What can I say about this? Nothing. My shoulders ached. Very painfully. As if I had been carrying too many sacks too heavy for me. I leaned forward. Through a green transparency I saw sea bottom so close that I could make out all the details. Then the wind's hand brushed the picture away.

In an hour and twenty minutes I had succeeded in climbing to nine hundred feet. A little to the south—that is, on my left—I could see a long trail on the surface of the sea, a sort of blue stream. I decided to let myself drift as far down as that stream. Here where I was, facing west, I was as good as motionless, unable either to advance or retreat. If I could reach that blue pathway, which must be lying in the shelter of something not the cyclone, I might be able to move in slowly to the coast. So I let myself drift to the left. I had the feeling, meanwhile, that the wind's violence had perhaps slackened.

It took me an hour to cover the five miles to shore. There in the shelter of a long cliff I was able to finish my journey south. Thereafter I succeeded in keeping enough altitude to fly inland to the field that was my destination. I was able to stay up at nine hundred feet. It was very stormy, but nothing like the cyclone I had come out of. That was over.

On the ground I saw a platoon of soldiers. They had been sent down to watch for me. I landed near by and we were a whole hour getting the plane into the hangar. I climbed out of the cockpit and walked off. There was nothing to say. I was very sleepy. I kept moving my fingers, but they stayed numb. I could not collect my thoughts enough to decide whether or not I had been afraid. Had I been afraid? I couldn't say. I had witnessed a strange sight. What strange sight? I couldn't say. The sky was blue and the sea was white. I felt I ought to tell someone about it, since I was back from so far away! But I had no grip on what I had been through. "Imagine a white sea . . . very white . . . whiter still." You cannot convey things to people by piling up adjectives, by stammering.

You cannot convey anything because there is nothing to convey. My shoulders were aching. My insides felt as if they had been crushed in by a terrible weight. You cannot make drama out of that, or out of the cone-shaped peak of Salamanca. That peak was charged like a powder magazine; but if I said so, people would laugh. I would myself. I respected the peak of Salamanca. That is my story. And it is not a story.

There is nothing dramatic in the world, nothing pathetic, except in human relations. The day after I landed I might get emotional, might dress up my adventure by imagining that I who was alive and walking on earth was living through the hell of a cyclone. But that would be cheating, for the man who fought tooth and nail against that cyclone had nothing in common with the fortunate man alive the next day. He was far too busy.

Wind, Sand and Stars, by Antoine de Saint-Exupéry

MADAME MARIE CURIE

*"She was to remember forever this evening
of glowworms, this magic."*

The life of the scientist is one of very little glamour; it seldom
brings much material gain; it is the exception whose work receives
any great degree of recognition. Yet there is no field in which the
rewards can be so great. To contribute knowledge that will benefit
not only self—or company or country—but all mankind forever must
produce a satisfaction impossible to equal. Such were the rewards
won by Marie and Pierre Curie.

Encouraged by her father, professor of physics at the University
of Warsaw, and by authorities who were not pleased with her student political activities, Marie Sklowdovska came to Paris, and the
Sorbonne in 1891, when she was 24. She had tremendous energy
and a drive to work. In 1895 she married Pierre Curie, a young
professor in the Sorbonne's school of physics and chemistry, and
with him began her investigations in the search for the new element
whose presence had been indicated by other scientists. They found
success in 1898 when Marie was barely thirty years old. They discovered radium.

The excerpt that follows is from the famous biography of her
mother by Eve Curie, published in 1937 and translated into some
twenty-five languages. The end of the long struggle. . . .

WHILE A YOUNG wife kept house, washed her baby daughter and put
pans on the fire, in a wretched laboratory at the School of Physics a
woman physicist was making the most important discovery of modern
science.

At the end of 1897 the balance sheet of Marie's activity showed two
university degrees, a fellowship and a monograph on the magnetiza-
tion of tempered steel. No sooner had she recovered from childbirth
than she was back again at the laboratory.

The next stage in the logical development of her career was the
doctor's degree. Several weeks of indecision came in here. She had to

choose a subject of research which would furnish fertile and original material. Like a writer who hesitates and asks himself questions before settling the subject of his next novel, Marie, reviewing the most recent work in physics with Pierre, was in search of a subject for a thesis.

At this critical moment Pierre's advice had an importance which cannot be neglected. With respect to her husband, the young woman regarded herself as an apprentice: he was an older physicist, much more experienced than she. He was even, to put it exactly, her chief, her "boss."

But without a doubt Marie's character, her intimate nature, had a great part in this all-important choice. From childhood the Polish girl had carried the curiosity and daring of an explorer within her. This was the instinct that had driven her to leave Warsaw for Paris and the Sorbonne, and had made her prefer a solitary room in the Latin Quarter to the Dluskis' downy nest. In her walks in the woods she always chose the wild trail or the unfrequented road.

At this moment she was like a traveler musing on a long voyage. Bent over the globe and pointing out, in some far country, a strange name that excites his imagination, the traveler suddenly decides to go there and nowhere else: so Marie, going through the reports of the latest experimental studies, was attracted by the publication of the French scientist Henri Becquerel of the preceding year. She and Pierre already knew this work; she read it over again and studied it with her usual care.

After Roentgen's discovery of X rays, Henri Poincaré conceived the idea of determining whether rays like the X ray were emitted by "fluorescent" bodies under the action of light. Attracted by the same problem, Henri Becquerel examined the salts of a "rare metal," uranium. Instead of finding the phenomenon he had expected, he observed another, altogether different and incomprehensible: he found that uranium salts *spontaneously* emitted, without exposure to light, some rays of unknown nature. A compound of uranium, placed on a photographic plate surrounded by black paper, made an impression on the plate through the paper. And, like the X ray, these astonishing "uranic" salts discharged an electroscope by rendering the surrounding air a conductor.

Henri Becquerel made sure that these surprising properties were not caused by a preliminary exposure to the sun and that they persisted when the uranium compound had been maintained in darkness for several months. For the first time, a physicist had observed the phenomenon to which Marie Curie was later to give the name of *radio-*

activity. But the nature of the radiation and its origin remained an enigma.

Becquerel's discovery fascinated the Curies. They asked themselves whence came the energy—tiny, to be sure—which uranium compounds constantly disengaged in the form of radiation. And what was the nature of this radiation? Here was an engrossing subject of research, a doctor's thesis! The subject tempted Marie most because it was a virgin field: Becquerel's work was very recent and so far as she knew nobody in the laboratories of Europe had yet attempted to make a fundamental study of uranium rays. As a point of departure, and as the only bibliography, there existed some communications presented by Henri Becquerel at the Academy of Science during the year 1896. It was a leap into great adventure, into an unknown realm.

There remained the question of where she was to make her experiments—and here the difficulties began. Pierre made several approaches to the director of the School of Physics with practically no results: Marie was given the free use of a little glassed-in studio on the ground floor of the school. It was a kind of storeroom, sweating with damp, where unused machines and lumber were put away. Its technical equipment was rudimentary and its comfort nil.

Deprived of an adequate electrical installation and of everything that forms material for the beginning of scientific research, she kept her patience, sought and found a means of making her apparatus work in this hole.

It was not easy. Instruments of precision have sneaking enemies: humidity, changes of temperature. Incidentally the climate of this little workroom, fatal to the sensitive electrometer, was not much better for Marie's health. But this had no importance. When she was cold, the young woman took her revenge by noting the degrees of temperature in centigrade in her notebook. On February 6, 1898, we find, among the formulas and figures: "Temperature here 6°25." Six degrees . . . !* Marie, to show her disapproval, added ten little exclamation points.

The candidate for the doctor's degree set her first task to be the measurement of the "power of ionization" of uranium rays—that is to say, their power to render the air a conductor of electricity and so to discharge an electroscope. The excellent method she used, which was to be the key to the success of her experiments, had been invented for the study of other phenomena by two physicists well known to her: Pierre and Jacques Curie. Her technical installation consisted of an "ionization chamber," a Curie electrometer and a piezoelectric quartz.

* About 44° Fahrenheit.

At the end of several weeks the first result appeared: Marie acquired the certainty that the intensity of this surprising radiation was proportional to the quantity of uranium contained in the samples under examination, and that this radiation, which could be measured with precision, was not affected either by the chemical state of combination of the uranium or by external factors such as lighting or temperature.

These observations were perhaps not very sensational to the uninitiated, but they were of passionate interest to the scientist. It often happens in physics that an inexplicable phenomenon can be subjected, after some investigation, to laws already known, and by this very fact loses its interest for the research worker. Thus, in a badly constructed detective story, if we are told in the third chapter that the woman of sinister appearance who might have committed the crime is in reality only an honest little housewife who leads a life without secrets, we feel discouraged and cease to read.

Nothing of the kind happened here. The more Marie penetrated into intimacy with uranium rays, the more they seemed without precedent, essentially unknown. They were like nothing else. Nothing affected them. In spite of their very feeble power, they had an extraordinary individuality.

Turning this mystery over and over in her head, and pointing toward the truth, Marie felt and could soon affirm that the incomprehensible radiation was an *atomic* property. She questioned: Even though the phenomenon had only been observed with uranium, nothing proved that uranium was the only chemical element capable of emitting such radiation. Why should not other bodies possess the same power? Perhaps it was only by chance that this radiation had been observed in uranium first, and had remained attached to uranium in the minds of physicists. Now it must be sought for elsewhere. . . .

No sooner said than done. Abandoning the study of uranium, Marie undertook to examine *all known chemical bodies,* either in the pure state or in compounds. And the result was not long in appearing: compounds of another element, thorium, also emitted spontaneous rays like those of uranium and of similar intensity. The physicist had been right: the surprising phenomenon was by no means the property of uranium alone, and it became necessary to give it a distinct name. Mme. Curie suggested the name of *radioactivity.* Chemical substances like uranium and thorium, endowed with this particular "radiance," were called *radio elements.*

Radioactivity so fascinated the young scientist that she never tired of examining the most diverse forms of matter, always by the same method. Curiosity, a marvelous feminine curiosity, the first virtue of a scientist, was developed in Marie to the highest degree. Instead of limiting her observation to simple compounds, salts and oxides, she had the desire to assemble samples of minerals from the collection at the School of Physics, and of making them undergo almost at hazard, for her own amusement, a kind of customs inspection which is an electrometer test. Pierre approved, and chose with her the veined fragments, hard or crumbly, oddly shaped, which she wanted to examine.

Marie's idea was simple—simple as the stroke of genius. At the crossroads where Marie now stood, hundreds of research workers might have remained, nonplussed, for months or even years. After examining all known chemical substances, and discovering—as Marie had done—the radiation of thorium, they would have continued to ask themselves in vain whence came this mysterious radioactivity. Marie, too, questioned and wondered. But her surprise was translated into fruitful acts. She had used up all evident possibilities. Now she turned toward the unplumbed and the unknown.

She knew in advance what she would learn from an examination of the minerals, or rather she thought she knew. The specimens which contained neither uranium nor thorium would be revealed as totally "inactive." The others, containing uranium or thorium, would be radioactive.

Experiment confirmed this prevision. Rejecting the inactive minerals, Marie applied herself to the others and measured their radioactivity. Then came a dramatic revelation: the radioactivity was a *great deal stronger* than could have been normally foreseen by the quantity of uranium or thorium contained in the products examined!

"It must be an error in experiment," the young woman thought; for doubt is the scientist's first response to an unexpected phenomenon.

She started her measurements over again, unmoved, using the same products. She started over again ten times, twenty times. And she was forced to yield to the evidence: the quantities of uranium and of thorium found in these minerals were by no means sufficient to justify the exceptional intensity of the radiation she observed.

Where did this excessive and abnormal radiation come from? Only one explanation was possible: the minerals must contain, in small quantity, a *much more powerfully radioactive substance* than uranium and thorium.

But what substance? In her preceding experiments, Marie had already examined *all known chemical elements*.

The scientist replied to the question with the sure logic and the magnificent audaciousness of a great mind: The minerals certainly contained a radioactive substance, which was at the same time a chemical element unknown until this day: *a new element.*

A new element! It was a fascinating and alluring hypothesis—but still a hypothesis. For the moment this powerfully radioactive substance existed only in the imagination of Marie and of Pierre. But it did exist there. It existed strongly enough to make the young woman go to see Bronya one day and tell her in a restrained, ardent voice:

"You know, Bronya, the radiation that I couldn't explain comes from a new chemical element. The element is there and I've got to find it. We are sure! The physicists we have spoken to believe we have made an error in experiment and advise us to be careful. But I am convinced that I am not mistaken."

These were unique moments in her unique life. The layman forms a theatrical—and wholly false—idea of the research worker and of his discoveries. "The moment of discovery" does not always exist: the scientist's work is too tenuous, too divided, for the certainty of success to crackle out suddenly in the midst of his laborious toil like a stroke of lightning, dazzling him by its fire. Marie, standing in front of her apparatus, perhaps never experienced the sudden intoxication of triumph. This intoxication was spread over several days of decisive labor, made feverish by a magnificent hope. But it must have been an exultant moment when, convinced by the rigorous reasoning of her brain that she was on the trail of new matter, she confided the secret to her elder sister, her ally always. . . . Without exchanging one affectionate word, the two sisters must have lived again, in a dizzying breath of memory, their years of waiting, their mutual sacrifices, their bleak lives as students, full of hope and faith.

It was barely four years before that Marie had written:

> Life is not easy for any of us. But what of that? we must have perseverance and above all confidence in ourselves. We must believe that we are gifted for something, and that this thing, at whatever cost, must be attained.

That "something" was to throw science upon a path hitherto unsuspected.

In a first communication to the Academy, presented by Prof. Lippmann and published in the *Proceedings* on April 12, 1898, "Marie Sklodovska Curie" announced the probable presence in pitchblende ores of a new element endowed with powerful radioactivity. This was the first stage of the discovery of radium.

By the force of her own intuition the physicist had shown to herself that the wonderful substance must exist. She decreed its existence. But its incognito still had to be broken. Now she would have to verify hypothesis by experiment, isolate this material and see it. She must be able to announce with certainty: "It is there."

Pierre Curie had followed the rapid progress of his wife's experiments with passionate interest. Without directly taking part in Marie's work, he had frequently helped her by his remarks and advice. In view of the stupefying character of her results, he did not hesitate to abandon his study of crystals for the time being in order to join his efforts to hers in the search for the new substance.

Thus, when the immensity of a pressing task suggested and exacted collaboration, a great physicist was at Marie's side—a physicist who was the companion of her life. Three years earlier, love had joined this exceptional man and woman together—love, and perhaps some mysterious foreknowledge, some sublime instinct for the work in common.

The available force was now doubled. Two brains, four hands, now sought the unknown element in the damp little workroom in the Rue Lhomond. From this moment onward it is impossible to distinguish each one's part in the work of the Curies. We know that Marie, having chosen to study the radiation of uranium as the subject of her thesis, discovered that other substances were also radioactive. We know that after the examination of minerals she was able to announce the existence of a new chemical element, powerfully radioactive, and that it was the capital importance of this result which decided Pierre Curie to interrupt his very different research in order to try to isolate this element with his wife. At that time—May or June 1898—a collaboration began which was to last for eight years, until it was destroyed by a fatal accident.

We cannot and must not attempt to find out what should be credited to Marie and what to Pierre during these eight years. It would be exactly what the husband and wife did not want. The personal genius of Pierre Curie is known to us by the original work he had accomplished before this collaboration. His wife's genius appears to us in the first intuition of discovery, the brilliant start; and it was to reappear to us again, solitary, when Marie Curie the widow unflinchingly carried the weight of a new science and conducted it, through research, step by step, to its harmonious expansion. We therefore have formal proof that in the fusion of their two efforts, in this superior alliance of man and woman, the exchange was equal.

Let this certainty suffice for our curiosity and admiration. Let us not attempt to separate these creatures full of love, whose handwriting

alternates and combines in the working notebooks covered with
formulae, these creatures who were to sign nearly all their scientific
publications together. They were to write "We found" and "We observed"; and when they were constrained by fact to distinguish between their parts, they were to employ this moving locution:

> Certain minerals containing uranium and thorium (pitch-
> blende, chalcolite, uranite) are very active from the point of view
> of the emission of Becquerel rays. In a preceding communication,
> *one of us* showed that their activity was even greater than that of
> uranium and thorium, and stated the opinion that this effect was
> due to some other very active substance contained in small quan-
> tity in these minerals.
>
> (Pierre and Marie Curie: *Proceedings of the Academy of
> Science*, July 18, 1898.)

Marie and Pierre looked for this "very active" substance in an ore
of uranium called pitchblende, which in the crude state had shown
itself to be four times more radioactive than the pure oxide of uranium
that could be extracted from it. But the composition of this ore had
been known for a long time with considerable precision. The new
element must therefore be present in very small quantity or it would
not have escaped the notice of scientists and their chemical analysis.

According to their calculations—"pessimistic" calculations, like
those of true physicists, who always take the less attractive of two
probabilities—the collaborators thought the ore should contain the
new element to a maximum quantity of one per cent. They decided
that this was very little. They would have been in consternation if they
had known that the radioactive element they were hunting down did
not count for more than a millionth part of pitchblende ore.

They began their prospecting patiently, using a method of chemical
research invented by themselves, based on radioactivity: they separated all the elements in pitchblende by ordinary chemical analysis
and then measured the radioactivity of each of the bodies thus obtained. By successive eliminations they saw the "abnormal" radioactivity take refuge in certain parts of the ore. As they went on, the field
of investigation was narrowed. It was exactly the technique used by the
police when they search the houses of a neighborhood, one by one, to
isolate and arrest a malefactor.

But there was more than one malefactor here: the radioactivity
was concentrated principally in two different chemical fractions of the
pitchblende. For M. and Mme. Curie it indicated the existence of
two new elements instead of one. By July 1898 they were able to
announce the discovery of one of these substances with certainty.

"You will have to name it," Pierre said to his young wife, in the same tone as if it were a question of choosing a name for little Irène. The one-time Mlle. Sklodovska reflected in silence for a moment. Then, her heart turning toward her own country which had been erased from the map of the world, she wondered vaguely if the scientific event would be published in Russia, Germany and Austria— the oppressor countries—and answered timidly:

"Could we call it 'polonium'?"

In the *Proceedings of the Academy* for July 1898 we read:

> We believe the substance we have extracted from pitchblende contains a metal not yet observed, related to bismuth by its analytical properties. If the existence of this new metal is confirmed we propose to call it *polonium*, from the name of the original country of one of us.

The choice of this name proves that in becoming a Frenchwoman and a physicist Marie had not disowned her former enthusiasms. Another thing proves it for us: even before the note "On a New Radioactive Substance Contained in Pitchblende" had appeared in the *Proceedings of the Academy*, Marie had sent the manuscript to her native country, to that Joseph Boguski who directed the little laboratory at the Museum of Industry and Agriculture where she had made her first experiments. The communication was published in Warsaw in a monthly photographic review called *Swiatlo* almost as soon as in Paris.

Life was unchanged in the little flat in the Rue de la Glacière. Marie and Pierre worked even more than usual; that was all. When the heat of summer came, the young wife found time to buy some baskets of fruit in the markets and, as usual, she cooked and put away preserves for the winter, according to the recipes used in the Curie family. Then she locked the shutters on her windows, which gave on burned leaves; she registered their two bicycles at the Orleans station, and, like thousands of other young women in Paris, went off on holiday with her husband and her child.

This year the couple had rented a peasant's house at Auroux, in Auvergne. Happy to breathe good air after the noxious atmosphere of the Rue Lhomond, the Curies made excursions to Mende, Puy, Clermont, Mont-Dore. They climbed hills, visited grottoes, bathed in rivers. Every day, alone in the country, they spoke of what they called their "new metals," polonium and "the other"—the one that remained to be found. In September they would go back to the damp workroom and the dull minerals; with freshened ardor they would take up their search again. . . .

In spite of their prosaic character—or perhaps because of it—some notes written by Mme. Curie in that memorable year 1898 seem to us worth quoting. Some are to be found in the margins of a book called *Family Cooking*, with respect to a recipe for gooseberry jelly:

I took eight pounds of fruit and the same weight in crystallized sugar. After an ebullition of ten minutes, I passed the mixture through a rather fine sieve. I obtained fourteen pots of very good jelly, not transparent, which "took" perfectly.

In a school notebook covered with gray linen, in which the young mother had written little Irène's weight day by day, her diet and the appearance of her first teeth, we read under the date of July 20, 1898, some days after the publication of the discovery of polonium:

Irène says "thanks" with her hand. She can walk very well now on all fours. She says "Gogli, gogli, go." She stays in the garden all day at Sceaux on a carpet. She can roll, pick herself up, and sit down.

On August 15, at Auroux:

Irène has cut her seventh tooth, on the lower left. She can stand for half a minute alone. For the past three days we have bathed her in the river. She cries, but today (fourth bath) she stopped crying and played with her hands in the water.

She plays with the cat and chases him with war cries. She is not afraid of strangers any more. She sings a great deal. She gets up on the table when she is in her chair.

Three months later, on October 17, Marie noted with pride:

Irène can walk very well, and no longer goes on all fours.

On January 5, 1899:

Irène has fifteen teeth!

Between these two notes—that of October 17, 1898, in which Irène no longer goes on all fours, and that of January 5 in which Irène has fifteen teeth—and a few months after the note on the gooseberry preserve, we find another note worthy of remark.

It was drawn up by Marie and Pierre Curie and a collaborator called G. Bémont. Intended for the Academy of Science, and published in the *Proceedings* of the session of December 26, 1898, it announced the existence of a second new chemical element in pitch-blende.

Some lines of this communication read as follows:

The various reasons we have just enumerated lead us to be-lieve that the new radioactive substance contains a new element to which we propose to give the name of RADIUM.

The new radioactive substance certainly contains a very strong proportion of barium; in spite of that its radioactivity is considera-ble. The radioactivity of radium therefore must be enormous.

A man chosen at random from a crowd to read an account of the discovery of radium would not have doubted for one moment that radium existed: beings whose critical sense has not been sharpened and simultaneously deformed by specialized culture keep their imag-inations fresh. They are ready to accept an unexpected fact, however extraordinary it may appear, and to wonder at it.

The physicist colleagues of the Curies received the news in slightly different fashion. The special properties of polonium and radium up-set fundamental theories in which scientists had believed for centuries. How was one to explain the spontaneous radiation of the radioactive bodies? The discovery upset a world of acquired knowledge and con-tradicted the most firmly established ideas on the composition of mat-ter. Thus the physicist kept on the reserve. He was violently interested in Pierre and Marie's work, he could perceive its infinite develop-ments, but before being convinced he awaited the acquisition of de-cisive results.

The attitude of the chemist was even more downright. By defini-tion, a chemist only believes in the existence of a new substance when he has seen the substance, touched it, weighed and examined it, con-fronted it with acids, bottled it, and when he has determined its "atomic weight."

Now, up to the present, nobody had "seen" radium. Nobody knew the atomic weight of radium. And the chemists, faithful to their prin-ciples, concluded: "No atomic weight, no radium. Show us some ra-dium and we will believe you."

To show polonium and radium to the incredulous, to prove to the world the existence of their "children," and to complete their own conviction, M. and Mme. Curie were now to labor for four years.

The aim was to obtain pure radium and polonium. In the most strongly radioactive products the scientists had prepared, these sub-stances figured only in imperceptible traces. Pierre and Marie already knew the method by which they could hope to isolate the new metals, but the separation could not be made except by treating very large quantities of crude material.

Here arose three agonizing questions:

How were they to get a sufficient quantity of ore? What premises could they use to effect their treatment? What money was there to pay the inevitable cost of the work?

Pitchblende, in which polonium and radium were hidden, was a costly ore, treated at the St. Joachimsthal mines in Bohemia for the extraction of uranium salts used in the manufacture of glass. Tons of pitchblende would cost a great deal: a great deal too much for the Curie household.

Ingenuity was to make up for wealth. According to the expectation of the two scientists, the extraction of uranium should leave, intact in the ore, such traces of polonium and radium as the ore contains. There was no reason why these traces should not be found in the residue. And, whereas crude pitchblende was costly, its residue after treatment had very slight value. By asking an Austrian colleague for a recommendation to the directors of the mine of St. Joachimsthal would it not be possible to obtain a considerable quantity of such residue for a reasonable price?

It was simple enough: but somebody had to think of it.

It was necessary, of course, to buy this crude material and pay for its transportation to Paris. Pierre and Marie appropriated the required sum from their very slight savings. They were not so foolish as to ask for official credits. . . . If two physicists on the scent of an immense discovery had asked the University of Paris or the French government for a grant to buy pitchblende residue they would have been laughed at. In any case their letter would have been lost in the files of some office, and they would have had to wait months for a reply, probably unfavorable in the end. Out of the traditions and principles of the French Revolution, which had created the metric system, founded the Normal School, and encouraged science in many circumstances, the State seemed to have retained, after more than a century, only the deplorable words pronounced by Fouquier-Tinville at the trial in which Lavoisier was condemned to the guillotine: "The Republic has no need for scientists."

But at least could there not be found, in the numerous buildings attached to the Sorbonne, some kind of suitable workroom to lend to the Curie couple? Apparently not. After vain attempts, Pierre and Marie staggered back to their point of departure, which is to say to the School of Physics where Pierre taught, to the little room where Marie had done her first experiments. The room gave on a courtyard, and on the other side of the yard there was a wooden shack, an abandoned shed, with a skylight roof in such bad condition that it admitted the rain. The Faculty of Medicine had formerly used the place as a dissecting room, but for a long time now it had not even been considered fit to house the cadavers. No floor: an uncertain layer of bitumen covered the earth. It was furnished with some worn kitchen tables, a blackboard which had landed there for no known reason, and an old cast-iron stove with a rusty pipe.

A workman would not willingly have worked in such a place: Marie and Pierre, nevertheless, resigned themselves to it. The shed had one advantage: it was so untempting, so miserable, that nobody thought of refusing them the use of it. Schutzenberger, the director of the school, had always been very kind to Pierre Curie and no doubt regretted that he had nothing better to offer. However that may be, he offered nothing else; and the couple, very pleased at not being put out into the street with their material, thanked him, saying that "this would do" and that they would "make the best of it."

As they were taking possession of the shed, a reply arrived from Austria. Good news! By extraordinary luck, the residue of recent extractions of uranium had not been scattered. The useless material had been piled up in a no-man's-land planted with pine trees, near the mine of St. Joachimsthal. Thanks to the intercession of Professor Suess and the Academy of Science of Vienna, the Austrian government, which was the proprietor of the State factory there, decided to present a ton of residue to the two French lunatics who thought they needed it. If, later on, they wished to be sent a greater quantity of the material, they could obtain it at the mine on the best terms. For the moment the Curies had to pay only the transportation charges on a ton of ore.

One morning a heavy wagon, like those which deliver coal, drew up in the Rue Lhomond before the School of Physics. Pierre and Marie were notified. They hurried bareheaded into the street in their laboratory gowns. Pierre, who was never agitated, kept his calm; but the more exuberant Marie could not contain her joy at the sight of the sacks that were being unloaded. It was pitchblende, *her* pitchblende, for which she had received a notice some days before from the freight station. Full of curiosity and impatience, she wanted to open one of the sacks and contemplate her treasure without further waiting. She cut the strings, undid the coarse sackcloth and plunged her two hands into the dull brown ore, still mixed with pine needles from Bohemia.

There was where radium was hidden. It was from there that Marie must extract it, even if she had to treat a mountain of this inert stuff like dust on the road.

Marya Sklodovska had lived through the most intoxicating moments of her student life in a garret; Marie Curie was to know wonderful joys again in a dilapidated shed. It was a strange sort of beginning over again, in which a sharp subtle happiness (which probably no woman before Marie had ever experienced) twice elected the most miserable setting.

The shed in the Rue Lhomond surpassed the most pessimistic expectations of discomfort. In summer, because of its skylights, it was as stifling as a hothouse. In winter one did not know whether to wish for rain or frost; if it rained, the water fell drop by drop, with a soft, nerve-racking noise, on the ground or on the worktables, in places which the physicists had to mark in order to avoid putting apparatus there. If it froze, one froze. There was no recourse. The stove, even when it was stoked white, was a complete disappointment. If one went near enough to touch it one received a little heat, but two steps away and one was back in the zone of ice.

It was almost better for Marie and Pierre to get used to the cruelty of the outside temperature, since their technical installation—hardly existent—possessed no chimneys to carry off noxious gases, and the greater part of their treatment had to be made in the open air, in the courtyard. When a shower came the physicists hastily moved their apparatus inside: to keep on working without being suffocated they set up draughts between the opened door and windows.

Marie probably did not boast to Dr. Vauthier of this very peculiar cure for attacks of tuberculosis.

We had no money, no laboratory and no help in the conduct of this important and difficult task [she was to write later]. It was like creating something out of nothing, and if Casimir Dluski once called my student years "the heroic years of my sister-in-law's life," I may say without exaggeration that this period was, for my husband and myself, the heroic period of our common existence. . . . And yet it was in this miserable old shed that the best and happiest years of our life were spent, entirely consecrated to work. I sometimes passed the whole day stirring a mass in ebullition, with an iron rod nearly as big as myself. In the evening I was broken with fatigue.

In such conditions M. and Mme. Curie worked for four years from 1898 to 1902.

During the first year they busied themselves with the chemical separation of radium and polonium and they studied the radiation of the products (more and more active) thus obtained. Before long they considered it more practical to separate their efforts. Pierre Curie tried to determine the properties of radium, and to know the new metal better. Marie continued those chemical treatments which would permit her to obtain salts of pure radium.

In this division of labor Marie had chosen the "man's job." She accomplished the toil of a day laborer. Inside the shed her husband was absorbed by delicate experiments. In the courtyard, dressed in her old dust-covered and acid-stained smock, her hair blown by the wind, surrounded by smoke which stung her eyes and throat, Marie was a sort of factory all by herself.

> I came to treat as many as twenty kilograms of matter at a time [she writes], which had the effect of filling the shed with great jars full of precipitates and liquids. It was killing work to carry the receivers, to pour off the liquids and to stir, for hours at a stretch, the boiling matter in a smelting basin.

Radium showed no intention of allowing itself to be known by human creatures. Where were the days when Marie naïvely expected the radium content of pitchblende to be *one per cent?* The radiation of the new substance was so powerful that a tiny quantity of radium, disseminated through the ore, was the source of striking phenomena which could be easily observed and measured. The difficult, the impossible thing, was to isolate this minute quantity, to separate it from the gangue in which it was so intimately mixed.

The days of work became months and years: Pierre and Marie were not discouraged. This material which resisted them, which defended its secrets, fascinated them. United by their tenderness, united by their intellectual passions, they had, in a wooden shack, the "anti-natural" existence for which they had both been made, she as well as he.

> At this period we were entirely absorbed by the new realm that was, thanks to an unhoped-for discovery, opening before us [Marie was to write]. In spite of the difficulties of our working conditions, we felt very happy. Our days were spent at the laboratory. In our poor shed there reigned a great tranquillity: sometimes, as we watched over some operation, we would walk up and down, talking about work in the present and in the future; when we were cold a cup of hot tea taken near the stove comforted us. We lived in our single preoccupation as if in a dream. . . .

Marie continued to treat, kilogram by kilogram, the tons of pitchblende residue which were sent her on several occasions from St. Joachimsthal. With her terrible patience, she was able to be, every day for four years, a physicist, a chemist, a specialized worker, an engineer and a laboring man all at once. Thanks to her brain and muscle, the old tables in the shed held more and more concentrated products— products more and more rich in radium. Mme. Curie was approaching the end: she no longer stood in the courtyard, enveloped in bitter smoke, to watch the heavy basins of material in fusion. She was now at the stage of purification and of the "fractional crystallization" of strongly radioactive solutions. But the poverty of her haphazard equipment hindered her work more than ever. It was now that she needed a spotlessly clean workroom and apparatus perfectly protected against cold, heat and dirt. In this shed, open to every wind, iron and coal dust was afloat which, to Marie's despair, mixed itself into the products purified with so much care. Her heart sometimes constricted before these little daily accidents, which took so much of her time and her strength.

Pierre was so tired of the interminable struggle that he would have been quite ready to abandon it. Of course, he did not dream of dropping the study of radium and of radioactivity. But he would willingly have renounced, for the time being, the special operation of preparing pure radium. The obstacles seemed insurmountable. Could they not resume this work later on, under better conditions? More attached to the meaning of natural phenomena than to their material reality, Pierre Curie was exasperated to see the paltry results to which Marie's exhausting effort had led. He advised an armistice.

He counted without his wife's character. Marie wanted to isolate radium and she would isolate it. She scorned fatigue and difficulties, and even the gaps in her own knowledge which complicated her task. After all, she was only a very young scientist: she still had not the certainty and great culture Pierre had acquired by twenty years' work, and sometimes she stumbled across phenomena or methods of calculation about which she knew very little, and for which she had to make hasty studies.

So much the worse! With stubborn eyes under her great brow, she clung to her apparatus and her test tubes.

In 1902, forty-five months after the day on which the Curies announced the probable existence of radium, Marie finally carried off the victory in this war of attrition: she succeeded in preparing a decigram of pure radium, and made a first determination of the atomic weight of the new substance, which was 225.

The incredulous chemists—of whom there were still a few—could only bow before the facts, before the superhuman obstinacy of a woman.

Radium officially existed.

It was nine o'clock at night. Pierre and Marie Curie were in their little house at 108 Boulevard Kellermann, where they had been living since 1900. The house suited them well. From the boulevard, where three rows of trees half hid the fortifications, could be seen only a dull wall and a tiny door. But behind the one-story house, hidden from all eyes, there was a narrow provincial garden, rather pretty and very quiet. And from the "barrier" of Gentilly they could escape on their bicycles toward the suburbs and the woods. . . .

Old Dr. Curie, who lived with the couple, had retired to his room. Marie had bathed her child and put it to bed, and had stayed for a long time beside the cot. This was a rite. When Irène did not feel her mother near her at night she would call out for her incessantly, with that "Mé!" which was to be our substitute for "Mamma" always. And Marie, yielding to the implacability of the four-year-old baby, climbed the stairs, seated herself beside the child and stayed there in the darkness until the young voice gave way to light, regular breathing. Only then would she go down again to Pierre, who was growing impatient. In spite of his kindness, he was the most possessive and jealous of husbands. He was so used to the constant presence of his wife that her least eclipse kept him from thinking freely. If Marie delayed too long near her daughter, he received her on her return with a reproach so unjust as to be comic:

"You never think of anything but that child!"

Pierre walked slowly about the room. Marie sat down and made some stitches on the hem of Irène's new apron. One of her principles was never to buy ready-made clothes for the child: she thought them too fancy and impractical. In the days when Bronya was in Paris the two sisters cut out their children's dresses together, according to patterns of their own invention. These patterns still served for Marie.

But this evening she could not fix her attention. Nervous, she got up; then, suddenly:

"Suppose we go down there for a moment?"

There was a note of supplication in her voice—altogether superfluous, for Pierre, like herself, longed to go back to the shed they had left two hours before. Radium, fanciful as a living creature, endearing as a love, called them back to its dwelling, to the wretched laboratory.

The day's work had been hard, and it would have been more reasonable for the couple to rest. But Pierre and Marie were not always reasonable. As soon as they had put on their coats and told Dr. Curie of their flight, they were in the street. They went on foot, arm in arm, exchanging few words. After the crowded streets of this queer district, with its factory buildings, wastelands and poor tenements, they arrived in the Rue Lhomond and crossed the little courtyard.

Pierre put the key in the lock. The door squeaked, as it had squeaked thousands of times, and admitted them to their realm, to their dream.

"Don't light the lamps!" Marie said in the darkness. Then she added with a little laugh:

"Do you remember the day when you said to me 'I should like radium to have a beautiful color'?"

The reality was more entrancing than the simple wish of long ago. Radium had something better than "a beautiful color": it was spontaneously luminous. And in the somber shed where, in the absence of cupboards, the precious particles in their tiny glass receivers were placed on tables or on shelves nailed to the wall, their phosphorescent bluish outlines gleamed, suspended in the night.

"Look . . . Look!" the young woman murmured.

She went forward cautiously, looked for and found a straw-bottomed chair. She sat down in the darkness and silence. Their two faces turned toward the pale glimmering, the mysterious sources of radiation, toward radium—their radium. Her body leaning forward, her head eager, Marie took up again the attitude which had been hers an hour earlier at the bedside of her sleeping child.

Her companion's hand lightly touched her hair.

She was to remember forever this evening of glowworms, this magic.

Madame Curie, by Eve Curie

FERDINAND MAGELLAN

"The region seemed beyond lawful entry."

On September 20, 1519, Ferdinand Magellan, a Portuguese commanding an armada of five vessels under a Spanish flag, set off to circle the world. On September 6, 1522, one of those ships returned to Sanuecar de Barrameda. The leader of the expedition was dead, killed by natives in the Philippines. The other four ships had been sunk, burned, or had turned back before the voyage was complete. Yet with all this, a dream had been realized, a milestone had been passed.

History has given Magellan little credit for this fantastic feat of navigation—in many ways more dangerous and more daring than Columbus' voyage. Magellan proved *the world was round. He proved that the Americas are a land mass completely separated from Asia. He was the first man to cross the Pacific* (which he named) *and was responsible for changing the entire concept of the relationship of the earth's land and water areas. This is his moment of triumph.*

ON THE eighteenth day of October the Armada, with Álvaro de la Mezquíta in command of the *San Antonio*, Duárte Barbósa in command of the *Vittoria*, and Juan de Serrano in the *Concepción*, set sail after the flagship. Magellan, watching the weather, noted the lengthening of the day and felt that the season was turning in spite of continued storms. It would be soon or never to the mouth of that elusive opening he hoped to find. Because there was always the fear in his mind that a strait might be passed during the night, he shortened down at dark, standing off and on to pick up his marks or range hills, and continued south by daylight. Too much was at stake to take chances as they worked down, increasing their latitude. For centuries after this initial voyage, Cape Horn ships were to sail those seas with caution, but with knowledge; Magellan, as able a sailor as any of them, knew the hazards without knowing where they lay. So, when three days had passed, none of them could believe they had come to an immense opening in the shore line, lying to the west and south.

Magellan, a devoutly religious man, as were many of the great commanders of the Age of Discovery, noted the day of the calendar, October 21, to be that of St. Ursula and her Virgins. The Promontory lying to the west, terminating solid land that extended northward, and the coast against which they had been contending for months, he named the Cape of the Eleven Thousand Virgins. Today seamen and geographers call it Cape Virgins. At noon, when they measured their altitudes, they placed it in latitude 52 degrees south of equinoctial—only a quarter of a degree out (latitude 52° 18′ 35″ S.).

As they hauled in, the ships coming close together for instruction, a wide, deep bay was disclosed trending far to the west. Nothing like this had been sighted before. A mouth stretched five leagues across to land that faded back into the south and west, while directly into the mighty bay there loomed outlines of mountains trembling in the air—a phantasmagoric aspect—lifting high walls above the sea as if suspended in the heavens, the waters apparently running under them over the edge of the world. Refractings confused the religious; the region seemed beyond lawful entry.

The Armada, taking advantage of favorable weather, stood to the south, and anchored outside of a line of breaking shoals four miles off the shore, and north of Cabo Espiritu Santo (which Magellan named), a striking steep white cliff, one hundred and ninety feet high. The tides were enormous, even higher than in San Julian, lifting forty feet above low water. When they receded, the shallow sands seemed to march out into the sea. And at nightfall the wind began to boom, coming from the east. The Captain General, showing four lights, hastily got under way, standing on the starboard tack, followed by the other ships. What the tidal currents were no one knew; what the water was could be told only by constant sounding. The cold grew intense. Nothing could be seen as the ships stood off and on between invisible capes. As the wind dropped, toward meridian of the next day, the *San Antonio* and the *Concepción* were ordered to run in as far as safe, and to report, while the flagship and the *Vittoria* kept their station, sailing back and forth across the entrance. Magellan knew that there would be no deserting him via the strait, if it was a strait, and he had trust in Serrano. In the falling dark the ships seemed to be returning, their courses like black squares set against the shore line. Then suddenly they began to veer, as if caught by some hand of the sea dragging their keels; the two reconnaissance ships were swept around a point and out of sight.

No one knew what had happened. Disaster might have sucked the two consorts into some foul bight. If the *Trinidada* and the *Vittoria* were also caught and cast ashore? Caution and vigilance kept the Captain General on edge. A long, anxious night, and no news; a day of terrible forebodings and another crucifying night. Then on the breaking of day, the wind having shifted offshore, a sudden shout came down from the lookouts. The *San Antonio* and the *Concepción* appeared beyond a point of the First Narrows (as we know them now), spewed out by the racing tidal stream, bowling before the wind. The current through the narrows runs up to eight knots; the wind sent them another five knots; they loomed up as they ran to seaward, approaching Magellan with incredible speed.

De Serrano, in the *Concepción* (a faster sailer than the heavy *San Antonio*), clung to the tilting poop rail as his ship ran past the flagship's quarter. "The Strait!" he called, his ship plowing by, plunging in the lumpy sea, spray booming from her bows. The *San Antonio* rounded to on the other side, and again "The Strait, the Strait!" Álvaro de la Mezquíta shouted as he pointed inland. Then the *San Antonio's* bombards were discharged, the smoke clouding over the flagship.

Cheers were returned from the *Trinidada* and the *Vittoria*. The two adventuring ships, as if the winners of a mighty joust, tacked and wore about their consorts; slatting canvas, wreaths of rising spray showering over their forecastles when they came to the wind. But enough of this. Magellan called all captains to the flagship. The sails were backed, and the four ships bobbed in the middle of the entrance bay as the small boats were hoisted out and assembled at the *Trinidada*. At last the story was this. When they had entered a narrow, the tide being slowly with them, the ships had come to a large middle basin and were about to return, after having seen a further opening. Then, on heading out to the east, a current, beyond anything they had ever known, started suddenly and swept them back into the First Narrows and around into a wide bight, where they anchored. The ships had seen the Second Narrows, and beyond into a great southerly opening which De Serrano was positive trended to the sea.

Estéban Gómez, King's pilot, then pilot of the *San Antonio* spoke for reason. They had at last accomplished their mission, the discovery of an opening into the western sea seen by Balboa, he said. Better to return home now so that fresh ships could be sent, as provisions were low; they had hardly enough to take them back to Spain. If bad fortune met them in the South Sea, the result would be starvation.

At this, as Pigafetta faithfully reported, the Captain General replied, "If we have to eat the leather on the yards, I will still go on and discover what I have promised the King, and I trust that God will aid us and give us good fortune."

They then sailed through the double narrows, the tide sweeping them into a wide bay trending to the south. White-topped mountains were in the far distance, and at night they saw many fires lit in the hills to the south and moving about along the shores. Magellan called the country Tierra del Fuego, Land of Fire.

Then, leagues down the Strait, the Captain General descried a wide opening to the east and sent the *San Antonio* and the *Concepción* to explore this arm (marked on the charts as Useless Bay) with its maze of channels leading southward into what is Admiralty Sound. The flagship and the *Vittoria* stood toward the south, where rose a magnificent twin-peaked, snow-capped mountain; close it seemed, because of its size, as they sailed onward. This was Mount Sarmiénto, three great glaciers descending from its slopes, its peaks lifting over seven thousand feet from the sea. When they were twenty leagues down the southern reach, the waters began to narrow. It looked as if they might have been mistaken after all, for the wildness of the region surpassed anything man had ever seen. The way trended sharply to the northwest, past a grand and savage cape, a towering black mass of bare rock veined by rifts of snow, its top crowned with white. A squall struck them, sending the ships over on their beams. Sheets were let fly; the land was shut in by whirling gales of white; birds were swept over them. High, unscalable crags lifted above their mastheads. Glaciers blue-white were suspended in the air, their cold breaths coming down on the icy decks. The ships, making hundreds of tacks, were first turned by one shore, then by another. The pilots, so confused they could not name the capes, slowly worked through the narrowing reaches. They entered false arms and were turned back; they felt their way ahead, always expecting to arrive at the end. But Magellan noted the current, ebbing and flowing. Sometimes they anchored under the steep edges of topless mountains, the ships hanging on narrow shelves of bottom—for in most cases the channels were so deep there were no soundings. Long green and purple streamers of kelp moved with the tide, guiding them.

After incredible work they came to a cove only a short distance beyond Cape Froward (southmost mainland of America and turning point in the Strait), a bay lost in the vast numbers of indentations. It might have been Cordes Bay, foul with rocks; it might have been Port Gallant. They called it the Bay of Sardines, and hung on for rest and fishing. What lay ahead looked far more difficult than what had been gone through. The Captain General, now more cautious than ever, decided to wait. He was worried as to the fate of his principal ship with most of the stores on board. Where was the *San Antonio*? And what had become of De Serrano in the *Concepción*?

The *Trinidada's* longboat was provisioned and sent out to explore.

It was punishing work at the oars, but she also had her mast and sail. He would wait. A week later the boat returned. They had seen a cape, the Cape Deseado of Magellan's desire. And beyond, so the pilots reported, was the blue mist of an open sea, the great South Sea.

But where were the other two ships? The *Trinidada* and the *Vittoria* left the Bay of Sardines and stood back, with a fair wind. Rounding Cape Froward, they met with the *Concepción*. She had found nothing useful in the great bay, in Useless Bay. In the mist of snow the *San Antonio* had vanished. The three ships sailed northward and anchored behind an island inside of the Second Narrows. If the lost ship was anywhere, she might be there. But no sign of her was seen. The provisions, of which she held the greatest part, made her essential to the voyage. The *Vittoria* was sent out again to the east, running through the double narrows with the tides; already they were gaining the secret of navigating the Strait. Captain Barbósa was to plant a banner on some conspicuous point, and bury an earthen pot containing an order of instruction. He sailed out and back to the Cape of the Eleven Thousand Virgins; he set up his banner on a small hill, conspicuous on the seaward edge of the First Narrows, possibly on Delgada Point, and left the message. To make doubly sure, Barbósa left a second banner, with another note, on a small island inside the Second Narrows. This might have been the eastern point of Elizabeth Island. But Alvaro de la Mezquíta, commanding the *San Antonio*, had listened to the King's pilot Estéban Gómez. The heaviest ship of the Armada was already many leagues to the north and east, sailing back to Spain with news of discovery and of the loss of the foolhardy Captain General, and with the story of his tyranny and his executions. Mezquíta, on arrival at San Lúcar was thrown into a dungeon and there remained until the years brought back the *Vittoria*.

Magellan called a conference with his loyal captains, Juan de Serrano and Duárte Barbósa. Were they willing to go on? They were, and the three ships again beat back to the Bay of Sardines. Here they waited. The lost ship might still come out of the maze of Tierra del Fuego; she might find the instructions. But the banners whipped to shreds; the earthen pots with their historic notes were lost in the sands. At last the decision was to go on.

Only a seaman who has penetrated the Strait can have the least conception of the work that lay ahead of the three surviving ships. The cold water had kept their bottoms clean, but their rig was a clumsy thing in the constant beating to windward through the worst waters known to man. On every hand were submerged rocks, and treacherous cross currents ran without regularity or reason. Five weeks had been consumed in the Strait, the Strait of Magellan as it will be known as long as men and charts exist. On November 28, 1520, the three ships, catching a favoring slant of wind from the south, cleared Cape Deseado, still marked on the charts, outside and south of the now famous headland called Cape Pillar. They shaped their course to the northwest to sail over the South Sea, a far greater ocean than the most learned cartographers had ever imagined.

Pigafetta, in writing up his journal after the ordeal of the Strait, entered a note of exceeding interest to all students of the Land of Fire. "We found, by a miracle, a strait which we call the Strait of the Eleven Thousand Virgins; this strait is a hundred and ten leagues long which are four hundred and forty miles and almost as wide as less than half a league, and it issues into another sea which is called the Peaceful Sea; it is surrounded by very great and high mountains covered with snow. . . . I think there is not in the world a more beautiful country, or a better strait than this one." . . .

For ninety-eight days Magellan sailed across the South Sea, a seemingly endless ocean of fair winds, of bright skies, during which time the three ships grew trailing weeds and clustering barnacles, while the shipworm, the teredo, bored into their planks. For a few weeks the warmth revived the crews, then the fading and putrescent quarter rations brought on scurvy.

Pigafetta says: "We ate biscuit, but in truth it was biscuit no longer, but a powder full of worms, and in addition it was stinking with the urine of rats. So great was our want of food, we were forced to eat the hide with which the main yard was covered. These hides, exposed to the sun, rain and wind, had become so hard we were first obliged to soften them by putting them overboard for four or five days, after which we put them on the embers and ate them thus. We also used sawdust for food, and rats became such a delicacy that we paid half a ducat apiece for them."

They reached the Ladrónes, the Isles of Robbers, and then fetched the Philippines—later named so after King Philip II of Spain. In his eagerness to convert the heathen savages, Magellan, the zealot, was slain on the Isle of Mactan. The circumnavigation, after the burning of the worn-out *Concepción* and the sending of the *Trinidada* to again cross the Pacific to Mexico (which she failed to accomplish), was completed by the small *Vittoria*, in which Pigafetta returned to San Lúcar. This ship, laden to the hatches with cloves, more than paid for the expedition, but Christopher Haro got no return on his investment, nor did Diego Barbósa. The heirs of Magellan were forgotten. Rodrigo, Magellan's son, was dead; his second child had died at birth, and Doña Beatriz, learning of the death of her husband, "grievously sorrowing," also passed away.

Moderns, concerned as they have been by later comparatively puny achievements, have begun to appreciate the magnitude of Magellan's accomplishment. At the Panama-Pacific Historical Congress, John W. Draper, the historian, was quoted as being of the opinion that Magellan's voyage was "the greatest achievement in the history of the human race."

Cape Horn, by Felix Riesenberg

DWIGHT D. EISENHOWER

"So we talked ... on Senators and skunks and civet cats."

The war in Europe was five years old—and the tide had definitely turned. Now the Allies were about to launch their biggest offensive, across the English Channel—the final push that was to drive the Germans back within their borders. The man responsible for every facet of this gigantic operation was Dwight D. Eisenhower.

Eisenhower's rise from obscurity to international prominence is a well-documented story, frequently told. He was an obscure army officer—not a failure by the lights of his profession but surely not spectacularly successful—when the United States was catapulted into the Second World War. Ike was ready. The war gave him a chance to prove that he was not only a good tactician and a skillful diplomat but a superb administrator. His rise was meteoric. In five short years he had soared from unimportant staff positions to the command of an army made up of troops from twelve nations—the mightiest force in the world.

Captain Harry Butcher, Eisenhower's naval aide, was with him on the eve of D-Day—the night before the battle broke on June 6, 1944. Here is his memorable picture. . . .

D-DAY IS now almost irrevocably set for tomorrow morning [June 6, 1944], about 6:40, the time varying with tides at different beaches, the idea being to strike before high tide submerges obstacles which have to be cleared away.

"Irrevocable" becomes practically absolute around dusk, Ike said this afternoon while talking to the press and radio men, who heard him explain for more than an hour the "greatest operation we have ever attempted."

This morning Ike went to South Parade Pier in Portsmouth to see the loading of some British soldiers aboard LCILs 600, 601, and 602. He always gets a lift from talking with soldiers. He got one this morning, which partially offset the impatience with which he viewed the cloudy weather which had been predicted clear. While talking to the press he noticed through the tent door a quick flash of sunshine and said: "By George, there *is* some sun. . . ."

The actual decision was confirmed and made final this morning at 4:15 after all the weather dope had been assembled. During yesterday the weather looked as if we might have to postpone for at least two days, until Thursday, with possibility of two weeks. Pockets of "lows" existed all the way from western Canada across the United States and the Atlantic, and were coming our way. What was needed was a benevolent "high" to counteract or divert at least one of the parading lows. During the night that actually occurred. During the day, Force U, the U.S. task force which started from Falmouth at the western end of the Channel at 6 A.M. Sunday, had become scattered, owing to the galelike wind sweeping southern England and the Channel. . . .

Air Chief Marshal Tedder told me that at the Sunday night meeting when the decision was made to launch OVERLORD, subject to final review at the 4 A.M. meeting, Monday morning, the weatherman who had spoken for all the weather services, after having given a rather doleful report, was asked, "What will the weather be on D-Day in the Channel and over the French coast?" He hesitated, Tedder said, for two dramatic minutes and finally said, conscientiously and soberly, "To answer that question would make me a guesser, not a meteorologist."

Despite the refusal of the weatherman to be a "guesser," Ike had to take the responsibility of making the decision without satisfactory assurance from the meteorologist—a responsibility which Tedder said Ike took without hesitation.

What does the Supreme Commander do just now? Before lunch he played this aide "Hounds and Fox," he being the hounds, and he won consistently, there being a trick in being a hound. We played a game of crackerbox checkers, and just as I had him cornered with my two kings and his one remaining king, damned if he didn't jump one of my kings and get a draw.

At lunch we talked of old political yarns, he having known my old friend Pat Harrison when he was coming up as a young Congressman. I told the story of the Harrison-Bilbo campaign in which the latter supported Governor Conner for Senator against Pat. One of Pat's supporters told a rally the trouble with Pat was that he was too damned honorable and should use Bilbo's tactics. These he illustrated by the famous yarn of Mama and Papa Skunk and their nine children, which ends with Papa alluding to a new and terrible odor wafting into their nostrils, and adding, "I don't know what it is, Mama Skunk and children dear, but whatever it is, we must get some of it."

So we talked, during the lunch, on Senators and skunks and civet cats.

After lunch I shepherded the press and radio men to our little camp. . . . Ike took over in his tent, and as usual held them on the edge of their chairs. The nonchalance with which he announced that we were attacking in the morning and the feigned nonchalance with which the reporters absorbed it was a study in suppressed emotion. . . .

The landings have gone better than expected. Every outfit is ashore, but we have just had a report that Gee, Major General Gerow, with his V Corps, can't get off one of its beaches because of hostile mortar and artillery fire. This is Omaha Beach. . . . But to go back. Last night, starting from camp at six, with Ike . . . we hit out for the 101st Airborne Division around Newbury. We saw hundreds of paratroopers, with blackened and grotesque faces, packing up for the big hop and jump. Ike wandered through them, stepping over packs, guns, and a variety of equipment such as only paratroop people can devise, chinning with this one and that one. All were put at ease. He was promised a job after the war by a Texan who said he roped, not dallied, his cows, and at least there was enough to eat in the work. Ike has developed or disclosed an informality and friendliness with troopers that almost amazed me. . . .

We returned to camp about 1:15, sat around the nickel-plated office caravan in courteous silence, each with his own thoughts and trying to borrow by psychological osmosis those of the Supreme Commander, until I became the first to say to hell with it and excused myself to bed. There I expected a phone call from Lieutenant Colonel Hugh Barkley, an Intelligence officer of the 101st, who had said his headquarters would have radio word from the air transports the moment the jump was made, and that he would phone me just as quickly as that. Every half-hour or so during the remainder of the night I awakened, said to myself, have I heard from Barkley, and finding the answer no, went back to the D-Eve sleep. At H-Hour, by coincidence, I was awake, that being 6:40, and was contemplating the underside of the drab tent roof, wondering how come such a quiet night in contrast with other D-Nights, when this was supposed to be the biggest and most superduper of all, when suddenly there came the call.

But it was [Air Marshal] Leigh-Mallory, himself . . . filled with information, good information. Surprisingly, said the Air Marshal, only twenty-one of the American C-47s out of the 850 were missing.

Only four gliders were unaccounted for. On the British, eight C-47s were AWOL out of some 400. Amazing good luck. And an RAF Intruder had seen the British paras drop, and it went off smooth, smooth indeed. Grand, said I, grand. I'll tell the boss as soon as he wakes up. . . .

So I tiptoed down the cinder path to Ike's circus wagon to see if he was asleep and saw him silhouetted in bed behind a Western. Ike grinned as he lit a cigarette. I . . . gassed with the boss awhile, remembering the first D-Night at Gib, when after a tedious one for him and an hour's lie-down under a table for me, we had met at the salt-water basin of the stinking tunnel lavatory to hoe off our whiskers. Being up bright and early, as is my custom on D-Day only, I skedaddled back to my tent, shaved, dressed, and sauntered nonchalantly in the early-morning sun to the office caravan. Ike had done his D-Day toilet as well, this time with running, soft hot water, and looked in the pink. We stood in front of the caravan, enjoying the beautiful, oh, what a beautiful day. A GI came grinding along with the morning papers from Portsmouth, with headlines of the fall of Rome and the Fifth Army's crashing victory, with personal statement by Wayne Clark. Ike said, "Good morning, *good* morning," to the GI, most cheerfully indeed. . . .

My Three Years with Eisenhower, by Captain Harry C. Butcher

V. MAN IN ADVERSITY

Sweet are the uses of adversity;

Which, like the toad, ugly and venomous,

Wears yet a precious jewel in his head.

WILLIAM SHAKESPEARE

As You Like It, Act II, Scene 1

FRANKLIN DELANO ROOSEVELT

"... active re-entry into politics would assist him to get well."

In what is appropriately enough the thirteenth chapter of his biography of Franklin Roosevelt, John Gunther tells again the familiar story of the President's terrible struggle with polio. Vigorous, athletic, ambitious, Roosevelt was truly a man in his prime. His political star was rising fast. He had been the Democratic vice-presidential candidate the year before in 1920 and was being boomed as the next governor of New York. Thirty-nine years old, in vibrant good health, he was reaching toward the ultimate heights of success when the dreadful and unexpected blow hit him. It would not have been a surprise to anyone if on his recovery he had sought a life of retirement. He could stand only with constant support . . . he could not walk . . . he was doomed to wear heavy steel braces wherever he went.

Here Gunther tells the story of Roosevelt's decision to stay in public life—and of the monumental obstacles he had to overcome to do it. Here is a portrait of Roosevelt, not as President, but as a human being of incredible courage and unmatched determination.

ROOSEVELT HAD a fairly wide though not unusual experience of illness before paralysis struck him. He was capable of feats of exertion over short periods that amazed his friends—for instance he could tire out a horse on rough mountain trails—but in a curious way his vitality was mercurial; he could vault over a row of chairs at the San Francisco convention and play golf within two strokes of a course record, but in those days he was not what would be called a "strong" man. He was graceful rather than muscular; taut, not solid. His body was a sensitive mechanism, and photographs of the time give him a look almost fragile. He radiated energy, as a consumptive may do, but he sometimes burned himself out in doing so; time and again his resistance weakened, and he fell prey to minor illness.

Measles . . . kept him from enlisting in the Spanish-American War;

also at Groton he had a severe attack of scarlet fever. He had recurrent lumbago during his honeymoon, and several attacks of hives. In 1912 he had a long bout of typhoid fever; it kept him in bed during his second run for State Senator, and Louis Howe had to make his speeches for him. A stomach complaint afflicted him in 1913, and two years later came an operation for acute appendicitis. Lumbago troubled him again in 1915, and he began to have stubborn head colds and sinus attacks. He had a serious throat infection in 1916; he spent several weeks in Atlantic City recuperating, and then had some dental trouble. The throat infection recurred the next year, and he spent a week in the hospital. Then, returning from Europe in 1918, he had double pneumonia and was so ill that he had to be carried from the ship on a stretcher. Following this came a severe attack of flu.

One should not, of course, exaggerate the importance of these illnesses; perhaps all they indicate was that he was working too hard. Nothing at all was wrong in any deep organic sense, though his letters mention that he had trouble keeping his weight up; he weighed 170 at about this time, which is not a great deal for a man six feet two. It is a striking irony that just before poliomyelitis struck him, he had a brief period of exceptionally brilliant and vibrant health, even though he had not had a real holiday for years. Another irony is that he had an almost morbid fear that infantile paralysis might strike some member of his family. . . .

On August 10, 1921, Roosevelt took his wife and their sons for a sail on a small craft which he was teaching the boys how to handle. Returning to Campobello he saw a forest fire on the nearby shore; the whole family landed for the strenuous fun of fighting it. To cool off, he decided to take a swim in a nearby lake, Glen Severn, though he had been complaining for several days of feeling tired; then he and the children jog-trotted the mile and a half home. Later FDR wanted another swim, and he jumped into the ocean from the beach. The Bay of Fundy is ice-cold even at this time of year. Back in the house again, he found that a batch of mail had arrived; he sat down in his wet bathing suit and went through it for half an hour. Thereupon he had a sudden chill, and Mrs. Roosevelt persuaded him to go to bed. (Interestingly enough he had had a chill the day before, as a result of slipping and falling overboard.)

Thus the attack began—though nobody can know when, where, or under what circumstances the polio virus first entered his system. The first intimation to FDR himself that something might be wrong with his legs was a tenderness in the forepart of the thighs.

The next day, August 11, he had a high temperature and acute pain in the left leg. Mrs. Roosevelt acted promptly; she sent the children away to a nearby camp, and summoned the nearest physician, Dr. E. H. Bennett of Lubec, Maine. Bennett got there by 10 A.M. He was puzzled. FDR could walk, but had severe pains throughout his back and legs. On August 12 difficulty in walking supervened, and Mrs. Roosevelt and Bennett thought they ought to consult another doctor. It happened that a famous Philadelphia diagnostician, Dr. W. W. Keen, was summering in the neighborhood; he examined Roosevelt on the 13th and again the next day and decided "that a clot of blood from a sudden congestion has settled in the lower spinal cord temporarily removing the power to move though not to feel." Nobody thought then in terms of infantile paralysis. But Keen knew that this was a serious matter; he thought that recovery might "take some months." Roosevelt got worse in the next few days, not better. Keen changed his mind, discarded the clot theory, and decided that FDR must have "a lesion" in the spinal cord. Also he sent Mrs. Roosevelt a bill for $600. By this time FDR's bladder and the rectal sphincter were paralyzed. Mrs. Roosevelt insisted that a specialist in poliomyelitis from Boston, Dr. Robert W. Lovett, be called in. Lovett saw FDR on August 25, made a correct diagnosis, and stopped the massages which Keen had ordered. Roosevelt was in the fiercest kind of pain during all of this, and was completely helpless. He had to be catheterized until September 8, and the paralysis spread to affect—temporarily —his arms and back as well as legs.

Sara Roosevelt was away in Europe, about to return home. The whole brunt fell on Eleanor. She did all the nursing. Her letters to the family during this period are models of clarity, courage, and cool restraint. She wrote Rosy, FDR's half brother, on August 14th: "We have had a very anxious few days as on Wednesday evening Franklin was taken ill. . . . I have wired New York for a masseuse and . . . in the meantime Louis [Howe] and I are rubbing him as well as we can. . . . I have only told Franklin he [the doctor] said he could surely go down [to New York] the 15th of September . . . but it may have to be done on a wheel chair. . . . Do you think you can meet Mama when she lands? She has asked us to cable just before she sails and I have decided to say nothing. No letter can reach her now and it would simply mean worry all the way home." A few days later, again to Rosy: "I have asked Dr. Keen to try to get Dr. Lovett here . . . to determine if it is I.P. or not. Dr. Keen thinks *not* but the treatment at this stage differs in one particular and no matter what it costs I feel and I am sure Mama would feel we must leave no stone unturned to accomplish the best results." Then to Sara: "Dearest Mama, Franklin has been quite ill and so can't go down to meet you on Tuesday to his great regret, but Uncle Fred and Aunt Kassie both write they will be there so it will not be a lonely homecoming. We are so happy to have you home again dear, you don't know what it means to feel you are near again." This is as brave an upper lip as has ever been set against catastrophe. FDR with polio! It was unbelievable! Yet it had to be believed, faced, and fought through to a finish.

Meanwhile Louis Howe, a house guest, insisted that there should be as little publicity as possible and that, for the time being at least, the newspapers should not know that FDR was paralyzed. Dr. Lovett gave permission for the trip to New York in mid-September, with the prognosis that there was "a good possibility of considerable improvement." Frederic Delano, FDR's uncle, got a private railway car, and Howe worked out a stratagem whereby Roosevelt was slipped on the train with only a few people aware of what was going on. But getting him off the island to a launch, down a steep rough slope to the beach, then transferring the stretcher up the dock on the mainland and onto a baggage cart, then into the railway car through a window, was one of the grimmest jobs Howe ever had to tackle. Mrs. Roosevelt and all the children came along. The doctors had assured her that they could not catch the illness at this date. . . .

In New York Roosevelt was taken to the Presbyterian Hospital on Park Avenue, and one of Lovett's associates, Dr. George Draper, a brilliant young specialist who had known FDR well at school, became his doctor and took charge of the case. Through all the agony that followed, Draper and Mrs. Roosevelt were the closest allies; Draper, more than anybody except Eleanor and Howe, should have the credit for saving Roosevelt. Again we see the long and intricate chain of cause and effect that controls the seeming fortuitousness of human lives. Had not Draper, a friend, happened to be on hand, with exactly the right combination of technical skill and personal force, it is extremely doubtful if FDR would ever have recovered to the extent he did. . . .

Howe decided that the newspapers must be told something, and on September 16, the New York *Times* carried a front-page story with the following headline:

F. D. ROOSEVELT ILL
OF POLIOMYELITIS
Brought on Special Car from Campobello,
Bay of Fundy, to Hospital Here
RECOVERING, DOCTOR SAYS
Patient Stricken by Infantile Paralysis
A Month Ago, and Use of Legs Affected

The first paragraph says that Roosevelt had lost the use of both legs below the knee "for more than a month." But one doctor is quoted as saying that "he definitely will not be crippled. No one need have any fear of permanent injury from this attack."

Dr. Lovett wrote Dr. Draper this hitherto unpublished letter:

With regard to Mr. R. I was called to see him in Campobello. There was some uncertainty about the diagnosis, but I thought it perfectly clear so far as the physical findings were concerned and I never feel that the history is of much value anyway.

He had I thought some facial involvement, apparently no respiratory, but a weakness in the arms, not very severe and not grouped at all. There was some atrophy of the left thenar eminence. . . . There was a scattered weakness in the legs, most marked in the hips when I saw him, very few muscles were absent, and in those that were recovering there was a pretty fair degree of power at the end of two weeks. No deformities were present, and the general aspect of the thing was a mild, rather scattered attack without excessive tenderness, coming on promptly and not in a sneaking way, with spontaneous improvement beginning almost at once and progressing.

It seems to me that it was a mild case within the range of possible complete recovery. I told them very frankly that no one could tell where they stood, that the case was evidently not of the severest type, that complete recovery or partial recovery to any point was possible, that disability was not to be feared, and that the only out about it was the long continued character of the treatment. It is dangerous to speak from impressions at the end of the second week, but my feeling about him was that he was probably going to be a case where the conservation of what muscular power he has may be very important, and it looked to me as if some of the important muscles might be on the edge where they could be influenced either way—toward recovery, or turn into completely paralyzed muscles. I was as noncommittal as I could be about who should conduct the treatment, and I asked them to put themselves in your hands and follow your advice.

But things were not to go as well as Lovett hoped. In fact Draper thought presently that FDR might never be able to sit up again, much less stand or walk. On September 24 he wrote Lovett the following letter, which has not been published before:

Just a line to report to you about Franklin R. I am much concerned at the very slow recovery both as regards the disappearance of *pain*, which is very generally present, and as to the recovery of even slight power to twitch the muscles. There is marked falling away of the muscle masses on either side of the spine in the lower lumbar region, likewise the buttocks. There is marked weakness of the right triceps; and an unusual amount of gross muscular twitching in the muscles of both forearms. He coordinates on the fine motions of his hands very well now so that he can sign his name and write a little better than before.

The lower extremities present a most depressing picture. There is a little motion in the long extensors of the toes of each foot, a little in the perinei of the right side, a little ability to twitch the bellies of the gastrocnemii, but not really extend the feet. There is little similar power in the left vastus, and on both sides similar voluntary twitches of the ham-string masses can be accomplished.

He is very cheerful and hopeful, and has made up his mind that he is going to go out of the hospital in the course of two or three weeks on crutches. What I fear more than anything else is that we shall find a much more extensive involvement of the great back muscles than we have suspected and *that when we attempt to sit him up he will be faced with the frightfully depressing knowledge that he cannot hold himself erect.* It has occurred to me that it might be possible for you to devise some kind of support for him which we can put on while he is in bed, just preparatory to getting him up in a chair for the first time, so that he will not realize too suddenly that his back will not hold him.

I feel so strongly . . . that the psychological factor in his management is paramount. *He has such courage, such ambition, and yet at the same time such an extraordinarily sensitive emotional mechanism that it will take all the skill which we can muster to lead him successfully to a recognition of what he really faces without crushing him.*

My thought was that as soon as the tenderness has left completely so that you could move him about as you please . . . you would come to New York to see him. At present I feel that we should not get the greatest value from your presence because of the impossibility of manipulating him.

I have studiously refrained from examining his upper extremities because he believes them to be untouched by the disease. It is fortunate that one does not have much opportunity in the recumbent position in bed to call upon the deltoids or the triceps —the biceps are fortunately pretty good so that he is able to pull himself up by the strap over his head and so help himself to turn in bed. This of course gives him a great sense of satisfaction.

Lovett replied that he would of course come to New York at any time, and recommended immersion in strong saline baths and the "use of electric light." He predicted that the involvement in the arms would clear up, which indeed it eventually did. . . .

During all this period Roosevelt of course suffered the most harrowing agonies, mental as well as physical. When did it first become unequivocally clear to him that there was no prospect that he would ever walk again? Was he told? Or did he guess it for himself? Did he ever know with full consciousness that his back and arms were in jeopardy too—that he might never be able to sit up again, never even regain the full use of his hands? Who broke it to him that leg braces would be necessary? Of course nature provides a cushion for shocks so grievous as these; the very fact of his complete nervous depression probably helped him, and mercifully he was under mild opiates a good part of the time.

There were excruciating ups and downs, as in all serious illnesses. On November 19–20 he had a mysterious relapse; his temperature went up to 101, and his eyes began to hurt. Momentarily it was even feared that, as if fate had not mutilated him enough, his eyesight might become affected. Later the tendons of the right knee tightened, bending the leg like a jackknife, and both legs had to be put in plaster casts as a remedial measure. The pain of this was the worst in the whole experience. Day by day, for several weeks, a wedge was tapped into each cast, a little deeper each time, to force the legs to become unlocked. But two items of good news compensated for this torture. First, the arms began to recover. Second, the "great muscles of the back" that Draper was so worried about resumed their normal function. He could sit up!

His mother wanted him to come to Hyde Park immediately after his discharge from the hospital, but he and Eleanor insisted on going to the 65th Street house in town. In his later convalescence, of course, he did spend much time at Hyde Park. Mrs. Roosevelt has recorded the "somewhat acrimonious" disputes that attended the decision to stay in New York City. This is to understate. What really happened during these agonizing months was a battle to the finish between these two remarkable women for Franklin's soul. Harsh words were seldom spoken; the intensity burned beneath the surface; the struggle was fierce just the same. Sara wanted FDR to submit gracefully to the disaster, and live out the rest of his years in vegetative retirement as an invalided country squire; Eleanor wanted him to continue active participation in every realm of life so far as this would not impede his recovery. She would not give an inch to the illness. She thought in fact that active re-entry into politics would assist him to get well. She was right, and in any case she won.

Anybody who has ever known and loved a person helplessly ill will understand the peculiarly harrowing nature of what Mrs. Roosevelt went through—the jagged alternations between hope and despair; the necessity of giving blind trust to a physician even when the physician, cruelly pressed, could scarcely trust himself; the fearsome responsibility involved; above all the unpredictable oscillations of mood in the patient himself, which had to be ministered to with the utmost firmness, subtlety, and tenderness. Only once, so far as is known, did Mrs. Roosevelt break down. The house was crowded to bursting, and she slept in a cot in one of the boys' rooms. FDR seemed no better, the worried children were on edge, and one day, while reading to the two youngest boys, she started to sob, and could not stop. Eventually, she records, she pulled herself together by going into an empty room in Sara's house next door; it was the only time in her whole life she ever went to pieces. Of course she herself was enlarged and steeled by the very intensity of an experience so grievous, no less than was her husband. They both came through the ravaging horrors of the ordeal with their characters—far from being diminished—magnificently enhanced.

By the spring of 1922 FDR was substantially better, though he could not walk, and by early autumn, a year after the illness first struck, he was able to do some work, and to hobble around on crutches. That he was able to make such progress was a triumph of pure grit, the conquest of flesh by will and spirit.

Now we must go into quite explicit and painful detail, because no appreciation at all of Roosevelt's later life is possible without concrete realization of what he went through. Dr. Draper taught him to "walk." Actually, though he himself might have disputed this, he never truly walked again. From the moment the illness struck him, he was "a goner below the waist," as one of the doctors put it. The major leg muscles never came back. Nor could he even *stand* (unless supported by someone's arm) without a prop, and even with braces he was like a man on stilts, because, being unable to flex with his toes, he had no balance. The braces were heavy, cumbersome, and a perpetual nuisance to manipulate. He could not put them on or take them off himself, and he "hated and mistrusted them." Without braces his helplessness was almost complete. Until the end of his life, he could not rise from a chair or sit down, even with the braces on, without help or at the cost of the most strenuously fatiguing effort. To get up he would have to lift out one leg with a hand, snap the brace tight, do the same with the other leg, then, with his legs absolutely stiff, as stiff as the legs of a pair of dividers, push himself up from the arms of the chair by the sheer power of his arms, wriggle, hold himself completely rigid from shoulder to ankle, tilt forward and upward slowly, very slowly, and then hope not to tip too far and fall. . . .

For relaxation he liked to sit in an easy chair on the east porch with Louis Howe, making ship models. Sometimes he would be alone; he would drop a knife or tool, and then, if it fell any distance away, be unable to pick it up again. To sail the models, he would go rowing in the Hudson; that is, Howe would get in the bow of the boat, he in the stern, with Mr. Depew at the oars. He even continued teaching the boys how to swim, by sitting on the edge of a pool and holding out a long pole. He did a good deal of carpentry, and, lying on his back hour after hour, played with his stamps and started a catalogue of all his books. Early in 1923 he began to write a little; he started a History of the United States (the text of which may be found in the second volume of his letters) and his book on John Paul Jones. He refused to be downhearted, and never conceded that he would not be able to walk again.

The legend is that his morale, his spirit, were so good that he was never even irritable. Of course that is not true; he *had* to be fretful on occasion. Once or twice he lost his temper with Anna, whom he loved best; she would weep and, overcome by this frightful tragedy that had assaulted her father, rush wildly from the room. But on the whole he was indefatigably patient, indomitable, and serene. He made his own bed of Procrustes bearable. Above all he was never bored; at the very deepest moments of strain and irritation he could save himself by his own curiosity and technical interest in what was being done for his cure; even when the heavy casts were stretching his legs slowly and painfully into shape he was fascinated by every detail of the treatment. . . .

A member of the family tells of one series of episodes almost too painful to be borne. FDR got a considerable amount of exercise by crawling. This man over forty who had been one of the most graceful, vital, and handsome youths of his generation spent hour after hour crawling over his library floor like a child. Then he determined to learn how to get upstairs by himself; day after day he would haul his dead weight up the stairs by the power of his hands and arms, step by step, slowly, doggedly; the sweat would pour off his face, and he would tremble with exhaustion. Moreover he insisted on doing this with members of the family or friends watching him, and he would talk all the time as he inched himself up little by little, talk, talk, and make people talk back. It was a kind of enormous spiritual catharsis—

as if he had to do it, to prove his independence, and had to have the feat witnessed, to prove that it was nothing.

Much of his energy went in the early days into experiments with such things as a kind of pincers on a stick, to reach for books, and a leaf-picker's device with which he could lift papers off the floor. Sometimes he would carry a book with his teeth. His wheel chairs were usually small, so that they would fit the narrowish corridors both in New York and Hyde Park, cushionless, and armless; underneath the seat was a concealed ash tray on a swivel, so that he would not drop ashes on the floor. Big casters made them easy to steer. He seldom wheeled himself, but when he did he scooted from room to room at a considerable rate of speed.

Roosevelt had after his illness four means of locomotion: (a) he could walk on somebody's arm with the braces and a cane, (b) he could walk with braces and crutches, (c) the wheel chair, (d) he could be carried. He hated to be carried, and Louis Howe laid it down as an iron rule that he must *never* be carried in public. But in private he was carried, like an infant, thousands of times. For instance, in later years, at dinner in the White House or elsewhere, he would usually be carried in to his place at the table before the company arrived. Often, however, he used the chair. His servants and helpers acquired a marvelous dexterity in manipulating the change from the wheel chair to another so quickly and unobtrusively that few people ever noticed. . . .

One of FDR's secretaries contributes this reminiscence. He was about to sign some checks in his capacity as head of the Woodrow Wilson Foundation and he said, "Wait a moment. I want to show you something." Then he proceeded to pick up one leg by the trouser crease and crossed it on the other one. "Now what do you think of that!" he exclaimed happily. Later she rode back to 65th Street with him. "He asked me to sit still when the car arrived home. He got out of the car and moved on crutches up the ramp that had been laid down to the front door. Then he gave the crutches to the chauffeur, and, using the railing along the ramp as support, *pulled* himself to the door. It was something he had just mastered."

Roosevelt, with great detachment and objectivity, once wrote a very good account of his own illness. His advice to fellow sufferers from polio was to go in for gentle exercise, skin massage, sun-bathing, and swimming in warm water; and to avoid overexertion, cold, deep massage, and getting fat.

In the autumn of 1924—I am skipping political developments to which we will return soon—began the great adventure of Warm

Springs. Here again we confront the extraordinary capriciousness of history; or perhaps it was determined by fate ten thousand years ago that (a) a dilapidated hotel with an adjacent warm pool should exist at Warm Springs, Georgia; (b) Dr. Lovett should have found that swimming in warm water helped some of his patients; (c) Roosevelt became a friend of a New York banker named George Foster Peabody; (d) Peabody bought the Warm Springs resort and leased it to a friend, Tom Loyless, a former editor of the Atlanta *Constitution*; (e) Loyless wrote Peabody that a Southern lad named Louis Joseph had been stricken by infantile paralysis two years before and had benefited greatly by the Warm Springs water. Who was this boy Louis Joseph? What has ever happened to him? Every human life is somehow associated with every other human life. Not one person in twenty million has ever heard of Louis Joseph; yet, by this combinative play and thrust of circumstance, this inextricably conjoined and mysterious chain of events, he became, by the mere fact of his existence, a major factor in the Roosevelt story.

Peabody thought that Roosevelt might be interested in the Joseph case, and passed on what information he had. At first the water did the boy little good; then after a summer he was able to stand up in the pool; then a year later "he could walk on land with the aid of canes." At once Roosevelt, breaking everything else off, set out for Warm Springs to see what this miracle might mean.

The Warm Springs pool is fed by a subterranean spring which gives it a constant temperature of about 88 degrees; the water, full of mineral salts, is of exceptionally high specific gravity. Its peculiar property is that patients can stay in it for extended periods, up to two hours or even longer, without the enervation or fatigue that usually accompanies bathing in water at this temperature. Immersion in *any* water will help a paralytic to some extent because water removes the weight of gravity. If, in a polio patient, any musculature remains at all, or any vestige of the neuromuscular coordinating mechanism, *some* degree of rehabilitation is possible if the muscles are exercised in circumstances where the force of gravity does not operate. But the beneficent effects of the Warm Springs pool seemed to go far beyond this minimum.

Roosevelt stayed six weeks on his first visit, and made more progress than in the preceding three long years. "He felt life in his toes for the first time since August, 1921." Not only did he help himself; he helped other patients too, by working out a series of underwater exercises. A good deal of publicity, contrary to his wish, attended his first visit; when he returned the next spring a dozen crippled persons had arrived without warning or invitation and were waiting for him. This provoked something of a crisis in the affairs of the local hotel; the healthy visitors were afraid to mix with the invalids, for fear of "catching" polio. Roosevelt took this in hand, arranged for the paralysis sufferers (his "gang" as he expressed it) to eat at a separate table, and even saw to it that a new segregated pool was built. Promptly he became "Dr." Roosevelt and, in close cooperation with the local physician, took effective charge of the establishment. He has recorded his struggle teaching two very fat ladies to get their feet down to the bottom of the pool, for a special exercise he invented. "I would take one large knee of one of the ladies and I would force this large knee and leg down. . . . And then I would say, 'Have you got it?' and she would say, 'Yes,' and I would say, 'Hold it, hold it.' Then I would reach up and get hold of the other knee very quickly, and start to put it down and then No. 1 knee would pop up again. . . . But before I left . . . I could get both those knees down at the same time."

But Warm Springs was not the only therapy FDR tried. Only someone in the grip of an intolerable illness can know with what soaring hope, tempered with anguished skepticism, one clasps at every straw. In 1925 he heard of a neurologist named William MacDonald of Marion, Massachusetts, who had devised a "walking board" for polio patients; he spent two summers with Dr. MacDonald, trying to walk round and round on this apparatus. One incident of this period is described by Mrs. Charles H. Hamlin, a close family friend: "One night Franklin and Eleanor came to visit me in Mattapoisett. Two men carried him in to a seat at the dining room table. He told the men not to return until 9:30. When dinner was over, Franklin pushed back his chair and said, 'See me get into the next room.' He got down on the floor and went in on his hands and knees and got up into another chair himself." Dr. MacDonald had taught him how to perform this feat, so that he "would have a feeling of freedom to move, if necessary."

But Warm Springs remained his chief hope. Not only did he return again and again (usually his only companions were Missy LeHand and a valet); he rented a house there, and eventually built one; it is striking that he should have named it the "Little White House," though his mother testifies that this was not because of any future "aspirations." Warm Springs became, in fact, his winter home. More and more he came to love the bland, soothing Georgia sun and the gentle quality of the countryside. . . .

It is time now to estimate some of the results of this extraordinary experience to Roosevelt. First, in the realm of the purely physical. Nobody with legs can easily appreciate what it is like to be without them. I do not mean in such obvious realms as that FDR could never take a hike, kick a football, dance, climb a fence, skate, or play with his toes in the sand. So long as he lived, he was never able to climb a stair more than two or three inches high, lean deeply to kiss a child, crouch to catch an object, scuff with his feet, squat on the grass, tap a foot, do a deep bend, or kneel in prayer. Beyond this were countless other deprivations and discomforts. Consider the thousands of times a day a man with normal legs and feet uses them instinctively, without thought: to hold balance in a veering automobile, to give emphasis while speaking, to brace the body in all manner of reflexes. All this—and much else—Roosevelt lost.

I do not even mention such items as that his physical movements were of necessity severely circumscribed; that special ramps and the like had to be set up whenever he traveled; that, by and large, he could not speak in halls where the platform was not easily accessible from street level; that the simple business of getting in and out of an automobile was an almost intolerable strain; that he could not completely dress or undress himself; that he wore a cape instead of an overcoat, and a sweater instead of a bathrobe, because they were easier to get into; that he could never fulfill one tenth or one twentieth of all manner of ideas that came to him. It was a pleasant notion that, when President, he should call on Mr. Justice Holmes. But just how he could be lugged up the narrow stairs in the Holmes dwelling had to be carefully planned out. It was imperative at the Atlantic Charter conference that he should visit Mr. Churchill on the *Prince of Wales*. But *how* to get him up the side of that battleship!

Hundreds of thousands of people saw Roosevelt wave or heard him say a few words from the observation car of his campaign train. The torture caused by these appearances, particularly toward the end, is seldom realized. Before each stop Pa Watson or Sam Rosenman would come into his compartment and say something like, "Mr. President, we'll be in Springfield in about ten minutes." FDR would put down what work he was doing, call for his valet, and his trousers would be taken off (sometimes he did this himself); then the braces were put on, and he locked and tested them; then, this accomplished, he got into his trousers again. During all this he talked incessantly. He would walk to the end of the car when the train eased to a stop, squeezing sideways down the aisle on the arm of a companion; then hold himself erect on the platform, smile, and say his few words or perhaps make a speech of some length; then be slowly turned around by whoever was helping him and return to his compartment where the process was duplicated in reverse (if you were one of those holding him you had to learn to let him down in his seat very carefully); he would whip off his trousers and unlock the braces with the greatest delight; then dress again and go back to work until it was time for the next stop. . . .

If he were making a speech in a hall he had to brace himself accurately on the lectern. This was always tested beforehand, to see if it would bear his weight.

He slipped, almost fell, or fell not more than five or six times in more than twenty years, a remarkable record. Once, crawling in his houseboat off Miami, he tore several leg ligaments in a bad fall. During the first presidential campaign, while making a speech in Georgia, he toppled over when the table against which he was leaning slipped. Members of his entourage quickly helped him to his feet; he kept on with his speech at the exact point where it had been broken off, and made no reference to the mishap; the audience cheered wildly. In Philadelphia four years later, a bolt in one of the braces became unlocked just before he was to address the Democratic convention, and he lost balance. The pages of his speech splashed to the floor, but Gus Gennerich, his bodyguard, and Mike Reilly caught him before he actually fell. They reached down and relocked the brace while Jim Farley and his son James closed in around him to keep the mishap from the eyes of the crowd. . . .

But the worst agony lay in subtler fields. For instance the President could never, except when he slept, be left alone; once he told Ambassador Winant that his utter lack of privacy was the hardest single thing he had to bear. Occasionally, by error, he *was* left alone. Once Frances Perkins was with him in the Oval Room just before he was going to bed; he rang, but unaccountably no one answered; finally he turned to Miss Perkins and said, "Please find Prettyman [the valet]; I am helpless without him." Also it was difficult for him to dismiss a visitor who overstayed his time, since he could not employ such ordinary gestures as rising from the chair or leading the visitor to the door. Again his immobility made it tedious, even arduous, to do routine business in a conference—he could not rise suddenly, move from chair to chair, talk standing, or otherwise do what everybody else does all the time, to relax the mood of a gathering, stiffen an argument, or emphasize a point. Try sitting for four or five hours in serious conversation with an argumentative group without once moving from your chair.

Psychologically one can trace dozens of minor characteristics that developed as a result of the paralysis. He loved gossip so much because he himself could not get around; talk was an outlet for all his suppressed energy. He loved holding the tiller of a boat because this gave him a sense of controlling motion. He had the close consciousness of time, of the passage of time and the intervals in time, so characteristic of people who have had prolonged illnesses; for instance his meals had to be served on the split second. He had a very serious conception (no matter how much he dallied in conversation) of the difference between 7:29 and 7:30.

Another point is that—understandably—he was somewhat timid of minor illnesses; when he had a cold, he needed to be babied a good deal. He hated to be near sick people, except Howe and Hopkins.

Roosevelt's own attitude to his affliction, as this became cemented into his character during the years, was to disregard it completely so far as externals were concerned. He had the special type of courage of the cripple who will not admit that he is crippled; this was a kind of defense mechanism since, at all costs, he had to protect himself from the invasion of any doubt or underconfidence. Almost never did he refer to his disability; for instance his mother testifies that she never once heard him mention it, incredible as this may seem. The artist Walter Tittle quotes him with an offhand remark, "Oh, yes, I could walk with crutches then," but even such casual references were very rare. He never under any circumstances used the illness as a political weapon. One minor point is that, for years, he would not say the word "golf" aloud, and nobody who knew him well ever talked about golf; it wounded him too deeply to think that he could never play again. He never returned to Campobello, much as he loved it, until 1933, because its associations were too painful. He wanted to discard utterly from his mind anything that had to do with the illness. He tried to seize everything that was normal. Above all he wanted to live like a normal man.

Nor would he permit anybody else to be sorry for him or show pity; nothing irritated him so much as special solicitude from friends or visitors. "No sob stuff!" was his stern warning to reporters who saw him after the attack, and he once told a biographer, "It's ridiculous to tell me that a grown man cannot conquer a child's disease." Above all, he never traded on his affliction, no matter how it might, as Mr. Ickes once put it, be exhausting his emotional reserves. Even healthy presidents ask for sympathy on occasion; Roosevelt never did. His attitude was, "I'm on top, I need your help, let's work together."

FDR himself could ignore his illness; other people couldn't. Members of the family had little, if any, self-consciousness about his disability, if only because he had no self-consciousness himself. But outsiders seeing him and his methods of conveyance for the first time were almost always profoundly shocked; even hard-boiled newspapermen who knew that he could not walk as well as they knew their own names could never quite get over being startled when FDR was suddenly brought into a room. The shock was greater when he wheeled himself and, of course, was greatest of all when he was carried; he seemed, for one thing, very small. Beyond this it was impossible not to feel emotion at realizing tangibly that the President of the United States was powerless to move. Yet in a few seconds, so relaxed was Roosevelt himself, the feeling of disconcertment would pass away. One reason why many visitors were so dumfounded was the voluntary conspiracy of silence about his illness that the newspapers maintained for many years. Caricatures never stressed his lameness; photographs were usually taken from the waist up: news stories seldom, if ever, mentioned that he was a cripple; and the fact that he used a wheel chair was never printed at all until the very end. In fact many people never even knew that he was paralyzed. During the 1930's when I lived in Europe I repeatedly met men in important positions of state who had no idea that the President was disabled.

Nobody but the most crassly callow visitors to Roosevelt ever made reference to his handicap. Madame Chiang Kai-shek, however, once committed the *gaffe* of telling the President, when she was about to leave the room, not to bother to get up. He "thanked her for the compliment." . . .

Several consolations and compensations attended Roosevelt's affliction. For instance it is an extraordinary fact that, paradoxical as it may seem, the blight of illness made him robust.

FDR had always been somewhat given to illness and very thin; now all the energy of his body seemed to go into a prodigious development of the torso, neck and arms. His face had been sensitive and narrow, with some marks of weakness; now it broadened out. Almost overnight, the head became Herculean. A minor contrary point is that he lost two inches in height. Jack Dempsey once said that FDR had the most magnificent development of shoulder muscles he had ever seen; on one occasion—and with no power in his legs, remember— he landed a 237-pound shark after a two-hour fight. Ask any fisherman what that means.

There is a curious double paradox here. His illness made him robust, yes, and for many years he was one of the sturdiest and healthiest men alive. Yet something oddly perverse attends a man who, wonderfully healthy, cannot walk.

Other compensations were more orthodox. He always had a good excuse not to do things that might bore him. He dropped out of society altogether and had time to work things out and evaluate; he discovered that what he previously thought was "thinking" had been merely "looking out of the window." He didn't have to exhaust himself on games, celebrations, and interminable public functions and private gatherings. Once he said to an ambassador, "How do you stand all the dinner parties?—I'll bet my stomach is in better shape than yours!" Once he confided to his son James, "The reason I get so much done is that I don't have to waste time with my legs." He said to Bernard M. Baruch once, "I save a lot of energy. What does a fellow need legs for, if we have elevators?"

But the more important transformations occurred in the ripe realm of the spirit. Roosevelt learned what suffering was; he learned compassion. Just as the muscles of his chest acquired a superdevelopment, so did he grow colossally in such attributes as serenity and will. He could not balance on his legs; he did learn to balance with his mind. Maybe he couldn't walk; but his feet were certainly on the ground. He learned the need for courage, and hence could transmit courage to the nation. In some respects it might almost be said that polio was God's greatest gift to him. Through the fires of this ordeal he established a power over his own mind that he had never had before, and this gave him power over the minds of others. The supreme experience of his life was to beat Death off, and then conquer indomitably the wounding traces that Death left.

Before the illness, all his charm and accomplishment notwithstanding, Roosevelt had something of the lightweight in him; even friends like Henry Stimson called him "an untried rather flippant young man." (Of course, later, he was to have another teacher almost as Draconian as illness—the Presidency.) But many people will testify to the fact that until the middle 20's, they liked FDR very much but thought that he was nothing more than an attractive, somewhat spurious, and highly amiable young man—almost a glad-hander, a playboy. He had promise, yes, but no great stature. He had brilliance, yes, but it was superficial. They were stunned, two or three years later, to discover that the ribs underneath this affable exterior had become steel; that the tremendous struggle he survived had etched ineradicable lines of power in every aspect of his character.

One interesting result of all this was superconfidence. Because he had beaten his illness, Roosevelt thought that he could beat anything. "The guy," Harry Hopkins once told Raymond Swing, "*never* knows when he is licked," and Hopkins thought that this was his chief defect.

Finally, one should reject the notion that it was primarily illness that made Franklin Roosevelt President. Obviously he must have had a good deal of character in the first place, not only to reach the stations in life that he did reach before illness struck him, but to have been able to get through the shattering ordeal of the attack itself. There are, after all, plenty of victims of infantile paralysis who never become great men. Once a friend asked Mrs. Roosevelt if she thought he would have been President if he had not been ill. Her answer was, "He would certainly have been President, but a president of a different kind."

Roosevelt in Retrospect, by John Gunther

ADMIRAL RICHARD E. BYRD

"No night had ever seemed so dark."

Exploration is a lonely business—and explorers belong to a dedicated race. And the loneliest kind of exploration is the kind that takes men to the poles—to the icy wastes of cold and freezing snow —and the unbelievable horrors of the arctic storm. Admiral Byrd spent much of his life at the poles—he made his first flight over the North Pole in 1925—and when he died in 1957 he had just returned from his third expedition to Little America—a region he had been the first to explore.

In a world like ours, surrounded as we are on all sides by the safeguards of civilization, it is difficult to encompass the concept of the explorer's life. He is faced unceasingly with a threatening unknown—he can never let up his guard lest he be overpowered by a danger he had no way of foreseeing. Nobody has ever written more truly or more vividly of exploration and of the life of the explorer than Admiral Byrd. Here is a selection from his finest work, "Alone," in which he describes one night on the Ross Ice Barrier at the southern tip of the world.

MAY WAS a round boulder sinking before a tide. Time sloughed off the last implication of urgency, and the days moved imperceptibly one into the other. . . . On getting up in the morning, it was enough for me to say to myself: Today is the day to change the barograph sheet, or, Today is the day to fill the stove tank. The night was settling down in earnest. By May 17th, one month after the sun had sunk below the horizon, the noon twilight was dwindling to a mere chink in the darkness, lit by a cold reddish glow. Days when the wind brooded in the north or east, the Barrier became a vast stagnant shadow surmounted by swollen masses of clouds, one layer of darkness piled on top of the other. This was the polar night, the morbid countenance of the Ice Age. Nothing moved; nothing was visible. This was the soul of inertness. One could almost hear a distant creaking as if a great weight were settling.

Out of the deepening darkness came the cold. On May 19th, when

I took the usual walk, the temperature was 65° below zero. For the first time the canvas boots failed to protect my feet. One heel was nipped, and I was forced to return to the hut and change to reindeer mukluks. That day I felt miserable; my body was racked by shooting pains—exactly as if I had been gassed. Very likely I was; in inspecting the ventilator pipes next morning I discovered that the intake pipe was completely clogged with rime and that the outlet pipe was two-thirds full. Next day—Sunday the 20th—was the coldest yet. The minimum thermometer dropped to 72° below zero; the inside thermograph, which always read a bit lower than the instruments in the shelter, stood at —74°; and the thermograph in the shelter was stopped dead—the ink, though well laced with glycerine, and the lubricant were both frozen. . . . The frost in the iron cleats went through the fur soles of the mukluks, and froze the balls of my feet. My breath made little explosive sounds on the wind; my lungs, already sore, seemed to shrivel when I breathed.

Seldom had the aurora flamed more brilliantly. For hours the night danced to its frenetic excitement. And at times the sound of Barrier quakes was like that of heavy guns. My tongue was swollen and sore from drinking scalding hot tea, and the tip of my nose ached from frostbite. A big wind, I guessed, would come out of this still cold; it behooved me to look to my roof. I carried gallons of water topside, and poured it around the edges of the shack. It froze almost as it hit. The ice was an armor plating over the packed drift.

At midnight, when I clambered topside for an auroral "ob," a wild sense of suffocation came over me the instant I pushed my shoulders through the trapdoor. My lungs gasped, but no air reached them. Bewildered and perhaps a little frightened, I slid down the ladder and lunged into the shack. In the warm air the feeling passed as quickly as it had come. Curious but cautious, I again made my way up the ladder. And again the same thing happened; I lost my breath, but I perceived why. A light air was moving down from eastward; and its bitter touch, when I faced into it, was constricting the breathing passages. So I turned my face away from it, breathing into my glove; and in that attitude finished the "ob." Before going below, I made an interesting experiment. I put a thermometer on the snow, let it lie there awhile, and discovered that the temperature at the surface was actually 5° colder than at the level of the instrument shelter, four feet higher. Reading in the sleeping bag afterwards, I froze one finger, although I shifted the book steadily from one hand to the other, slipping the unoccupied hand into the warmth of the bag.

Out of the cold and out of the east came the wind. It came on gradually, as if the sheer weight of the cold were almost too much to be moved. On the night of the 21st the barometer started down. The night was black as a thunderhead when I made my first trip topside; and a tension in the wind, a bulking of shadows in the night indicated that a new storm center was forming. Next morning, glad of an excuse to stay underground, I worked a long time on the Escape Tunnel by the light of a red candle standing in a snow recess. That day I pushed the emergency exit to a distance of twenty-two feet, the farthest it was ever to go. My stint done, I sat down on a box, thinking how beautiful was the red of the candle, how white the rough-hewn snow. Soon I became aware of an increasing clatter of the anemometer cups. Realizing that the wind was picking up, I went topside to make sure that everything was secured. It is a queer experience to watch a blizzard rise. First there is the wind, rising out of nowhere. Then the Barrier unwrenches itself from quietude; and the surface, which just before had seemed as hard and polished as metal, begins to run like a making sea. Sometimes, if the wind strikes hard, the drift comes across the Barrier like a hurrying white cloud, tossed hundreds of feet in the air. Other times the growth is gradual. You become conscious of a general slithering movement on all sides. The air fills with tiny scraping and sliding and rustling sounds as the first loose crystals stir. In a little while they are moving as solidly as an incoming tide, which creams over the ankles, then surges to the waist, and finally is at the throat. I have walked in drift so thick as not to be able to see a foot ahead of me; yet, when I glanced up, I could see the stars shining through the thin layer just overhead.

Smoking tendrils were creeping up the anemometer pole when I finished my inspection. I hurriedly made the trapdoor fast, as a sailor might batten down a hatch; and knowing that my ship was well secured, I retired to the cabin to ride out the storm. It could not reach me, hidden deep in the Barrier crust; nevertheless the sounds came down. The gale sobbed in the ventilators, shook the stovepipe until I thought it would be jerked out by the roots, pounded the roof with sledge-hammer blows. I could actually feel the suction effect through the pervious snow. A breeze flickered in the room and the tunnels. The candles wavered and went out. My only light was the feeble storm lantern.

Even so, I didn't have any idea how really bad it was until I went aloft for an observation. As I pushed back the trapdoor, the drift met me like a moving wall. It was only a few steps from the ladder to the instrument shelter, but it seemed more like a mile. The air came at me in snowy rushes; I breasted it as I might a heavy surf. No night had ever seemed so dark. The beam from the flashlight was choked in its throat; I could not see my hand before my face.

My windproofs were caked with drift by the time I got below. I had a vague feeling that something had changed while I was gone, but what, I couldn't tell. Presently I noticed that the shack was appreciably colder. Raising the stove lid, I was surprised to find that the fire was out, though the tank was half full. I decided that I must have turned off the valve unconsciously before going aloft; but, when I put a match to the burner, the draught down the pipe blew out the flame. The wind, then, must have killed the fire. I got it going again, and watched it carefully.

The blizzard vaulted to gale force. Above the roar the deep, taut, thrumming note of the radio antenna and the anemometer guy wires reminded me of wind in a ship's rigging. The wind direction trace turned scratchy on the sheet; no doubt drift had short-circuited the electric contacts, I decided. Realizing that it was hopeless to attempt to try to keep them clear, I let the instrument be. There were other ways of getting the wind direction. I tied a handkerchief to a bamboo pole and ran it through the outlet ventilator; with a flashlight I could tell which way the cloth was whipped. I did this at hourly intervals, noting any change of direction on the sheet. But by 2 o'clock in the morning I had had enough of this periscope sighting. If I expected to sleep and at the same time maintain the continuity of the records, I had no choice but to clean the contact points.

The Barrier shook from the concussions overhead; and the noise was as if the entire physical world were tearing itself to pieces. I could scarcely heave the trapdoor open. The instant it came clear I was plunged into a blinding smother. I came out crawling, clinging to the handle of the door until I made sure of my bearings. Then I let the door fall shut, not wanting the tunnel filled with drift. To see was impossible. Millions of tiny pellets exploded in my eyes, stinging like BB shot. It was even hard to breathe, because snow instantly clogged the mouth and nostrils. I made my way toward the anemometer pole on hands and knees, scared that I might be bowled off my feet if I stood erect; one false step and I should be lost forever.

I found the pole all right; but not until my head collided with a cleat. I managed to climb it, too, though ten million ghosts were tearing at me, ramming their thumbs into my eyes. But the errand was useless. Drift as thick as this would mess up the contact points as quickly as they were cleared; besides, the wind cups were spinning so fast that I stood a good chance of losing a couple of fingers in the process. Coming down the pole, I had a sense of being whirled violently through the air, with no control over my movements. The trapdoor was completely buried when I found it again, after scraping around for some time with my mittens. I pulled at the handle, first with one hand, then with both. It did not give. It's a tight fit, anyway, I mumbled to myself. The drift has probably wedged the corners. Standing astride the hatch, I braced myself and heaved with all my strength. I might just as well have tried hoisting the Barrier.

Panic took me then, I must confess. Reason fled. I clawed at the three-foot square of timber like a madman. I beat on it with my fists, trying to shake the snow loose; and, when that did no good, I lay flat on my belly and pulled until my hands went weak from cold and weariness. Then I crooked my elbow, put my face down, and said over and over again, You damn fool, you damn fool. Here for weeks I had been defending myself against the danger of being penned inside the shack; instead, I was now locked out; and nothing could be worse, especially since I had only a wool parka and pants under my windproofs. Just two feet below was sanctuary—warmth, food, tools, all the means of survival. All these things were an arm's length away, but I was powerless to reach them.

There is something extravagantly insensate about an Antarctic blizzard at night. Its vindictiveness cannot be measured on an anemometer sheet. It is more than just wind: it is a solid wall of snow at gale force pounding like surf. The whole malevolent rush is concentrated upon you as upon a personal enemy. In the senseless explosion of sound you are reduced to a crawling thing on the margin of a disintegrating world; you can't see, you can't hear, you can hardly move. The lungs gasp after the air sucked out of them, and the brain is shaken. Nothing in the world will so quickly isolate a man.

Half-frozen, I stabbed toward one of the ventilators, a few feet away. My mittens touched something round and cold. Cupping it in my hands, I pulled myself up. This was the outlet ventilator. Just why, I don't know—but instinct made me kneel and press my face against the opening. Nothing in the room was visible, but a dim patch of light illuminated the floor, and warmth rose up to my face. That steadied me.

Still kneeling, I turned my back to the blizzard and considered what might be done. I thought of breaking in the windows in the roof, but they lay two feet down in hard crust, and were reinforced with wire besides. If I only had something to dig with, I could break the crust and stamp the windows in with my feet. The pipe cupped between my hands supplied the first inspiration; maybe I could use that to dig with. It, too, was wedged tight; I pulled until my arms ached, without budging it; I had lost all track of time, and the despairing thought came to me that I was lost in a task without end. Then I remembered the shovel. A week before, after leveling drift from the last light blow, I had stabbed a shovel handle up in the crust somewhere to leeward. That shovel would save me. But how to find it in the avalanche of the blizzard?

I lay down and stretched out full length. Still holding the pipe, I thrashed around with my feet, but pummeled only empty air. Then I worked back to the hatch. The hard edges at the opening provided another grip, and again I stretched out and kicked. Again no luck. I dared not let go until I had something else familiar to cling to. My foot came up against the other ventilator pipe. I edged back to that, and from the new anchorage repeated the maneuver. This time my ankle struck something hard. When I felt it and recognized the handle, I wanted to caress it.

Embracing this thrice-blessed tool, I inched back to the trapdoor. The handle of the shovel was just small enough to pass under the little wooden bridge which served as a grip. I got both hands on the shovel and tried to wrench the door up; my strength was not enough, however. So I lay down flat on my belly and worked my shoulders under the shovel. Then I heaved, the door sprang open, and I rolled down the shaft. When I tumbled into the light and warmth of the room, I kept thinking, How wonderful, how perfectly wonderful.

Alone, by Richard E. Byrd

ANDREW JACKSON

"Nobody ever laughed at Andrew Jackson in a fury..."

When Andrew Jackson took office as the seventh President of
the United States in March of 1829, the country's conservative fac-
tions feared for the safety of the nation. Unlike his predecessors,
Jackson had not been born among the landed gentry or the intellectual aristocracy. His early life as the youngest son of a widowed
mother was almost unbelievably hard. He got nothing without fighting for it. And he learned to fight hard. He was one of those who
thrive on adversity and who grow strong on hardship. Crude, with
immovable convictions, yet sensitive to the wants and needs of the
people, he gave the young country a new kind of leadership.

Gerald Johnson shows Jackson here as a boy—in the circumstances
that made him a man.

THE TIME was March, 1767. The woman in the case was the Widow
Jackson, relict of the late Andrew Jackson, pioneer farmer. But the
place has been for generations, and still is, the subject of endless and
acrimonious dispute between two sovereign commonwealths.

Within a few hundred yards to the farmhouse where George
McKemey lived ran the boundary line between His Majesty's Prov-
inces of North and South Carolina. On March 15, 1767, Mrs. Jackson,
widowed a few weeks earlier, bore a son in George McKemey's house.
But was the boundary line, less than a quarter of a mile away, to the
east of that house, or west of it? . . .

The point at the time seemed as insignificant as anything well could
be, seeing who were the actors in this backwoods drama. For the Jack-
sons were worse than poor. They were luckless. Not much is known
of their life in Carrickfergus, Ireland, where Andrew Jackson and
Elizabeth Hutchinson, his wife, carried on the business of linen
drapers; but obviously fortune never smiled upon them conspicuously,
for in 1765 they joined the flood of immigrants to America, a step
then as now rarely taken by anyone in good circumstances.

And they found no magic in the New World. Jackson obtained possession of certain lands, uncleared, on Twelve Mile Creek, in North Carolina. . . . It is a frightful task to clear for cultivation land covered with virgin forest. It is a task fit to appall a seasoned woodsman accustomed to the use of ax and maul, toughened to long and arduous labor out of doors. What it must have been to the linen draper from Carrickfergus is beyond imagination. But he attacked the forest resolutely and not without success, for the record testifies that he cleared his land, raised at least one crop and built his log house by the beginning of the year 1767.

History is full of the battles of the Scotch-Irish, and they are usually well fought. The struggle of the immigrant Jackson against the harsh New World is not in the list, yet there is no reason to doubt that it was as gallant as any of them. But in the end it was a lost battle, for early in 1767, with his two sons still small and a third expected soon, he lay down and died.

The forest had conquered. In a rude farm-wagon they brought his body down to old Waxhaw churchyard and buried it there without a stone to mark the place. The family came down at the same time, and never saw their hard-won home on Twelve Mile Creek again. Mrs. Jackson had relatives in South Carolina to whom she turned. A brother-in-law, who lived close to the church, realizing that she was in no fit condition for the ordeal of travel over the roads that then existed, all unwittingly saved his own name from oblivion by offering her shelter. For he was George McKemey, and in his house a few nights later was born the boy who was named Andrew, after the dead linen draper.

So there was another Andrew Jackson to carry on the fight of the Scotch-Irish against the wilderness, and this one did not die when his work was but well begun. On the contrary, he broke the forces of the wilderness. He swept clear a broad path for settlers from the Tennessee to the Gulf of Mexico. He swept Florida. He burst the last barrier that threatened to bar the way of all Mississippi Valley folk to the highway of the sea. He became the scourge of the children of the wilderness, and the warden of white civilization in a territory immensely greater than all Ireland.

The linen draper was avenged. . . .

This was the origin of Andrew Jackson: troubled, dark, difficult to determine exactly. It was the hard beginning of a hard career. The man rarely knew ease of body or of soul. In his mother's womb he seemed to be foreordained to travel a stony road, to cut his way through wildernesses, to contend against darkness, to fight often alone and always against great odds. . . .

It is always a bitter world to the boy who enters it without family, or influential friends, or money; and this boy had the additional ill luck to enter it at a moment when it was growing bitter to the great, not to mention the penniless son of an immigrant. In 1767 war clouds were already high and in the Carolinas, as in the other colonies, thoughtful men were already regarding the future with foreboding. Already, too, the inevitable first symptom of war fever was revealing itself in party division between neighbors and quondam friends—a division that was to deepen and widen until after ten years' festering it was to break out in murder, rapine, pillaging, burning and all the other horrors of civil war.

It was in this atmosphere of increasing tension that little Andrew spent his childhood. Three weeks after his birth, his mother resumed her interrupted journey into South Carolina and was received into the house of another brother-in-law, Crawford by name, whose wife was an invalid. . . . She made shift somehow to put her sons in the best schools available, and it appears that for Andrew, in particular, her aspirations were practically limitless. She hoped to make him a Presbyterian minister! . . .

There is something ludicrous in thinking of Andrew Jackson as a theologian, but to all the other functions of the ministry of that time he was temperamentally well adapted. . . .

Yet the meagre evidence that is available all indicates that even in his childhood Andrew Jackson was plainly no candidate for holy orders. In 1859 Parton found the countryside still full of tales of a schoolboy who was a terror by reason of a tremendous fund of energy coupled with an equally tremendous temper. These tales refer somewhat vaguely to all sorts of devilment into which Andy led his companions, but they are clearest on the point of the fury with which the lad turned upon any incautious practical joker who undertook to render him ridiculous. There is, for example, the story of the group of boys who loaded a gun with an excessive charge and then handed it to Andy to fire, expecting to enjoy seeing him knocked flat. They saw him knocked flat, but the enjoyment was cut short when he leaped to his feet, his eyes blazing, and ripped out:

"By God, if one of you laughs, I'll kill him!"

Nobody laughed. Nobody ever laughed at Andrew Jackson in a fury. . . .

War burst upon the country when he was nine years old, and in the Carolinas it was a war of such ferocity as is unparalleled in American history, except, perhaps, in some Indian campaigns. For the first four years the fighting was more or less regularized, although passions ran higher and higher. The Highland Scotch in large numbers fought for the King, and Tories were everywhere. Then in 1780 Lincoln was caught in Charleston, and all the regulars, the Continentals, of the two Carolinas were lost with him. Cornwallis swept northward and the Tories rose behind him. At Camden, Gates was smitten such a blow that the American army of the South virtually ceased to exist. Then Greene came down to take command and rounding up every available man of military age fell slowly back before Cornwallis, consolidating his forces as he went. Cornwallis, concentrating his columns and leaving Lord Rawdon with a small command in Camden, moved after Greene. Thus the country around the Waxhaws was swept bare of regular troops of both armies, whereupon bands of bushwhackers, Whig and Tory, began to harry the region, and the war degenerated into a hideous orgy of murder, arson and pillage, characterized by countless treasons and innumerable atrocities.

Andrew's elder brother, Hugh, had joined the command of Colonel Davie, had fought at the battle of Stono, and had died of fatigue and exposure. Then the dreaded Tarleton burst upon the Waxhaws and Andrew Jackson got his first close view of war when he went with his mother to the church to attend the wounded gathered there.

What would a pugnacious, red-headed boy do in such circumstances? At fourteen Andrew was already tall, although extremely thin and gangling. But the bushwhackers were not scrupulous about age-limits. A rifle was a rifle, and a British soldier or, better, a Tory, shot by a fourteen-year-old boy was as dead as any other corpse. So it was inevitable that Andrew and his remaining brother, Robert, should presently find themselves in a Whig band.

But the Waxhaw Whigs had grown so active that Rawdon sent from Camden a patrol of dragoons to suppress them. The patrol surprised the Jackson brothers' band and scattered it, the boys saving themselves by breakneck flight through the woods. Late at night they crept back to a kinsman's house, where they were promptly betrayed by a Tory neighbor. The house was quietly surrounded by dragoons, the doors secured, and the boys captured.

The subaltern in command presumably was none too well pleased when he entered the house and found that his haul consisted of a couple of children. At any rate, he was in no pleasant temper when the prisoners were brought before him, and Andrew Jackson found himself for the first time facing a representative of the King's Majesty. Chagrined, enraged, frightened, but still defiant, the two youngsters waited to hear their doom. It was more terrible, when it came, than the worst they had feared. They were not to be given the death of a soldier by shooting. They were not even to have the poor dignity of death on the gallows as spies. The order was nothing so glorious, even if terrible. The order was simply to clean the officer's mud-spattered jack-boots.

The officer got precisely what was given the boys who had overloaded the gun—an explosion of wrathful defiance. It was too much for his overstrained temper. His sabre flashed. Andrew's left hand flew up, and checked, but did not stop the blow. Blood gushed from gashes in hand and scalp, and from that day he carried a great scar across his head.

The infuriated Briton then turned upon Robert and struck him to the floor. He never entirely recovered from the wound.

Such was Andrew Jackson's first face-to-face encounter with the British. Aching, bleeding, half stunned, the boys were marched off, surrounded by dragoons, to the prison camp at Camden.

It was forty long miles to Camden town and when one travels with a gashed hand and a split scalp forty miles on horseback are a journey to be remembered. When, in addition, one is only fourteen years old, and has seen the promise of a glorious military career end in an order to clean jack-boots; when one has been captured without firing a shot, wounded without honor, fallen into the hands of a derisive and undamaged enemy, then a ride of forty miles without medical attention, without food, without water, is an ordeal fit to create in one's breast a raging hell able to sear one's mind for life.

This was the beginning of young Andrew Jackson's experience of the reality of war. But it was only the beginning. Arrived at Camden, the prisoners were thrown into a stockade around the jail, with two hundred and fifty other unfortunates.

The horrors of Libby and Elmira and the prison hulks of the Civil War are well remembered, but the most noisome of them was no worse than Camden during the British occupation. The blithe informality of the Revolution was well illustrated by the refusal of either side to take seriously its responsibility for prisoners. . . .

The prisoners had no beds or bedding. They had no medicines. Many of them were wounded, but they had no medical attention. Their only food was a little bad bread, although, to do Lord Rawdon justice, that apparently was due to the thieving of a rascally contractor, presumably an American. There is a story to the effect that young Jackson, having caught the attention of a British subaltern, explained the food situation and horrified the Briton, who instituted an investigation that partially corrected it. Possibly Jackson's distaste for army contractors had its inception there. At any rate when he laid hands on half a dozen men of that trade at New Orleans forty years later, it was with the greatest difficulty that he was dissuaded from hanging them without much inquiry as to their guilt or innocence of the charges on which they had been taken. Such gusto in prosecution argues a long-standing, ingrained dislike, although it must be admitted that it seems to be the soldier's customary attitude toward men who provision the army.

The prisoners were in many instances improperly clothed, and it is said that such clothing as they had was sometimes stolen from them. Fortunately, spring comes early in South Carolina, or probably none would have survived; but, at that, suffering from cold was added to suffering from hunger, from festering, unattended wounds, and from filth, in that pestilential hole. Ere long a worse thing happened. Small-pox broke out.

Robert Jackson had never fully recovered from the sabre-cut he received on the night of his capture, and he was now down with small-pox. A few days after the fight on Hobkirk's Hill Andrew sickened also. The annals of the house of Jackson seemed about to be closed.

But Elizabeth, the indomitable, was still alive and vigorously at work. From a Whig bushwhacker she secured the promise of thirteen British soldiers for exchange, and with them she purchased the liberty of her sons and five other Americans. But she came almost too late. Robert was more dead than alive. He could not stand, or even sit on horseback without being held, while Andrew was burning with fever. Nevertheless, the start was made toward home. Two horses were secured, and on one of them Robert was held, while the mother rode the other. Andrew dragged along on foot with the other freed men.

They had almost traversed the endless forty miles when a terrific rainstorm overtook them and the sick boys were drenched with cold water. The smallpox, in the vernacular of the time, "struck in." Within forty-eight hours Robert was dead and Andrew was raving in delirium. But Elizabeth Jackson was not yet beaten. What a battle she fought for the life of her sole remaining child can never be known, but she pulled him through. For months he was a wreck, but within a few weeks he was clearly out of danger.

The war, however, was not through with Andrew Jackson yet. At Camden his mother had seen what a prison camp might be, and it was now with a new understanding that she heard the terrible wail that came up from the prison ships at Charleston, where many of the men of the Waxhaws, her friends and neighbors, were confined. Having obeyed the Scriptural injunction to care first for them of her own house, she turned now toward others. This new country had exacted a frightful toll from her. She had given it her husband. She had given it her first-born, Hugh. She had given it Robert. Only grudgingly had it left to her Andrew, her baby, and it had left him spent and broken.

But patriotism thrives on sacrifice. None know so well how to love a country as those whose hearts it has broken. None are so ready to respond to its call as those who have already given it tribute of blood and tears without stint. Elizabeth Jackson, who had already, God knows, done her part, could not rest idly while there remained anything she could do. Therefore, having seen Andy out of the shadow of death, in the summer of 1781 she set out for Charleston to help relieve the sufferings of his comrades-in-arms.

The good that women do does not always live after them. The record of that journey is simply non-existent. Tradition has it that Elizabeth Jackson trudged the hundred and sixty miles on foot; but it is more probable—and her son so believed—that she made the trip on horseback, leading a pack-animal loaded with medicines and small comforts for the imprisoned men.

But the tale of her ministrations is lost altogether. All we know is that she arrived at her destination, and there is tragic evidence that she worked with the prisoners, for presently she contracted ship-fever and at the house of one William Barton, two and a half miles from Charleston, she died and was buried on the open plain.

So passed the last of the family of Andrew Jackson, none killed by an enemy bullet, but all victims of the war. Patriots all, all dead on the field of honor, yet they gained no glory and no renown. To this day they lie in unmarked graves, and except for the fortuitous circumstance that the sole survivor of the family later gained distinction, the story of their struggles, of their anguish and their sorrow would have been utterly lost as the stories of millions of other sufferers in that and other wars have been lost.

And so, ere he had passed his fifteenth birthday, Andrew Jackson knew about war. Some maker of epigrams has said that no man is really educated until he knows the three great verities of life, poverty, and love, and war. In two of these the child was already so well instructed that the lessons could never be forgotten. Poverty had been his familiar since his birth; now war also was known to him.

The feeble, disease-racked body crawled slowly back to health, although a lingering, intermittent fever clutched him long after the smallpox had disappeared. But the numbed soul was past recovery. Andrew Jackson, a romanticist in so many ways, was the sharpest of realists in all matters touching war. . . . His idea of war was gained from intimate contact with the grim reality, in the hellish campaign of the Carolinas. It began with close-range observation of the harvest of a battlefield gathered in old Waxhaw church. "The men were dreadfully mangled," says one account. "Some had as many as thirteen wounds and none had less than three." It included observation of

Sumter's fight at Hanging Rock, which was lost through poor discipline, and Andrew did not forget the lesson. It proceeded with days and nights of terror when Tory bands ranged through the country, massacring, burning and pillaging. It comprised two experiences of that most miserable of all war's calamities, the flight of refugees. It involved the brutality of the British officer with the sabre, and the experience of being a wounded prisoner in a pestilence-ridden camp. Above all, with Hugh and Robert dead of exposure and disease and Elizabeth dead through her ministrations to prisoners, it steeled him to contemplate without revulsion what war brings to non-combatants. At fifteen he did not know soldiering, but he knew war. As a child it was already burnt into him that regardless of the panoply and all the brave array, the banners, the music, the parades and pageants, the end and aim of the whole business is death.

At fifteen the harrows of hell had passed over him, and forever after in the war he was a grim realist. Inveterate romanticist as he was, in this particular romance had been cauterized. It was thenceforth impossible for him to become a bandbox soldier. He might, indeed, strut in gaudy uniforms and receive gracefully the plaudits of the ladies while in garrison, but in the field he stripped off the frippery and became a hard and dangerous man, a killer, pure and simple.

Incidentally, he became a winner.

Andrew Jackson, by Gerald W. Johnson

*"The Justice went to the root of the matter at once.
'Why do you hurt these children?'"*

The selection that follows might properly be thought not to belong in a book dealing with the turning points in the lives of individual men and women, for it is the story of a town. It does have a
place, though, as a human document, for the people of Salem are
a symbol of man's reactions to circumstances that overpower and
frighten him—that deafen him to the voices of reason.

Here is a retelling of the fantastic story of the witch trials of
Salem in which in one year twenty people were executed by Fear
in the name of Justice.

. . . SALEM VILLAGE had got a new minister—the Reverend Samuel
Parris, ex-merchant in the West Indies. The most important thing
about Samuel Parris was the fact that he brought with him to Salem
Village two West Indian servants—a man known as John Indian and
a woman named Tituba. And when he bought those two or their
services in the West Indies, he was buying a rope that was to hang
nineteen men and women of New England—so odd are the links in
the circumstantial chain.

Perhaps the nine-year-old Elizabeth Parris, the daughter of the parsonage, boasted to her new friends of the odd stories Tituba told and
the queer things she could do. Perhaps Tituba herself let the report
of her magic powers be spread about the village. She must have been
as odd and imagination-stirring a figure as a parrot or a tame monkey
in the small New England town. And the winters were long and white
—and any diversion a godsend.

In any case, during the winter of 1691–92 a group of girls and
women began to meet nightly at the parsonage, with Tituba and her
fortunetelling as the chief attraction. Elizabeth Parris, at nine, was the
youngest; then came Abigail Williams, eleven, and Ann Putnam,
twelve. The rest were older—Mercy Lewis, Mary Wolcott, and Elizabeth Hubbard were seventeen; Elizabeth Booth and Susan Sheldon,

eighteen; and Mary Warren and Sarah Churchill, twenty. Three were servants—Mercy Lewis had been employed by the Reverend George Burroughs, a previous minister of Salem Village, and now worked for the Putnams; Mary Warren was a maid at the John Procters'; Sarah Churchill, at the George Jacobs'. All, except for Elizabeth Parris, were adolescent or just leaving adolescence.

The elder women included a pair of gossipy, superstitious busy-bodies—Mrs. Pope and Mrs. Bibber; and young Ann Putnam's mother, Ann Putnam, Sr., who deserves a sentence to herself.

For the Putnams were a powerful family in the neighborhood and Ann Putnam, married at seventeen and now only thirty, is described as handsome, arrogant, temperamental, and high-strung. She was also one of those people who can cherish a grudge and revenge it.

The circle met—the circle continued to meet—no doubt with the usual giggling, whispering, and gossip. From mere fortunetelling it proceeded to other and more serious matters—table rapping, perhaps, and a little West Indian voodoo—weird stories told by Tituba and weird things shown, while the wind blew outside and the big shadows flickered on the wall. Adolescent girls, credulous servants, superstitious old women—and the two enigmatic figures of Tituba, the West Indian, and Ann Putnam, Sr.

But soon the members of the circle began to show hysterical symptoms. They crawled under tables and chairs; they made strange sounds; they shook and trembled with nightmare fears. The thing became a village celebrity—and more. Something strange and out of nature was happening—who had ever seen normal young girls behave like these young girls? And no one—certainly not the Reverend Samuel Parris —even suggested that a mixed diet of fortunetelling, ghost stories, and voodoo is hardly the thing for impressionable minds during a long New England winter. Hysteria was possession by an evil spirit; patho-logical lying, the devil putting words into one's mouth. The Reverend Samuel became very busy. Grave ministers were called in to look at the afflicted children. A Dr. Gregg gave his opinion. It was almost too terrible to believe, and yet what else could be believed? Witchcraft!

Meanwhile, one may suppose, the "afflicted children," like most hysterical subjects, enjoyed the awed stares, the horrified looks, the respectful questions that greeted them, with girlish zest. They had been unimportant girls of a little hamlet; now they were, in every sense of the word, spot news. And any reporter knows what that does to certain kinds of people. They continued to writhe and demonstrate— and be the center of attention. There was only one catch about it. If they were really bewitched, somebody must be doing the bewitching.

On the twenty-ninth of February, 1692, in the midst of an appropriate storm of thunder and lightning, three women—Sarah Good, Sarah Osburn, and Tituba—were arrested on the deadly charge of bewitching the children.

The next day, March 1, two magistrates, Justice Hawthorne and Justice Corwin, arrived with appropriate pomp and ceremony. The first hearing was held in the crowded meetinghouse of the village; and all Salem swarmed to it, as crowds in our time have swarmed to other sleepy little villages suddenly notorious.

The children—or the children and Tituba—had picked their first victims well. Sarah Good and Sarah Osburn were old women of no particular standing in the community.

We can imagine that meetinghouse—and the country crowd within it—on that chill March day. At one end was the majesty of the law—and the "afflicted children," where all might see them and observe. Dressed in their best, very likely, and with solicitous relatives near at hand. Do you see Mercy Lewis? Do you see Ann Putnam? And then the whole crowd turned to one vast, horrified eye. For there was the accused—the old woman—the witch!

The justices—grim Justice Hawthorne in particular—had, evidently, arrived with their minds made up. For the first question addressed to Sarah Good was, bluntly:

"What evil spirit have you familiarity with?"

"None," said the piping old voice. But everybody in the village knew worthless Sarah Good. And the eye of the audience went from her to the deadly row of "afflicted children" and back again.

"Have you made no contracts with the devil?" proceeded the Justice.

"No."

The Justice went to the root of the matter at once.

"Why do you hurt these children?"

A rustle must have gone through the meetinghouse at that. Aye, that's it; the Justice speaks shrewdly; hark to the Justice! Aye, but look, too! Look at the children! Poor things, poor things!

"I do not hurt them. I scorn it," said Sarah Good defiantly. But the Justice had her now; he was not to be brushed aside.

"Who, then, do you employ to do it?"

"I employ nobody."

"What creature do you employ then?" For all witches had familiars.

"No creature, but I am falsely accused." But the sweat must have been on the old woman's palms by now.

The Justice considered. There was another point, minor but illuminating.

"Why did you go away muttering from Mr. Parris, his house?"

"I did not mutter, but I thanked him for what he gave my child."

The Justice returned to the main charge, like any prosecuting attorney.

"Have you made no contract with the devil?"

"No."

It was time for Exhibit A. The Justice turned to the children. Was Sarah Good one of the persons who tormented them? Yes, yes!—and a horrified murmur running through the crowd. And then, before the awe-stricken eyes of all, they began to be tormented. They writhed; they grew stiff; they contorted; they were stricken moaning or speechless. Yet, when they were brought to Sarah Good and allowed to touch her, they grew quite quiet and calm. For, as everyone knew, a witch's physical body was like an electric conductor—it reabsorbed, on touch, the malefic force discharged by witchcraft into the bodies of the tormented. Everybody could see what happened—and everybody saw. When the meetinghouse was quiet, the Justice spoke again.

"Sarah Good, do you not see now what you have done? Why do you not tell us the truth? Why do you torment these poor children?"

And with these words Sarah Good was already hanged. For all that she could say was, "I do not torment them." And yet everyone had seen her, with their own eyes.

Sarah Osburn's examination followed the same course, the same prosecutor's first question, the same useless denial, the same epileptic feats of the "afflicted children," the same end.

Then Tituba was examined and gave them their fill of marvels, prodigies, and horrors.

The West Indian woman, a slave in a strange land, was fighting for her life, and she did it shrewdly and desperately. She admitted, repentantly, that she had tormented the children. But she had been forced to do so. By whom? By Goody Good and Goody Osburn and two other witches whom she hadn't yet been able to recognize. Her voodoo knowledge aided her—she filled the open ears of Justices and crowd with tales of hairy familiars and black dogs, red cats and black cats and yellow birds, the phantasm of a woman with legs and wings. And everybody could see that she spoke the truth. For, when she was first brought in, the children were tormented at her presence; but as soon as she had confessed and turned King's evidence, she was tormented herself, and fearfully. To Boston Jail with her—but she had saved her neck.

The hearing was over; the men and women of Salem and its outlying farms went broodingly or excitedly back to their homes to discuss the fearful workings of God's providence. Here and there a common-

sense voice murmured a doubt or two—Sarah Good and Sarah Osburn were no great losses to the community; but still, to convict two
old women of heinous crime on the testimony of greensick girls and a
West Indian slave! But, on the whole, the villagers of Salem felt relieved. The cause of the plague had been found; it would be stamped
out and the afflicted children recover. The Justices, no doubt, con-
gratulated themselves on their prompt and intelligent action. The
"afflicted children" slept, after a tiring day—they were not quite so
used to such performances as they were to become.

As for the accused women, they went to Boston Jail—to be chained
there while waiting trial and gallows.

Meanwhile, on an outlying farm, Giles Corey, a turbulent, salty old
fellow of eighty-one, began to argue the case with his wife, Martha.
He believed, fanatically, in the "afflicted children." She did not, and
said so—even going so far as to say that the magistrates were blinded
and she could open their eyes. It was one of those marital disputes
that occur between strong-willed people. And it was to bring Martha
Corey to the gallows and Giles Corey to an even stranger doom.

Yet now there was a lull, through which people whispered.

As for what went on in the minds of the "afflicted children," during
that lull, we may not say. But this much is evident. They had seen
and felt their power. The hearing had been the greatest and most
exciting event of their narrow lives. And it was so easy to do; they
grew more and more ingenious with each rehearsal. You twisted
your body and groaned—and grown people were afraid.

Add to this the three girl-servants, with the usual servants' grudges
against present or former masters. Add to this that high-strung, domi-
nant woman Ann Putnam, Sr., who could hold a grudge and remember it. Such a grudge as there might be against the Towne sisters, for
instance—they were all married women of the highest standing, particularly Rebecca Nurse. So suppose—just suppose—that one of them
were found out to be a witch? And hadn't Tituba deposed that there
were other women, besides Good and Osburn, who made her torment
the children?

On March 19 Martha Corey and Rebecca Nurse were arrested on
the charge of witchcraft. On March 21 they were examined and committed. And with that the real reign of terror began.

Salem Village, as a community, was no longer sane.

Let us get it over quickly. The Salem witches ceased to be Salem's
affair—they became a matter affecting the whole colony. Sir William
Phips, the new governor, appointed a special court of oyer and ter-
miner to try the cases. And the hangings began.

On January 1, 1692, no one, except possibly the "circle children," had heard of Salem witches. On June 10 Bridget Bishop was hanged. She had not been one of the first accused, but she was the first to suffer. She had been married three times, kept a roadhouse on the road to Beverley where people drank rum and played shovelboard, and dressed, distinctively for the period, in a "black cap and black hat and red paragon bodice broidered and looped with diverse colors." But those seem to have been her chief offenses. When questioned, she said, "I never saw the devil in my life."

All through the summer the accusations, the arrests, the trials, came thick and fast till the jails were crowded. Nor were those now accused friendless old beldames like Sarah Good. They included Captain John Alden (son of Miles Standish's friend), who saved himself by breaking jail, and the wealthy and prominent Englishes, who saved themselves by flight. The most disgraceful scenes occurred at the trial of the saintly Rebecca Nurse. Thirty-nine citizens of Salem were brave enough to sign a petition for her, and the jury brought in a verdict of "not guilty." The mob in the sweating courtroom immediately began to cry out, and the presiding judge as much as told the jury to reverse their verdict. They did so, to the mob's delight. Then the governor pardoned her. And "certain gentlemen of Salem"—and perhaps the mob—persuaded him into reversing his pardon. She was hanged on Gallows Hill on July 19 with Sarah Good, Sarah Wilds, Elizabeth How, and Susanna Martin.

Susanna Martin's only witchcraft seems to have been that she was an unusually tidy woman and had once walked a muddy road without getting her dress bedraggled. No, I am quoting from testimony, not inventing. As for Elizabeth How, a neighbor testified, "I have been acquainted with Goodwife How as a naybor for nine or ten years and I never saw any harm in her but found her just in her dealings and faithful to her promises. . . . I never heard her revile any person but she always pitied them and said, 'I pray God forgive them now.'" But the children cried, "I am stuck with a pin. I am pinched," when they saw her—and she hanged.

It took a little more to hang the Reverend George Burroughs. He had been Salem Village's second minister—then gone on to a parish in Maine. And the cloth had great sanctity. But Ann Putnam and Mercy Lewis managed to doom him between them, with the able assistance of the rest of the troupe. Mr. Burroughs was unfortunate enough to be a man of unusual physical strength—anyone who could lift a gun by putting four fingers in its barrel must do so by magic arts. Also, he had been married three times. So when the ghosts of his first two wives, dressed in winding sheets, appeared in a sort of magic-lantern show to Ann Putnam and cried out that Mr. Burroughs had murdered them—the cloth could not save him then.

Here and there in the records gleams a flash of frantic common sense. Susanna Martin laughs when Ann Putnam and her daughter go into convulsions at her appearance. When asked why, she says, "Well I may, at such folly. I never hurt this woman or her child in my life." John Procter, the prosperous farmer who employed Mary Warren, said sensibly, before his arrest, "If these girls are left alone, we will all be devils and witches. They ought all to be sent to the whipping post." He was right enough about it—but his servant helped hang him.

Judge, jury, and colony preferred to believe the writhings of the children; the stammerings of those whose sows had died inexplicably; the testimony of such as Bernard Peach, who swore that Susanna Martin had flown in through his window, bent his body into the shape of a "whoope," and sat upon him for an hour and a half.

One hanging on June 10, five on July 19, five on August 19, eight on September 22, including Mary Easty and Martha Corey. And of these the Reverend Noyes remarked, with unction, "What a sad thing it is to see eight firebrands of hell hanging there!" But for stubborn Giles Corey a different fate was reserved.

The old man had begun by believing in the whole hocus-pocus. He had quarreled with his wife about it. He had seen her arrested as a witch, insulted by the magistrates, condemned to die. Two of his sons-in-law had testified against her; he himself had been closely questioned as to her actions and had made the deposition of a badgered and simple man. Yes, she prayed a good deal; sometimes he couldn't hear what she said—that sort of thing. The memory must have risen to haunt him when she was condemned. Now he himself was in danger.

Well, he could die as his wife would. But there was the property—his goods, his prospering lands. By law, the goods and property of those convicted of witchcraft were confiscated by the state and the name attainted. With a curious, grim heroism, Giles Corey drew up a will leaving that property to the two sons-in-law who had not joined in the prevailing madness. And then at his trial, he said, "I will not plead. If I deny, I am condemned already in courts where ghosts appear as witnesses and swear men's lives away."

A curious, grim heroism? It was so. For those who refused to plead either guilty or not guilty in such a suit were liable to the old English punishment called *peine forte et dure*. It consisted in heaping weights or stones upon the unhappy victim till he accepted a plea—or until his chest was crushed. And exactly that happened to old Giles Corey. They heaped the stones upon him until they killed him—and two days before his wife was hanged, he died. But his property went to the two loyal sons-in-law, without confiscation—and his name was not attainted. So died Giles Corey, New England to the bone.

And then, suddenly and fantastically as the madness had come, it was gone.

The "afflicted children," at long last, had gone too far. They had accused the governor's lady. They had accused Mrs. Hall, the wife of the minister at Beverley and a woman known throughout the colony for her virtues. And there comes a point when driven men and women revolt against blood and horror. It was that which ended Robespierre's terror—it was that which ended the terror of the "afflicted children." The thing had become a *reductio ad absurdum*. If it went on, logically, no one but the "afflicted children" and their protégées would be left alive.

In 1706 Ann Putnam made public confession that she had been deluded by the devil in testifying as she had. She had testified in every case but one. And in 1711 the colony of Massachusetts paid fifty pounds to the heirs of George Burroughs, twenty-one pounds to the heirs of Giles Corey—five hundred and seventy-eight pounds in all to the heirs of various victims. An expensive business for the colony, on the whole.

What happened to the survivors? Well, the Reverend Samuel Parris quit Salem Village to go into business in Boston and died at Sudbury in 1720. And Ann Putnam died in 1716 and from the stock of the Putnams sprang Israel Putnam, the Revolutionary hero. And from the stock of the "witches," the Nurses and the others, sprang excellent and distinguished people of service to state and nation. And hanging Judge Hawthorne's descendant was Nathaniel Hawthorne.

We have no reason to hold Salem up to obloquy. It was a town, like another, and a strange madness took hold of it. But it is no stranger thing to hang a man for witchcraft than to hang him for the shape of his nose or the color of his skin. We are not superstitious, no. Well, let us be a little sure we are not. For persecution follows superstition and intolerance as fire follows the fuse. And once we light that fire we cannot foresee where it will end or what it will consume—any more than they could in Salem two hundred and sixty-seven years ago.

We Aren't Superstitious, by Stephen Vincent Benét

HERMAN MELVILLE

"... within, there is change and tumult ...
a creature tearing at his vitals ..."

W̲hen Herman Melville died in 1891 his mourners were few.
At the time of his death he was retired from the job of customs
inspector on the New York docks, a position he had held for some
twenty years. True, his obituary mentioned that in his youth he had
been a writer, and had published a number of novels. They had
created quite a stir in literary circles—Typee, Omoo, Moby-Dick
. . . but they had been written some forty years earlier and were
all but forgotten.

It wasn't until the nineteen-twenties that the Melville genius was
"rediscovered," and Moby-Dick took its place as one of the greatest
of American novels.

Here is Melville at thirty, in his prime as a writer, engaged in
his terrible struggle with the White Whale. The selection here is
from Lewis Mumford's fine biography of Melville, written some
twenty-five years ago but still one of the best pictures of the writer
ever drawn.

IT WAS TIME for Melville to begin work again. In February, 1850, he
owed his publisher, Harper's, more than seven hundred dollars in advances not covered by royalties. He did what he could to reduce the
scale of his living. In the spring, he left New York and went up to
Broadhall with his family—the old homestead that his Grand-Uncle
Thomas had sold when he emigrated to Ohio, had now been converted into an inn; his grandfather's old desk was still mildewing in
the barn, and Melville brought it to light, cleaned it up for his own
use, and sat down to it.

The Berkshires were "home" for Melville quite as much as Albany
or New York; perhaps more so, for he had a feeling for the open
country and its ways. By October he had found a near-by farmstead,
with a house that had been an inn during the eighteenth century, an
apple orchard on the south side, broad hay fields to the north, and

pasture rising back of the house to the west, which ended in a wood lot on the summit of the hill. The countryside was well cultivated. Maple trees lined the highroad on each side, the willows dropped lazily over the banks of the Housatonic and, on the poorer upland soils, where the amaranth grew, the white threads of birch trees stood out against the dark pattern of the woods. Pittsfield, a village with metropolitan pretensions, the capital of the Berkshires and the resort of palpable celebrities, was only two miles or so away by a road that led down the valley and across the river, past a sawmill, and through the parklike streets of the village itself.

Judge Shaw advanced Melville funds on a friendly sort of mortgage to purchase Arrowhead; and Melville doubtless intended by modest and spasmodic farming, with a vegetable garden, hay fields, a wood lot, a cow, and a horse, to eke out the narrow income derived from his books. For a man in prime health there was nothing injudicious in this arrangement; winter leaves a considerable amount of free time from farm work, and, with only a few hundred dollars in ready cash every year, Melville might have made a pretty good go of it. But there were handicaps. He had a wife and child to support; other children came presently, four in all; and Elizabeth Melville was a duffer as a housekeeper; try as she would, she could not cook without strain nor manage a servant; and her chief equipment for facing the work and the winter was an admirable set of party dresses and slippers. Melville's picked-up knowledge of cookery must have been called upon for service during the first weeks they were definitely on their own; and presently Mrs. Maria Melville and his sisters came to join the household, in order to teach Elizabeth the rudiments of the household arts. It was a humiliating experience for Elizabeth; but there was no help for it; to the end of her days she did not like housekeeping; the art of "managing" was apparently not in her. The many hands in Arrowhead doubtless made light work; they also made inroads upon the larder, and what the Melvilles gained in service they lost in supplies. The house itself was commodious in rooms, but cramped in space, since it did not so much exist in its own right, as it did as a sort of annex to the chimney, a vast brick structure, with a circumference of forty-eight feet at the base; the chimney was ample enough, but it swallowed wood on a winter day as a whale swallows little fishes, and the rooms that were left were none too large.

On any realistic canvas, this new move, with all its unexpected burdens, was a dubious one. But in 1850 Melville was at the top of his energies; the impetus from *Typee* and *Omoo* had not been lost; the reception in England had probably added to his confidence; and when he looked around him, the American scene itself reinforced his courage and his convictions, and gave him new strength.

Sometime in 1850, towards the close of summer, Herman Melville must have begun to write *Moby-Dick*; for the book, which is a long one, was finished in the summer of 1851. In back of the actual writing went a considerable amount of preparation; and one does not know how long before the theme of the book had begun to root itself in Melville's mind. The work itself shows that he had reached out for every book on whaling he could lay hands on, practically every book that had been written, and, in addition, he had made note of every quotation and allusion to the whale he had met in his wide miscellaneous reading. Scholarship as well as personal experience went into his writing: one of the best modern writers upon whaling, Frank Bullen, the author of *The Cruise of the Cachalot*, confesses he would never have gone farther with his own work had he known about the wealth of information and detail that went into *Moby-Dick* before he set out. Did Melville consciously save the greatest of his ocean experiences for his maturity? Did he wait for Leviathan to develop his soul? Did he begin another *White-Jacket* or *Typee*, and become conscious, in the act of writing, of this deepening of his insight, this integration of his powers, and of the vast fable that was now at his command?

One cannot make a reasonable conjecture about the matter. All one knows are the actual conditions under which *Moby-Dick* was written, the reactions of the writing itself upon Melville, and its final result—the story of the White Whale.

Conceive of Melville in his new home, as he embarks upon the most extensive of his spiritual voyages. The furniture has been removed to his new house, the beds put up, the heavier articles shifted and re-shifted, and, by a month's work outdoors, the woodpile has grown and the hay been stowed into the hayloft. For the moment, all his relations are well poised, Barney is through the period of teething, Elizabeth has help in her housework, and the first tension of removal is over; Mr. Duyckinck occasionally, with the most tactful sort of generosity, sends up a case of champagne in a wicker cradle or a fine bundle of cigars, or he suggests a review to be written. He even tries to nourish Melville's reputation by abetting some one who is writing about him in the papers and who wishes to publish a photograph of the famous author. Here alone Melville's pride rebuffs this rudimentary effort at an art which has become a loathsome sore in our own time; he refuses his picture. "The fact is," he explains, "almost everybody is having his 'mug' engraved nowadays, so that this test of distinction is getting to be reversed; and therefore, to see one's 'mug' in

a magazine is presumptive evidence that he's a nobody. . . . I respect-
fully decline to be *oblivionated*. . . ." But when a journeyman painter
made the rounds of the neighborhood Melville sat for him—and the
portrait, which slightly resembles Allan's, remains a just punishment
for his vanity.

Below the edge of Melville's horizon is this new friend, Nathaniel
Hawthorne, and, as he raises his eyes from the desk in his second-story
chamber and looks through the single small window that faces the
north, he sees the wide valley sweeping across to successive ridges of
hills, dominated by Mt. Greylock—otherwise called, from the double
hump in the ridge, Saddleback. The red clover that incarnadined the
summer fields is gone; or rather, its color has mounted to the crown
of the landscape; the maples are a still more glorious red. The spirits
caper in the autumn air; there are glowing Byzantine days when the
heavens reflect the hues of the October apples, when the sky is so ripe
and ruddy it seems there must be harvest home for the angels and
that Charles' Wain is heaped as high as Saddleback with autumn
sheaves. The sunrises and the sunsets glow side by side in the woods,
and momentarily moult in the falling leaves. Neither the Rhine nor
the Moselle produces anything as heady as the landscape of the Berkshires in autumn. Now is the time to begin. When Melville writes his
first words, "Call me Ishmael," he is writing out of his health and
ecstasy; he himself is not an outcast, nor is his spirit drooping with
the "hypos"; his first touch is a black one because his canvas demands
it. He is about to build up a vast pyramid of contrasts, between the
whiteness of external evil and the blackness of man's inner doom; and
he faces this drama with his full powers.

The apples are gathered; the autumn plowing is done; Melville is
at work. The mood of creation is upon him; he is ready not for one
book but for fifty books; if Mr. Duyckinck would only send him about
fifty fast-writing youths with an easy style, not averse to polishing their
letters, he might set them all at work. "It is not so much the paucity,
as the superabundance of material that seems to incapacitate modern
authors," he had written that summer. In this autumn ferment, Melville has scarcely enough time to think about his future books sepa-
rately; in lieu of using fifty youths, he must pack as much as possible
into one book. Melville scarcely breaks his way through a chapter or
two before he realizes that he has found his theme; and the only question is how to quarry this marble, how to get it out. "Youth," Melville
said in another place, "must wholly quit, then, the quarry for a while;
and not only go forth and get tools to use in the quarry, but must go
and thoroughly discover architecture. Now the quarry-discoverer is
long before the stone-cutter; and the stone-cutter is long before the

architect; and the architect is long before the temple; for the temple is the crown of the world." His apprenticeship is at last definitely over; he is at work on the temple itself—such a temple as Dante, Shakespeare, Webster, Marlowe, Browne, might each in his way have conceived and designed.

The days go by; the leaves fall; the candlelight comes early; the mice creep into the cupboard and make nests for themselves in the woodpile; the wide meadows become as bleak as a gray sea. In this most inland scene, with only the Housatonic to connect him with the watery world, Melville still dreams of the sea; his thought centers on the sea, its creatures, its boats, its fish, its men, its deeper monsters. Oh! for a dash of salt spray! he cries; and as substitute he draws upon experience and memory for the savor. The days grow cold. Snow hems in the roof and chimney of Arrowhead. Melville has a sea-feeling all the more; when he looks out of his little window on rising, he feels as if he were looking out of his port-hole in the midst of the Atlantic; his room seems a ship's cabin, and at nights, when he wakes up and hears the wind shrieking, he can almost fancy there is too much sail on the house, and he had better go up on the roof and rig in the chimney. On a winter morning he rises at eight, helps his horse to his hay and the cow to her pumpkin, stands around to take in the grateful complacency of the cow, she moves her jaws so mildly and with such sanctity; then, with his own breakfast over, he goes to his workroom and lights the fire, runs rapidly through the MS. and starts to work. At half past two a knock comes. He does not answer. Again the knock and again, till he rises from his writing, almost mechanically, and resumes the external round; feed for the horse and cow; then dinner; then he rigs up his sleigh and goes off to the village for the mail, for supplies, for a little friendly chaffer perhaps round the tavern bar. So one day follows another on the surface; but within, there is change and tumult. Melville, like Ahab, finds a creature tearing at his vitals, and that creature the thing he has created.

"How then with me, writing of this Leviathan? Unconsciously, my chirography expands into placard capitals. Give me a condor's quill! Give me Vesuvius' crater for an inkstand. Friends! hold my arms! For in the mere act of penning my thoughts of this Leviathan, they weary me, and make me faint with the outreaching comprehensiveness of sweep, as if to include the whole circle of the sciences, and all the generations of whales, and men, and mastodons, past, present, and to come, with all the revolving panoramas of empire on earth, and throughout the whole universe, not excluding its suburbs. Such, and so magnifying, is the virtue of a large and liberal theme! We expand to its bulk. To produce a mighty volume you must choose a mighty theme. No great and enduring volume can ever be written upon the flea, though many there be who have tried it."

Such intensity of effort, so many hours of writing and reading, are as exhausting as the direction of a battle; but there is no lying up in winter quarters, no delegation of responsibility. The writer does not live outside his book; the world, the familiar, homely world, becomes a weak picture, and his imagination is the body and blood of reality. Taking a book off the brain, Melville exclaims while in the midst of it, "is akin to the ticklish and dangerous business of taking an old painting off a panel: you have to scrape off the whole brain in order to get at it with due safety—and even then the painting may not be worth the trouble." Well, *Moby-Dick* is worth the trouble; the very writing of it becomes a powerful instrument in his own development. What absorbs so much of his time and life is not the book alone, "but the primitive elementalizing of the strange stuff, which in the act of attempting the book, has upheaved and upgushed in his soul. Two books are being writ; of which the world shall only see one, and that the bungled one. The larger book, and the infinitely better, is for . . . his own private shelf. That it is whose unfathomable cravings drunk his blood; the other only demands ink."

Melville knows he must not let up on this work; he flogs himself to get his uttermost into it; the application ruins his eyesight. This small aperture and northern light are bad for his eyes. No matter; he writes with one eye closed and the other blinking. By December, in the evening, he is exhausted: he spends the aftermath of the day in a sort of physical trance; but already his mind is anticipating the developments of the next day, and he is up early, and goes back to his task.

Spring comes; but it is no spring for Melville. He will not even be bothered for dinner. Some days he sits at his desk till 4:30 without writing a word; in the spring twilight, when the catkins of the maples glow in the mild sunset and the bluebirds dart about the field like unfettered flowers, he at last comes out and creeps about like an owl. If Melville plows and plants, he does it mechanically; his heart is not in it; and he is not nourished by it. In the midst of his writing, his soul reaches a pitch of exaltation, as it does defiantly in a terrible gale, when the hand is firmly on the wheel, and the dangerous seas that wash the decks do not loosen the hold; the letters that he writes to Hawthorne then are prophetic, and deep, and full of proud mastery. In building up his vast symbol of the whale, he strips the universe down to his own ego; like Ahab himself, he says no to all the powers and dominions that lie beyond it. Does not Hawthorne do as much?

But the soft milky air of June gets the better of Melville's humors;

every breath of the warm earth, the spicy perfume of wild strawberries, the honeyed odor of the locust trees, the dank green fragrance of ferns, the sight of buttercups making the fields sunny even on dull days, or the daisies turning the high grass into the whitish green color of the ocean when the waves disperse on the beach, the warm feeling of animal contentment that the sun itself pours into a man—all these things renewed his energies and revived his spirits. Melville relaxed and refreshed himself in the sunlight, building an addition to the house, and plowing and sowing, and watching the green shoots rise. He does not doubt the reality of his black moments; for, as he tells Hawthorne, in the boundless, trackless, but still glorious wilderness of the universe, where he and Hawthorne are outposts, there are savage Indians as well as mosquitoes; still, one does not go on fighting them forever. As for the crotchety and overdoleful chimeras, "the like of you and me, and some others, forming a chain of God's outposts around the world, must be content to encounter now and then, and fight them as best we can."

Melville goes down to New York to see the first part of *Moby-Dick* through the press; but the oppressive, humid days in that Babylonish brick-kiln, and the long delays of the printers, disgust him; he comes back to the country, and purposes to end the book, if possible, reclining on the grass, or watching the clouds play on a summer afternoon around old Greylock, from the newly built porch he has added to the north side of the house, where the view lies. The tail of *Moby-Dick* is not cooked yet; though the hell-fire in which the book was broiled might not unreasonably have charred it before this. Melville's intention is sane enough, if only he had the leisure to cultivate the calm, grass-growing mood; but no, he must keep on patching and tinkering at his buildings. In July the hay waits for no author to finish his chapter; there are a hundred chores to keep him away from his book, still more from deep questions about the universe and its meaning, and evil, and truth, and all those aspects of reality that need a Hawthorne for perfect communication. There is no help for it; he must go back to New York to finish the book in a third-story room, where there is no cow to milk, no horse to feed, no sister or wife or mother to be a little hurt or concerned by his inattentiveness or moodiness.

These last straining days in New York were not unlike, one might guess, those that Pierre experienced: the book that was begun in health and exuberance in the keen, mountain air of October in the Berkshires was finished in exacerbation and depression and desolation in the humid dog days of a dirty, unkempt city, days of unrelieved sunlight, followed by afternoon thunderstorms that leave the air even heavier than before, the pavements steaming, the waves of warm, unpleasant air, carrying slight odours of putrefaction, wafted upward into even the third story.

"In the earlier progress of the book, he had found some relief in making his regular evening walk through the greatest thoroughfares of the city: and so the utter desolation of his soul might feel itself more intensely against the bodies of the hurrying thousands. Then he began to be sensible of more fancying stormy nights than pleasant ones; for then the great thoroughfares were less thronged, and the innumerable shop-awnings flapped and beat like schooners' broad sails in a gale, and the shutters banged like lashed bulwarks; and the slates fell hurtling like displaced ships' blocks from aloft. Stemming such tempers through the deserted streets, Pierre felt a dark triumphant joy; that while others had crawled in fear to their kennels, he alone defied the storm—admiral, whose most vindictive pelting of hailstones—striking his non-framed fiery furnace of a body—melted into soft dew, and so, harmlessly trickled off him. By-and-by, of such howling, pelting nights, he began to bend his steps down the narrow side streets, in quest of the more secluded and mysterious taprooms. There he would feel a singular satisfaction in sitting down all dripping in a chair ordering half a pint of ale before him, and, drawing over his cap to protect his eyes from the light, eye the varied faces of the social castaways, who here had their haunts from bitterest midnights. But at last he began to feel a distaste for even these; and now nothing but the utter night-desolation of the obscurest warehousing lanes would content him or be at all sufferable to him."

"Dollars damn me," he wrote Hawthorne, "and the malicious devil is forever grinning in upon me, holding the door ajar. My dear Sir, a presentiment is upon me.— I shall at last be worn out and perish, like an old nutmeg-grater, grated to pieces by the constant attrition of the wood, that is, the nutmeg. What I feel most moved to write, that is banned—it will not pay. Yet, altogether write the *other* way I cannot. So the product is a final hash; and all my books are botches. . . . But I was talking about the 'whale.' As the fishermen say, 'he was in his flurry' when I left him some three weeks ago. I'm going to take him up by his jaw, however, before long and finish him up in some fashion or another. What's the use of elaborating what, in its very essence, is so short-lived as a modern book? Though I wrote the Gospels in this century, I should die in the gutter. What reputation H. M. has is horrible. Think of it! To go down to posterity as the man who lived among the cannibals. When I speak of posterity in reference to myself, I only mean the babies who will probably be born in the moment immediately ensuing upon my giving up the ghost. . . . I shall go down to them in all likelihood. . . . I have come to regard this matter of Fame as the most transparent of all vanities. I read Solomon more and more, and every time see deeper and deeper and unspeakable meanings in him. I did not think of Fame, a year ago, as I do now. My development has all been within a few years past. I am like one of those seeds taken out of the Egyptian pyramids which, after being three thousand years a seed, and nothing but a seed, being planted in English soil, it developed itself, grew to greenness, and then fell to mold. So I. Until I was twenty-five, I had no development at all. From my twenty-fifth year I date my life. Three weeks have scarcely passed, at any time between then and now, that I have not unfolded within myself. But I feel that I am now come to the utmost leaf of the bulb, and that shortly the flower must fall to the mold."

If it was in a mood of confidence and creative delight that he sounded his depths in *Moby-Dick*, it was in this other mood, chastened, almost fearful, that his stripped ego rose to the surface after this extreme plunge. He had looked into the abyss; he was dizzy, terrified, appalled. His letters to Hawthorne have this mingled sense of awe and exaltation: they are the mood of the last part of *Moby-Dick*. Melville's notes to Mr. Duyckinck are still jocular and robust; they might be the words of the imperturbable Stubb or the jaunty Flask, but that is because Melville gave Mr. Duyckinck only a part of himself, the polite, free-and-easy, effervescent side, meant for appreciative eating and solicitous drinking, the side he doubtless turned to his family and housemates, when weariness did not bury him from their sight—the last people who could share or understand his quest, his insight, his triumph. There is no question of wearing a mask: both sides of Melville are authentic, but the deeper part of him, which would under happier circumstances have served as ballast and made him face the waves more steadily, claimed too much of his inner space. He lost buoyancy; the water crept above the waterline; the ship rode dangerously. Now, however, we are speaking of the consequences of Melville's writing *Moby-Dick*. The book itself was published towards the end of 1851 by Bentley, in England, and a little later in the same year by Harper's in New York.

Whether it was an angel or a devil that Melville had struggled with this long year, he had wrestled magnificently, and the book was done, the most important of Melville's books, and surely one of the most important books of the century.

Herman Melville, by Lewis Mumford

STEPHEN FOSTER

"Dear friends and gentle hearts."

Stephen Foster lived a tragic life—tragic because so much of what he had to give was wasted. Although he gave America some of its best-loved songs—Oh! Susanna, My Old Kentucky Home and Old Black Joe—he had within him the genius to produce much more. Alexander Woollcott draws a touching portrait of Foster, the gentle man who was never quite able to cope with the harsh realities of life.

THIS IS the story of a scrap of paper with five words scribbled on it. It was found among the effects of a hapless young derelict who, on a January day toward the close of the Civil War, died in a charity ward of Bellevue Hospital in the city of New York. Three days before, the police had found him lying naked in the hallway of a Bowery lodging-house—naked and bleeding from an unexplained wound in the head, a wound still unexplained. He was not yet forty, but for some years he had been adrift from his folks, and already drink and loneliness and despair had done for him. Yet he had lived long enough to unpack his heart for the consolation of his countrymen for generations to come.

In a pocket of the clothes the police had gathered up at his lodgings and deposited at Bellevue when they delivered him there, a battered purse was found. It contained a quarter and a dime in the dingy paper money so often circulated in wartime. There was also some hard money—three coppers. This sum of 38 cents was his entire fortune. Yet he bequeathed to us certain legacies now as clearly a part of the national wealth as Yellowstone Park or the Gettysburg Address. He left us "Old Black Joe" and "My Old Kentucky Home" and "Old Folks at Home." His name was Stephen Collins Foster.

Foster's death caused so little stir at the time that it was not mentioned in the New York papers until more than two weeks later and then only in the briefest of obituaries. Now he gazes pensively into eternity from the gallery of the Hall of Fame.

What is important is that just as one heard the songs of Stephen Foster round all the campfires on both sides of the line in the Civil

War, so the doughboys in the last war sang and whistled them on the coast of Africa and in the islands of the South Seas and in Japan. One can't help wishing that one could go back through time long enough to visit that charity ward in Bellevue and whisper to the dying man that this is the way it was going to be.

If so many of Foster's famous works pretend to be plaintive Negro ballads, it was not because his roots were in the South. He was never "way down upon the Suwannee River" any more than Al Jolson ever had a mammy. Indeed the very word Suwannee was a correction in the original manuscript, an afterthought which he got out of a gazetteer he consulted in the Pittsburgh bank where his brother was employed. No, it was because he plied a trade that had few outlets in his day and the best of these was the minstrel show. Foster's lyric yearning for the deep South was a matter of dollars and cents and burnt cork. That is why old black Joe was black.

But not all of Foster's songs were of this pattern. He did write the words and music of "Massa's in de Cold Cold Ground" and "Nellie Was a Lady" and "de Camp Town Races" and "Uncle Ned" and "Oh! Susanna" and "Hard Times, Come Again No More." He also wrote "Beautiful Dreamer" and "Old Dog Tray" and "Gentle Annie" and "Come Where My Love Lies Dreaming." . . . Abundance is one of the attributes of genius as it is of nature. It is the whole point of this gentle and luckless troubadour that he wrote not one song but 200. Not one but a half dozen of these will be sung and loved in America as long as there is an America.

The greatest of these—including all the best—were written before he was thirty. He was thirty-eight when he died. Of the unproductive years one can only guess whether he lost his gift because he had taken to the bottle or took to the bottle because he had lost his gift. We know it from that scrap of paper. It was a memo pencilled in Foster's own handwriting. The five words were "Dear Friends and Gentle Hearts." Who can doubt that this was the title or refrain of a song he meant to write? Maybe it was singing itself to him there in the charity ward. One has the notion that it would have been the best of all. But we shall not hear it this side of Heaven.

Long, Long Ago, by Alexander Woollcott

MARY WHITE

"She never fell from a horse in her life."

Mary White never knew fame. Her accomplishments were not the sort that would mark her for immortality. She was sixteen when she died, killed by a foolish accident that shouldn't have happened. Mary White was a schoolgirl who lived in a typical midwestern city-town, a kind of Centerville, U.S.A., an American heartland. She was a leader among her peers, and a genuinely good human being.

William Allen White, editor and publisher of the Emporia Gazette, wrote Mary White's obituary—a simple tribute to a beloved daughter, lost forever. It is one of the most moving memorials ever written.

THE ASSOCIATED PRESS reports carrying the news of Mary White's death declared that it came as the result of a fall from a horse. How she would have hooted at that! She never fell from a horse in her life. Horses have fallen on her and with her—"I'm always trying to hold 'em in my lap," she used to say. But she was proud of few things, and one was that she could ride anything that had four legs and hair. Her death resulted not from a fall, but from a blow on the head which fractured her skull, and the blow came from the limb of an overhanging tree on the parking.

The last hour of her life was typical of its happiness. She came home from a day's work at school, topped off by a hard grind with the copy on the High School Annual, and felt that a ride would refresh her. She climbed into her khakis, chattering to her mother about the work she was doing, and hurried to get her horse and be out on the dirt roads for the country air and the radiant green fields of the spring. As she rode through the town on an easy gallop she kept waving at passers-by. She knew everyone in town. For a decade the little figure with the long pigtail and the red hair ribbon has been familiar on the streets of Emporia, and she got in the way of speaking to those who nodded at her. She passed the Kerrs, walking the horse, in front of the Normal Library, and waved at them; passed another friend a few hundred feet farther on, and waved to her. The horse was walking and as she turned into North Merchant Street she took off her cowboy hat, and the horse swung into a lope. She passed the Tripletts and waved her cowboy hat at them, still moving gayly north on Merchant Street. A *Gazette* carrier passed—a high-school boy friend—and she waved at him, but with her bridle hand; the horse veered quickly, plunged into the parking where the low-hanging limb faced her, and, while she still looked back, waving, the blow came. But she did not fall from the horse; she slipped off, dazed a bit, staggered, and fell in a faint. She never quite recovered consciousness.

But she did not fall from the horse, neither was she riding fast. A ycar or so ago she used to go like the wind. But that habit was broken, and she used the horse to get into the open to get fresh, hard exercise, and to work off a certain surplus energy that welled up in her and needed a physical outlet. That need has been in her heart for years. It was back of the impulse that kept the dauntless, little brown-clad figure on the streets and country roads of this community and built into a strong, muscular body what had been a frail and sickly frame during the first years of her life. But the riding gave her more than a body. It released a gay and hardy soul. She was the happiest thing in the world. And she was happy because she was enlarging her horizon. She came to know all sorts and conditions of men. Charley O'Brien, the traffic cop, was one of her best friends. W. L. Holtz, the Latin teacher, was another. Tom O'Connor, farmer-politician, and Rev. J. H. J. Rice, preacher and police judge, and Frank Beach, music master, were her special friends, and all the girls, black and white, above the track and below the track, in Pepville and Stringtown, were among her acquaintances. And she brought home riotous stories of her adventures. She loved to rollick; persiflage was her natural expression at home. Her humor was a continual bubble of joy. She seemed to think in hyperbole and metaphor. She was mischievous without malice, as full of faults as an old shoe. No angel was Mary White, but an easy girl to live with, for she never nursed a grouch five minutes in her life.

With all her eagerness for the out-of-doors, she loved books. On her table when she left her room were a book by Conrad, one by Galsworthy, *Creative Chemistry* by E. E. Slosson, and a Kipling book. She read Mark Twain, Dickens, and Kipling before she was ten—all of their writings. Wells and Arnold Bennett particularly amused and diverted her. She was entered as a student in Wellesley in 1922; was assistant editor of the High School Annual this year, and in line for election to the editorship of the Annual next year. She was a member of the executive committee of the High School Y.W.C.A.

Within the last two years she had begun to be moved by an ambition to draw. She began as most children do by scribbling in her school books, funny pictures. She bought cartoon magazines and took a course—rather casually, naturally, for she was, after all, a child, with no strong purposes—and this year she tasted the first fruits of success by having her pictures accepted by the High School Annual. But the thrill of delight she got when Mr. Ecord, of the Normal Annual, asked her to do the cartooning for that book this spring was too beautiful for words. She fell to her work with all her enthusiastic heart. Her drawings were accepted, and her pride—always repressed by a lively sense of the ridiculousness of the figure she was cutting—was a really gorgeous thing to see. No successful artist ever drank a deeper draft of satisfaction than she took from the little fame her work was getting among her schoolfellows. In her glory, she almost forgot her horse—but never her car.

For she used the car as a jitney bus. It was her social life. She never had a "party" in all her nearly seventeen years—wouldn't have one; but she never drove a block in the car in her life that she didn't begin to fill the car with pick-ups! Everybody rode with Mary White—white and black, old and young, rich and poor, men and women. She liked nothing better than to fill the car full of long-legged high-school boys and an occasional girl, and parade the town. She never had a "date" nor went to a dance, except once with her brother Bill, and the "boy proposition" didn't interest her—yet. But young people—great, spring-breaking, varnish-cracking, fender-bending, door-sagging carloads of "kids"—gave her great pleasure. Her zests were keen. But the most fun she ever had in her life was acting as chairman of the committee that got up the big turkey dinner for the poor folks at the county home; scores of pies, gallons of slaw, jam, cakes, preserves, oranges, and a wilderness of turkey were loaded in the car and taken to the county home. And, being of a practical turn of mind, she risked her own Christmas dinner by staying to see that the poor folks actually got it all. Not that she was a cynic; she just disliked to tempt folks. While there she found a blind colored uncle, very old, who could do nothing but make rag rugs, and she rustled up from her school friends rags enough to keep him busy for a season. The last engagement she tried to make was to take the guests at the county home out for a car ride. And the last endeavor of her life was to try to get a rest room for colored girls in the high school. She found one girl reading in the toilet, because there was no better place for a colored girl to loaf, and it inflamed her sense of injustice and she became a nagging harpy to those who, she thought, could remedy the evil.

The poor she had always with her, and was glad of it. She hungered and thirsted for righteousness; and was the most impious creature in the world. She joined the Congregational Church without consulting her parents; not particularly for her soul's good. She never had a thrill of piety in her life, and would have hooted at a "testimony." But even as a little child she felt the church was an agency for helping people to more of life's abundance, and she wanted to help. She never wanted help for herself. Clothes meant little to her. It was a fight to get a new rig on her; but eventually a harder fight to get it off. She never wore a jewel and had no ring but her high-school class ring, and never asked for anything but a wrist watch. She refused to have her hair up, though she was nearly seventeen. "Mother," she protested, "you don't know how much I get by with, in my braided pigtails, that I could not with my hair up." Above every other passion of her life was her passion not to grow up, to be a child. The tomboy in her, which was big, seemed to loathe to be put away forever in skirts. She was a Peter Pan, who refused to grow up.

Her funeral yesterday at the Congregational Church was as she would have wished it; no singing, no flowers save the big bunch of red roses from her Brother Bill's Harvard classmen—Heavens, how proud that would have made her! and the red roses from the *Gazette* force—in vases at her head and feet. A short prayer, Paul's beautiful essay on "Love," from the thirteenth chapter of First Corinthians, some remarks about her democratic spirit by her friend, John H. J. Rice, pastor and police judge, which she would have deprecated if she could, a prayer sent down for her by her friend, Carl Nau, and opening the service the slow, poignant movement from Beethoven's "Moonlight Sonata," which she loved, and closing the service a cutting from the joyously melancholy first movement of Tchaikovsky's *Symphonie Pathétique*, which she liked to hear in certain moods on the phonograph; then the Lord's Prayer by her friends in the high school.

That was all.

For her pall bearers, only her friends were chosen: her Latin teacher, W. L. Holtz; her high-school principal, Rice Brown; her doctor, Frank Foncannon; her friend, W. W. Finney; her pal at the *Gazette* office, Walter Hughes; and her brother Bill. It would have made her smile to know that her friend, Charley O'Brien, the traffic cop, had been transferred from Sixth and Commercial to the corner near the church to direct her friends who came to bid her good-by.

A rift in the clouds in a gray day threw a shaft of sunlight upon her coffin as her nervous, energetic little body sank to its last sleep. But the soul in her, the glowing, gorgeous, fervent soul of her, surely was flaming in eager joy upon some other dawn.

Mary White's Obituary, by William Allen White

LUDWIG VAN BEETHOVEN

"I must live like an exile ..."

The genius of Ludwig van Beethoven was a powerful force—in ways it seemed a thing apart from the man to whom it belonged. His childhood and early adult years had been harsh ones—he had been forced while still in his teens to take charge of the household from a drunken wastrel father who was not competent to manage for himself—but by the time he was 25 he had reached a full awareness of his powers. Arrogant and condescending, he felt quite certain that his genius set him apart from the "dolls," the "little men" of the world. Beethoven was not a vicious man, but he was supremely conscious of the difference between himself and others.

In his masterful Beethoven, J. W. N. Sullivan notes that it was probably in 1798, when he was 28, that Beethoven first noticed the signs of approaching deafness. Overcome by panic and fearful lest this terrible news be known, he swore his friends to secrecy, pretended the malady did not exist, consulted doctors—and quacks, anyone who would tell him he would get better. It was not until years later when his deafness became entirely apparent that Beethoven admitted his affliction.

It would be natural to equate deafness for a composer to blindness to an artist . . . but for Beethoven that was not so . . . his genius was not to be curbed by his bodily frailties. The masterpiece of his life, The Ninth Symphony, was written in 1823 after he had been totally deaf for years. Yet Beethoven's affliction did change him—for it was his deafness and the realization of his human frailties that really made him a man.

. . . BEETHOVEN FOUND, that his philosophy of power was, on the whole, successful. It had not been very severely tested. The death of his father, towards the end of 1792, could not have distressed him very greatly, and he assumed the extra share of responsibility for his brothers with equanimity. In 1795 he proposed marriage to a former Bonn colleague, Magdalena Willman, now famous in Vienna as a singer, but her refusal does not seem to have given him much concern.

Being a really strong man Beethoven could never have taken his morality of power with the seriousness of a Nietzsche. His ideal was the hero, not the strong man. But strength cannot become heroism until the soul has known despair, and just now Beethoven found everything easy. He became careless and forgot to fear God or his fellowmen. His overbearing manners, about which we have evidence even when he was known merely as a pianist, were not those of an uncouth provincial, misbehaving himself in all innocence. They were the expression of one of Beethoven's most lasting characteristics, a profound contempt for the great bulk of his fellow-men. This contempt was by no means always savage; it was often robustly good-humoured. But there can be no question but that it was there. It was perfectly compatible with that love for humanity he afterwards professed, for that love was based on the vision that came to him of humanity as a suffering humanity. But all his life he had the contempt of *"eine Natur"* for the *"süsse Puppe."* To such a man the majority of human beings are more or less random collections of borrowed emotions and borrowed ideas. They are, to an extent he finds it difficult to understand, the result of their accidental circumstances. He feels in them an entire absence of the integrating strength and courage that dwells in himself. Their culture and morality, their aims in life, even their joys and sorrows, seem to him merely characterless reflections of their environment. They have none of his passion for heroic achievement, and in any case they would be incapable of paying the price for it. They are never honest, for the last thing they would face is themselves in their essential loneliness. With such creatures a man of Beethoven's kind could never be really intimate. He could treat them with rough good-humour or, if they offended him, he could blaze out in contemptuous wrath. But he could never treat them with the consideration and respect that a man shows towards his equals. He could hurt their feelings with careless indifference, believing that their feelings were of no consequence even if they really existed. The only attitude a *"süsse Puppe"* can take up towards such a man is either one of admiration or one of hatred. Beethoven had plenty of enemies who could not forget the wounds to their vanity that he had inflicted. But also, besides the men he genuinely respected, he had plenty of friends who put up with his contemptuous lack of restraint. At times he tried to be coldly diplomatic with people and to conceal from them the contempt he felt. Thus, he notes in the 1814 diary: "Never show to men the contempt they deserve, one never knows to what use one may want to put them." Even during the early years in Vienna he adopted this diplomatic attitude. Thus, speaking of men who doubtless considered themselves his intimate friends, he describes one as "too weak for friendship" and goes on: "I consider him and . . . mere instruments on which, when it pleases me, I play; but they can never become noble witnesses of my inner and outer activity, nor be in true sympathy with me; I value them according as they are useful to me." Usually, however, he felt no need of such restraint. Even for so considerable a genius as Haydn he did not conceal a certain sneering condescension. Smaller men had to endure being tossed up and down as the mood took him. Two letters to the composer J. N. Hummel, on two consecutive days, run as follows:

"Do not come to me any more. You are a false fellow, and the knacker take all such."

*   *   *

"Good friend Nazerl,
"You are an honourable fellow, and I see you were right. So come this afternoon to me. You will also find Schuppanzigh, and both of us will bump, thump and pump you to your heart's delight."

His relations with most of his fellow-men remained at this stage throughout his life. His rapid alternations of feeling for one and the same person are often comic, and seem to testify to a complete lack of insight on his part. But his apparent lack of "human understanding" is due to the lack of anything there he particularly wanted to understand. He was, almost more than any man that ever lived, "eine Natur," and the "süsse Puppes" never seemed to him to be real people at all. Even Goethe found this attitude in him a little disconcerting, as he complains in a letter to Zelter. "His talent amazed me; unfortunately he is an utterly untamed personality, not altogether in the wrong in holding the world to be detestable, but who does not make it any the more enjoyable either for himself or for others by his attitude." Even Goethe found Beethoven excessive, although he understood the attitude. He had earlier written: "A more self-contained, energetic, sincere artist I never saw. I can understand right well how singular must be his attitude towards the world."

But this attitude was complicated by the very quick and rich emotional nature he possessed. Beethoven, especially at this time, was no misanthrope. The whole man was intensely alive and lived in a vivid world. Everything interested him. He was eager for society, and for anything that contributed to the wealth of impressions that poured in upon him every day. His art was not yet a refuge to him, a mystery to be served, the only region in which his soul could escape all trammels and become completely free, but a glorious vehicle for the expression of the vivid experiences life presented to him. He enjoyed conversation and reading, brilliant social functions, and unconstrained laughter in taverns. He travelled. And, at this time, according to Wegeler, he was always in love, "and made many conquests which would have been difficult if not impossible for many an Adonis." All this made an excellent setting for the morality of power. Beethoven's real strength, his contempt for others, and his success, must have made this doctrine thoroughly congenial to him. He was, in fact, admirably constructed to be an exponent of the morality of power. But a higher destiny was reserved for him.

It would appear that Beethoven first noticed symptoms of his deafness in 1798. His first reference to it, however, occurs in a letter, dated June 1, 1801. The letter is most interesting as showing us Beethoven's attitude, at this time, towards the impending calamity. His first reaction, as we should expect, is rage at the *senselessness* of the hideous affliction. That he, of all men, should lose this particular sense must, indeed, have seemed the most abominable of ironies.

"Your Beethoven is most unhappy," he writes, "and at strife with nature and Creator. I have often cursed the latter for exposing his creatures to the merest accident, so that often the most beautiful buds are broken or destroyed thereby. Only think that my noblest faculty, my hearing, has greatly deteriorated."

But still he has hopes, although he fears the worst, and his self-confidence remains indomitable.

". . . it is said to be due to my bowels and so far as they are concerned I am nearly restored to health. I hope, indeed, that my hearing will also improve, but I am dubious, because such diseases are the most incurable. How sad is my lot! I must avoid all things that are dear to me and live amongst such miserable and egotistical men as . . . and . . . and others. I must say that amongst them all Lichnowsky is the most satisfactory, since last year he has settled an income of 600 florins on me and the good sale of my works enables me to live without care. I could sell everything I compose five times over and at a good price. . . . Oh, how happy could I be if my hearing were completely restored; then would I hurry to you, but as it is I must refrain from everything and the most beautiful years of my life must pass without accomplishing the promise of my talent and powers. A sad resignation to which I must resort although, indeed, I am resolved to rise superior to every obstacle. But how will that be possible? . . . My affliction causes me the least trouble in playing and composing, the most in association with others, and you must be my companion. I am sure my fortune will not desert me. With whom need I be afraid of measuring my strength? Since you have been gone I have composed every sort of music except operas and church music. . . . I beg of you to keep the matter of my deafness a profound secret to *be confided to nobody no matter who it is.* . . ."

In a letter to his doctor friend Wegeler, written at the end of the same month, he goes more into detail.

". . . my hearing has grown steadily worse for three years for which my bowels, which you know were always wretched and have been getting worse, since I am always troubled with a dysentery, in addition to unusual weakness, are said to be responsible. Frank wanted to tone up my body by tonic medicines and restore my hearing with almond oil, but, *prosit*, nothing came of the effort; my hearing grew worse and worse, and my bowels remained as they had been. This lasted till the autumn of last year, and I was often in despair. Then came a medical ass who advised me to take cold baths, a more sensible one to take the usual lukewarm Danube bath. That worked wonders; my bowels improved, my hearing remained, or became worse. I was really miserable during this winter; I had frightful attacks of colic and I fell back into my previous condition, and so things remained until about four weeks ago, when I went to Vering, thinking that my condition demanded a surgeon, and having great confidence in him. He succeeded almost wholly in stopping the awful diarrhœa. He prescribed the lukewarm Danube bath, into which I had each time to pour a little bottle of strengthening stuff, gave me no medicine of any kind until about four weeks ago, when he prescribed pills for my stomach and a kind of tea for my ear. Since then I can say I am stronger and better; only my ears whistle and buzz continually, day and night. I can say I am living a wretched life; for two years I have avoided almost all social gatherings because it is impossible for me to say to people: 'I am deaf.' If I belonged to any other profession it would be easier, but in my profession it is an awful state, the more since my enemies, who are not few, what would they say? In order to give you an idea of this singular deafness of mine I must tell you that in the theatre I must get very close to the orchestra in order to understand the actor. If I am a little distant I do not hear the high tones of the instruments, singers, and if I be put a little farther away I do not hear at all. Frequently I can hear the tones of a low conversation, but not the words, and as soon as anybody shouts it is intolerable. It seems singular that in conversation there are people who do not notice my condition at all, attributing it to my absent-mindedness. Heaven knows what will happen to me. *Vering says that there will be an improvement if no complete cure.* I have often—cursed my existence. *Plutarch* taught me resignation. If possible I will bid defiance to my fate, although there will be moments in my life when I shall be the unhappiest of God's creatures. . . . Resignation! What a wretched refuge—and yet the only one open to me. . . ."

In November he again writes to Wegeler. His hearing has become no better, but rather worse. The slight hope of improvement that he had seems to have abandoned him, so that now he clutches eagerly at any chance. He thinks of changing his physician, accusing Vering of negligence. And he has been collecting stories of marvellous cures. "Miracles are told of *galvanism*; what have you to say about it? A doctor told me that he had seen a deaf and dumb child recover his hearing (in Berlin) again—and a man who had been deaf 7 years got well."

Then comes a reference to "*a dear, fascinating* girl who loves me and whom I love. There have been a few blessed moments within the last two years and it is the first time that I feel marriage might bring me happiness. Alas! she is not of my station—and now—it would be impossible for me to marry. I must still hustle about actively." It is highly probable that the "dear fascinating girl" referred to was the Countess Julia Guicciardi, at the date of this letter just one week less than seventeen years of age. But there is no convincing evidence that she ever played any important part in Beethoven's life. And it does not appear that the impossibility of marriage to which he refers was in any way due to his affliction. But doubtless the general exaltation produced by "being in love" intensified Beethoven's perceptions of the desirability of those aspects of life that his deafness was making inaccessible to him.

"Oh, if I were rid of this affliction I could embrace the world! I feel that my youth is just beginning and have I not always been ill? My physical strength has for a short time past been steadily growing more than ever and also my mental powers. Day by day I am approaching the goal which I apprehend but cannot describe. It is only in this that your Beethoven can live. Tell me nothing of rest. I know of none but sleep, and woe is me that I must give up more time to it than usual. Grant me but half freedom from my affliction and then—as a complete, ripe man I shall return to you and renew the old feelings of friendship. You must see me as happy as it is possible to be here below—not unhappy. No! I cannot endure it. I will take Fate by the throat; it shall not wholly overcome me. Oh, it is so beautiful to live—to live a thousand times! I feel that I am not made for a quiet life."

During the winter of 1801–2 Beethoven did change his physician, the new one being Dr. Schmidt, and on his advice spent the summer of 1802 at the near but quiet and secluded village of Heiligenstadt. Schmidt seems to have given Beethoven hopes that the quiet, by lessening the demands on his hearing, would effect an improvement. Up till now, as we see quite clearly from the letters, Beethoven's reaction to the impending calamity was defiance. He felt that he must assert his will in order not to be overcome. He would summon up all his strength in order to go on living and working in spite of his fate. "I will take Fate by the throat." He was, as it were, *defending* his creative power. But by the end of this summer he found that his genius, that he had felt called upon to cherish and protect, was really a mighty force using him as a channel or servant. It is probable that every genius of the first order becomes aware of this curious relation towards his own genius. Even the most fully conscious type of genius, the scientific genius, as Clerk Maxwell and Einstein, reveals this feeling of being *possessed*. A power seizes them of which they are not normally aware except by obscure premonitions. With Beethoven, so extraordinarily creative, a state of more or less unconscious tumult must have been constant. But only when the consciously defiant Beethoven had succumbed, only when his pride and strength had been so reduced that he was willing, even eager, to die and abandon the struggle, did he find that his creative power was indeed indestructible and that it was its deathless energy that made it impossible for him to die. This new and profound realization of his nature is the most significant thing in the famous Heiligenstadt Testament, written in the autumn of this year, but not discovered till after his death. It marks the complete collapse of the old morality of power, and shows the experiences that made possible the erection of a new morality of power on the ruins of the old. The document must be quoted in full.

For my brothers Carl and —— Beethoven

O ye men who think or say that I am malevolent, stubborn or misanthropic, how greatly do ye wrong me, you do not know the secret causes of my seeming, from childhood my heart and mind were disposed to the gentle feelings of good will, I was even ever eager to accomplish great deeds, but reflect now that for 6 years I have been in a hopeless case, aggravated by senseless physicians, cheated year after year in the hope of improvement, finally compelled to face the prospect of a *lasting malady* (whose cure will take years or, perhaps, be impossible), born with an ardent and lively temperament, even susceptible to the diversions of society, I was compelled early to isolate myself, to live in loneliness, when I at times tried to forget all this, O how harshly was I repulsed by the doubly sad experience of my bad hearing, and yet it was impossible for me to say to men speak louder, shout, for I am deaf. Ah how could I possibly admit an infirmity in the one sense which should have been more perfect in me than in others, a sense which I once possessed in highest perfection, a perfection such as few surely in my profession enjoy or ever have enjoyed—O I cannot do it, therefore forgive me when you see me draw back when I would gladly mingle with you, my misfortune is doubly painful because it must lead to my being misunderstood, for me there can be no recreation in society of my fellows, refined intercourse, mutual exchange of thought, only just as little as the greatest needs command may I mix with society. I must live like an exile, if I approach near to people a hot terror seizes upon me, a fear that I may be subjected to the danger of letting my condition be observed—thus it has been during the last year which I spent in the country, commanded by my intelligent physician to spare my hearing as much as possible, in this almost meeting my present natural disposition, although I sometimes ran counter to it yielding to my inclination for society, but what a humiliation when one stood beside me and heard a flute in the distance and I *heard nothing,* or someone heard *the shepherd singing* and again I heard nothing, such incidents brought me to the verge of despair, but little more and I would have put an end to my life—only art it was that withheld me, ah it seemed impossible to leave the world until I had produced all that I felt called upon to produce, and so I endured this wretched existence—truly wretched, an excitable body which a sudden change can throw from the best into the worst state—Patience—it is said I must now choose for my guide, I have done so, I hope my determination will remain firm to endure until it pleases the inexorable Parcæ to break the thread, perhaps I shall get better, perhaps not, I am prepared. Forced already in my 28th year to become a philosopher, O it is not easy, less easy for the artist than for anyone else—Divine One thou lookest into my inmost soul, thou knowest it, thou knowest that love of man and desire to do good live therein. O men, when some day you read these words, reflect that ye did me wrong and let the unfortunate one comfort himself and find one of his kind who despite all the obstacles of nature yet did all that was in his power to be accepted among worthy artists and men. You my brothers Carl and —— as soon as I am dead if Dr. Schmid is still alive ask him in my name to describe my malady and attach this document to the history of my illness so that so far as possible at least the world may become reconciled with me after my death. At the same time I declare you two to be the heirs to my small fortune (if so it can be called), divide it fairly, bear with and help each other, what injury you have done me you know was long ago forgiven. To you brother Carl I give special thanks for the attachment you have displayed towards me of late. It is my wish that your lives may be better and freer from care than I have had, recommend virtue to your children, it alone can give happiness, not money, I speak from experience, it was virtue that upheld me in misery, to it next to my art I owe the fact that I did not end my life by suicide.—Farewell and love each other—I thank all my friends, particularly *Prince Lichnowsky* and *Professor Schmid*—I desire that the instruments from Prince L. be preserved by one of you but let no quarrel result from this, so soon as they can serve you a better purpose sell them, how glad will I be if I can still be helpful to you in my grave—with joy I hasten towards death—if it comes before I shall have had an opportunity to show all my artistic capacities it will still come too early for me despite my hard fate and I shall probably wish that it had come later—but even then I am satisfied, will it not free me from a state of endless suffering? Come when thou will I shall meet thee bravely.—Farewell and do not wholly forget me when I am dead, I deserve this of you in having often in life thought of you how to make you happy, be so—

LUDWIG VAN BEETHOVEN.

[Seal.]

Heiglnstadt,
October 6th, 1802.

For my brothers Carl and —— to be read and executed after my death.

Heiglnstadt, October 10th, 1802, thus do I take my farewell of thee—and indeed sadly—yes that beloved hope—which I brought with me when I came here to be cured at least in a degree—I must wholly abandon, as the leaves of autumn fall and are withered so hope has been blighted, almost as I came—I go away—even the high courage—which often inspired me in the beautiful days of summer—has disappeared—O Providence—grant me at last but one day of pure joy—it is so long since real joy echoed in my heart—O when—O when, O Divine One—shall I find it again in the temple of nature and of men—Never? no—O that would be too hard.

This document marks a crisis in Beethoven's life. Never again was his attitude towards life one of defiance, where the defiance was an expression of what is called his "strength of character." He had no such need of defiance, for he no longer had any fear. He had become aware within himself of an indomitable creative energy that nothing could destroy. It is this realization, become exultant, that makes him break off in sketching the theme of the great C major fugue of the third Rasoumowsky quartet to write in the margin that nothing can now hinder his composing: "In the same way that you are now able to throw yourself into the whirlpool of society, so you are able to write your works in spite of all social hindrances. Let your deafness no longer be a secret—even for art." He is no longer afraid for his art. He no longer fears that "the most beautiful years of my life must pass without accomplishing the promise of my talent and powers." And to this consciousness of indomitable creative power, the deepest thing in Beethoven, he continually gives expression in his music. The quartet fugue just mentioned is such an expression, although an even more irresistible manifestation of sheer force is to be found in the Scherzo of the ninth symphony. Such movements are in no sense programme music, although they may form a part of a programmatic whole. Such music expresses qualities, not experiences. The quality that survived the experience depicted in the first movement of the ninth symphony and enabled the composer to achieve the state depicted in the third movement was precisely the primitive unconquerable energy depicted in the Scherzo. This quality was the most primitive and most lasting thing in Beethoven. It is almost symbolic that his last recorded action, when lying unconscious on his death-bed, should have been the shaking of his fist towards heaven in response to a shattering peal of thunder.

His realization of the deep-rooted character of his own creative power, which we date from the Heiligenstadt Testament, changed the character of the problem of his attitude towards life. A rigid, strained defiance was no longer necessary. What he came to see as his most urgent task, for his future spiritual development, was *submission*. He had to learn to accept his suffering as in some mysterious way necessary.

Beethoven, by J. W. N. Sullivan

VI. THE MOMENT OF TRUTH

Truth is as impossible to be soiled

by any outward touch as the sunbeam.

JOHN MILTON

The Doctrine and Discipline of Divorce

PETER FREUCHEN

"I felt as if I had been rescued..."

The fascination that the arctic has for some men is a profound
and devastating thing. It pulls them back to the white wastes again
and again until they can no longer travel—or until they are lost forever in the overpowering, everlasting ice and snow. Peter Freuchen
was more truly a citizen of the poles than of his native Denmark.
He was not yet 20 when he made his first expedition to Greenland
to collect geological specimens. When he died of a heart attack at
Elmendorf Air Force Base in Alaska in 1957 he was 71.

In this selection from his autobiography, Arctic Adventure, published in 1935, he tells of his first Greenland expedition. It does not
take a profound situation to try a man's character. Here, simply and
beautifully told, is the story of a supreme test, a test from which
Freuchen had to emerge true to himself.

I HAD BEEN in the harness all day and now that no traces held me
back, it was easy just to walk, just to put one foot ahead of the other.
Acute hunger seems to sharpen the other senses and, while my movements were automatic and I was too tired to sit down and rest, my
brain was unnaturally alert.

It was my first spring in Greenland, 1907. Three of us, Gundahl,
Jarner and I, had left the base of the Denmark Expedition to north-
east Greenland, to familiarize ourselves with the landscape and collect such stray geological specimens as we could find. We had chosen
to pull the sledges ourselves. You get to know the land much better
that way than by sitting on the sledge, occupying yourselves with the
dogs and looking straight ahead.

Food and kerosene had been cached for us along the way, but when
we reached the cache we found that a bear had been there before us.
Even the canned goods were gone—the animal had chewed open the
tins and eaten everything. He had examined the kerosene tank and,
finding that it was of no use to him, given it a slap with his big paw,
crashing it open. We knew that we could expect to find neither musk

oxen, rabbits nor ptarmigans. The bear who had visited the spot some days before had not bothered to wait for us.

There was another cache for us to return to at the Koldewey Islands, enough food to last us several days while we studied geological formations. But even if we could, by hurrying, cover twice as much ground as we had anticipated, it would still take us three days to reach the Islands. We set out. There was nothing else to do.

We made slow progress. It was our fifth day now without anything to eat. We were weak and when we camped that night we cut some pieces of wood from the sledge and built a fire in order to melt ice for drinking water. After the tent was up there seemed nothing to say. It was useless to try to forget our present situation; we were too far sunk to think of anything else. We were so wretched that we were irritated at the sight of each other's faces.

In desperation I took my gun and walked away. I saw traces of rabbits, a few foxes and ptarmigans, but nothing living. I trudged uphill and downhill—there was no use going back to look into the haggard eyes of those two poor fellows.

At length I saw a rabbit. Unless I had been terribly hungry, I doubt very much that I would have spotted him. A cute, white little thing among the boulders. Unfamiliar with men, he paid me slight heed and allowed me to come near. When he decided to run I fired, and he disappeared over the top of the hill. When I finally reached the spot where I had last seen him, the rabbit lay dead only a few paces distant.

I felt as if I had been hauled suddenly out of the sea after all hope of rescue was gone! I took the dead rabbit in my hands, hefted it— rabbits often weigh eight pounds up north—and realized what it would mean to us—a fine stew for three men and a chance, after what seemed months, of feeling that heavenly filled-up sensation.

I was so weak after the excitement subsided that I sat down on a stone to rest. I thought about eating the rabbit. Should we eat it all today, or keep some for tomorrow? Better eat all of it at once, and then walk as fast as possible for the cache. Chances were that we would find something else on the way. I sat and made plan after plan, each born of the fact that I had a rabbit and an hour ago I had none.

At last I got up, and started back toward camp. The rabbit was heavy and, hanging on a string over my shoulder, interfered with my progress. I thought, "If I cut it open and take out the guts it will be much lighter." But back of that was the idea of eating the raw liver and heart, and not sharing it with the other two men who lay starving in the tent. I was ashamed of my treason, and hurried on, but soon I had to sit down again and rest, and temptation returned doubly strong.

Since I had killed the rabbit, and walked so far to get it, wasn't I entitled to half of it? If I ate it, wouldn't I be much stronger and able to do a greater share of the work? Yet if I ate a mouthful of the rabbit I might not be able to stop until I had devoured the whole of it. Suppose I did eat it all?—I would never have to tell Jarner and Gundahl that I had killed a rabbit.

It was not possible for me to resist as long as I sat still. I jumped up again.

I remember the voices that talked within me. With eight pounds of meat dangling from my shoulder, all the gnawing pangs of hunger returned tenfold. I commenced to sing in order to drown out any thoughts prompted by my stomach. Half singing, half crying, fighting the temptation to steal the food from the two men in camp, I walked on, hardly able to put one foot before the other. Whenever I sank to the ground from exhaustion I could think of nothing but my stomach.

I told myself that I could at least take the legs and chew on them. And surely nobody would want the ears—I could eat them. Finally I decided to eat it all, and then confess to myself that I was not fit for Arctic exploration, and give it all up. Then I felt calmer. I said to myself: "No, I'll wait until I reach the next hilltop." But when I reached the next hilltop something made me decide that this was not the place to eat—I would try to make the next.

And so, playing this trick upon my stomach time after time, I reached a hill from which I could see our tent in the valley below, a tiny white spot against the rocks. There my two friends waited patiently and trustingly for my return. I felt as if I had been rescued, but I was more ashamed than I had ever been in my life. I am sure that if I had not seen the tent at that moment nothing could have prevented my selfish betrayal of my comrades. And I could never have felt any pride in myself after that.

It was like reaching a friendly shore after the hazards of an uncharted sea, and my strength returned. Jarner and Gundahl saw me coming and greeted me with weak, but excited yells. I was close to tears, but I tried to conceal them while my two friends prepared the meal. We had camped in a patch of cassiope, that fine fuel which the Arctic produces—a small plant which covers the ground like a carpet and can be burned, either wet or dry, and will hold a fire for twenty-four hours in its ashes.

Jarner and Gundahl acted as though they were celebrating Christmas. I lay inside the tent, tired and faint, and every time I heard them exclaim over the quality of the meat and the excellent hindquarters, and say, "Freuchen gets the best piece because he found the rabbit and killed it," I felt that I was having my ears boxed. Even as we were eating, I could not feel as jubilant as they.

In the Arctic one's job is accomplished against a backdrop of continual struggle—continual struggle for existence. A great deal depends on the individual. If he gives less than his best he is finished, and his failure may be fatal to the men of his outfit as well as to himself.

I have heard it said that Arctic explorers are inferior men who would be lost in the civilized world. This may be true of some of them, but character and an iron will are frequently demanded of a man in the North. I have seen bravery there among explorers and more generally among the natives, a quiet bravery seldom found or required in civilization. It is taken for granted. And I learned that no man should go into the Arctic until he is sure of himself. As for me, I was lucky. I saw my tent in time.

Arctic Adventure: My Life in the Frozen North, by Peter Freuchen

FATHER DAMIEN

*"He spoke of it with the fond warmth and
enthusiasm that men feel for such visions."*

Sent to the Pacific as a missionary priest, young Father Damien
was appalled by the condition of the lepers, lodged by the Hawaiian
government on Molokai Island. Here they lived without physical,
medical, or spiritual comfort. Deportation to Molokai was a sentence of slow death by torture. Father Damien's request to join
these poor sufferers was granted and for twelve years he lived among
them, helping improve their lot, fighting constantly and tirelessly
to help these poor unfortunate men and women. Then one morning,
at Mass, he spoke to his flock in words of truth they—and the world—
were destined never to forget.

MUCH TO his discomfort and before the interested eyes of his parish-
ioners Damien was formally invested with the insignia of the decora-
tion on the steps of his chapel at Kalawao by Bishop Koeckmann who
placed the gold and scarlet ribbon around the priest's neck and read
aloud the royal decree. Other than that it showed the Princess' favor
Damien had no great interest in the bauble and sought to remove it
as quickly as possible, giving as an excuse that its glitter went ill with
the patches of his faded cassock. The Bishop sternly commanded him
to wear it, but that night the medal was placed back in its box and
there it remained, never to be seen again, until discovered after the
priest's death.

More important to him than any medal was Liliuokalani's gracious
letter. His hopes mounted high as he thought of how governmental
aid to the lepers could be spurred and increased under her patronage.
In his happiness he disclosed many plans to the Bishop. All were of
course connected with the condition of his lepers. He talked enthusi-
astically of the hospitals and orphanages that were to be conducted
on a vast and scientific scale. He painted a picture of a settlement,
indeed almost a principality, that would be under ecclesiastical rule
like the larger monasteries and lazar houses of the Middle Ages. Nuns

would nurse the sick and teach the children. Monks would be trained as physicians and chemists, and other monks would attend to the more menial duties. Excepting for the lepers, there would be no place for laymen in this establishment, the workers would all be volunteers under Church discipline, sworn to remain among the lepers for life, without fear, without family ties and without any hope of earthly reward. Occupations and industries suitable to the strength and ability of the lepers were to be founded and in this haven of the future there was to be a laboratory where scientists and technicians could systematically study and fight the disease.

It was his dream, his ambition. He spoke of it with the fond warmth and enthusiasm that men feel for such visions.

Hope he might, and dream he did, but as the months passed, and then the years, the consciousness slowly came to him that the goodwill of Royalty does not necessarily mean the help of governments. It is true that after the Regent's visit there was an improvement in the Board of Health's attitude towards the colony but to the priest who saw men die—sometimes only because of the conditions—almost every day, the efforts of the authorities seemed pitifully insufficient against the picture of the efficient institution his hopes had painted. The charity of the nuns in Honolulu and his own work seemed of little account, subject as they were to the vagaries of time and circumstance. His heart sank as he studied reports of the disease in India, China, South America and other parts of the world. It was the same depressing story of Hawaii: either the lepers were beggars and outcasts, shunned and loathed, or they were confined in the most primitive of "settlements" to be completely forgotten by their more fortunate fellows.

Humanity in general seemed determined to ignore the existence of lepers. When, because of poverty, the priest was forced to deny a poor wretch the solace of an adequate bandage for his sores, he could not but think of the fine houses and splendid carriages of the officials who were apparently so indifferent to the needs of Molokai and yet who talked so convincingly, so cruelly, of budget limitations.

Dreams vanished and his hope turned to a disillusionment which flavored many of his actions. The pace of his work never slackened. Nor did his consideration for his charges lessen, but in his dealings with those outside the ranks of the lepers he became abruptly harsh in manner, quick to take offense, and quick to quarrel. Always impatient with the ways of officialdom, his wranglings with them now increased in number and vehemence. There were many times when it was he who, undoubtedly, was in the wrong. . . .

This harsher side of him was revealed only to ordinary men, for his ill-temper never touched the lepers. To them he always remained the same, a kind father, sometimes stern perhaps, but always just and understanding and ready to help. No matter how violent his rages or how wrong his quarrels, it must be remembered that they were never motivated by selfishness. Whatever he did, he did for his lepers. Their life was his life; he had made it so since he first put foot on the island.

Then he had been a young man, splendid in health and burning with zeal, to whom no obstacle was too large to overcome. But now, after twelve years on Molokai, he seemed, to the interested eyes of a visiting official, "an embittered old man," undeniably devout and courageous, but soured with disappointment. This was in 1885 when he actually was only forty-five years old.

That same year, on the morning of the first Sunday in June, he was celebrating early Mass in the chapel of Kalawao with his customary fervor, chanting the Latin in his deep, steady voice and showing no other emotion than his usual devotion. In fact during the entire ritual of that morning he did nothing to indicate that the Mass might be different from the many he had celebrated before; the *Introit* was said and the *Gloria* was sung with spirit, genuflections were made with the requisite pomp, and the altar boys concluded that their priest was in the best of humors when, in stumbling over their responses, they received no frown.

It was a hot day. In the sultry, crowded interior, the congregation, all of whom were invalids in varying stages of the disease, probably welcomed the relaxation that comes with the end of the Gospel. Perhaps, even, there were a few that, with a torpor induced by the heat, might have been inclined to drowsiness as the priest, standing before the altar, divested himself of chasuble and maniple in preparation for the sermon. But after he had advanced to the sanctuary rail (he had no pulpit), and began to talk, all signs of lethargy among his listeners quickly vanished. There was a sudden shocked stir, for instead of addressing them with his usual *My brethren*, he said, slowly and significantly, *We lepers* . . .

It was his way of telling them that he had contracted their disease.

Damien the Leper, by John Farrow

"... we were about to pass the rest of our life as orphans."

The simplicity—and the truth—of Socrates' teachings have kept them alive in the minds of men for nearly twenty-five hundred years. When the Delphic oracle said of him that he was the wisest man in Greece, his ironical response was, that if he was wise it was because he recognized his own ignorance while others did not. Socrates never stated a proposition—rather, his method of teaching was to first destroy preconceived notions and then point the way to truth and let the student find his way himself.

That there is no compromise with truth is in itself perfect truth. This was the touchstone of Socrates' life. When he was accused, in 399 B.C., of corrupting the youth of Athens, and "practicing religious novelties," his prosecutors hoped and believed that he would remove himself from the jurisdiction of the court, or at least plead a lesser charge for they were not anxious to put him to death. Socrates refused to flee—or to ask for a lesser sentence. The resolute, quiet and humble way he died has become almost a legend.

Plato was not actually present at the end, but his re-creation of the scene as it was described to him by Crito and others who were with Socrates is one of his greatest pieces of writing.

I WILL BEGIN [says Phaedo] at the beginning. . . . On the previous days we had been in the habit of assembling early in the morning at the court in which the trial took place, and which is not far from the prison. There we used to wait talking with one another until the opening of the doors (for they were not opened very early); then we went in and generally passed the day with Socrates. On the last morning we assembled sooner than usual, having heard on the day before when we quitted the prison in the evening that the sacred ship had come from Delos; and so we arranged to meet very early at the accustomed place. On our arrival the jailer who answered the door, instead of admitting us, came out and told us to stay until he called us. "For the

Eleven," he said, "are now with Socrates; they are taking off his chains, and giving orders that he is to die today." He soon returned and said that we might come in.

On entering we found Socrates just released from chains, and Xanthippe, whom you know, sitting by him and holding his child in her arms. When she saw us she uttered a cry and said, as women will, "O Socrates, this is the last time that either you will converse with your friends, or they with you."

Socrates turned to Crito and said: "Crito, let some one take her home." Some of Crito's people accordingly led her away, crying out and beating herself. And when she was gone . . . he arose and went into a chamber to bathe; Crito followed him, and told us to wait. So we remained behind, talking and thinking . . . he was like a father of whom we were being bereaved, and we were about to pass the rest of our life as orphans. When he had taken his bath his children were brought to him—(he had two young sons and an elder one); and the women of the family also came, and he talked to them and gave them a few directions in the presence of Crito; then he dismissed them and returned to us.

Now the hour of sunset was near, for a good deal of time had passed while he was within. When he came out, he sat down with us again after his bath, but not much was said. Soon the jailer, who was the servant of the Eleven, entered and stood by him, saying:—To you, Socrates, whom I know to be the noblest and gentlest and best of all who ever came to this place, I will not impute the angry feelings of other men, who rage and swear at me, when, in obedience to the authorities, I bid them drink the poison—indeed, I am sure that you will not be angry with me for others, as you are aware, and not I, are to blame. And so fare you well, and try to bear lightly what must needs be—you know my errand. Then bursting into tears he turned away and went out.

Socrates looked at him, and said: I return your good wishes, and will do as you bid. Then turning to us, he said, How charming the man is: since I have been in prison he has always been coming to see me, and at times he would talk to me, and was as good to me as could be, and now see how generously he sorrows on my account. We must do as he says, Crito; and therefore let the cup be brought, if the poison is prepared; if not, let the attendant prepare some.

Yet, said Crito, the sun is still upon the hill-tops, and I know that many a one has taken the draught late, and after the announcement has been made to him, he has eaten and drunk, and enjoyed the society of his beloved; do not hurry—there is time enough.

Socrates said: Yes, Crito, and they of whom you speak are right in so acting, for they think that they will be gainers by the delay; but I am right in not following their example, for I do not think that I should gain anything by drinking the poison a little later; I should only be ridiculous in my own eyes for sparing and saving a life which is already forfeit. Please then to do as I say, and not to refuse me.

Crito made a sign to the servant, who was standing by; and he went out, and having been absent for some time, returned with the jailer carrying the cup of poison. Socrates said: You, my good friend, who are experienced in these matters, shall give me directions how I am to proceed. The man answered: You have only to walk about until your legs are heavy, and then to lie down, and the poison will act. At the same time he handed the cup to Socrates, who in the easiest and gentlest manner, without the least fear or change of colour or feature, looking at the man with all his eyes . . . as his manner was, took the cup and said: What do you say about making a libation out of this cup to any god? May I, or not? The man answered: We only prepare, Socrates, just so much as we deem enough. I understand, he said: but I may and must ask the gods to prosper my journey from this to the other world—even so—and so be it according to my prayer. Then raising the cup to his lips, quite readily and cheerfully he drank off the poison. And hitherto most of us had been able to control our sorrow; but now when we saw him drinking, and saw too that he had finished the draught, we could no longer forbear, and in spite of myself my own tears were flowing fast; so that I covered my face and wept, not for him, but at the thought of my own calamity in having to part from such a friend. Nor was I the first; for Crito, when he found himself unable to restrain his tears, had got up, and I followed; and at that moment, Appollodorus, who had been weeping all the time, broke out in a loud and passionate cry which made cowards of us all.

Socrates alone retained his calmness: What is this strange outcry? he said. I sent away the women mainly in order that they might not misbehave in this way, for I have been told that a man should die in peace. Be quiet then, and have patience.

When we heard his words we were ashamed, and refrained our tears; and he walked about until, as he said, his legs began to fail, and then he lay on his back, according to the directions, and the man who gave him the poison now and then looked at his feet and legs; and after a while he pressed his foot hard, and asked him if he could feel; and he said, No; and then his leg, and so upwards and upwards, and showed us that he was cold and stiff. And he felt them himself, and said: When the poison reaches the heart, that will be the end.

He was beginning to grow cold about the groin, when he uncovered his face, for he had covered himself up, and said—they were his last words—he said: Crito, I owe a cock to Asclepius; will you remember to pay the debt?

The debt shall be paid, said Crito; is there anything else? There was no answer to this question; but in a minute or two a movement was heard, and the attendants uncovered him; his eyes were set, and Crito closed his eyes and mouth.

Such was the end of our friend . . . concerning whom I may truly say, that of all the men of his time whom I have known, he was the wisest and justest and best.

The Four Socratic Dialogues of Plato, translated by Benjamin Jowett

JOAN OF ARC

"... a vision so exalted ..."

J oan of Arc was a product—and a victim of her times. The end of the Middle Ages was an era of constant civil war and factional fighting—a time when western Europe was emerging from a thousand years of sleep, when nations were once again beginning to rise out of a chaos. It was a cruel time—and brutal; a time when the devil still roamed the earth in human form and witches whispered with their evil spirits.

The daughter of a peasant, Joan first heard her voices when she was thirteen years old—Saint Michael and Saint Catherine and Saint Margaret. Their message was simple—she had been chosen to lead the French to victory over the English and to crown the rightful king of France . . . and all this came to be. Fired by her zeal, the army lifted the siege at Orléans and marched victoriously on to Reims, where the dauphin was crowned as Charles VII. It was the beginning of the end of English rule in France. But it was also the end for the Maid—her comet had been burned out. Captured by the English, she was tried by the Church and condemned to burn. Joan the Maid of Orléans was just nineteen years old.

There is no sadder—and no more inspiring story than that of Joan's recantation—and then of her return to her truths.

JOAN KNEW the day of her trial had come when Father Jean Massieu, a young priest attached to the Rouen cathedral and for the present clerk to the prosecutor Jean d'Estivet, read her the bishop's order citing her "to appear before us on Wednesday, the 21st of February, at eight o'clock in the morning, in the chapel royal of the Castle, to answer to a questioning . . . under pain of excommunication. . . ."

And so, in the early morning of the 21st of February, 1431, Joan of Arc, held under grave suspicion of offending Holy Mother Church, stepped into the light of day for the first time in nearly three months, to take part in the second act, the *processus ordinarius* of the Inquisitorial drama.

A little before eight o'clock, Father Massieu came to conduct her from the prison to the court, his special duty while the trial lasted. Did he seek to help Joan when, walking without irons after so long, she took like a child the eight steps that led down from her cell? Perhaps that first day, in his fear of witchcraft, Father Massieu may have had qualms about reaching the royal chapel without mishap, knowing how wily the Devil could be in looking after his own. Joan, however, walked meekly beside him, guarded by three of her jailers. When they entered the chapel none of the mischief happened which is said to occur when an evil thing sets foot in a holy place.

In that atmosphere of incense and burning tapers the court made an impressive sight. Silent and stern, the examiners, luminaries from the faculties of theology and law, doctors of medicine, archbishops, bishops, abbots, canons and promising sprigs of the holy vine, sat in the posts suited to their degree. Vermeil and vair marked the high dignitaries, dark gowns and furred bonnets the scholars. Awesome in his official robes, one of which, the seamless garment, signified charity, Pierre Cauchon presided that day as sole judge, an honor which Jean Lemaistre would gladly have resigned to him for the duration of the trial.

Pierre Cauchon could not have been too well pleased with the attendance. Forty-two judges—they too were given that title by courtesy —out of a panel of more than one hundred and fifty. Enough were present, however, for the business of the day. For the rest, a fine for truancy would call them to duty.

Joan was led to a chair. The trial opened. The battle lines were arrayed. On one side the shrewdest intellects of the time, backed by English power and English money. On the other, an illiterate girl of nineteen, alone. On one side, men who believed in witchcraft and persecuted it as a crime dangerous to man and especially hateful to God. On the other, a visionary girl, burning with the faith that she had been sent by the King of Heaven for the good of France. On one side, men for the most part vowed to chastity, who looked upon woman as a sinful lure and could therefore feel nothing but loathing for a member of the sex who dressed in defiance of divine commandment. On the other, a small pathetic figure in the once-handsome garments of her mission—all that remained to Joan of those happy days.

The judges looked at the accused. The accused looked at the judges. To her they were all churchmen, and she had never been at ease with churchmen. At Poitiers she had convinced her examiners. Would she convince these? What did their faces tell her? Did she read a glacial scholarship in Thomas de Courcelles, the shining light of the University of Paris? And in his confrère, Nicolas Midi, fiery orator and canon of Rouen? What premonition had she from Guillaume Erard, doctor of theology and persuasive fisherman of souls? What from Jean Beaupère, and from the prosecutor Estivet? None at all. For Joan, plain Joan distinguished from the Maid, was so incredibly simple in her trusting innocence that she never detected even in the sly Loiseleur the sympathetic priest from Lorraine, nor in Jean d'Estivet another pious captive who, on the pretext of bringing her good advice, also found his way to her cell in convenient monkish disguise, according to the precepts of the trusty handbook.

The bishop spoke. He told of how Joan had been captured; then, turning toward her, he warned her to tell the truth on the questions that would be put to her. He called for the Book, the holy Book of the Evangel, for her to take the oath. Joan shook her head. How could she swear when there were things about which she could not speak? ("Answer boldly," her Voices had said.) "I cannot take the oath," she replied to the bishop.

Pierre Cauchon turned as purple as his robe. The judges murmured. "I do not know what you will question me about," she explained. "You may ask me things that I must not tell you."

Never before had such a thing happened. Pierre Cauchon expostulated with the girl. "You are asked only to tell the truth about matters of religion and other things that you know."

"I'll willingly swear concerning my father and mother, and whatever I've done since coming into France," she said. "As for my revelations from God, I've never disclosed them to anyone but Charles, my king, and I am not going to reveal them here, either—not even if you were to cut off my head. . . . Eight days from now I'll know whether I can tell you about them," she added, using for the first time the naïve dodge to which she resorted whenever she wished to gain time or to put off the questioner.

With admirable patience Pierre Cauchon endeavored to break down the girl's will. The minutes passed. The examiners fretted, impatient for their part in that contest. In the end Cauchon had to administer the oath on Joan's terms. Kneeling down, and laying both hands upon the Book, she swore to answer truly on all matters, excluding her revelations.

The questions now flew thick and fast.

"Your name and surname?"

"In my village they called me Little-Joan, in France, Joan. As for my surname—I know nothing about that." A surname? What was a surname?

"The names of your father and mother?"

"My father is called Jacques d'Arc and my mother Isabelle."

The examiners exchanged glances and smiles. The ignorant village girl did have a surname, after all.

"How old are you?"

"Nineteen, I think, or thereabout."

"Who taught you? Where did you learn your faith?"

"My mother taught me the *Pater Noster* and *Ave Maria* and the *Credo*. No one else taught me my faith—only my mother."

"Recite your *Pater Noster*, then."

"Gladly, if you will hear me in confession."

"Recite your *Pater Noster*. I command you."

"I will not say it unless you hear me in confession."

"Will you say it before two of these worthy doctors who speak the French tongue?"

Joan rejected that suggestion also.

It is difficult to know why so much was made of a recital of the *Pater Noster*. Joan may have persisted in her refusal in order to be allowed to go to confession. Also, she had too much respect for the sacred words to rattle them off for the curiosity of the examiners. They, for their part, may have sought to find out by that test not only whether Joan had received Catholic instruction, but also whether she was a sorceress. It was well known that no witch could recite the prayer without stumbling.

Much time was spent in arguing on that and other questions. The examiners began to wilt. Cauchon, so far, had had to make all the concessions in that unequal duel.

Before adjourning for the day, the bishop had . . . still to complete the ritual of authority. Summoning the three English guards, he swore them on the Book never to relax their vigilance or to permit the prisoner to see anyone without his leave. Ironically, one of the jailers bore the name of that same Talbot whom the French might have exchanged for Joan and did not.

Back in her cell Joan had the irons reclamped upon her wrists and ankles and was guarded more rigorously, if possible, than before. Here was a spirit the court had not counted on, an integrity and courage baffling to those scholastic minds whose icy logic had in itself the sterility of death. The following day, therefore, when the court reconvened, Joan had to meet the questioning of one of the subtlest brains of the University. The *salle d'honneur*, a reception room near the great hall of the castle, was now the place of meeting to accommodate the larger assemblage. Cauchon again presided, but it was Jean Beaupère who took up the examination.

As doctor of theology, Beaupère could split hairs with the best and count to the least wing feather the number of angels that could dance on the point of a pin. A fanatical servant of Mother Church, he was a very hammer of God in her service, seeking out and pitilessly crushing her offenders. The loss of his right hand limited his use of the effective gesture, but what he lacked in manner he supplied by the insidiousness of his method. . . .

Switching subtly to what apparently had no connection with Joan's admitted revelation, he questioned her about her childhood, her observance of the faith, the customs of Domremy, the Ladies' Tree, the healing fountain. With the simplicity that was so much part of the girl Joan, she gave him the naïve poetry of her native village, too innocent to know that with every mention of fairies and May-branches she was playing into Beaupère's hands. Only when he insisted on prying into matters that did not concern the trial would she bid him unceremoniously to "Pass on to something else." However, it was what Joan would have left out of the trial that the court wanted most to know.

Beaupère made the opening wedge into the heart of her mystery. He asked her bluntly when she had first had her visions.

Amazingly, she told him. As if the ecstasy of that first experience in her father's garden were again upon her, she spoke with a beauty she had never before commanded. She told of her vow, of Saint Michael and his escort of angels. "I saw them with the eyes of my body as clearly as I see you." She told of Saint Catherine and Saint Margaret. She described the rich crowns upon their heads, and their soft, sweet voices. She repeated their words. "I know that if I were in a wood, I should hear those Voices coming to me. . . . The name they often gave me was Joan the Maid, Child of God."

"What was the shape in which the Voice appeared?" Beaupère broke in.

"You won't get that from me now."

But she replied freely on many other matters, with every word involving herself more and more in the net Beaupère so cunningly spread about her. At his success, the other examiners began hurling questions, hardly waiting for Joan to finish answering one before assailing her with another. They saw her growing exhaustion but they had no pity. They knew that she was fasting in observance of Lent, but they kept her there for hours, in no hurry to interrupt such a profitable interrogatory. . . .

Joan's examination lasted through the 3rd of March, but the court uncovered little that had not been brought out earlier. It was as if by their insistence on statement and restatement, by their flying from one subject to another, they hoped to catch her in contradictions and undermine the strength of her defense. Over and over they posed the same questions as if for the first time, about her Voices, their appearance, the sign to the king, the superstitions of her village, her clothes, her help to the kingdom of France, and always she answered openly on all that pertained to the trial. Often she referred the court to "the book of Poitiers," the records of that earlier examination which had mysteriously disappeared.

Joan's moral strength, instead of discouraging her judges, acted as a challenge. If she was the oak, they would be the moles gnawing at the roots. She was one; they were many. So, with the blind patience of their bigotry, they returned again and again to their destructive work.

Q. "Which of the Voices appeared to you first?"

A. "I could not tell the difference as quickly as that. I knew once, but I have forgotten. . . . I had great comfort from Saint Michael."

Q. "How long ago did you first perceive the Voice of Saint Michael?"

A. "I did not say 'the Voice of Saint Michael.' I told you of great comfort."

Q. "Did God command you to put on men's clothes?"

A. "My clothes are a small matter, one of the very least. I did not put them on by any man's advice. . . . All I have done I did at God's bidding. Had He ordered me to put on other dress, I would have done so."

Q. "Was there any light when the Voice came to you?"

A. "There was light, as there should be. All light is not shed on you alone."

Q. "The first time you saw your king was there an angel above his head?"

A. "By Our Lady, if there was, I know nothing about it! I did not see it."

Q. "What were the revelations to your king?"

A. "You won't get that from me, now or this year."

Q. "Have your saints any hair?"

A. "That would be worth knowing!"

Q. "Is their hair long and flowing?"

A. "I don't know. And I don't know whether they have arms or other members. They spoke well and I understood them well."

Q. "How could they speak if they had no members?"

A. "I refer that to God. They speak the French tongue."

Q. "Does not Saint Margaret speak English?"

A. "Why should she, since she is not of the English party?"

Q. "In what shape did Saint Michael appear to you?"

A. "I did not see any crown. I know nothing about his garments."

Q. "Was he naked?"

A. "Do you think God has nothing with which to clothe him? . . . I feel great joy when I see him. Then I think I am not in mortal sin."

Q. "When you confess do you believe you are in mortal sin?"

A. "I don't know. . . . I do not believe I have done the deeds of mortal sin. . . . Please God I shall never do anything that would so burden my soul!"

Q. "What sign did you give your king?"

A. "You'll never have that from my lips. Go and ask him."

Q. "Have your Voices forbidden you to tell the truth?"

A. "Would you have me tell you what concerns the King of France? There are many things that do not belong to this trial. But I know that my king will win the kingdom of France. I know it as well as I know that you are here to judge me."

Q. "What promises have your Voices made you?"

A. "They promised that my king would have his kingdom, whether his enemies wished it or not, and that they would lead me to paradise, as I begged them to do."

Q. "Did they make you no other promise?"

A. "They made me another—which I will tell you three months from now."

Q. "Did they tell you that you would be released within three months?"

A. "That does not concern your case. I don't know when I shall be freed, but those who would put me out of this world may well leave it before me."

Q. "Do you know by revelation that you will escape from prison?"

A. "Would you have me give evidence against myself?"

Q. "Have your Voices told you anything about it?"

A. "They have indeed! They said I shall be freed, but I know neither the day nor the hour. And they have told me to be brave and put on a cheerful face. If not for the revelation that comforts me each day I would have died."

Q. "Have you any rings?"

A. (To Cauchon) "You have one that belongs to me. Give it back to me."

Q. "What have you done with your mandragora?"

A. "I have none and never had. . . . I know it is an evil thing. . . . It is said to bring money but I place no stock in such things at all."

Q. "Do the people of your party really believe that you are sent from God?"

A. "I do not know if they believe it. I leave that to their own hearts. But even if they do not believe it, I am still sent from God."

Q. "Do you think that in believing you are sent from God they believe rightly?"

A. "If they believe that I am sent from God they are not deceived."

Q. "Did you know what they believed when they kissed your hands and feet and your garments?"

A. "Many came because they wanted to see me, but they kissed my garments only when I could not help it. The poor came to me . . . because I did what I could for them."

By the end of the interrogatory the three notaries had amassed a quantity of material which Pierre Cauchon and his committee proposed to cast into a formal indictment.

For nearly a week the bishop and his committee pored over the evidence only to find themselves strangely embarrassed. They had hoped to prepare for the tribunal a neat statement of Joan's offenses, but the more they studied the minutes, the weaker their charges became. Although Joan's answers showed her to be far from innocent, they were still a long way from demonstrating her guilt, especially before the assessors who, although for the most part prejudiced against her in the beginning, had lately been showing signs of wanting the trial to be fair as well as notable. Those signs came timidly and from a minority so small that it appeared no bigger than a speck of doubt on the clear horizon of general certitude. But such a speck could easily grow into a storm cloud and that Pierre Cauchon could not risk. As it was, some of the favorable comments reached the ears of the English, who angrily reproved the bishop for not conducting the trial better.

Cauchon knew he must use more effective methods, both to appease his masters and to convince the doubters of Joan's guilt. Accordingly he proposed further questioning of the accused. However, he did not wish to inconvenience the whole tribunal, he said. Therefore, to gather this additional evidence, he appointed a small body of examiners to assist him. Also, he called off the open meetings for a while, as he intended to question Joan in prison.

From the 10th of March to the 18th, once, and often twice, a day, Cauchon went with his select committee to Joan's cell. Now Joan had not even the solace of her walk to the judgment hall. The spring was coming and with it the season of Christ's resurrection. Yet to her in her cell it might have been enduring winter and endless night, but for the tongues of the church bells that called off the hours for prayer. If, so far, she had cherished the hope that she could convince her judges of her innocence, as she had convinced the clergy at Poitiers, her king, and many other skeptics on matters even more difficult to believe, she was to realize by the end of the inquiry that she stood in peril of her life.

Time after time, in the same deliberate disorder, the apparently irrelevant questions were flung at her, as the examiners tried to make her admit that because of her capture she had been betrayed by her Voices, which therefore could not have come from God. Not a session passed without allusion to her clothes and her wickedness. Day after day they pursued the subject of the sign to the king and the angel who had brought it. With miraculous fortitude she retained her presence of mind under that deadly inquest. But even Joan, child of God, sometimes lost her temper, so that when the examiner plagued her with such a question as "Did you show reverence to the sign?" she retorted, "Yes, I went down on my knees many times and I also thanked the Lord for freeing me from the vexing arguments of the clergy." . . .

The question that followed was not prompted by real or assumed stupidity.

"Why should the angel have come to you?"

"Because," said Joan, "it pleased the Lord to defeat the king's enemies through a simple maid."

Her reply suggested an inquiry into the source of her victories. Indubitably many of the examiners believed that extraordinary powers had been behind her. Perhaps among them a few were willing to be convinced that those powers came from God. For the purpose of Cauchon's inquiry, however, God had to be kept entirely out of it. But the bishop was reckoning without Joan. Whenever the examiner tried to impute magic to her banner, or to her presence in battle Joan replied with such angelic candor that even the University men were confounded. And always she maintained, "The victory was all the Lord's."

If the sorcery did not reside in her sword, her armor, or her banner, it must be in Joan herself. Boldly, even for such a trial, the examiner initiated another group of questions.

"When you vowed to God to remain a virgin, was it to Him you spoke?"

"It should be enough to promise to those sent by God—Saint Catherine and Saint Margaret."

"Did you know by revelation that if you lost your virginity you would lose your luck?"

"I have had no revelation about that," she said.

"Do you believe your Voices would come to you if you were married?"

"I do not know. I refer that to God."

An embarrassed modesty kept her from saying more, just as it in-

variably sealed her lips on the very real necessity for her clinging to
her male garments. As the trial progressed her obduracy in that respect
so magnified her offense, that one might have thought her clothes were
the reason for her being where she was. What at first had been a matter
of expediency now became a matter of principle, and Joan defended
that principle with the same courageous loyalty that she showed
Messire and her saints. Her clothes were part of her task; by relinquish-
ing them she offended God at Whose command she had put them
on. . . .

For a while the court left her in peace while Estivet, the prosecutor,
drew up the articles of accusation. He must have been hard put to it
to convert Joan's answers into a convincing indictment, although even
the most fair-minded assessors could not but have been influenced by
her insubordination and her attitude toward Mother Church.

Nevertheless Estivet succeeded in producing against her an imposing
document of some seventy counts, charging heresy, sorcery, idolatry
and other crimes from her earliest years. All the charges derived from
her own words except one, in which the testimony of her jealous rival,
Catherine de la Rochelle, accused her of magic by declaring Joan had
employed the services of two Counselors of the Fountain and was on
familiar terms with the Devil. As for Joan's help to her king, Catherine
cited her as saying that she had been sent by God "for violence and
the effusion of blood."

The indictment sounded more than satisfactory to Cauchon and
his supporters. Still, he saw the danger of making too foolproof a case.
If his clique understood that Joan, guilty or innocent, must die, there
were still some who believed in the fairness of his fine trial. Therefore,
as he dragged his victim nearer and nearer to the place of judgment,
he increased his precautions in the conduct of the case, so that not
even Joan's partisans—he suspected three or four—could say he had
not given her every chance to save herself. . . .

It was already a month since the publication of the articles and Joan
remained unconvicted. The temper of the English was rising. Twice
the woman had almost been snatched out of their justice by sickness,
yet the court persevered in its inexcusable delay. The third time
she might escape them altogether. They fretted and stormed—and
threatened.

The bishop, for his part, was no less concerned. Had the English
merely wanted Joan killed, he could have burned her with as little
ceremony as Paris in burning Pieronne half a year ago. But Joan was
no simple visionary like the poor Breton peasant. She had put her
visions to work, and to such purpose that the whole world had heard
about them. For the trial to have any effect the whole world must

hear equally of her repentance or, more accurately, her denial of the divinity of her visions. . . .

The main object of that trial would still have to be attained. Although Loiseleur had been invaluable in his role of loyal and adroit softener of heretical hearts, Cauchon had failed to obtain from Joan any public confession. An approved method, however, remained, guaranteed not only to soften the heart but to crush body and soul as well, when that soul did not take its premature departure to a better world under the method's persuasiveness. Accordingly, on the 9th of May, Joan was brought to the torture chamber of the Great Tower where Cauchon awaited her with a small but chosen public for the third charitable warning. None could say that he had overlooked any legitimate means to save that hardened soul.

Joan saw the rack, the pincers for tearing the flesh from the living frame, the cords of the strappado and, beside them, the executioners, ready to apply the persuasion of their specialty. Cauchon, always thorough, made certain that Joan missed none of the horror. As he exhorted her to make a clean breast of those truths which she had withheld from the questioning, he pointed to the instruments that would else wring them out of her.

If Joan's body cowered before those terrors, her spirit held firm. "In truth, if you were to have me torn limb from limb, if you were to drive my soul out of my body, I would tell you nothing I have not already told you," she said. "And if I did, I would always say later that you had made me say it by force."

The executioner, Leparmentier, admired the girl's courage and marked the amazement of the judges as she defended her stand.

"I have asked my Voices whether I should submit to the Church, since the judges were urging me to do so. And they told me that if I wished God's help, I must lay all my actions before Him. . . . I also asked the Voices if I would burn," she added, betraying the dread that haunted her. "They told me to put myself in the Lord's hands and He would help me."

For that day Joan escaped the torture but not the anxiety that at any moment she might be taken before those men whose sunken eyes behind their masks already prefigured the hollow sockets of death. What cruel anguish for the girl whose strong young body had survived chains and sickness, the brutality of her jailers and the want of the sunlight and air that had nurtured her, to live in the apprehension of having that body torn like a fly's in the hands of wanton boys.

Indeed, for three days torture was more than a possibility, as Cauchon deliberated whether in Joan's present state of defiance it would do any good. When he put the matter to a vote before the

Vice-Inquisitor and thirteen members of the tribunal, they voted eleven against, and three for it. The triumvirate who wished at such cost to save the heretic consisted of Aubert Morel, a lawyer, the brilliant Thomas de Courcelles, and Loiseleur, who recommended it "for the cure of her soul."

At last, to Cauchon's relief, the delegates returned from Paris with the verdict of the University. It was no simple opinion that they brought, but an immoderate document. In it the University affirmed, supported by theology and canon law, that if Joan did not lie about her visions she was surely seduced by Belial, Satan and Behemoth. It found, moreover, that the twelve articles proved her to be bloodthirsty, cruel, seditious, blasphemous, apostate, schismatic and heretical. The findings were in themselves damning enough. The last two spelled doom, as they would have done, not only for Joan, but for anyone found guilty on either count.

Legally the verdict was unimpeachable. Since the Inquisition held heresy to be a religious error maintained in willful defiance of the truth after it had been defined and declared by the Church in an authoritative manner, Joan surely was chargeable. As for schism, understood in such a case as a breach of discipline in opposition to Catholic government, that crime too she had committed, and still committed, with every affirmation of her private judgment against the authority of the Church as incorporated in its court.

Since 1232, when Pope Gregory IX had founded the Inquisition, entrusting it to the Dominicans, those "hounds of God" had subjected to the most cruel tortures all they suspected of heresy and schism. The guilty out of regard for the Church's abhorrence to shedding blood, they handed over to the civil authorities which, having no such sensitiveness, carried out the execution, though generally in a manner that did not cause the blood to flow. It comes as something of a shock, nonetheless, that the boldest supporter Joan had in court, the Dominican Isambard de la Pierre, even while he recognized the passions and ambitions that motivated her trial, maintained to the end that the judgment was legally justified, since Cauchon had respected throughout the letter of the law. . . .

Even if Joan had not been formally summoned, she would have known by her many visitors that she was about to meet her gravest test. Not once had she faltered or compromised through fear of pain or death, or denied her visions and her king. In the face of every kind of trial she had kept faith with her conscience, trusting to the promises of her Voices and nurturing the hope of final deliverance. On the eve of her sentence, perhaps of her execution, she saw herself still in chains, in the prison of the English, at the mercy of her enemies. Even then she did not falter. . . .

Meanwhile, in a clearing of the cemetery of Saint-Ouen, adjoining the abbey church, two platforms had risen overnight in the provident manner of the times, which kept such structures at hand for mysteries as for executions. It was still dark when the crowds began milling about the place, drawn by the clatter of hammers that always announced some extraordinary event. Soon the whole city knew that Joan the Pucelle was to be sentenced that day. Many English soldiers mingled with the populace. They were tense and watchful and fully armed.

The larger of the stages could scarcely hold its load of judges and dignitaries. Beside Cauchon in his cope and heavy robes sown with carbuncles, his miter upon his head and in his hand the crosier from which fluttered the green maniple, stood the Vice-Inquisitor in his white gown and black mantle. About them, members of the tribunal, the Cardinal-Bishop of Winchester, Louis of Luxembourg, Bishop of Thérouanne, the Bishop of Norwich and the French Bishop of Noyon, stood rigid as metal statues in their stiff capes of gold. A boding shadow, the Earl of Warwick surrounded by his officers, loomed behind Pierre Cauchon.

A cart divided the crowd. Joan and Father Massieu stepped out of it and mounted the second stage where Guillaume Erard, doctor of theology, waited, to deliver the prescribed sermon. With him were his scribes and apparitors.

If Joan had not noticed him when she arrived, so small and shabby in the clothes she had not relinquished, she saw him now at the foot of the platform—Thirache, the executioner, standing beside his cart, ready at a word to take her where the pyre was waiting. Beyond, she could see the tombs, the funeral cypresses, the ranks of faces. What a dread spectacle to terrify one young girl! . . .

Amid the clamor Guillaume Erard took out a paper and read from it words in which Joan was made to declare that she was "a wretched miscreant, long enmeshed in sin but now returned to Holy Mother Church; that she had lied about her visions; transgressed the commandments of the Holy Scriptures; that she had violated decency in her dress; that she had borne arms and caused cruel bloodshed; that she had maintained against all truth to have done these deeds at God's behest; that she had been seditious, idolatrous and schismatic, but that thanks to Almighty God she had returned to the way of truth. Now she abjured and renounced all such wickedness and swore by Almighty God and His holy Gospels never in any way to relapse into her former sins."

It is doubtful if, in that confusion, Joan heard what the preacher read, or understood it if she heard. But now Erard was addressing her again. "Joan, abjure these things for which you stand condemned. Submit to our Holy Mother Church, Abjure—"

"Abjure! Abjure!" the priests took up the cry. "Abjure!" pleaded the judges, several coming over to her from the other stage to sway her by their presence. "Abjure!" the crowd joined in. Many, however, shouted insults. The soldiers rattled their arms. That was not the end they had been led to expect.

Joan looked wildly about her, at the terrifying mob, at the executioner whom the priests pointed out to her—as if she had not seen him.

"What does it mean—abjure?" she asked.

"Tell her," Erard commanded Massieu.

The good priest explained that if Joan contradicted any of the articles read to her she would die. "Say that you will refer to the Church Universal whether you should abjure or not," he prompted her.

Joan repeated his counsel.

"You will abjure now—or burn!" said Erard.

The terrible word was out. Its glare dimmed the light of her Voices. Other voices, of the priests, the clerks, the judges, again took up the chant. "Abjure! Abjure! Abjure or you will burn!" The crowd pushed against the stages. "Read your sentence!" someone shouted angrily to the bishop. "To the fire with her!" A few murmured that Joan was being coerced to sign.

Still she did nothing. "You take great pains to seduce me," she said finally with a weary smile.

In the tumult the bishop rose and began to read the sentence which would have concluded with the dread words, "that she be turned over to the secular arm, with the prayer that it deal mercifully with her." But Cauchon did not read the sentence through. Joan made a motion, murmured something. She spoke again. One heard her say, "I will do what you will have me do." Another heard, "I would rather sign than burn."

At this an English prelate shouted to Cauchon, "You are favoring her!"

"You lie!" the bishop shouted back, throwing his papers to the ground in anger.

They were gathered up and somehow the abjuration was thrust before Joan. She traced a sign which, evidently, was not satisfactory, since it was a circle, signifying—nothing. Someone held her hand and she was made to trace the suitable mark. . . .

Joan returned to the prison alive but the Maid, the brave defender

of her soul's integrity, was no more. Joan had killed her by her abjuration, which simultaneously converted all her deeds to works of sorcery
and branded Charles VII as her deluded fool. Neither the English
with their daggers nor Thirache with his pyre could have destroyed
her as completely as she destroyed herself. The Pucelle had ceased to
exist on the platform of the Saint-Ouen cemetery. Now, by a scholasti-
cal technicality, only the Armagnac witch survived, paradoxically released of excommunication and under tolerance of the Church. . . .

When Joan was led back to her cell from Saint-Ouen, the irons were
immediately clamped round her ankles, the chain was padlocked to
the post, while the guards, incensed like the rest of their countrymen
by the sentence, lost no time in venting their spite against the Armagnac Pucelle. So far nothing was changed for Joan by her abjuration.

Later in the afternoon the Vice-Inquisitor with Isambard de la
Pierre, Nicolas Midi, Courcelles and Loiseleur, came to bring her the
good will of Mother Church, who rejoiced in the return of one lamb
to her bosom. Lemaistre and Isambard spoke sincerely. Courcelles performed a duty. Midi and Loiseleur served Cauchon.

With them came a barber and a tailor, the one to crop Joan's hair
to obliterate the sinfulness of her mannish cut while inspiring her with
salutary humiliation, the other to bring her a dress. In everything she
let them do as they wished in a heartbreaking submissiveness. One
wonders what privacy the young girl had in that crowded cell. Where
did she shed her tunic and hose to put on the garment of her repentance? Her jailers were surely present. The men of the church perforce
had to assist to make sure that she fulfilled this, the major outward
condition of her abjuration. . . .

It was only when Joan found herself once more alone, in the shame
of her shorn hair and the dress that could not but remind her of her
cowardice, that she understood the full meaning of what she had done
that morning. In the hysteria, the terror, the threats and prayers, the
hubbub of the mob, she had signed the paper, in a moment of panic
weakness, thinking only to escape the fire. But her visitors, by coming
to congratulate her, had opened her eyes to the depths of her betrayal; for if, in the stress of the morning, she had not heard what
things she had abjured she knew now. By admitting that what she had
done was not well done, she had betrayed her Voices and denied her
mission. She had but to look about her to know that she too had been
betrayed. Why had she been ordered back to this prison, to these
guards? What had they done with the clothes they had taken from her?
What would they do to her now that she had denied her Voices?
Would her saints ever come to her again? How could she live without

their aid and counsel? What would she do, now that she most needed them?

Alone, worse than alone, she knew no peace of any kind. She suffered in mind the torments of remorse, and in body the outrages of her keepers whom her dress incited. Would her saints still watch over her? She had kept her body pure. Would they help her to keep it so?

In the records the deposition of one Jean Marcel tells of how the Rouen tailor who was helping Joan to try on the dress "subtly took her by the breasts, whereupon she was very indignant and slapped [his] face." If an honest tailor could subject her to such treatment, even among witnesses, how much more must Joan have had to fear from the men who had her entirely at their mercy day and night. And not only from them, if one may believe another witness, unimpeachable both for his office and for his source—Friar Martin Ladvenu, who heard Joan's last confession. It may be the good friar, who testified at Joan's rehabilitation, seventeen years later, wished out of sympathy for her martyrdom to show how much she had suffered at the hands of her enemies. Perhaps also he may have interpreted in its extreme sense Joan's account of the indignities which she had confided to him, a pious man and her confessor. His testimony is clear. "He depones that the innocent Maid revealed to him that after her abjuration and recantation they had violently tormented, molested, beaten and outraged her in prison, and that an English lord had violated her." Joan, however, on the morning of her death, cried out words which might be taken to mean that she went to the pyre as she had lived, a virgin. . . .

However it was, three days after the scene at Saint-Ouen, Cauchon heard that Joan had relapsed and could be seen again in her tunic and breeches. . . . What Cauchon had heard, indeed, what he had been hourly expecting, was true. Joan had resumed her male garments. Provocation, certainly, had not been wanting, but the true reason was as pathetic as it was terrible. She had been tricked into wearing them again by her guards, who could have done what they did only in the certainty of accomplishing what was pleasing to their masters.

Father Massieu gives the account. "Then, as she had been ordered, she put off her men's clothes and put on a dress, and her clothes were thrust away into a sack in the same room where she was prisoner. . . . At night when she slept, she was chained by the legs, by two pairs of irons, locked very fast to the post . . . so that she could not move. And when on the morning of Trinity Sunday she was about to rise (as she told me) she said to the Englishmen, her jailers, 'Unchain me so that I may get up.' Then one of them took away the dress she had on, and the others emptied the sack where they kept the men's clothes. And these garments they gave to her, saying 'Get up.' And she said to them, 'You know that it is forbidden me to wear them. I cannot put them on without falling into fault.' Yet they would not give her any other dress, so they went on arguing back and forth till the hour of midday. At length, for a bodily necessity, she was compelled to go out and so to put on those clothes, and when she came back they would give her none other, in spite of her pleading and prayers."

Then it was that the whole bitter anguish of her condition overwhelmed her. They had all forsaken her—the priests, the assessors, the good monks who had tried to help her. No one had given her the blessed sacrament although she was freed of the peril of excommunication. She was alone, alone and lost. She had done a cowardly and terrible thing, and this was her punishment. . . . Her remorse would not let her rest. She must speak or die. And she spoke to her jailers. They scarcely understood all she poured forth of her guilt and contrition, but they knew enough to report to Cauchon that she had returned to her former state.

On Monday, May 28 . . . Cauchon, and part of the court, gained admittance to Joan's cell. The bishop did not come to bring the sacrament; he had no comfort to give her. He brought the sorrowful displeasure of Mother Church, who nevertheless must be convinced that Joan had indeed relapsed before visiting upon her a condign punishment. The visitors found the poor girl so tortured and disfigured by her agony that they hardly knew her. Who would have believed that this crumpled bundle of rags from which a tear-grimed face looked up with accusing eyes had once been the leader of sixteen thousand soldiers and the wonder of the world!

If Lemaistre and Isambard felt compassion for the suffering of a fellow creature, Cauchon allowed no such emotion to interfere with his duty of establishing the fact of Joan's relapse. It was obvious enough, considering the clothes she was wearing. Nevertheless Cauchon had to ask the necessary questions for the documentation. . . . He pointed out that she had confessed to lying concerning her saints, that she had even made her mark on the paper of the abjuration.

"Whatever I said, I said through fear of fire," she repeated. "I have never done anything contrary to God and the Christian faith. . . . I would rather do penance once, with my life, than go on suffering in prison."

Cauchon left her. Outside, he turned to Warwick and the English who were there waiting and said in a loud voice, laughing: "Farewell! Farewell! Be of good cheer. The deed is done."

Indeed, it needed only the authoritative voice of the tribunal for him to declare Joan a relapsed heretic and let secular justice proceed from there. It had been a long trial. But to all things must come an end—and a reward.

The following day the court convened for the last time. Only about forty of the judges appeared, a sufficient number, however, for the business of the day. After Cauchon read them the minutes of the previous interview, a few still showed reluctance to utter the words from which there could be no redress. But before the close of the session they pronounced Joan a relapsed heretic, the unforgivable crime in the eyes of the Inquisition. They then instructed Father Massieu to call for her the following morning, before eight o'clock. This time he was to lead her to the place of execution. . . .

Joan prepared herself for death. More than two months since, she had foreseen what her end would be, and begged her judges that if she must go to her execution they give her a woman's smock and a kerchief for her head. The smock had been provided, a black robe of coarse stuff, the long penitential garment of those whom the Inquisition condemned. Instead of a kerchief there was a miter ready, the mocking crown of the outcast, painted with the words "Heretic, relapsed, apostate, idolater." . . .

It was time to leave the place of her greatest spiritual anguish to go where she would know the most cruel suffering of the body before release into the peace of death. She was resigned. Between Friar Ladvenu and Father Massieu she walked from the prison to the waiting cart, whose four horses knew their way blindfold to the Vieux Marché, the market place of Rouen, the heart and grave of that unhappy city. Isambard de la Pierre joined her to comfort her in her last hour.

A hundred soldiers with swords and battle axes surrounded the cart, while more than eight hundred men-at-arms mingled with the crowd. There was a momentary commotion when, through the bulwark of soldiers, through the surging mob, a man pushed his way to the cart, crying aloud for Joan to forgive him in the name of God. The English rushed at him and would have killed him had not Warwick recognized Loiseleur, too late repented of his dark transactions. The earl delivered him from the soldiers' fury and spirited him out of the city for a few days.

The cart lumbered into the market square. If the spectacle of Saint-Ouen had been calculated to chasten the soul by its silent reminders of mortality, the three platforms in the Vieux Marché gave to the scene the awfulness of a living mystery where nothing was simulated, not even death.

Two of the stages, hung with sumptuous cloths, were already oc-

cupied, one by Cauchon and his court, the other by honored specta-
tors, English nobles, visitors of note. The third was deserted and bare
but for a plaster stake the height of a girl and an untidy rooks' nest of
faggots beneath it. Nearby stood Thirache, the executioner, in his
frightening red suit. When Joan saw the dread preparations she burst
into tears.

On the stage that faced the church of Saint Sauveur, Nicolas Midi
stood ready to deliver the sermon, on the text, "If one member suffer,
all the members suffer with it." Joan was led to the judges' platform,
and sat in silence while Midi pronounced the justification in a ringing
voice for all to hear. The crowd stared at Joan's robe, at the miter on
her shaven head, and turned from her to the empty scaffold.

When Midi had done speaking Joan fell upon her knees. Even her
bitterest enemies, even the Cardinal-Bishop of Winchester and her
judges wept with her as she prayed, now crying out in horror of
her dreadful fate, and now so resigned that no one knew which was
more pitiful, her young girl's natural terror of death or her contrition.

The preliminaries of the promised show seemed unduly prolonged
to the multitude and the people grew restless. . . . The English had
had enough of praying and speechmaking. Besides, they feared Joan
might again elude them by some unforeseen technicality.

"Well, priest, do you intend us to dine here?" someone shouted to
Father Massieu. Others clamored to have Joan given over into their
hands, where she would not have to wait long to die.

Whether because of the turmoil or the court's uneasiness at the
rising frenzy, the formalities were cut short. Thus, although the bishop
handed Joan over to secular justice, that justice, represented by the
bailiff of Rouen, failed to pronounce the sentence of death. If he
did, no one heard it. Without further ceremony Joan was brought
down from the bishop's stage and rushed by the soldiers toward the
executioner's platform.

"You priests," she cried as she was being led away, "I beg you all to
say a mass for me." Then, with her old courage, "Whatever I have
done, I alone am responsible!"

At the foot of the scaffold she was given over to Thirache with the
command, "Do your duty."

She saw the board hung in front of the pyre that declared for the
crowd's benefit: "Joan, who let herself be called the Pucelle; liar, male-
factress, deceiver of the people; seeress, superstitious, blasphemer of
God, presumptuous; misbeliever in the faith of Jesus Christ; boastful,
idolatrous, cruel, corrupt, invoker of devils; apostate, schismatic,
heretic." Even if she had been able to read it, it could not now affect

her more than the knowledge that for her unalterable faith she had to die.

"A cross," she begged Ladvenu as she was being lifted to the high platform. "Give me a cross!"

In his pity for her an Englishman who heard her made a rude little cross from two pieces of wood and handed it to her. She took it and kissed it, calling on her Saviour Who had suffered on the cross, to give her strength in her agony; and then she placed it in her bosom between her body and her gown.

"Father Massieu, Isambard, I pray you bring me the crucifix from Saint Sauveur, that I may have Our Lord before my eyes until I am dead," she implored.

Isambard went to the neighboring church and returned with the crucifix. Joan clasped it devotedly and relinquished it only when her hands were fastened behind her, as her body was bound to the stake. She saw the sea of faces from the great height of the scaffold. She saw the city spread about her. "Rouen! Rouen!" she cried. "Is it here I must abide? Ah, Rouen! I greatly fear you will suffer for my death!"

Thirache set the torch to the faggots. They crackled and ignited. "Ah-h-h!" Joan gave a prolonged scream when she saw the fire. Slowly, from the bottom of the pyre it gained upward, first the breath of smoke and then the flames.

Their light summoned a greater light. "Saint Catherine! Saint Margaret! Saint Michael!" she called. As long as she could speak she said that all she had done her Voices had bade her do.

Slowly, with feline slowness, the flames climbed higher.

As the fire gained upon her, from her feet to her robe, from her robe to her flesh, she screamed dreadfully in the pitiful body's pain. The people made a forward movement like the sea, but they could not quench that fire. And always, that anguished screaming, cut by Joan's calling on her saints and "Jesus! Jesus!"

Isambard, braving the fire, stood on the scaffold holding the crucifix before her eyes. "Go! Go!" she begged him for fear he should be burned. Then he, too, left her alone with her agony. The smoke enveloped her, the flames formed a core of light. At last she dropped her head upon her breast and expired, the name of Jesus upon her lips.

So died Joan, martyr and patriot, for a vision so exalted that in her humbleness she had not dared to claim it for her own. . . .

So triumphed Joan, daughter of the people, herald of the modern world. She had shaken the entire feudal age by her concept of France as a national entity, as a people united and ready to assert itself by a struggle to the death, if need be, to put that idea to the test. The idea conquered. It conquered more than the English. It conquered the world.

So triumphed Joan, heroine of faith and loyal martyr who, because she could not maintain her vision yet live, had the courage to defend it and die.

The Saint and the Devil, by Frances Winwar

"And he went out, and wept bitterly."

Macauley said, "The English Bible, a book which, if everything else in our language should perish, would alone suffice to show the whole extent of its beauty and power."

Nowhere in the New Testament is the simplicity, beauty and truth of the writing more striking than in the chapter from the Gospel of St. Matthew which tells the story of the Last Supper, the denial by Peter and the arrest of Jesus. Here is a turning point for all Christianity—the moment when the sacrifice that Jesus is to make becomes known. It is a moment of eternal truth.

AND IT came to pass, when Jesus had finished all these sayings, he said unto his disciples, ye know that after two days is the feast of the passover, and the Son of man is betrayed to be crucified.

Then assembled together the chief priests, and the scribes, and the elders of the people, unto the palace of the high priest, who was called Caiaphas, and consulted that they might take Jesus by subtilty, and kill him. But they said, not on the feast day, lest there be an uproar among the people.

Now when Jesus was in Bethany, in the house of Simon the leper, there came unto him a woman having an alabaster box of very precious ointment, and poured it on his head, as he sat at meat. But when his disciples saw it, they had indignation, saying, to what purpose is this waste? For this ointment might have been sold for much, and given to the poor.

When Jesus understood it, he said unto them, why trouble ye the woman? For she hath wrought a good work upon me. For ye have the poor always with you; but me ye have not always. For in that she hath poured this ointment on my body, she did it for my burial. Verily I say unto you, wheresoever this gospel shall be preached in the whole world, there shall also this, that this woman hath done, be told for a memorial of her.

Then one of the twelve, called Judas Iscariot, went unto the chief priests and said unto them, what will ye give me, and I will deliver him unto you? And they covenanted with him for thirty pieces of silver. And from that time he sought opportunity to betray him.

Now the first day of the feast of unleavened bread the disciples came to Jesus, saying unto him, where wilt thou that we prepare for thee to eat the passover? And he said, go into the city to such a man, and say unto him, the Master saith, my time is at hand; I will keep the passover at thy house with my disciples. And the disciples did as Jesus had appointed them; and they made ready the passover.

Now when the even was come, he sat down with the twelve. And as they did eat, he said, verily I say unto you, that one of you shall betray me. And they were exceeding sorrowful, and began every one of them to say unto him, Lord, is it I?

And he answered and said, he that dippeth his hand with me in the dish, the same shall betray me. The Son of man goeth as it is written of him: but woe unto that man by whom the Son of man is betrayed! It had been good for that man if he had not been born.

Then Judas, which betrayed him, answered and said, Master, is it I?

He said unto him, thou hast said.

And as they were eating, Jesus took bread, and blessed it, and brake it, and gave it to the disciples, and said, take, eat; this is my body. And he took the cup and gave thanks, and gave it to them, saying, drink ye all of it. For this is my blood of the new testament, which is shed for many for the remission of sins. But I say unto you, I will not drink henceforth of this fruit of the vine, until that day when I drink it new with you in my Father's kingdom.

And when they had sung a hymn, they went out into the mount of Olives. Then saith Jesus unto them, all ye shall be offended because of me this night: for it is written, I will smite the shepherd, and the sheep of the flock shall be scattered abroad. But after I am risen again, I will go before you into Galilee.

Peter answered and said unto him, though all men shall be offended because of thee, yet will I never be offended.

Jesus said unto him, verily I say unto thee, that this night, before the cock crow, thou shalt deny me thrice.

Peter said unto him, though I should die with thee, yet will I not deny thee. Likewise said all the disciples.

Then cometh Jesus with them unto a place called Gethsemane, and saith unto the disciples, sit ye here, while I go and pray yonder. And he took with him Peter and the two sons of Zebedee, and began to be sorrowful and very heavy. Then saith he unto them, my soul is exceeding sorrowful, even unto death: tarry ye here, and watch with me. And he went a little farther, and fell on his face, and prayed, saying, O my Father, if it be possible, let this cup pass from me: nevertheless not as I will, but as thou wilt.

And he cometh unto the disciples, and findeth them asleep, and saith unto Peter, what, could ye not watch with me one hour? Watch and pray, that ye enter not into temptation: the spirit indeed is willing, but the flesh is weak.

He went away again the second time, and prayed, saying, O my Father, if this cup may not pass away from me, except I drink it, thy will be done.

And he came and found them asleep again: for their eyes were heavy. And he left them, and went away again, and prayed the third time, saying the same words.

Then cometh he to his disciples, and saith unto them, sleep on now, and take your rest: behold, the hour is at hand, and the Son of man is betrayed into the hands of sinners. Rise, let us be going: behold, he is at hand that doth betray me.

And while he yet spake, lo, Judas, one of the twelve, came, and with him a great multitude with swords and staves, from the chief priests and elders of the people. Now he that betrayed him gave them a sign, saying, whomsoever I shall kiss, that same is he: hold him fast. And forthwith he came to Jesus, and said, hail master; and kissed him. And Jesus said unto him, friend, wherefore art thou come?

Then came they, and laid hands on Jesus, and took him. And, behold, one of them which were with Jesus stretched out his hand, and drew his sword, and struck a servant of the high priest's, and smote off his ear. Then said Jesus unto him, put up again thy sword into his place: for all they that take the sword shall perish with the sword. Thinkest thou that I cannot now pray to my Father, and he shall presently give me more than twelve legions of angels? But how then shall the scriptures be fulfilled, that thus it must be?

In that same hour said Jesus to the multitudes, are ye come out as against a thief with swords and staves for to take me? I sat daily with you teaching in the temple, and ye laid no hold on me.

But all this was done, that the scriptures of the prophets might be fulfilled.

Then all the disciples forsook him, and fled. And they that had laid hold on Jesus led him away to Caiaphas the high priest, where the scribes and the elders were assembled. But Peter followed him afar off unto the high priest's palace, and went in, and sat with the servants, to see the end.

Now the chief priests, and elders, and all the council, sought false witness against Jesus, to put him to death; but found none: yea, though many false witnesses came, yet found they none.

At the last came two false witnesses. And said, this fellow said, I am able to destroy the temple of God, and to build it in three days. And the high priest arose, and said unto him, answerest thou nothing? What is it which these witness against thee?

But Jesus held his peace.

And the high priest answered and said unto him, I adjure thee by the living God, that thou tell us whether thou be the *Christ*, the Son of God.

Jesus saith unto him, thou hast said: nevertheless I say unto you, hereafter shall ye see the Son of man sitting on the right hand of power, and coming in the clouds of heaven.

Then the high priest rent his clothes, saying, he hath spoken blasphemy; what further need have we of witnesses? Behold, now ye have heard his blasphemy. What think ye?

They answered and said, he is guilty of death. Then did they spit in his face, and buffeted him with the palms of their hands, saying, prophesy unto us, thou *Christ*, who is he that smote thee?

Now Peter sat without in the palace: and a damsel came unto him, saying, thou also wast with Jesus of Galilee. But he denied before them all, saying, I know not what thou sayest. And when he was gone out into the porch, another maid saw him, and said unto them that were there, this fellow was also with Jesus of Nazareth. And again he denied with an oath, I do not know the man. And after a while came unto him they that stood by, and said to Peter, surely thou also art one of them; for thy speech betrayeth thee. Then began he to curse and to swear, saying, I know not the man.

And immediately the cock crew.

And Peter remembered the word of Jesus, which said unto him, before the cock crow, thou shalt deny me thrice.

And he went out, and wept bitterly.

King James Bible

PHILIP DUNAWAY, whose sudden death in September, 1957, came as a stunning shock to all who knew him, was an immensely versatile man of letters. In his many years in publishing he was, at one time or another, an author, an editor, a co-founder of a publishing house, and a bookseller. His general and specific knowledge was of a kind that allowed him to discuss Eastern philosophy, American politics, or English cricket standings with equal ease and authority. A *Treasury of the World's Great Diaries*, which he edited with Mel Evans, was published in 1956. This book was the product of his researches and reading in the field of biography.

GEORGE DE KAY has been connected with the book business in one way or another all his working life. After a stint in the Navy during World War II, he went to work for a large New York publishing house. There, during the next eight or ten years, he learned the hard facts of publishing—from the composing room to the front office. He was, at various times, salesman, book-club promotion man, editor, and for several years editor-in-chief of a well-known series of paper books. As an editor he has worked on scores of books, but this is the first to bear his name.